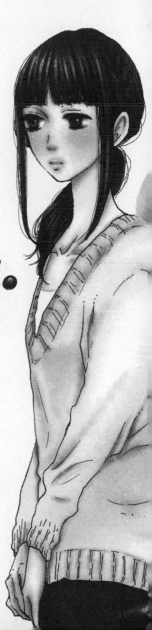

Say I Love You.

by
Kanae
Hazuki

Kanae Hazuki
presents

Chapter 61

Chapter 62

Chapter 63

Chapter 64

CHARACTER

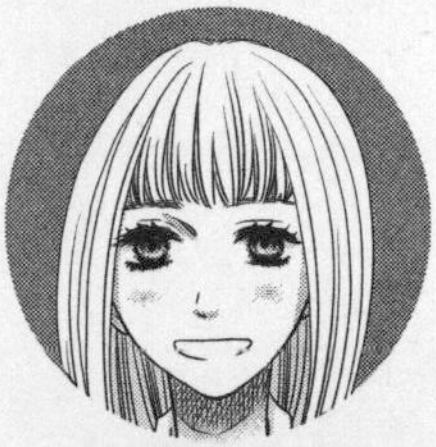

Mei Tachibana
A girl who hadn't had a single friend, let alone a boyfriend, for sixteen years. She started dating Yamato, the most popular boy in school, and is now growing as a woman. This spring marks the beginning of her stint at vocational school, where she is training to be a preschool teacher.

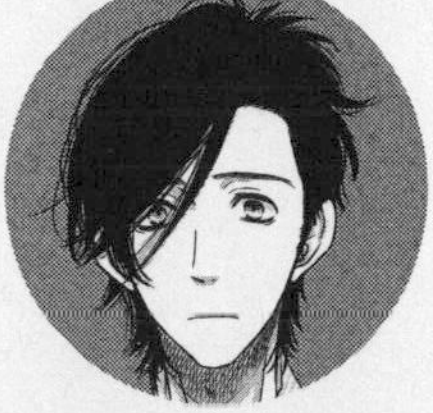

Yamato Kurosawa
The most popular boy at school. He was taken in by the charms of the brooding weirdo Mei, and they are now dating. He chose to go to college as he pursues a career in photography.

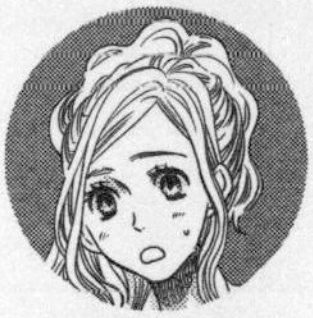

Asami Oikawa
An amiable girl, and Mei's first friend. Encouraged by Mei, she started dating Yamato's friend Nakanishi. Like Mei, she aspires to be a preschool teacher.

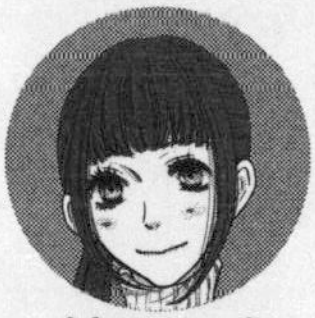

Megumi Kitagawa
An amateur model who was once extremely aggressive in her pursuit of Yamato. After he dumped her, she got serious about her career. Now that she's graduated high school, she is trying her hand at modeling in Paris.

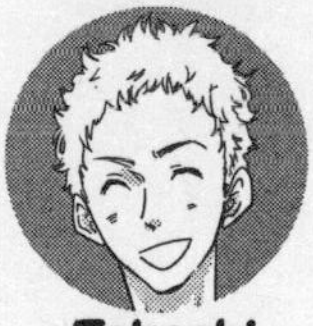

Takeshi Nakanishi
Yamato's friend and Asami's boyfriend. A bit of a jokester, he teased Mei at first, but that led to her encounter with Yamato. After high school, he decided to go to college.

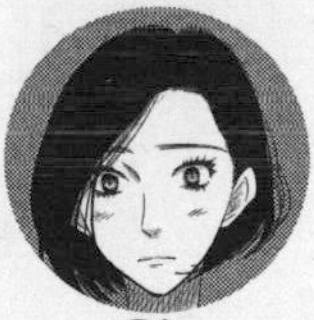

Rin Aoi
A second-year in high school, and Ren's twin sister. She's a popular model going by the name RIN. She fell in love with Kai at first sight, and they dated, but they're now broken up.

STORY

After spending sixteen years without a single friend or boyfriend, Mei Tachibana is now happily dating the most popular boy from school, Yamato Kurosawa. As third-years in high school, they thought hard about what they wanted to do after graduation; ultimately Mei decides to go to vocational school to be a preschool teacher, and Yamato decides to go to college while also pursuing a career in photography. Their friends all choose their own paths as well. And eventually the day comes for them to bid farewell to their high school lives, where they made so many memories. But as soon as the ceremony is over, Yamato stops Mei and...?!

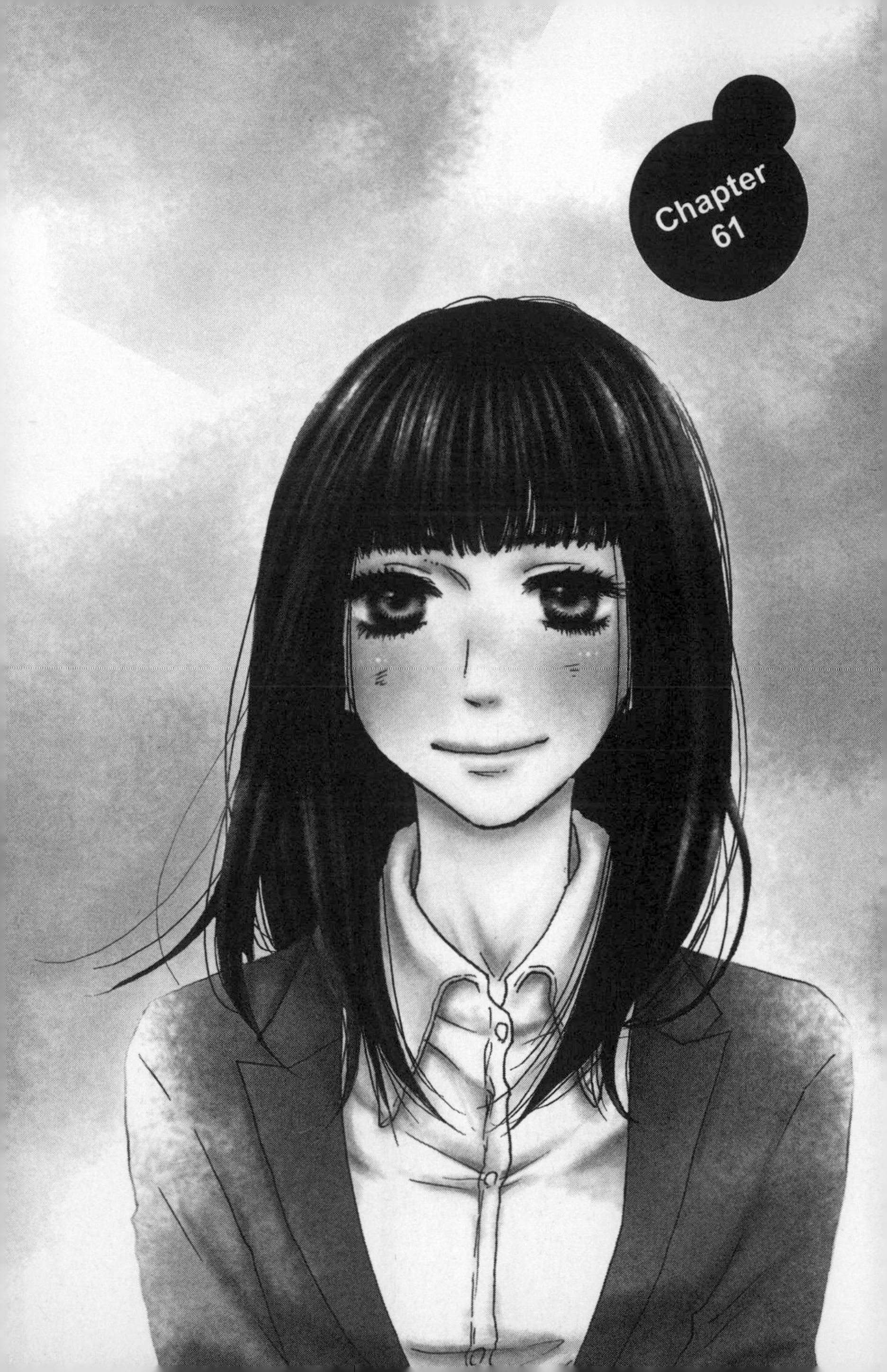
Chapter
61

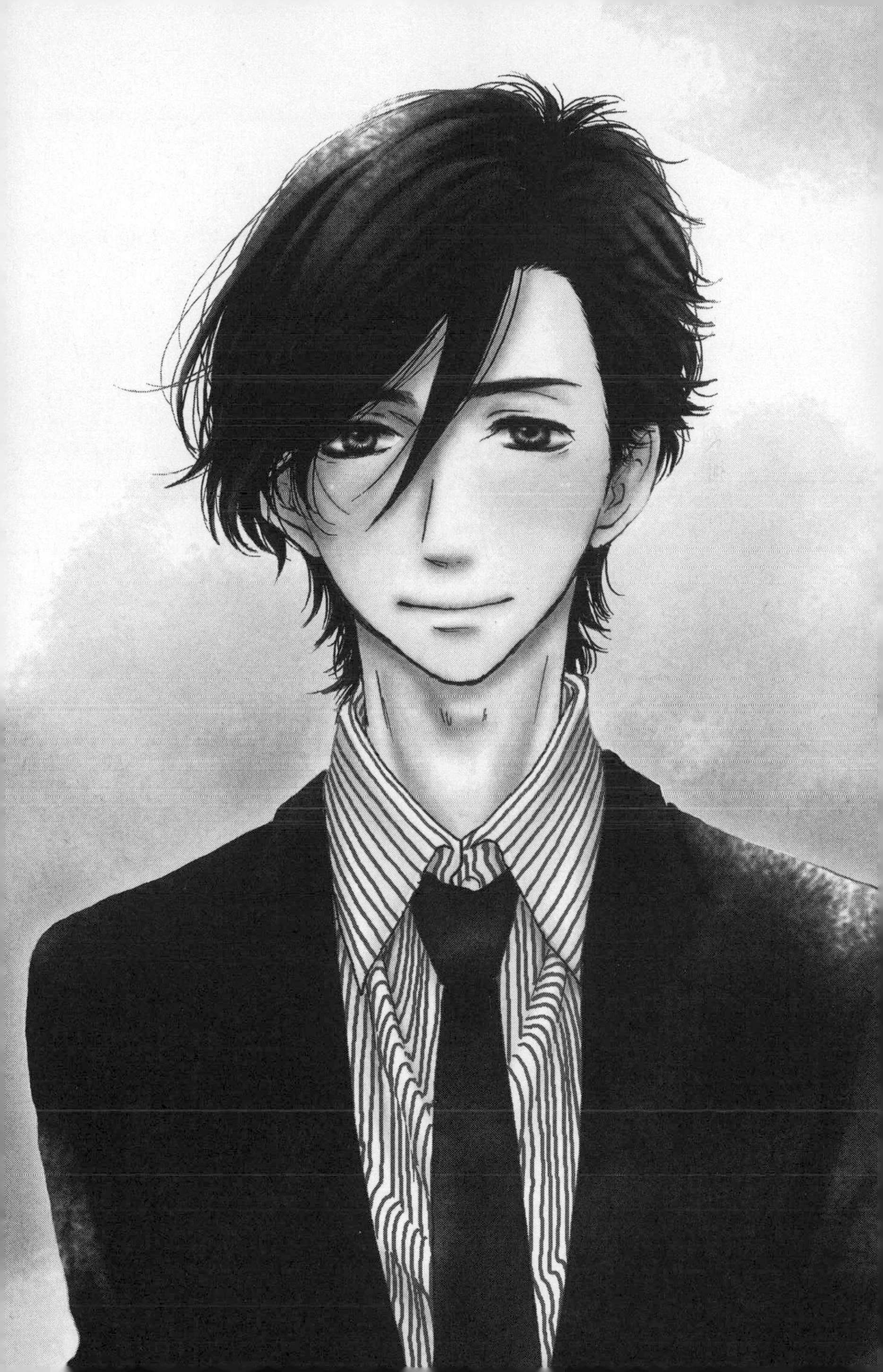

Say "I love you".

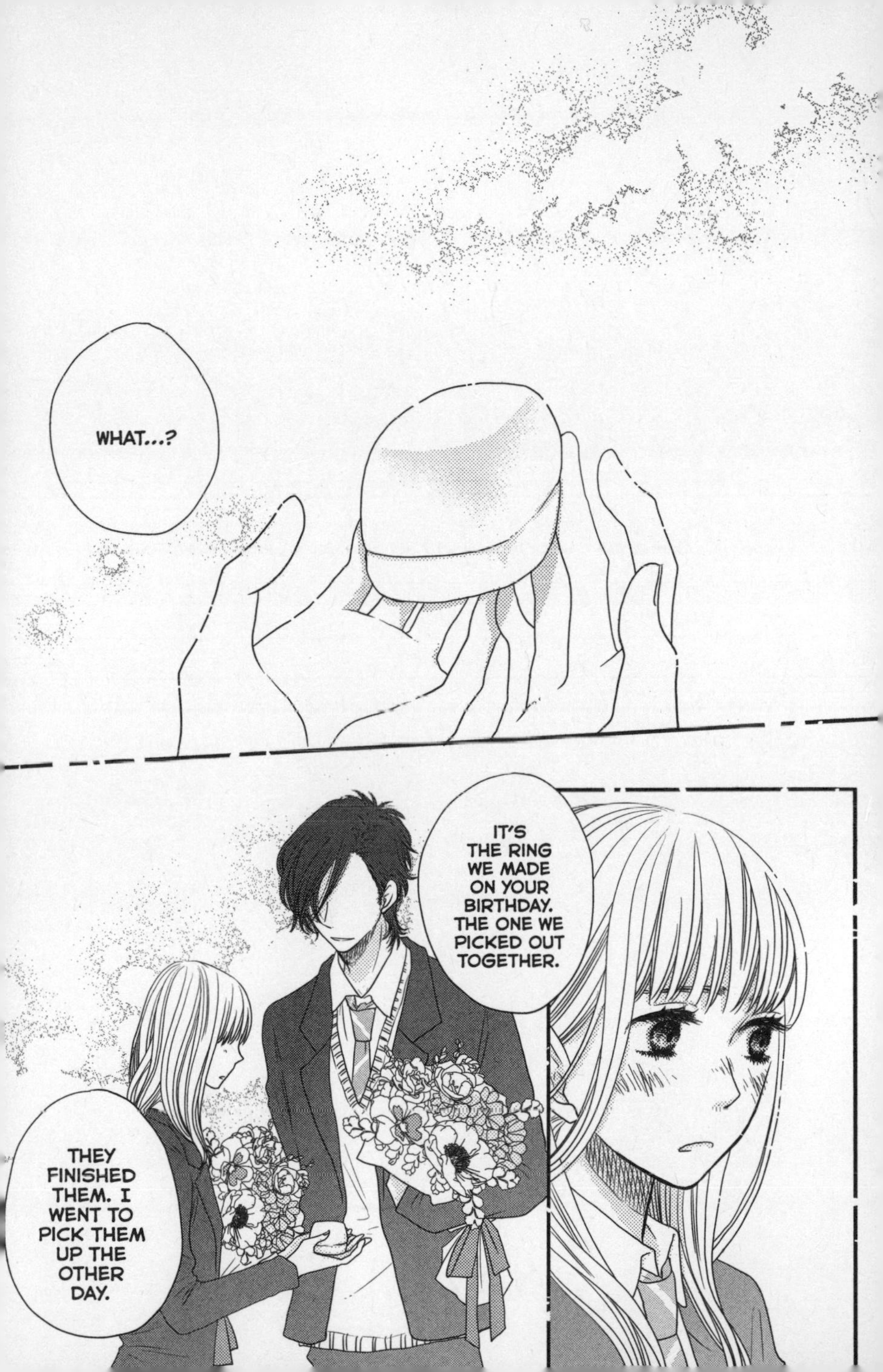
WHAT...?
IT'S THE RING WE MADE ON YOUR BIRTHDAY. THE ONE WE PICKED OUT TOGETHER.
THEY FINISHED THEM. I WENT TO PICK THEM UP THE OTHER DAY.

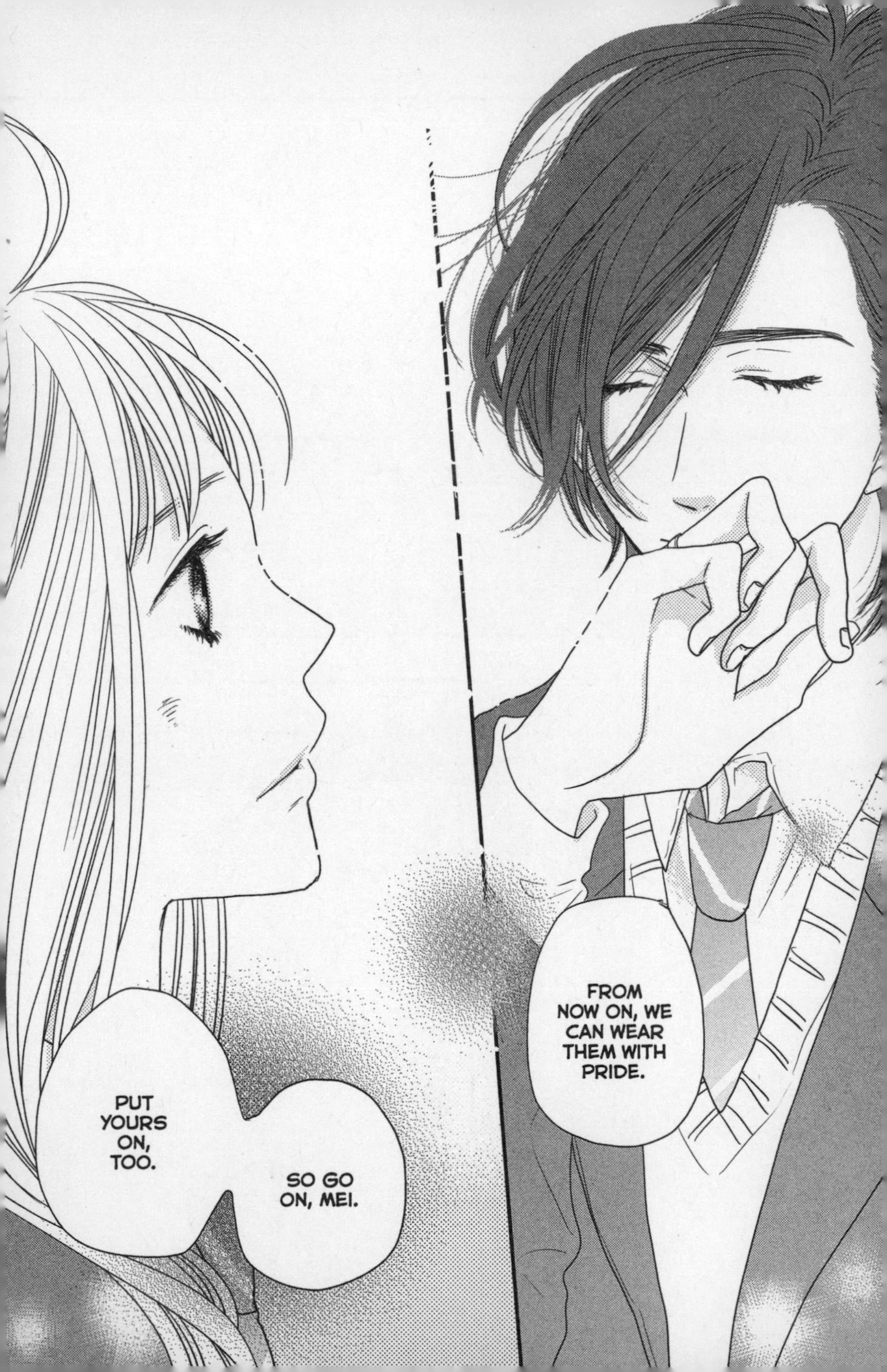
FROM NOW ON, WE CAN WEAR THEM WITH PRIDE.
SO GO ON, MEI.
PUT YOURS ON, TOO.

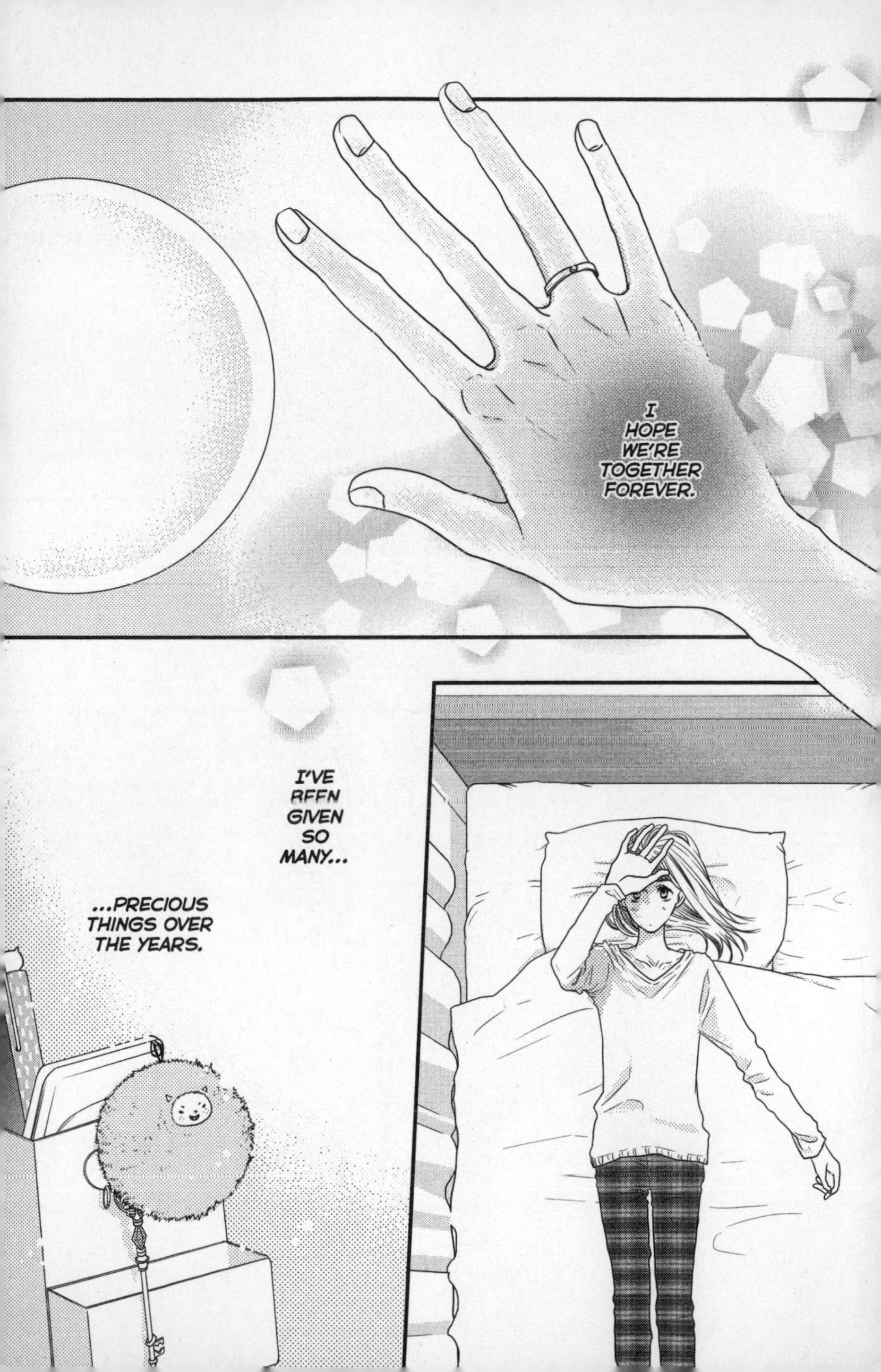
I HOPE WE'RE TOGETHER FOREVER.
I'VE BEEN GIVEN SO MANY...
...PRECIOUS THINGS OVER THE YEARS.

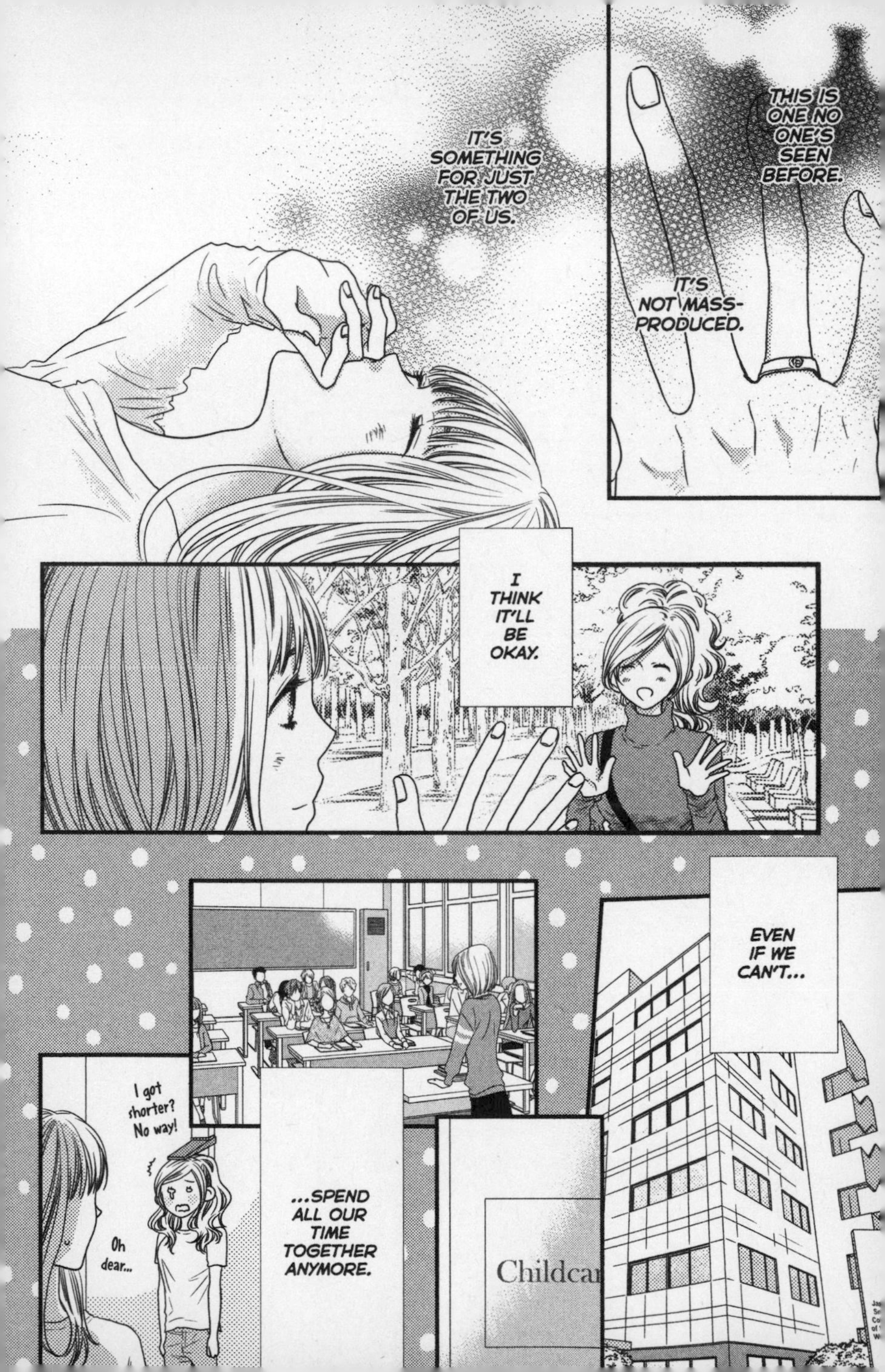
THIS IS ONE NO ONE'S SEEN BEFORE.
IT'S NOT MASS-PRODUCED.
IT'S SOMETHING FOR JUST THE TWO OF US.
I THINK IT'LL BE OKAY.
EVEN IF WE CAN'T...
Childcar
...SPEND ALL OUR TIME TOGETHER ANYMORE.
I got shorter? No way!
Oh dear...

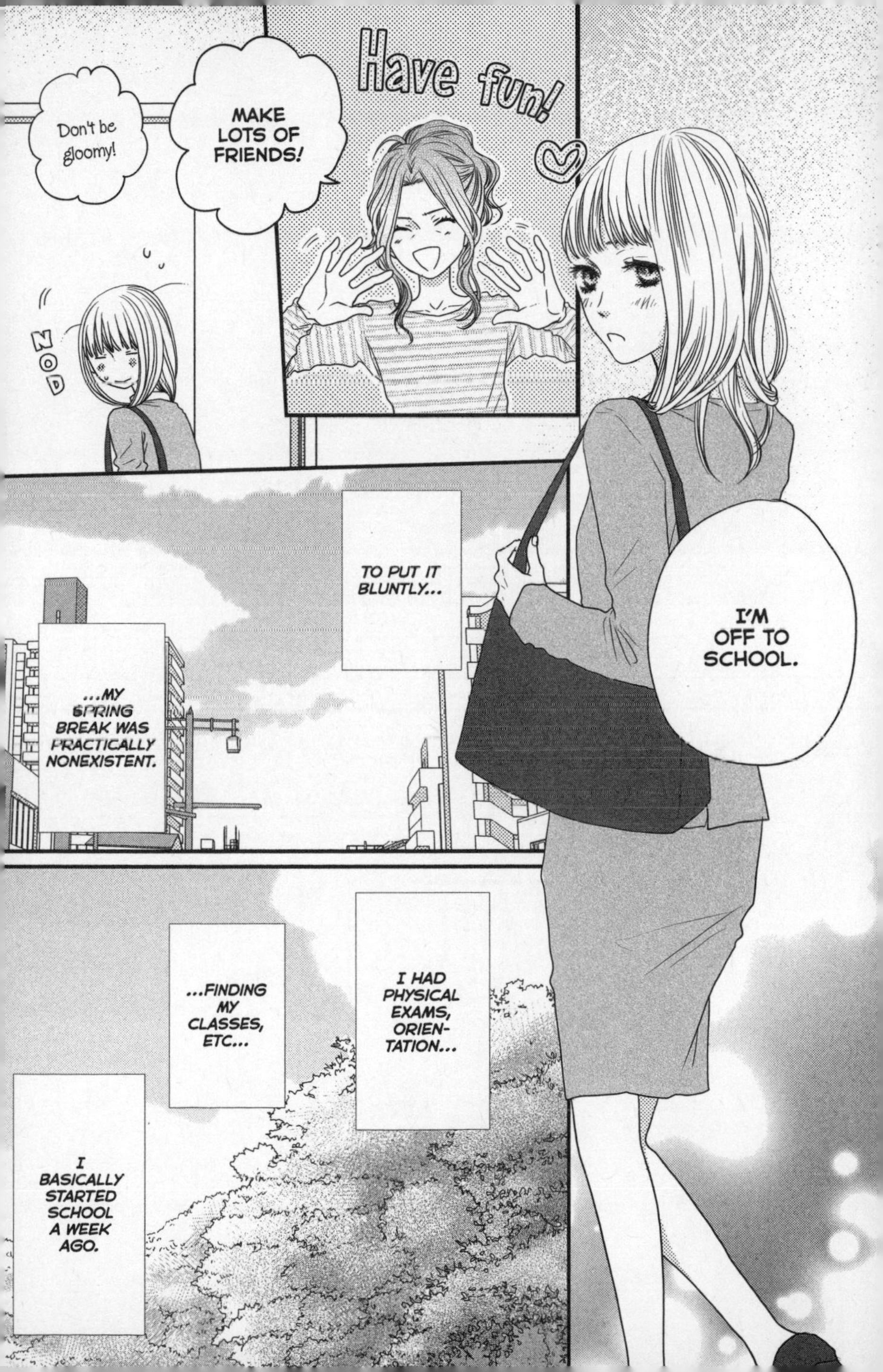
I'M OFF TO SCHOOL.
Have fun!
MAKE LOTS OF FRIENDS!
Don't be gloomy!
NOD
TO PUT IT BLUNTLY...
...MY SPRING BREAK WAS PRACTICALLY NONEXISTENT.
I HAD PHYSICAL EXAMS, ORIEN-TATION...
...FINDING MY CLASSES, ETC...
I BASICALLY STARTED SCHOOL A WEEK AGO.

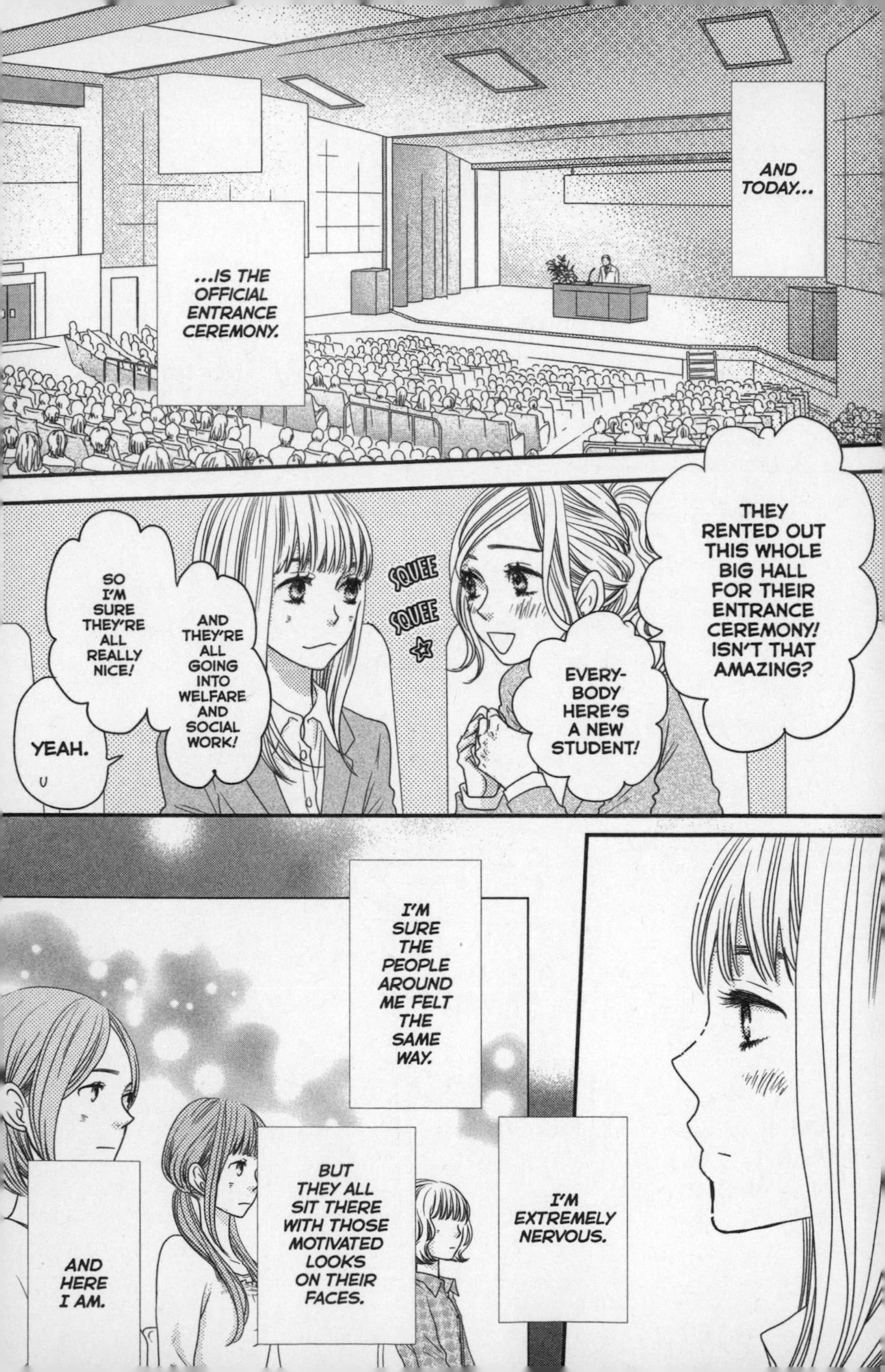
AND TODAY...
...IS THE OFFICIAL ENTRANCE CEREMONY.
THEY RENTED OUT THIS WHOLE BIG HALL FOR THEIR ENTRANCE CEREMONY! ISN'T THAT AMAZING?
EVERY-BODY HERE'S A NEW STUDENT!
SQUEE
SQUEE
AND THEY'RE ALL GOING INTO WELFARE AND SOCIAL WORK!
SO I'M SURE THEY'RE ALL REALLY NICE!
YEAH.
I'M EXTREMELY NERVOUS.
I'M SURE THE PEOPLE AROUND ME FELT THE SAME WAY.
BUT THEY ALL SIT THERE WITH THOSE MOTIVATED LOOKS ON THEIR FACES.
AND HERE I AM.

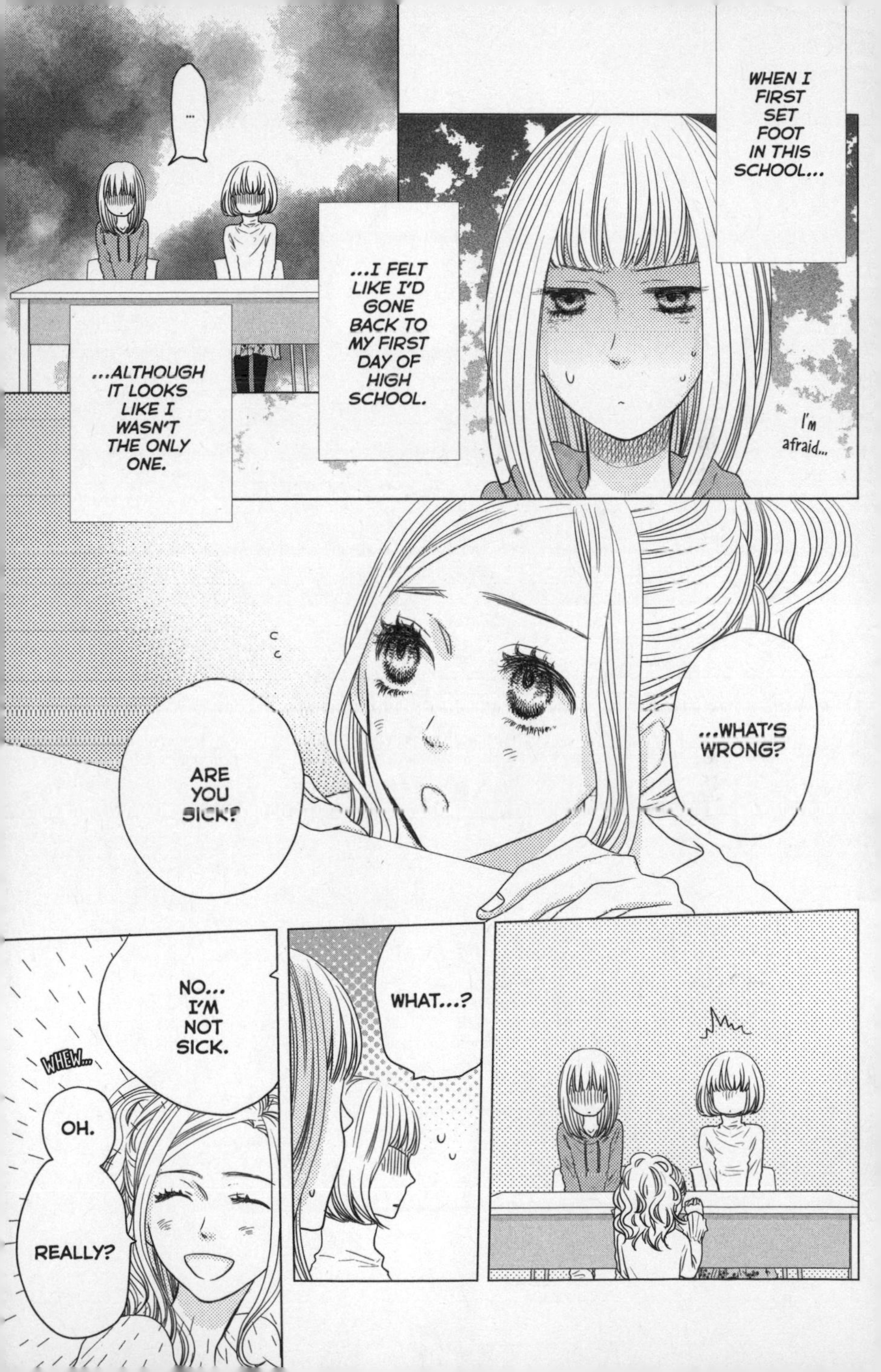
WHEN I FIRST SET FOOT IN THIS SCHOOL...
I'm afraid...
...I FELT LIKE I'D GONE BACK TO MY FIRST DAY OF HIGH SCHOOL.
...
...ALTHOUGH IT LOOKS LIKE I WASN'T THE ONLY ONE.
...WHAT'S WRONG?
ARE YOU SICK?
WHAT...?
NO... I'M NOT SICK.
WHEW...
OH.
REALLY?

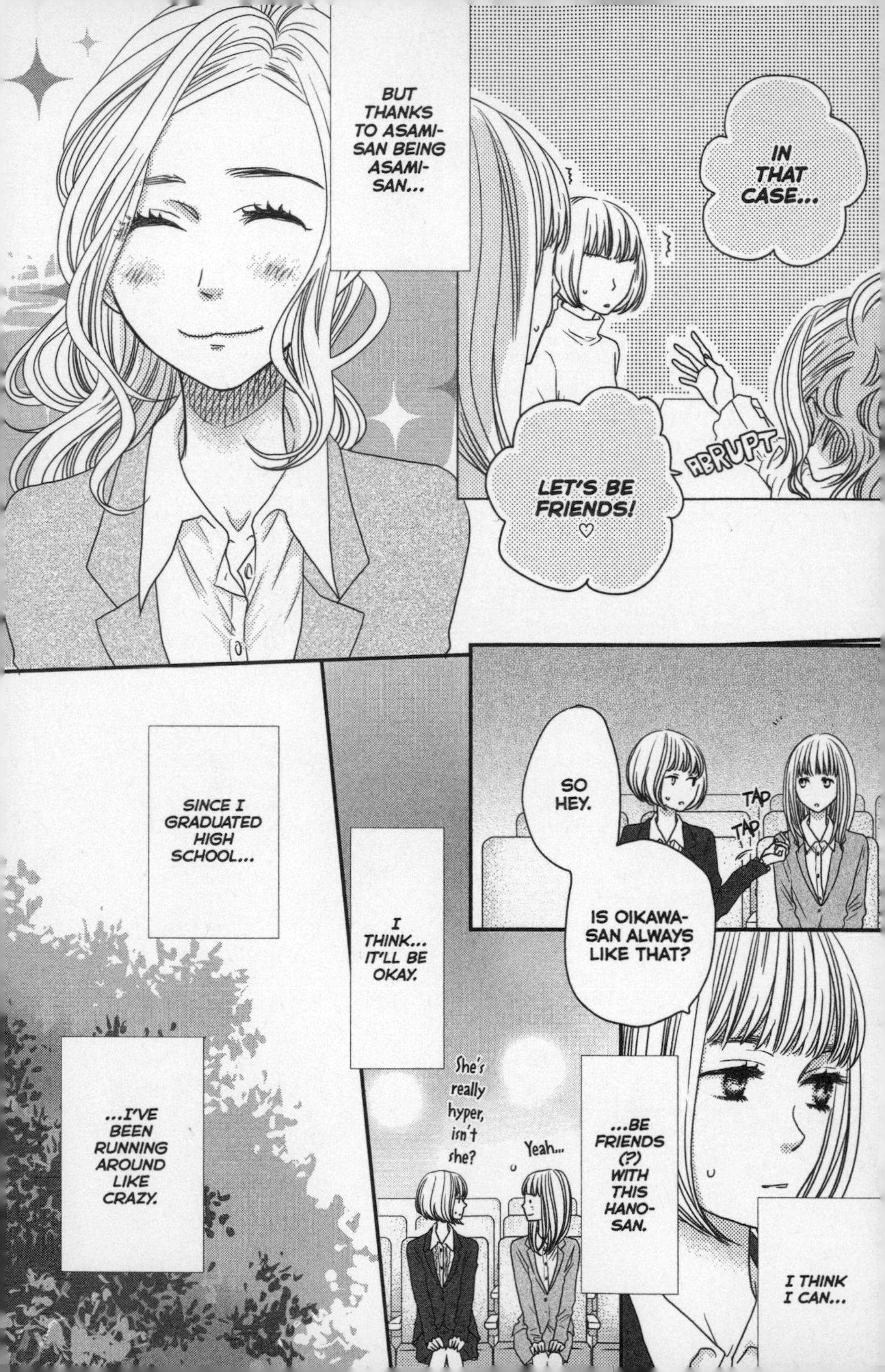
IN THAT CASE...
ABRUPT
LET'S BE FRIENDS! ♡
BUT THANKS TO ASAMI-SAN BEING ASAMI-SAN...
SO HEY.
TAP TAP
IS OIKAWA-SAN ALWAYS LIKE THAT?
I THINK I CAN...
...BE FRIENDS (?) WITH THIS HANO-SAN.
She's really hyper, isn't she?
Yeah...
I THINK... IT'LL BE OKAY.
SINCE I GRADUATED HIGH SCHOOL...
...I'VE BEEN RUNNING AROUND LIKE CRAZY.

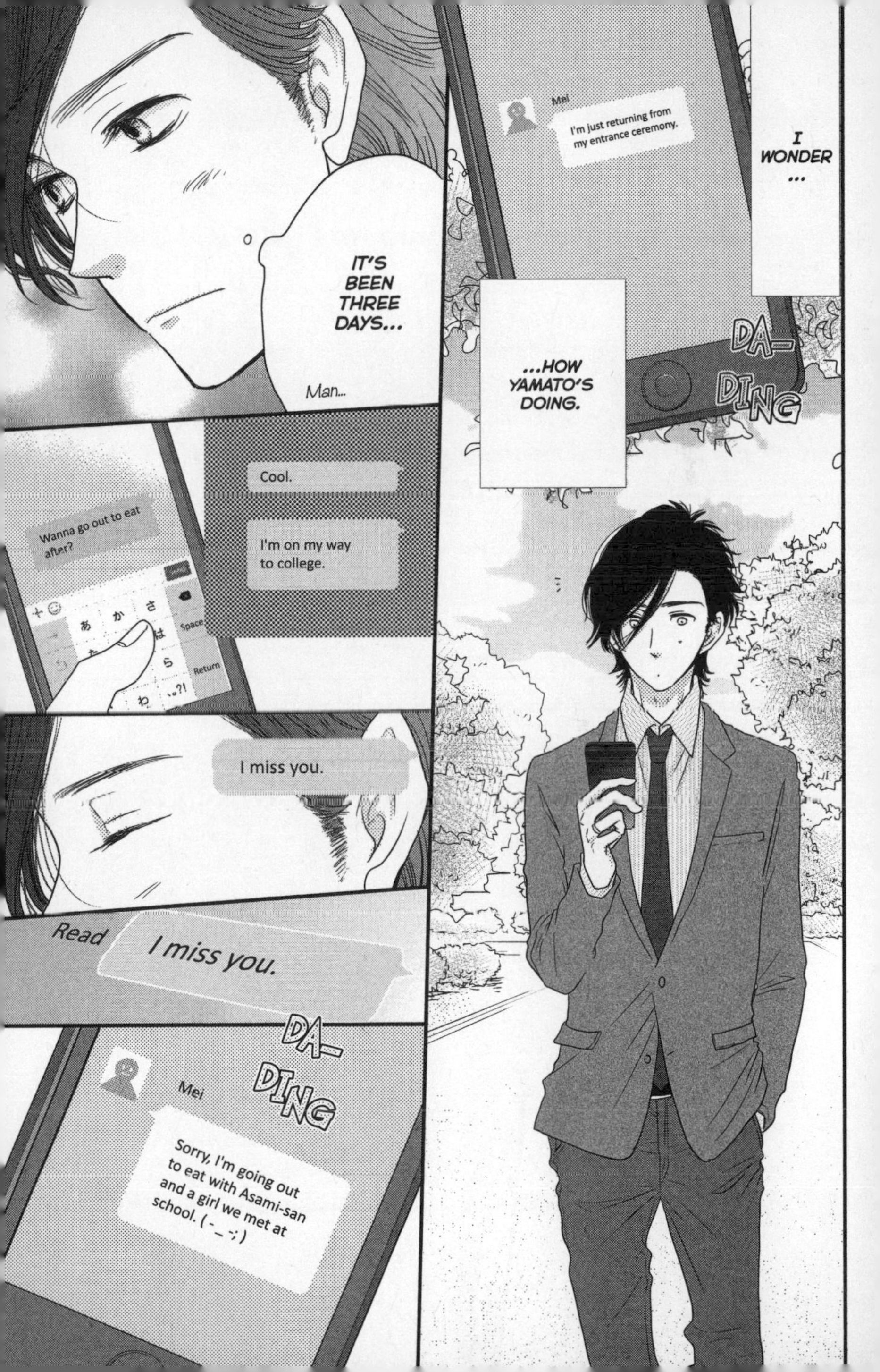

I WONDER ...
Mei
I'm just returning from my entrance ceremony.
DA-DING
...HOW YAMATO'S DOING.
IT'S BEEN THREE DAYS...
Man...
Cool.
I'm on my way to college.
Wanna go out to eat after?
I miss you.
Read
I miss you.
DA-DING
Mei
Sorry, I'm going out to eat with Asami-san and a girl we met at school. (-_-;)

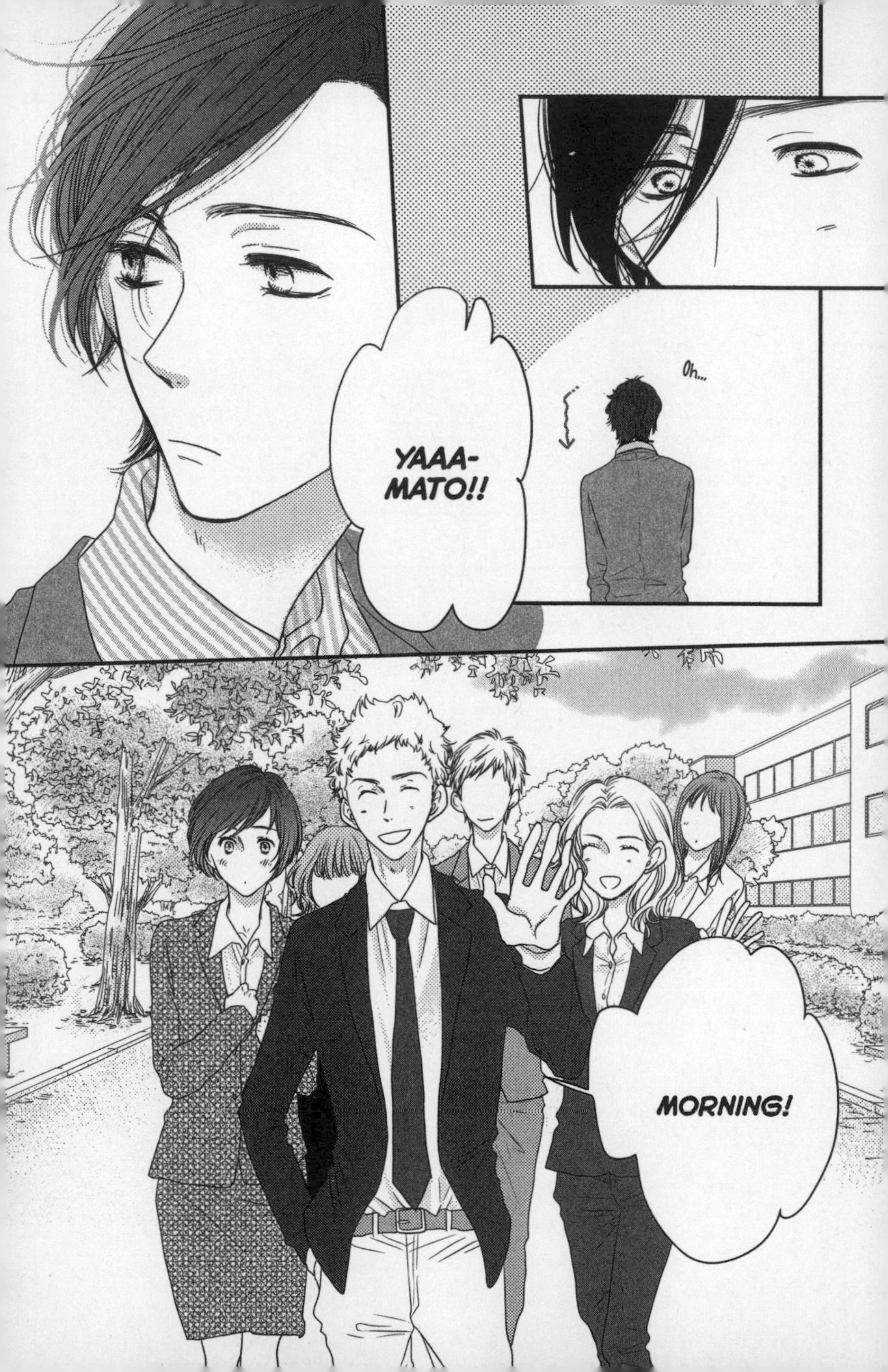
Oh...
YAAA-MATO!!
MORNING!

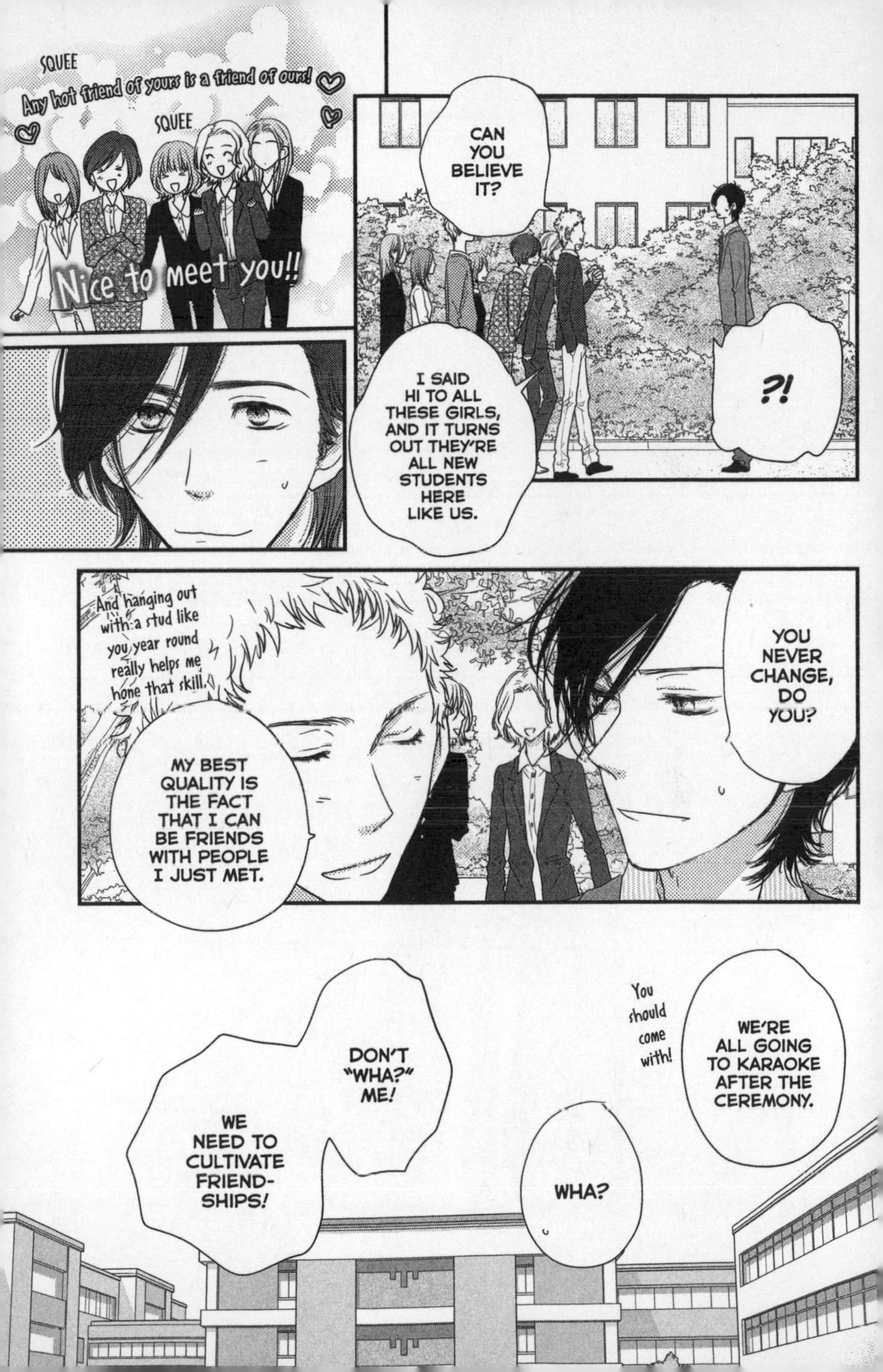
CAN YOU BELIEVE IT?
I SAID HI TO ALL THESE GIRLS, AND IT TURNS OUT THEY'RE ALL NEW STUDENTS HERE LIKE US.
?!
SQUEE
Any hot friend of yours is a friend of ours!
SQUEE
Nice to meet you!!
YOU NEVER CHANGE, DO YOU?
MY BEST QUALITY IS THE FACT THAT I CAN BE FRIENDS WITH PEOPLE I JUST MET.
And hanging out with a stud like you year round really helps me hone that skill.
WE'RE ALL GOING TO KARAOKE AFTER THE CEREMONY.
You should come with!
WHA?
DON'T "WHA?" ME!
WE NEED TO CULTIVATE FRIEND-SHIPS!

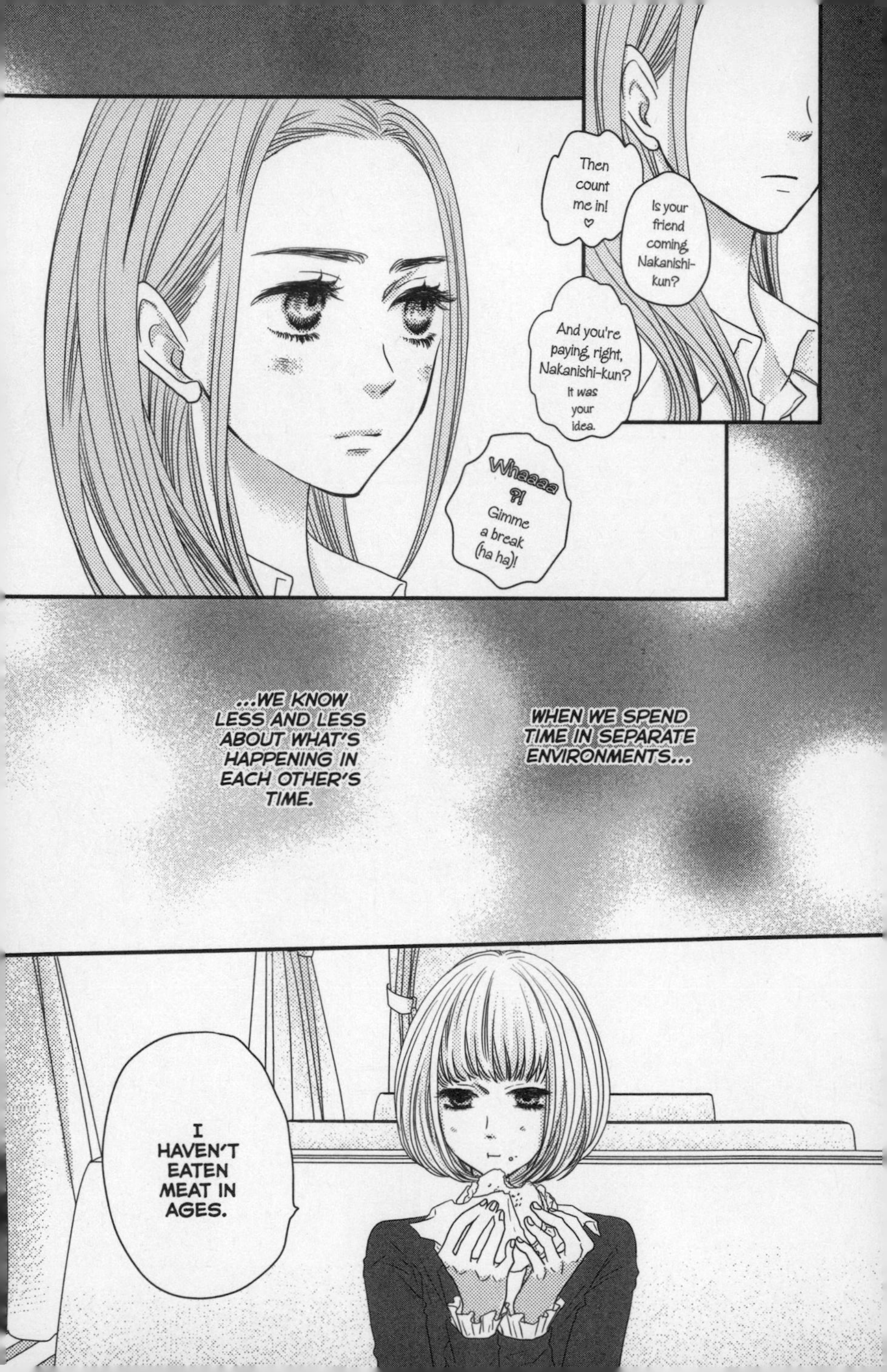
Is your friend coming, Nakanishi-kun?
Then count me in! ♡
And you're paying, right, Nakanishi-kun? It was your idea.
Whaaaa?! Gimme a break (ha ha)!
WHEN WE SPEND TIME IN SEPARATE ENVIRONMENTS...
...WE KNOW LESS AND LESS ABOUT WHAT'S HAPPENING IN EACH OTHER'S TIME.
I HAVEN'T EATEN MEAT IN AGES.

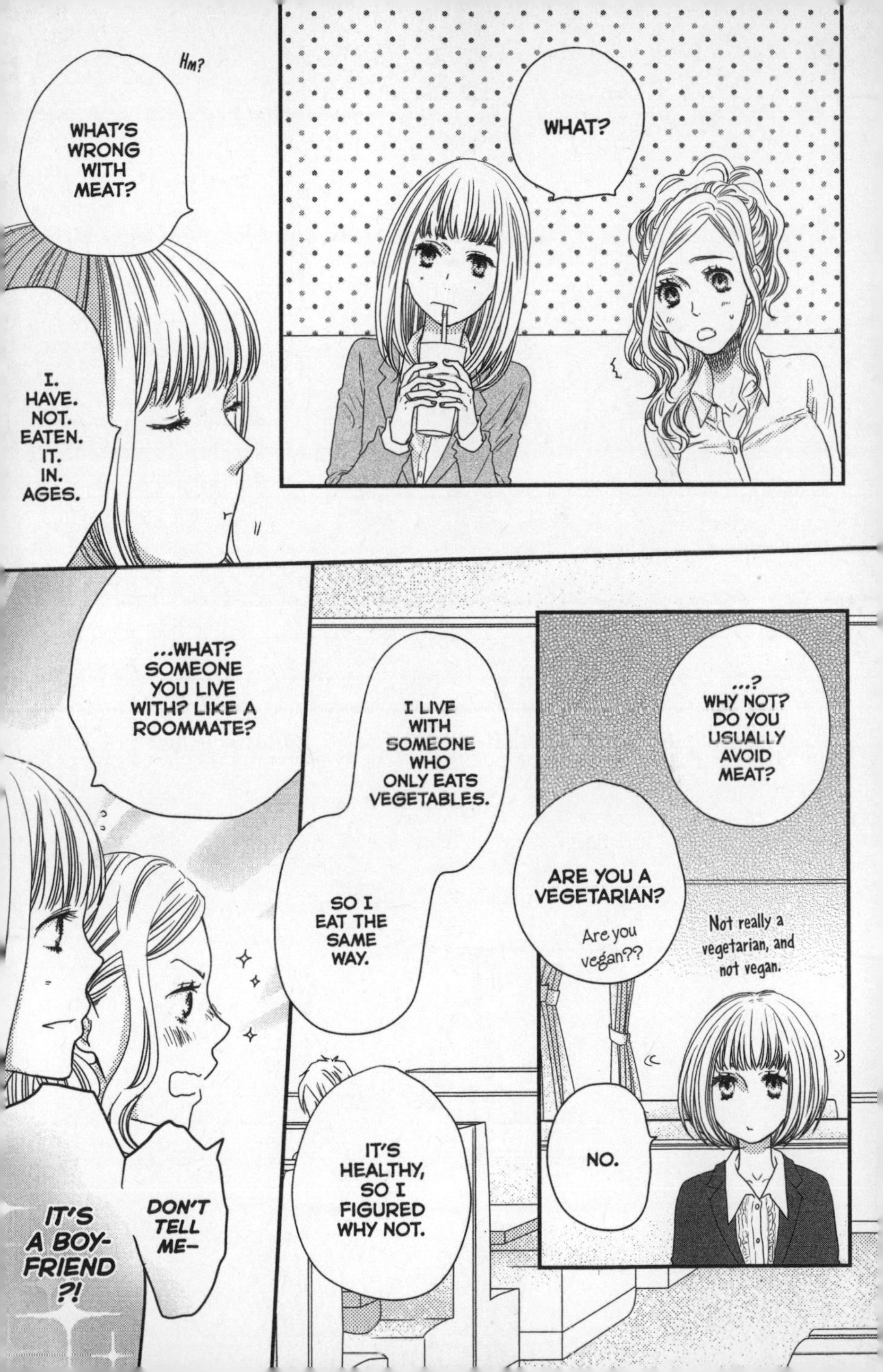
WHAT?
Hm?
WHAT'S WRONG WITH MEAT?
I. HAVE. NOT. EATEN. IT. IN. AGES.
...? WHY NOT? DO YOU USUALLY AVOID MEAT?
ARE YOU A VEGETARIAN?
Are you vegan??
Not really a vegetarian, and not vegan.
NO.
I LIVE WITH SOMEONE WHO ONLY EATS VEGETABLES.
SO I EAT THE SAME WAY.
IT'S HEALTHY, SO I FIGURED WHY NOT.
...WHAT? SOMEONE YOU LIVE WITH? LIKE A ROOMMATE?
DON'T TELL ME—
IT'S A BOY-FRIEND?!

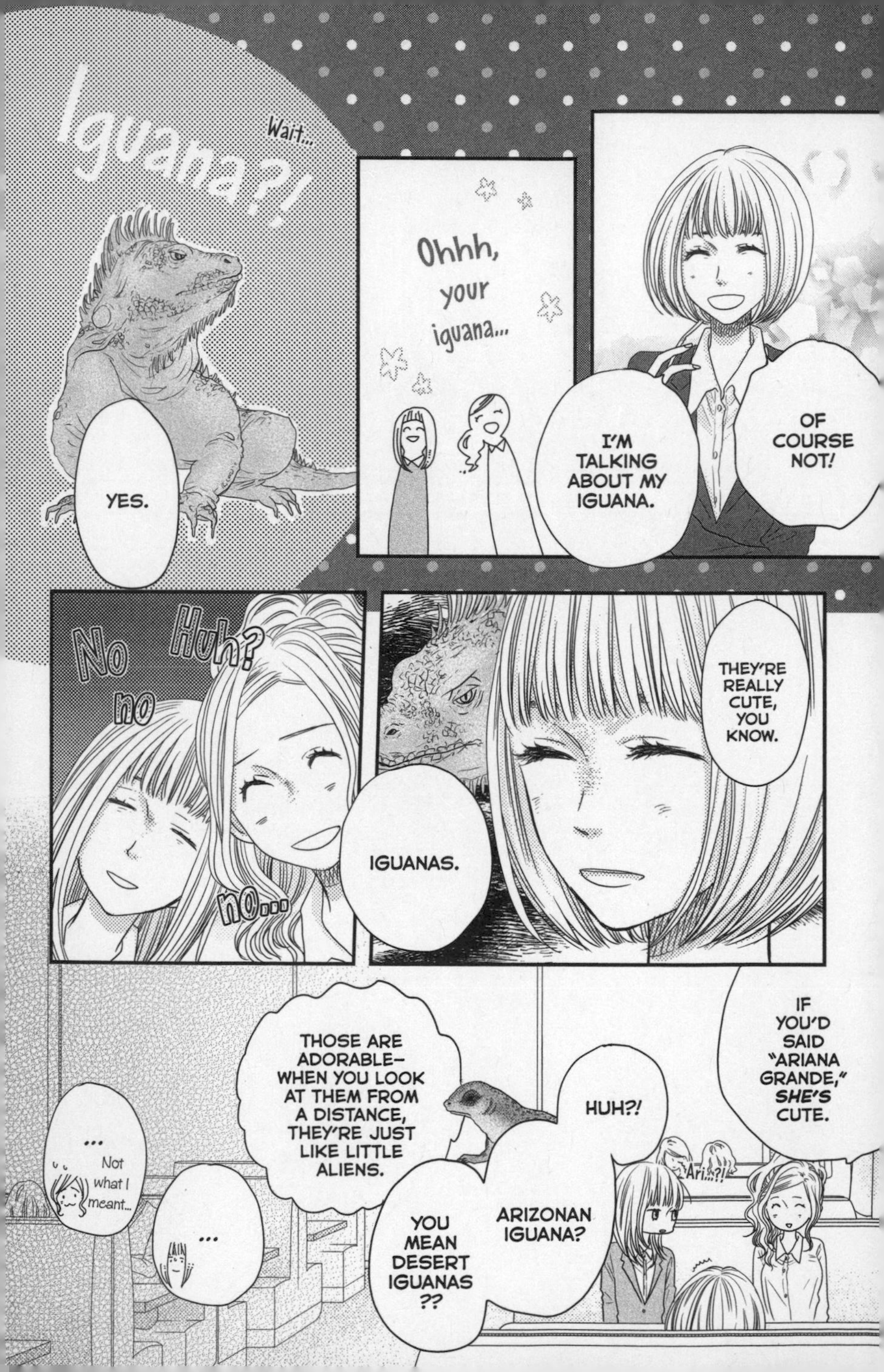
OF COURSE NOT!
I'M TALKING ABOUT MY IGUANA.
Ohhh, your iguana...
Wait...
Iguana?!
YES.
THEY'RE REALLY CUTE, YOU KNOW.
IGUANAS.
Huh?
No no no...
IF YOU'D SAID "ARIANA GRANDE," *SHE'S* CUTE.
Ari...?!
HUH?!
ARIZONAN IGUANA?
YOU MEAN DESERT IGUANAS??
THOSE ARE ADORABLE— WHEN YOU LOOK AT THEM FROM A DISTANCE, THEY'RE JUST LIKE LITTLE ALIENS.
...
... Not what I meant...

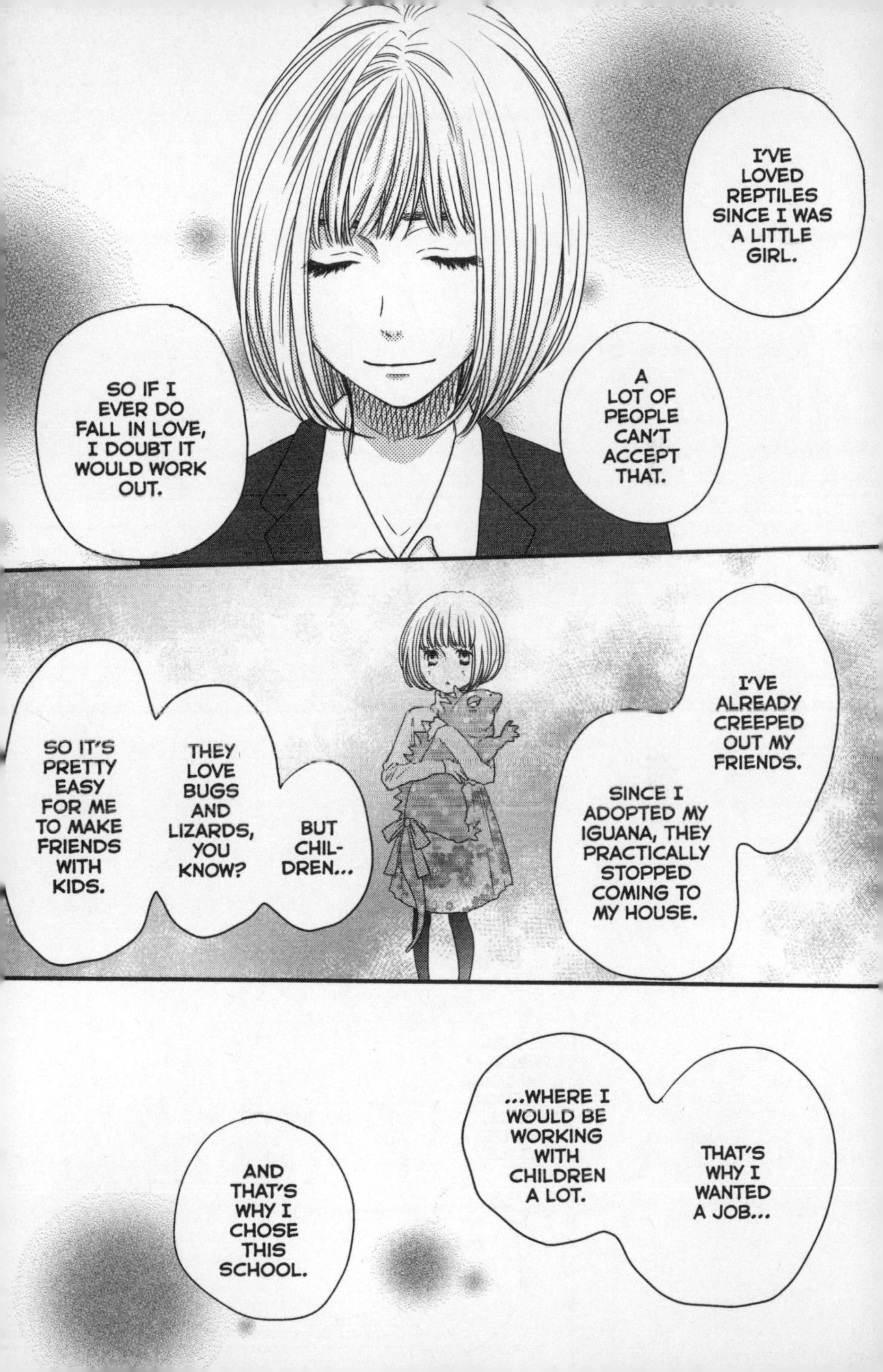
I'VE LOVED REPTILES SINCE I WAS A LITTLE GIRL.
A LOT OF PEOPLE CAN'T ACCEPT THAT.
SO IF I EVER DO FALL IN LOVE, I DOUBT IT WOULD WORK OUT.
I'VE ALREADY CREEPED OUT MY FRIENDS.
SINCE I ADOPTED MY IGUANA, THEY PRACTICALLY STOPPED COMING TO MY HOUSE.
BUT CHIL-DREN...
THEY LOVE BUGS AND LIZARDS, YOU KNOW?
SO IT'S PRETTY EASY FOR ME TO MAKE FRIENDS WITH KIDS.
THAT'S WHY I WANTED A JOB...
...WHERE I WOULD BE WORKING WITH CHILDREN A LOT.
AND THAT'S WHY I CHOSE THIS SCHOOL.

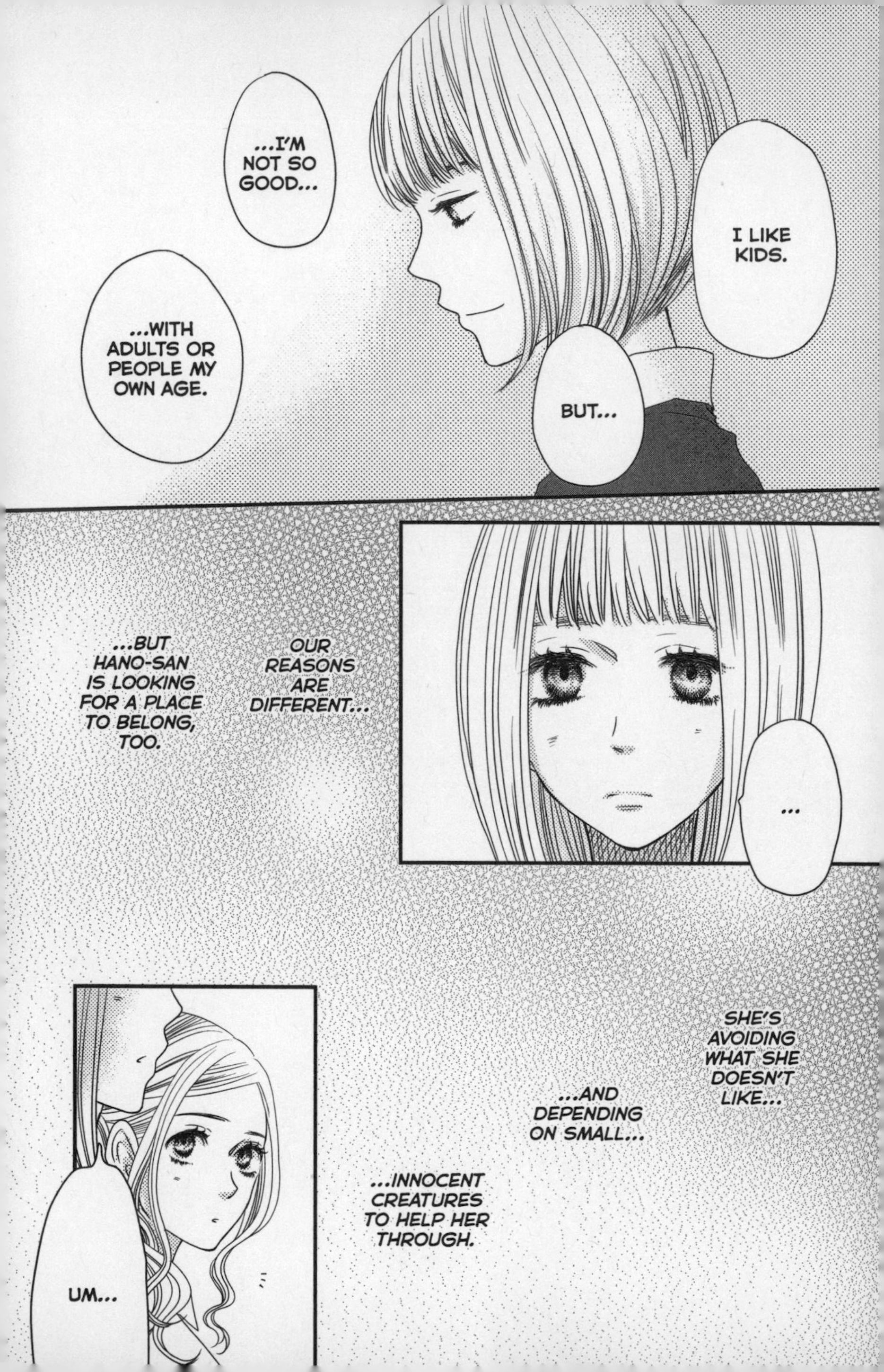
I LIKE KIDS.
BUT...
...I'M NOT SO GOOD...
...WITH ADULTS OR PEOPLE MY OWN AGE.
...
OUR REASONS ARE DIFFERENT...
...BUT HANO-SAN IS LOOKING FOR A PLACE TO BELONG, TOO.
SHE'S AVOIDING WHAT SHE DOESN'T LIKE...
...AND DEPENDING ON SMALL...
...INNOCENT CREATURES TO HELP HER THROUGH.
UM...

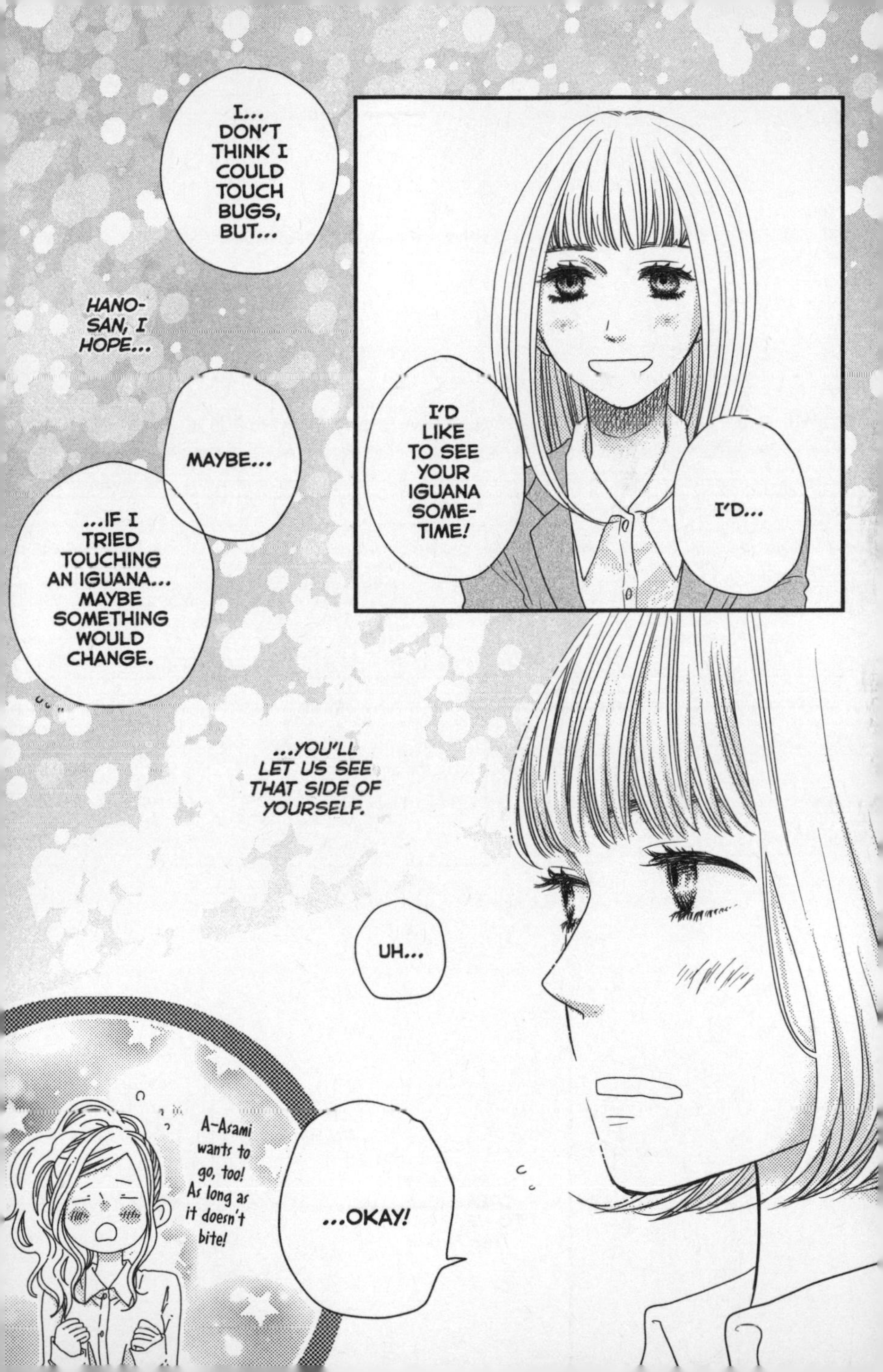
I'D...
I'D LIKE TO SEE YOUR IGUANA SOME-TIME!
I... DON'T THINK I COULD TOUCH BUGS, BUT...
MAYBE...
...IF I TRIED TOUCHING AN IGUANA... MAYBE SOMETHING WOULD CHANGE.
HANO-SAN, I HOPE...
...YOU'LL LET US SEE THAT SIDE OF YOURSELF.
UH...
...OKAY!
A-Asami wants to go, too! As long as it doesn't bite!

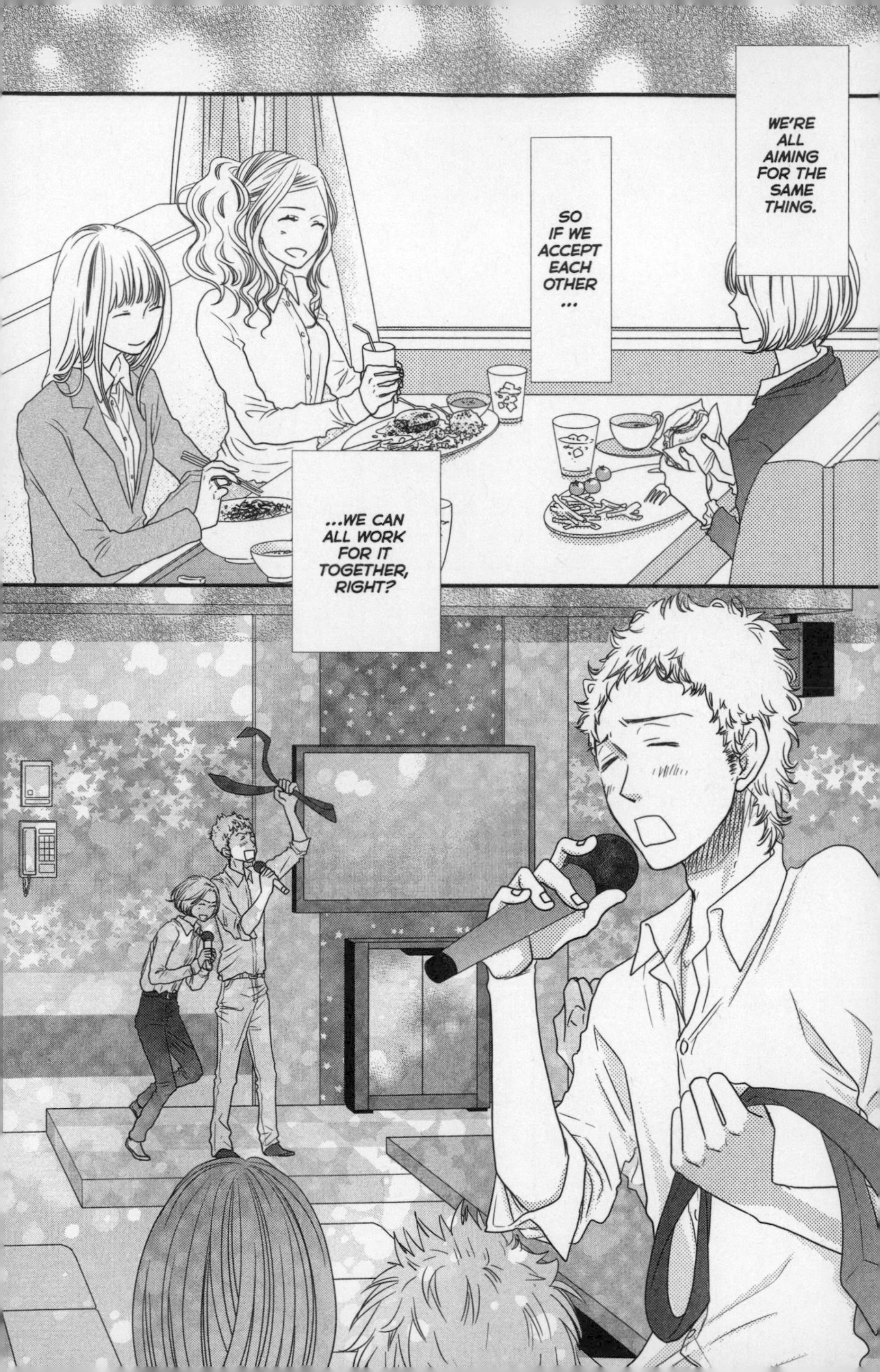
WE'RE ALL AIMING FOR THE SAME THING.
SO IF WE ACCEPT EACH OTHER ...
...WE CAN ALL WORK FOR IT TOGETHER, RIGHT?

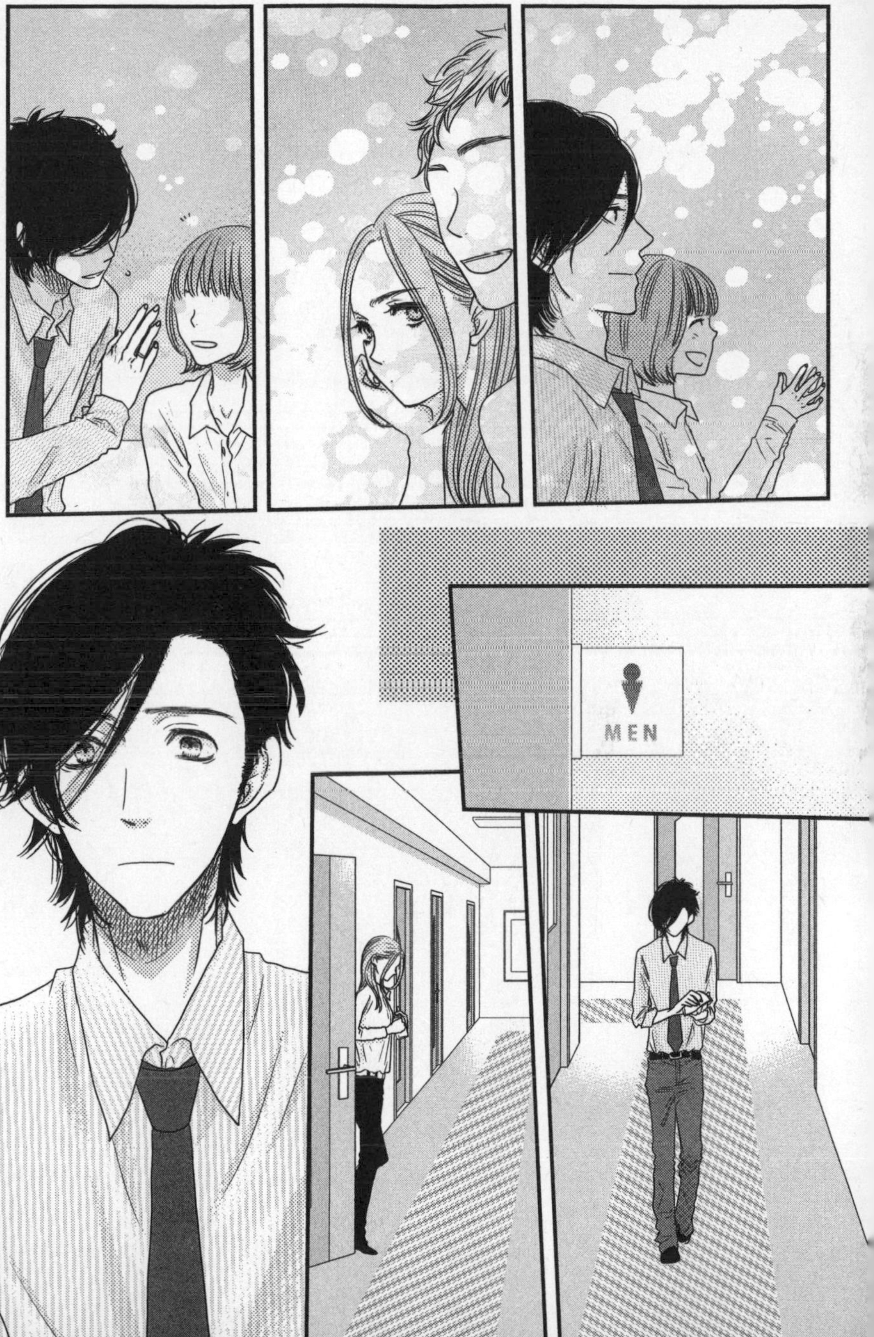
MEN

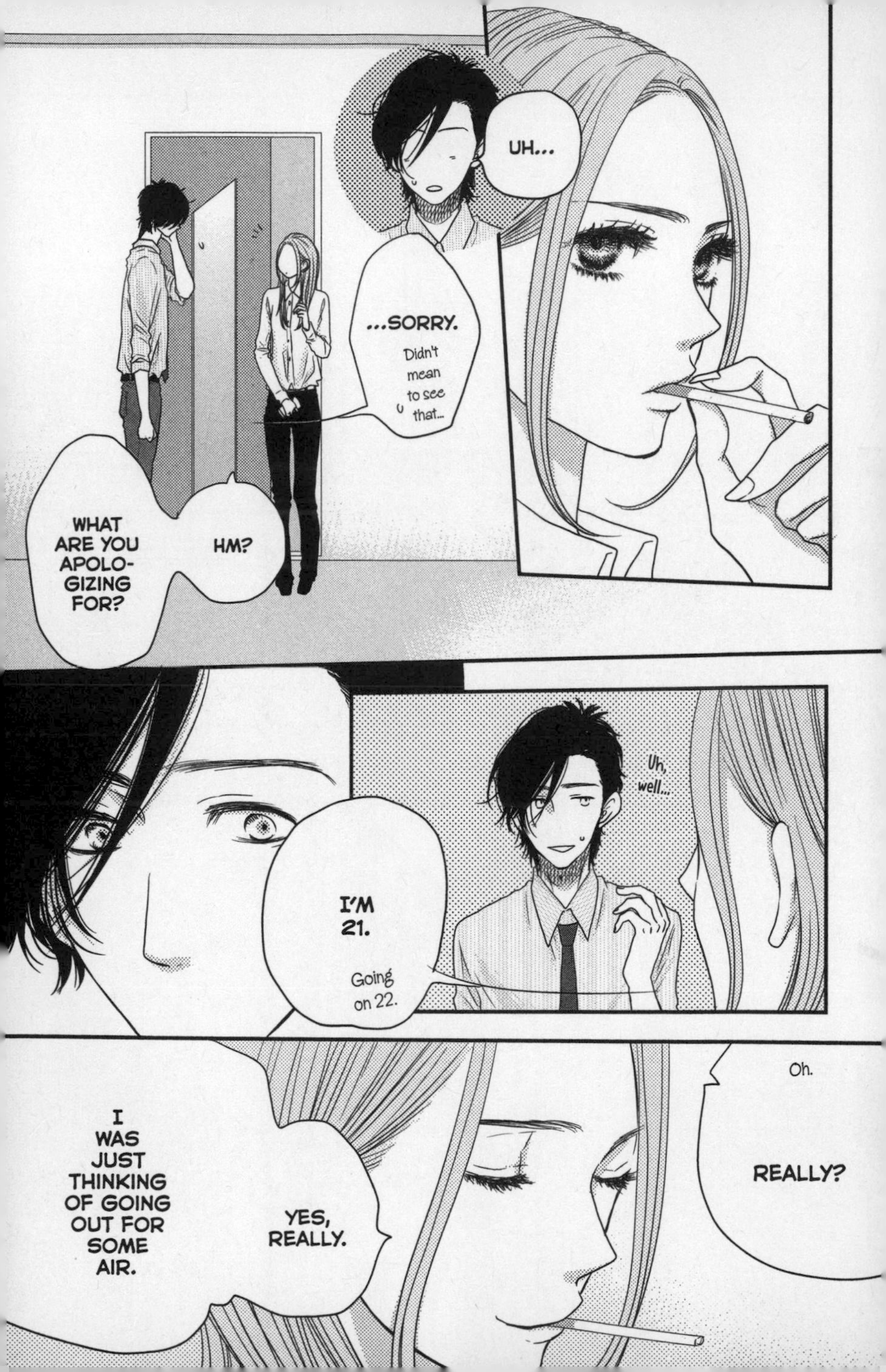
UH...
...SORRY.
Didn't mean to see that...
HM?
WHAT ARE YOU APOLOGIZING FOR?
Uh, well...
I'M 21.
Going on 22.
Oh.
REALLY?
YES, REALLY.
I WAS JUST THINKING OF GOING OUT FOR SOME AIR.

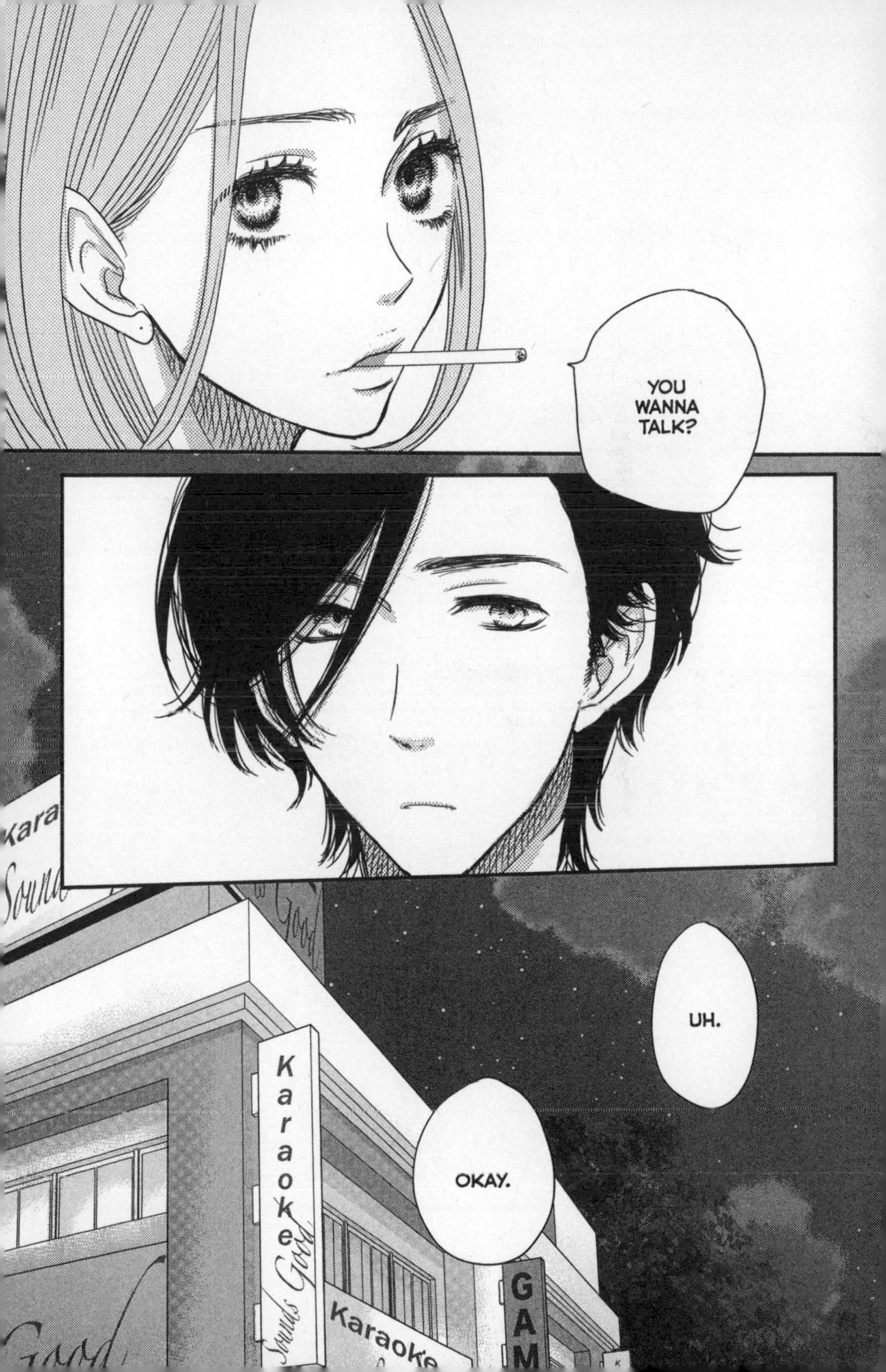
YOU WANNA TALK?
UH.
OKAY.
Karaoke
Sounds Good
Karaoke
GAM

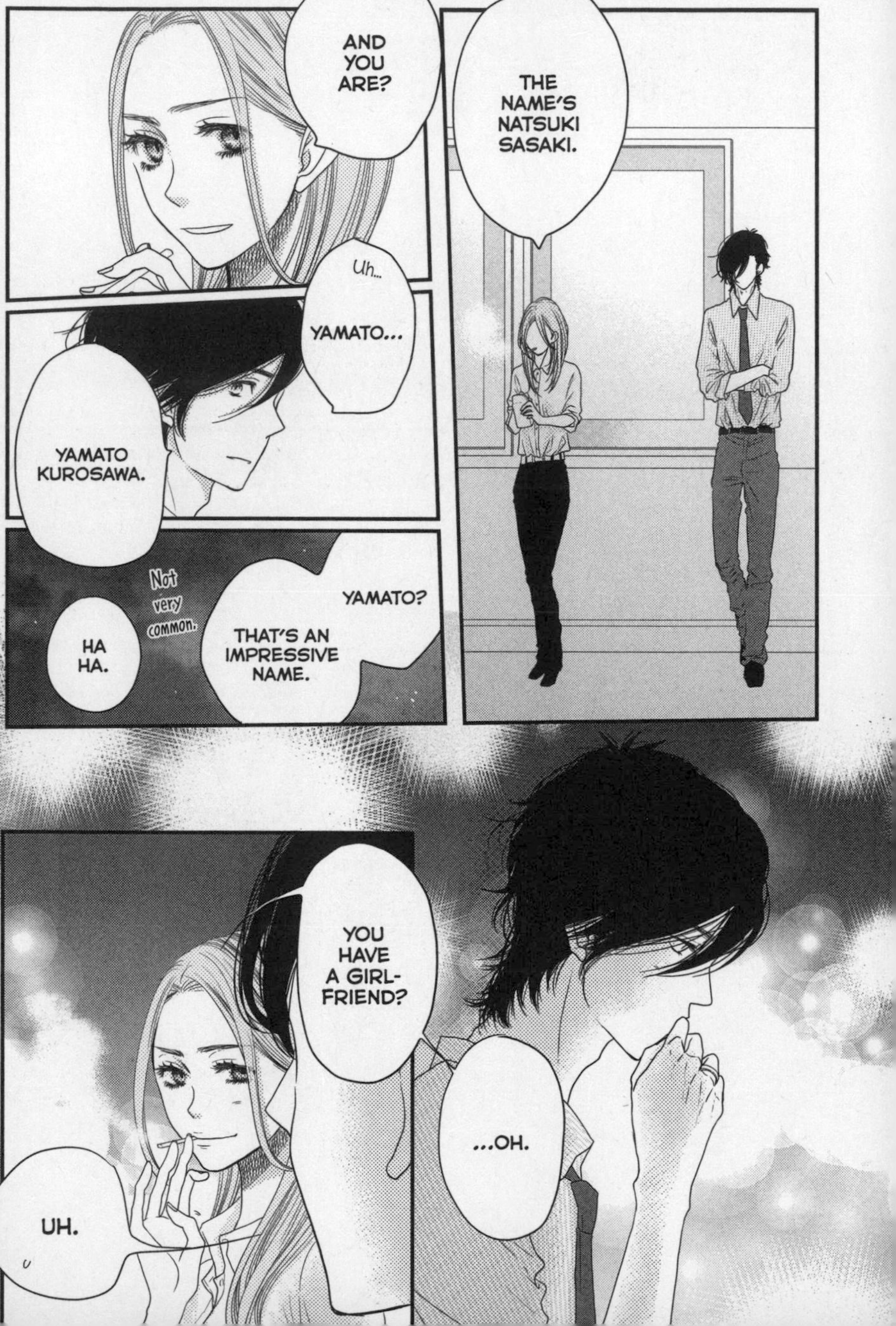
THE NAME'S NATSUKI SASAKI.
AND YOU ARE?
Uh...
YAMATO...
YAMATO KUROSAWA.
YAMATO?
THAT'S AN IMPRESSIVE NAME.
Not very common.
HA HA.
YOU HAVE A GIRL-FRIEND?
...OH.
UH.

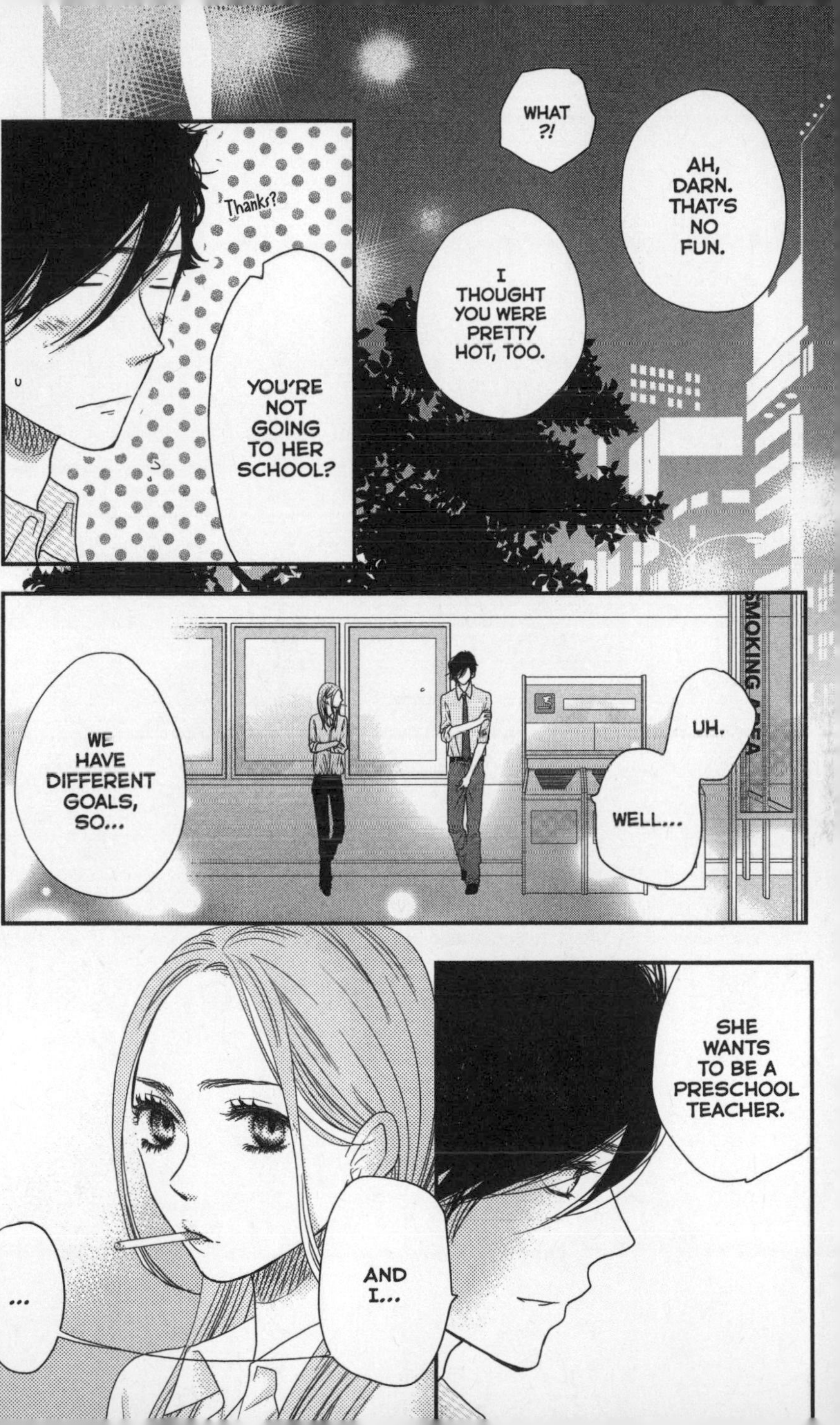
WHAT ?!
AH, DARN. THAT'S NO FUN.
I THOUGHT YOU WERE PRETTY HOT, TOO.
Thanks?
YOU'RE NOT GOING TO HER SCHOOL?
SMOKING AREA
UH.
WELL...
WE HAVE DIFFERENT GOALS, SO...
SHE WANTS TO BE A PRESCHOOL TEACHER.
AND I...
...

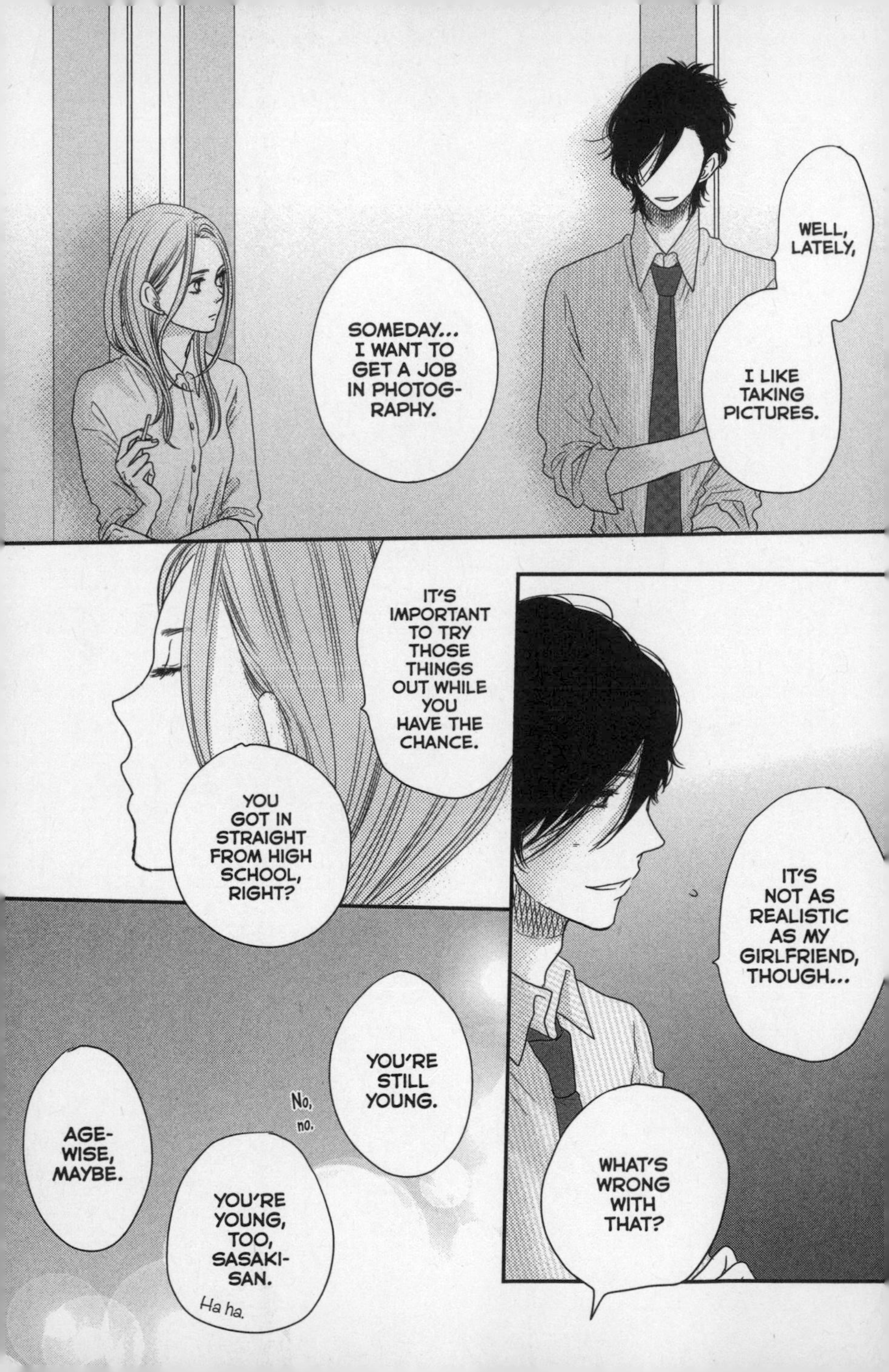
WELL, LATELY,
I LIKE TAKING PICTURES.
SOMEDAY... I WANT TO GET A JOB IN PHOTOG-RAPHY.
IT'S NOT AS REALISTIC AS MY GIRLFRIEND, THOUGH...
WHAT'S WRONG WITH THAT?
IT'S IMPORTANT TO TRY THOSE THINGS OUT WHILE YOU HAVE THE CHANCE.
YOU GOT IN STRAIGHT FROM HIGH SCHOOL, RIGHT?
YOU'RE STILL YOUNG.
No, no.
AGE-WISE, MAYBE.
YOU'RE YOUNG, TOO, SASAKI-SAN.
Ha ha.

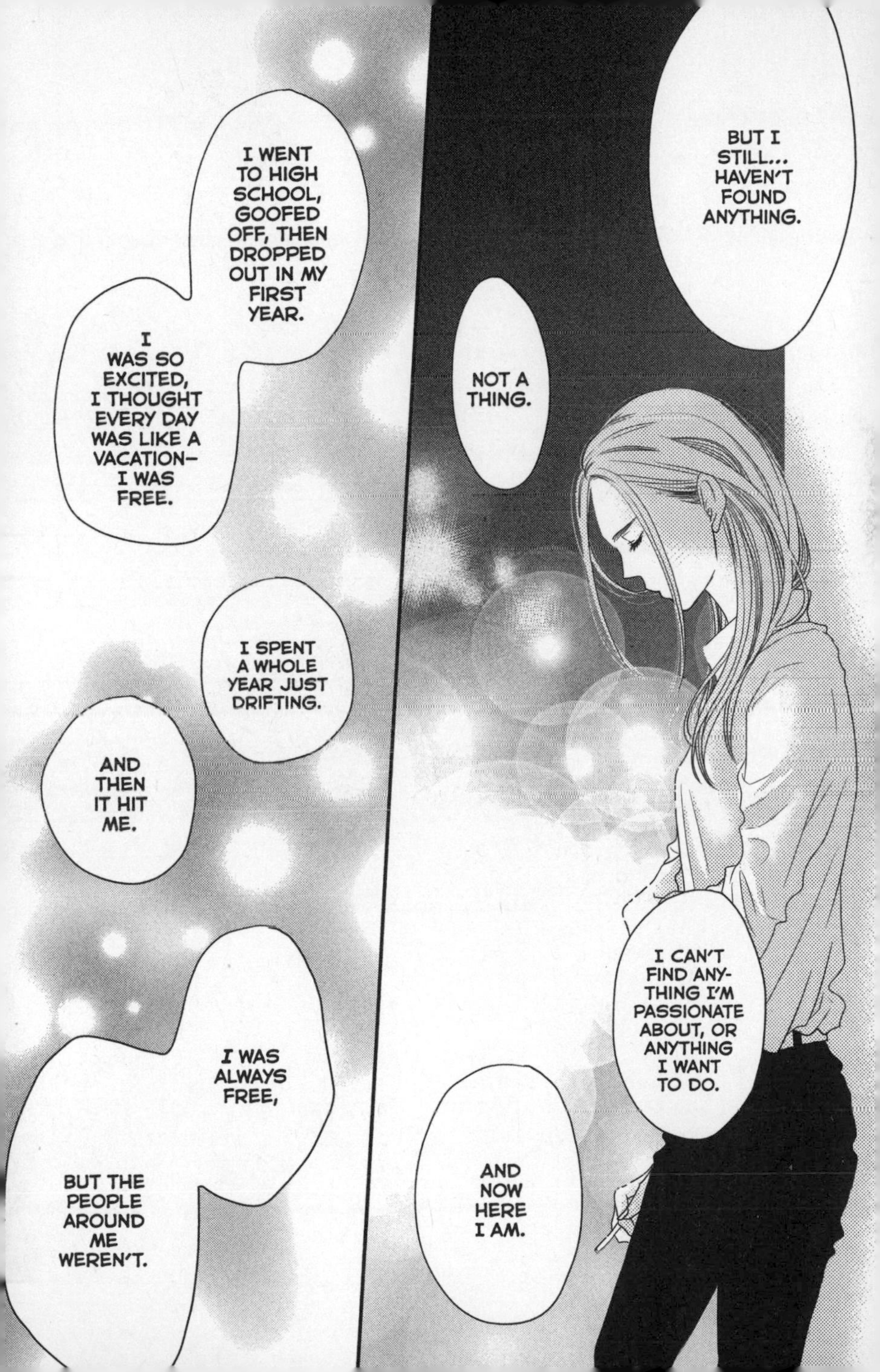
BUT I STILL... HAVEN'T FOUND ANYTHING.
NOT A THING.
I CAN'T FIND ANYTHING I'M PASSIONATE ABOUT, OR ANYTHING I WANT TO DO.
AND NOW HERE I AM.
I WENT TO HIGH SCHOOL, GOOFED OFF, THEN DROPPED OUT IN MY FIRST YEAR.
I WAS SO EXCITED, I THOUGHT EVERY DAY WAS LIKE A VACATION— I WAS FREE.
I SPENT A WHOLE YEAR JUST DRIFTING.
AND THEN IT HIT ME.
I WAS ALWAYS FREE,
BUT THE PEOPLE AROUND ME WEREN'T.

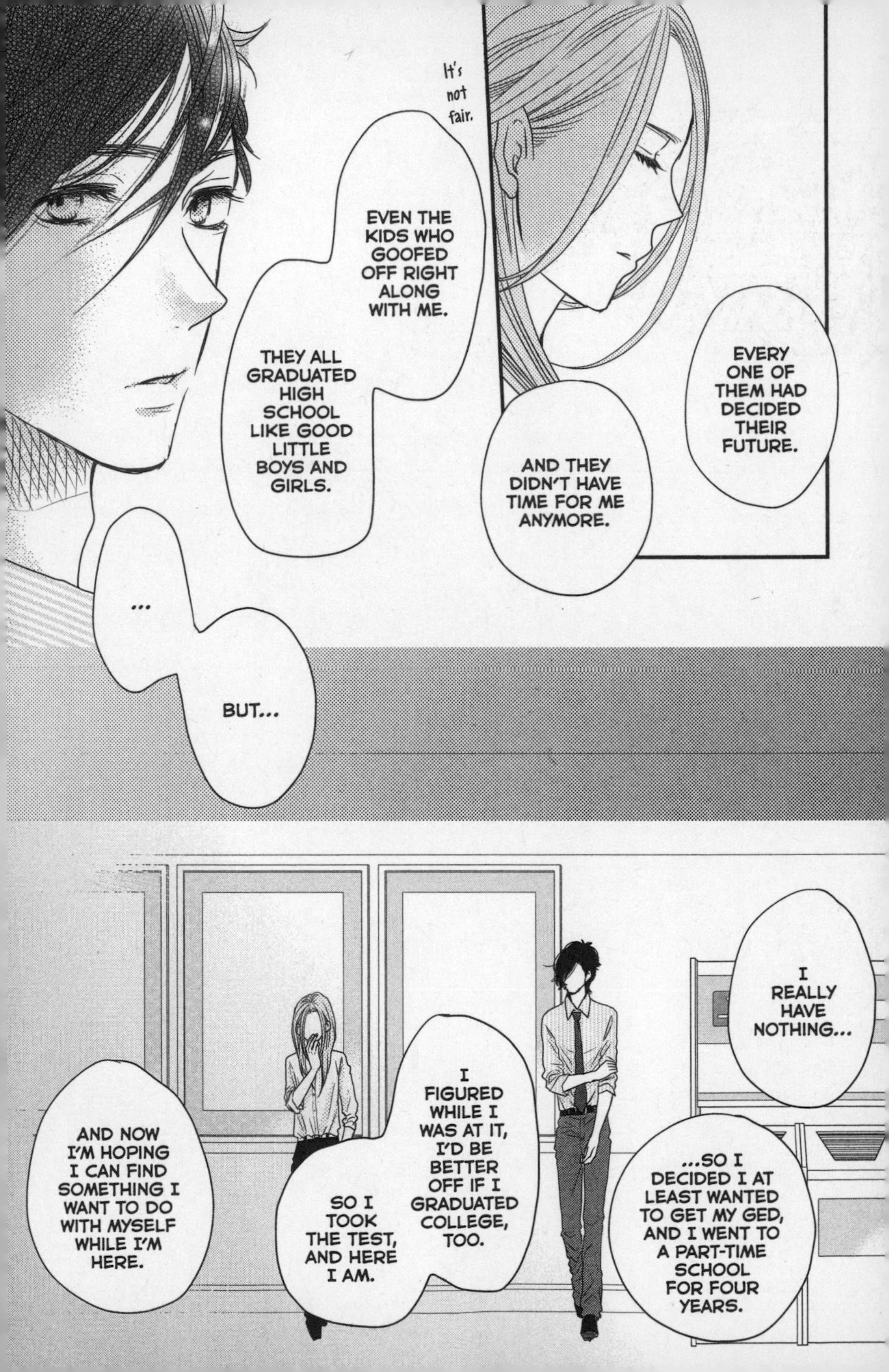
EVERY ONE OF THEM HAD DECIDED THEIR FUTURE.
AND THEY DIDN'T HAVE TIME FOR ME ANYMORE.
It's not fair.
EVEN THE KIDS WHO GOOFED OFF RIGHT ALONG WITH ME.
THEY ALL GRADUATED HIGH SCHOOL LIKE GOOD LITTLE BOYS AND GIRLS.
...
BUT...
I REALLY HAVE NOTHING...
...SO I DECIDED I AT LEAST WANTED TO GET MY GED, AND I WENT TO A PART-TIME SCHOOL FOR FOUR YEARS.
I FIGURED WHILE I WAS AT IT, I'D BE BETTER OFF IF I GRADUATED COLLEGE, TOO.
SO I TOOK THE TEST, AND HERE I AM.
AND NOW I'M HOPING I CAN FIND SOMETHING I WANT TO DO WITH MYSELF WHILE I'M HERE.

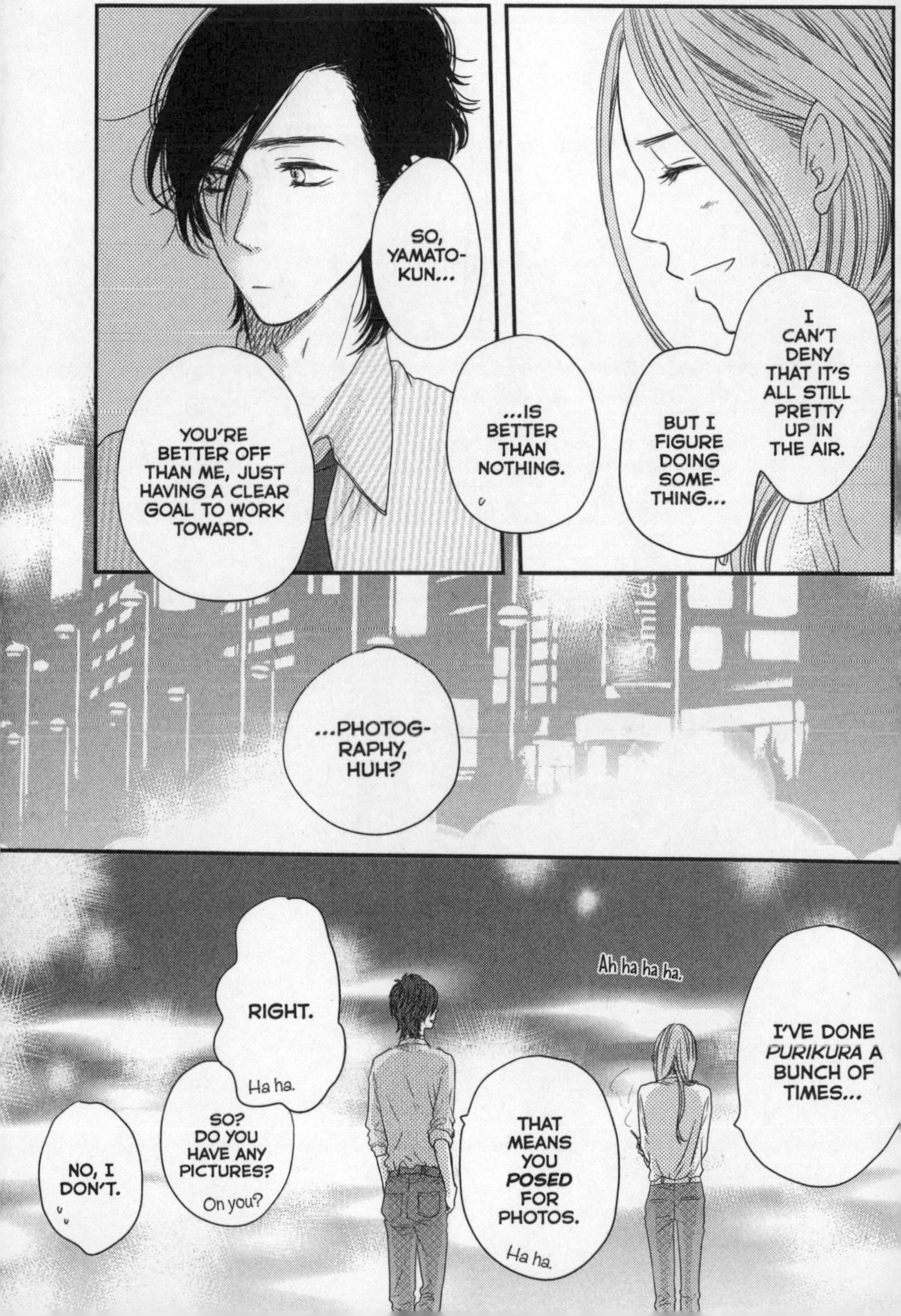
I CAN'T DENY THAT IT'S ALL STILL PRETTY UP IN THE AIR.
BUT I FIGURE DOING SOMETHING...
...IS BETTER THAN NOTHING.
SO, YAMATO-KUN...
YOU'RE BETTER OFF THAN ME, JUST HAVING A CLEAR GOAL TO WORK TOWARD.
...PHOTOGRAPHY, HUH?
Ah ha ha ha.
I'VE DONE *PURIKURA* A BUNCH OF TIMES...
THAT MEANS YOU *POSED* FOR PHOTOS.
Ha ha.
RIGHT.
Ha ha.
SO? DO YOU HAVE ANY PICTURES?
On you?
NO, I DON'T.

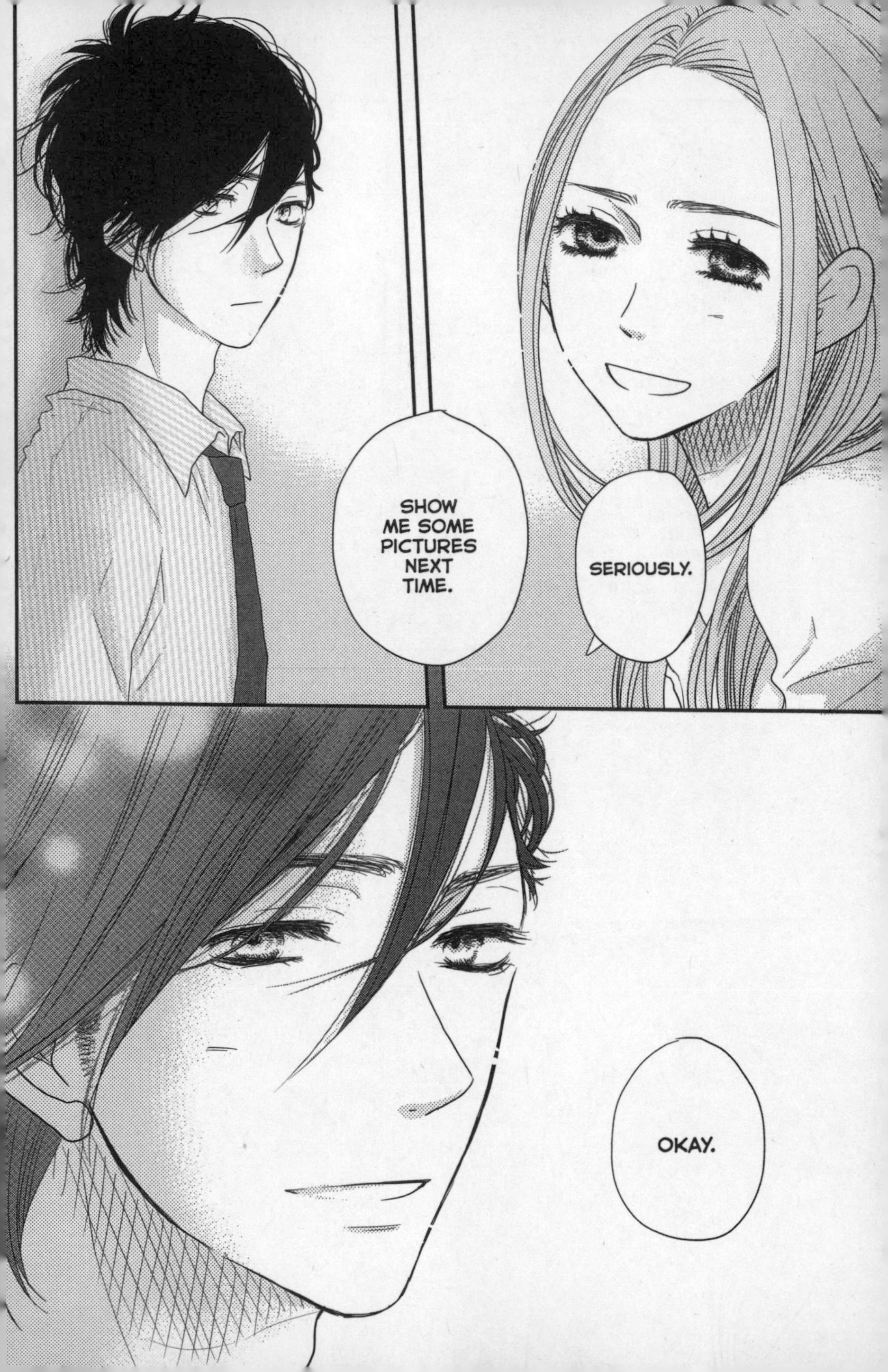
SERIOUSLY.
SHOW ME SOME PICTURES NEXT TIME.
OKAY.

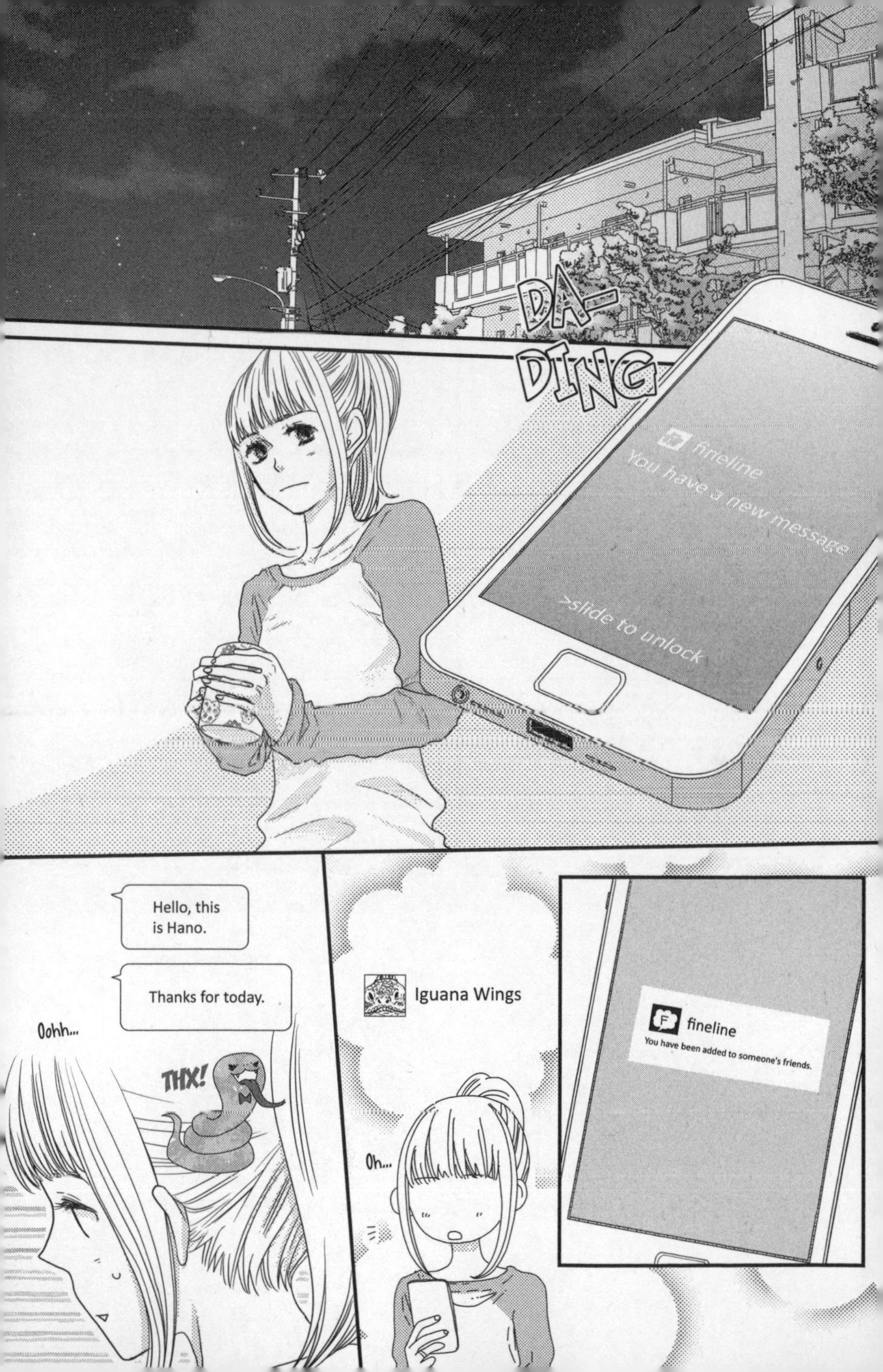
DA-DING
fineline
You have a new message
>slide to unlock
fineline
You have been added to someone's friends.
Iguana Wings
Oh...
Hello, this is Hano.
Thanks for today.
Oohh...
THX!

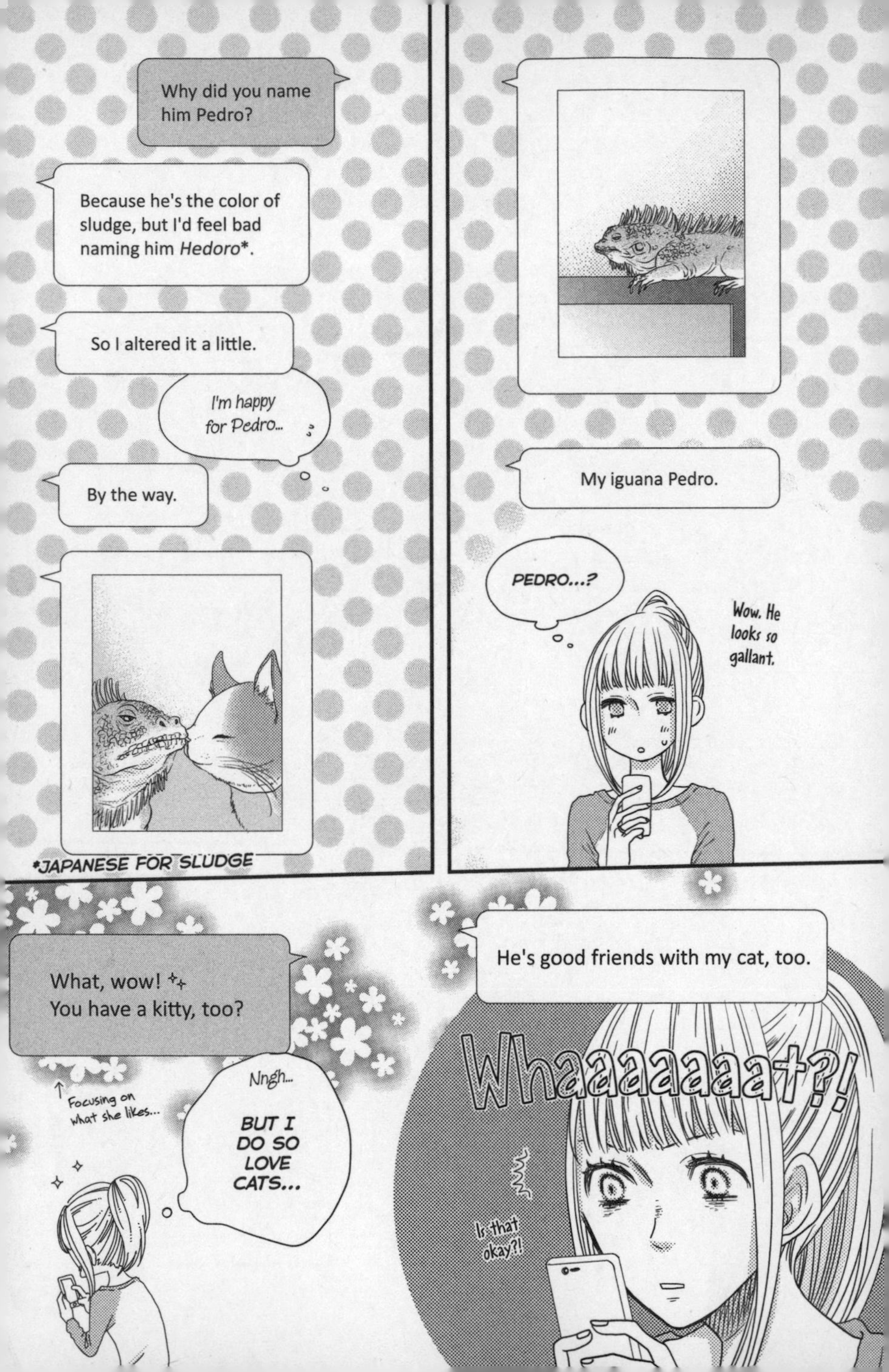
My iguana Pedro.
PEDRO...?
Wow. He looks so gallant.
Why did you name him Pedro?
Because he's the color of sludge, but I'd feel bad naming him *Hedoro**.
So I altered it a little.
I'm happy for Pedro...
By the way.
*JAPANESE FOR SLUDGE
He's good friends with my cat, too.
Whaaaaaaaat?!
Is that okay?!
What, wow! You have a kitty, too?
Nngh...
BUT I DO SO LOVE CATS...
Focusing on what she likes...

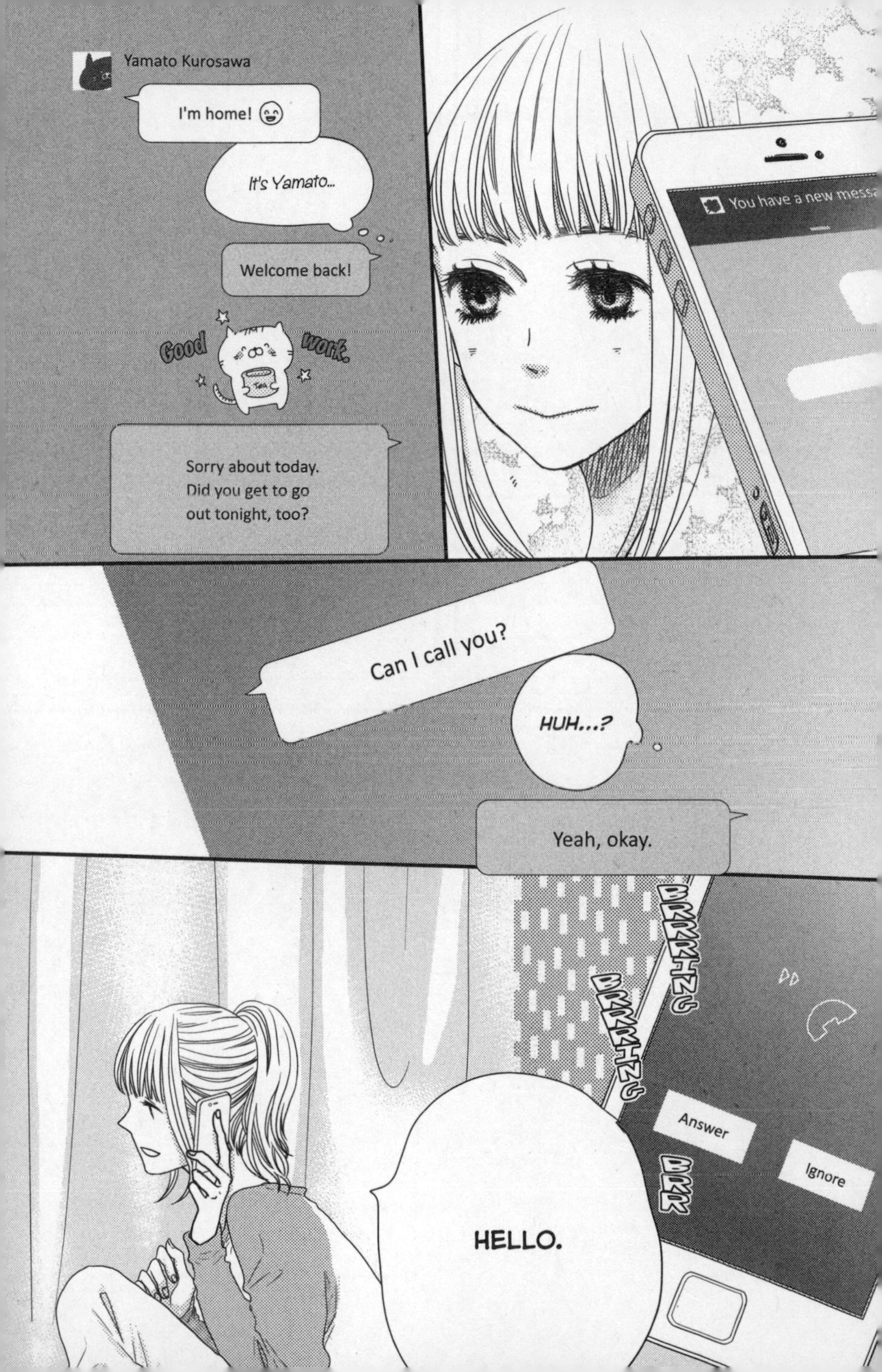
You have a new messa
Yamato Kurosawa
I'm home!
It's Yamato...
Welcome back!
Good work.
Sorry about today. Did you get to go out tonight, too?
Can I call you?
HUH...?
Yeah, okay.
BRRRING
BRRRING
Answer
Ignore
BRRR
HELLO.

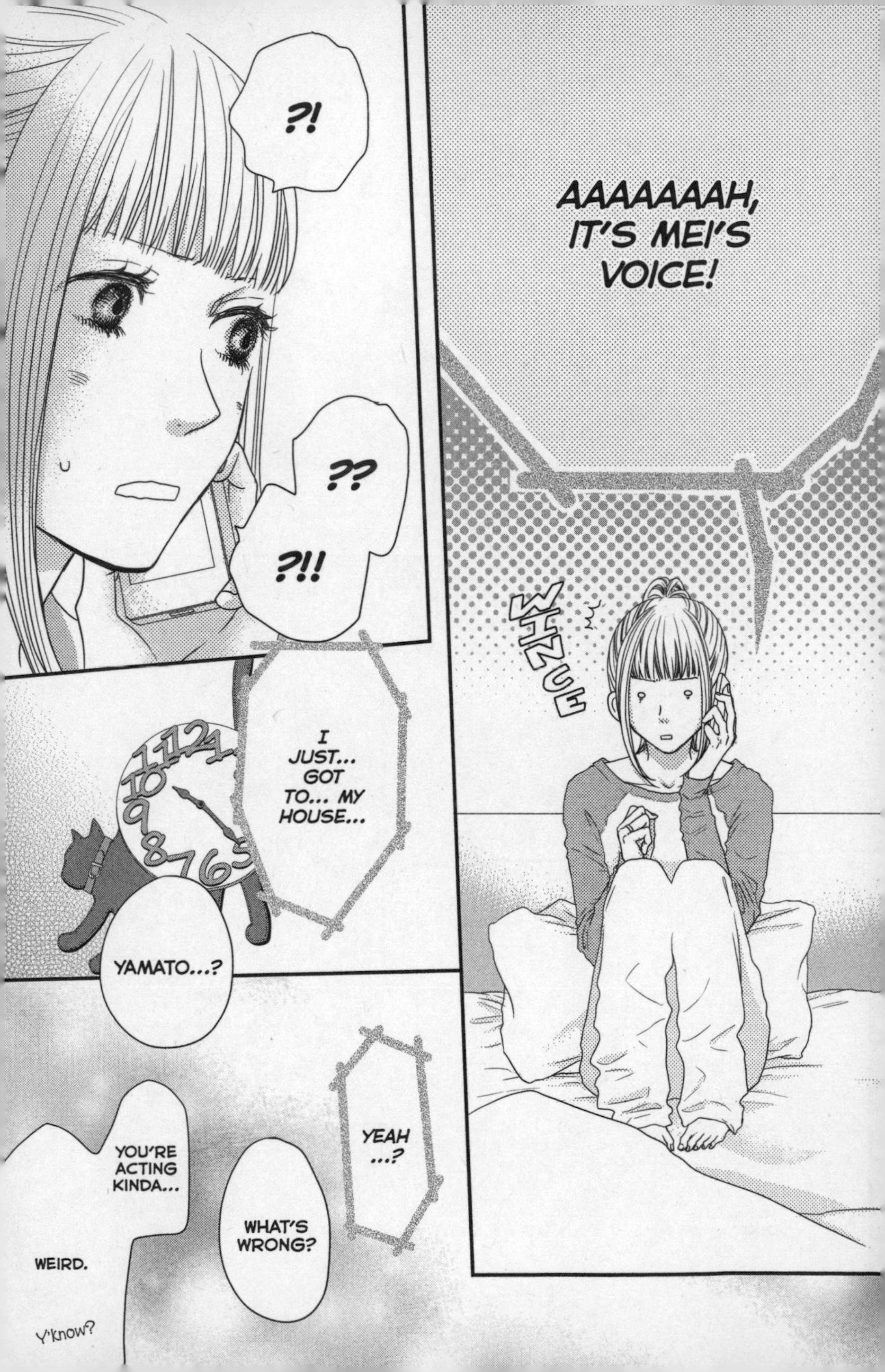
AAAAAAAH, IT'S MEI'S VOICE!
WINCE
?!
??
?!!
I JUST... GOT TO... MY HOUSE...
YAMATO...?
YEAH ...?
WHAT'S WRONG?
YOU'RE ACTING KINDA...
WEIRD.
Y'know?

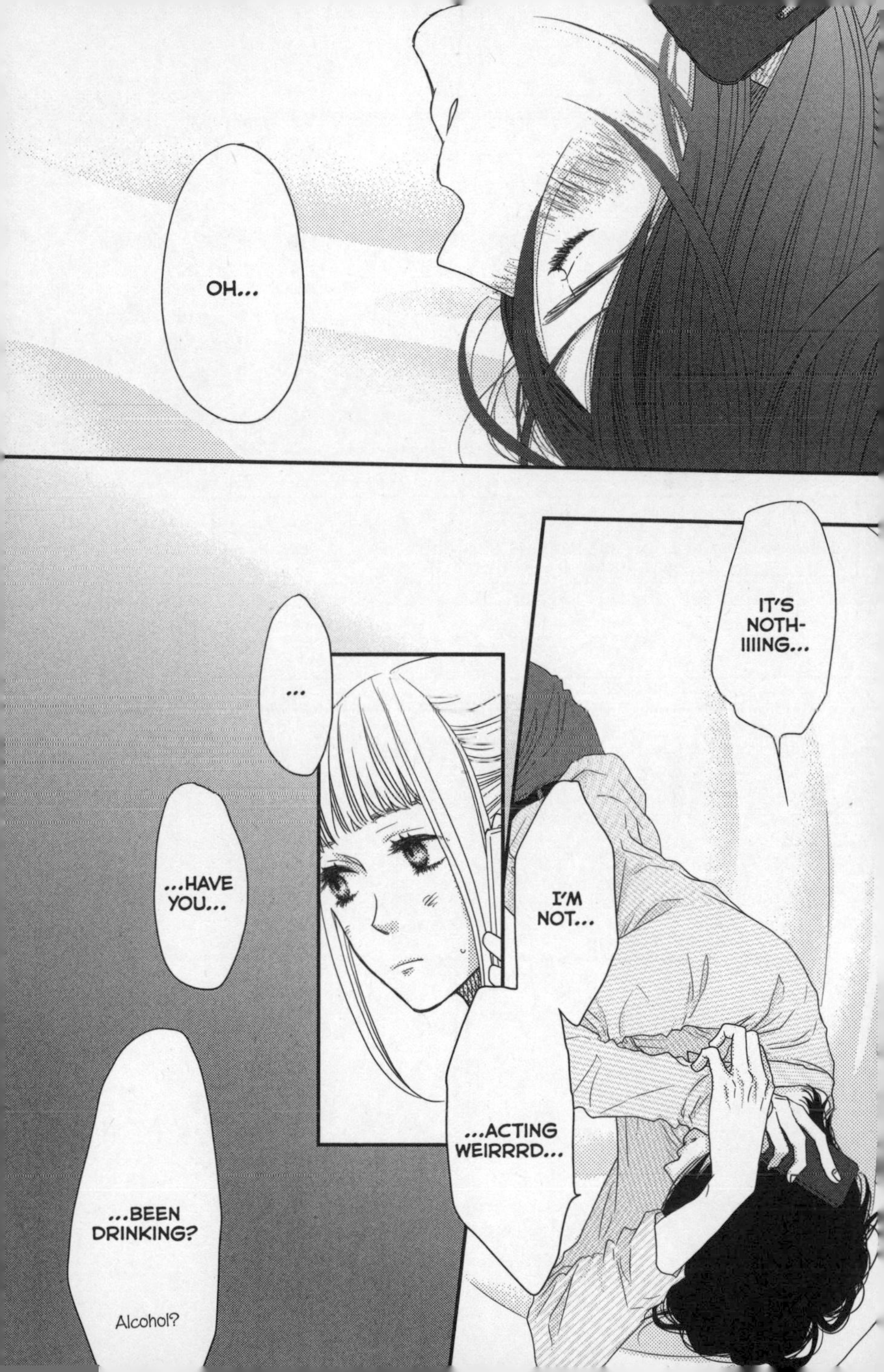
OH...
IT'S NOTH-IIIING...
I'M NOT...
...ACTING WEIRRRD...
...
...HAVE YOU...
...BEEN DRINKING?
Alcohol?

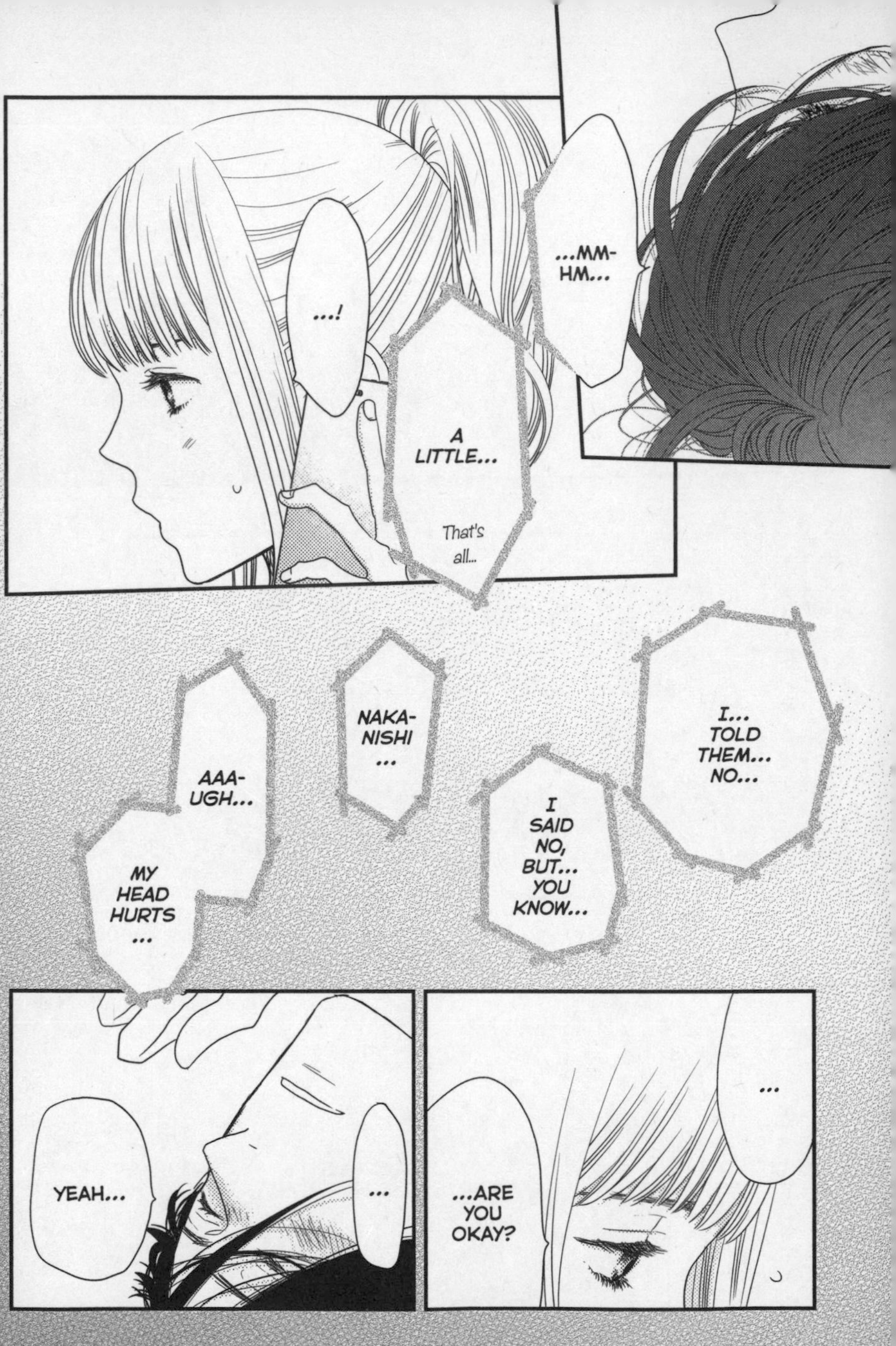
...MM-HM...
A LITTLE... That's all...
...!
I... TOLD THEM... NO...
I SAID NO, BUT... YOU KNOW...
NAKA-NISHI...
AAA-UGH... MY HEAD HURTS...
...
...ARE YOU OKAY?
...
YEAH...

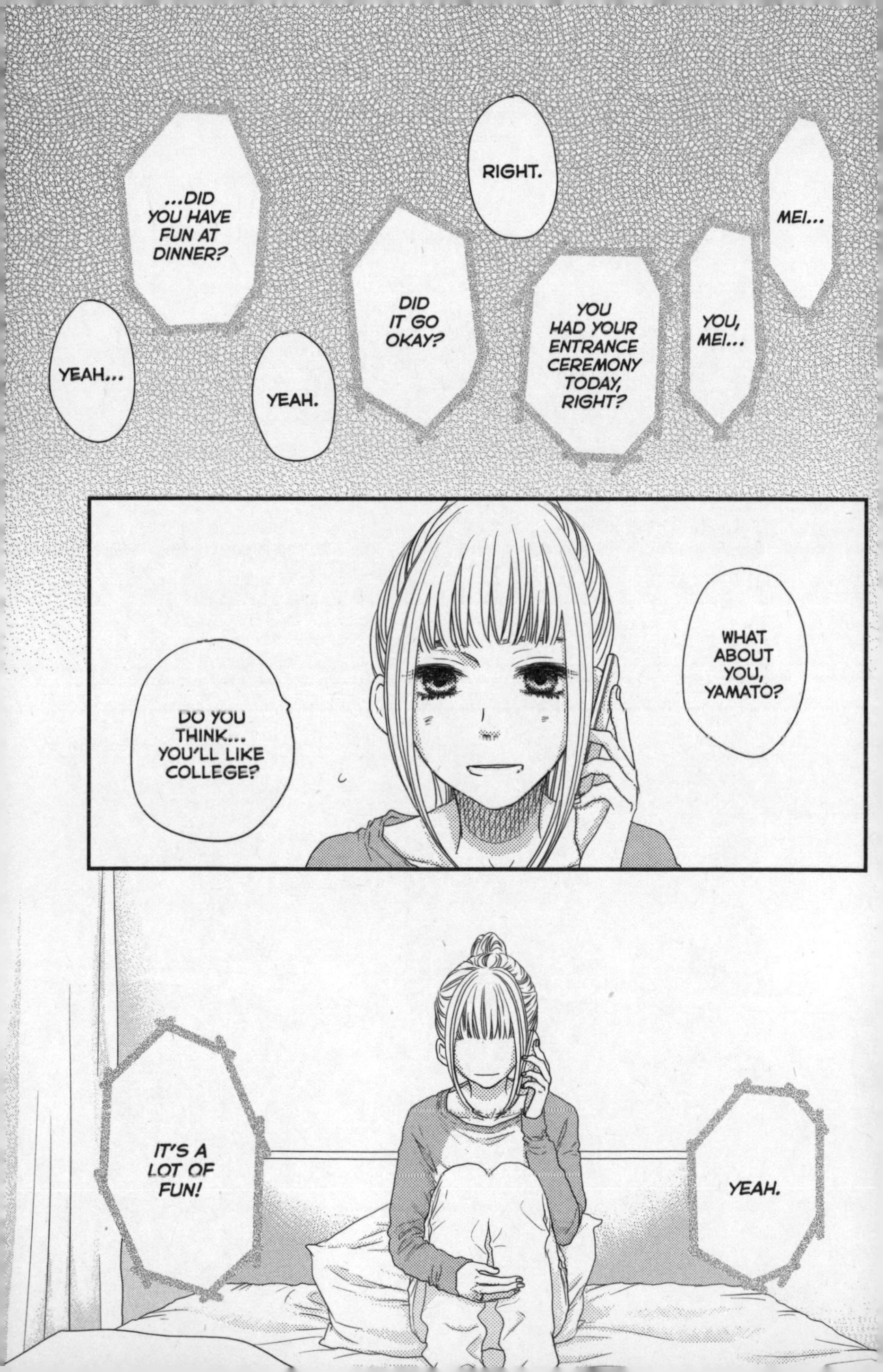
MEI...
YOU, MEI...
YOU HAD YOUR ENTRANCE CEREMONY TODAY, RIGHT?
RIGHT.
DID IT GO OKAY?
YEAH.
...DID YOU HAVE FUN AT DINNER?
YEAH...
WHAT ABOUT YOU, YAMATO?
DO YOU THINK... YOU'LL LIKE COLLEGE?
YEAH.
IT'S A LOT OF FUN!

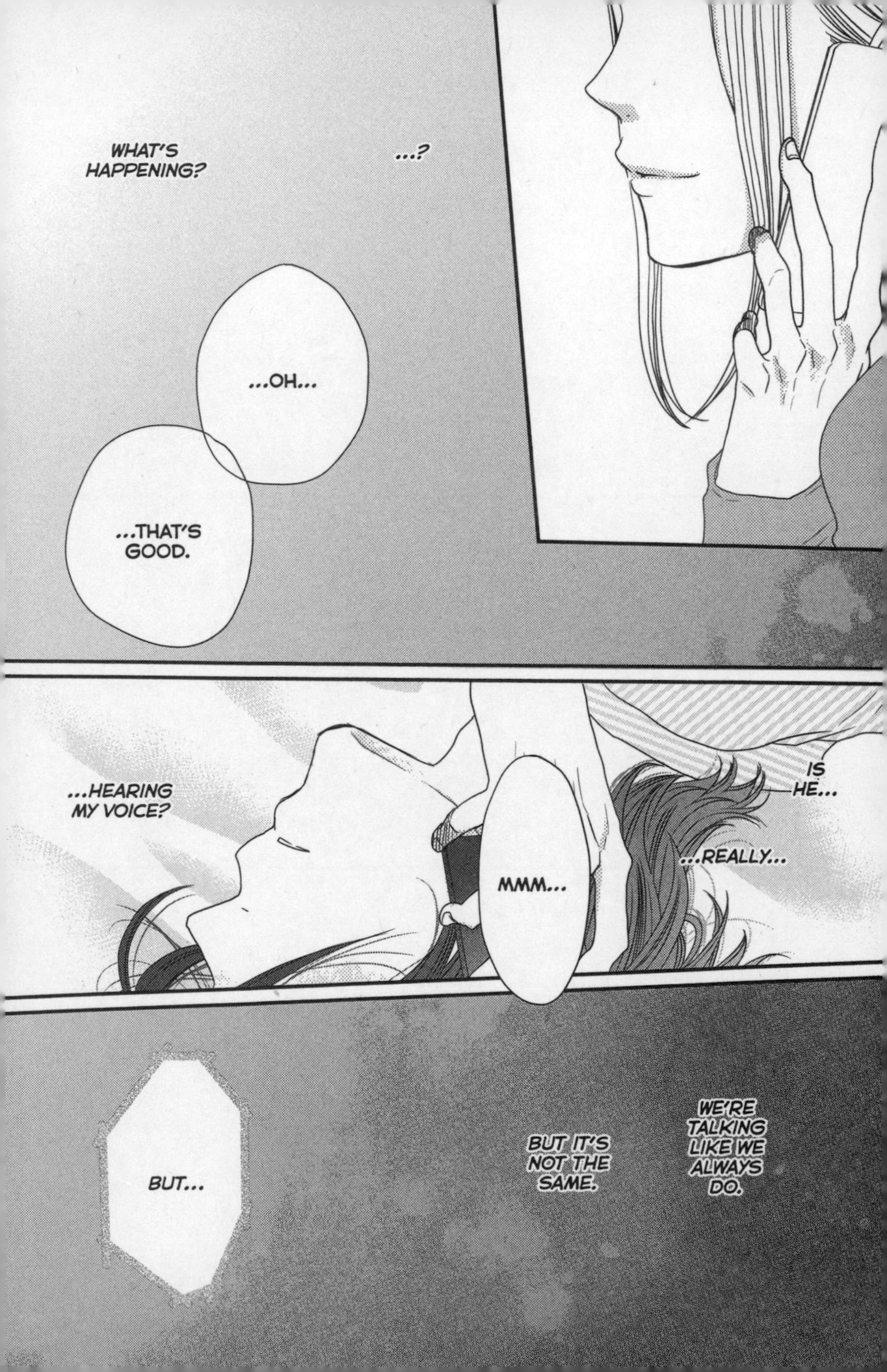
...?
WHAT'S HAPPENING?
...OH...
...THAT'S GOOD.
IS HE...
...REALLY...
MMM...
...HEARING MY VOICE?
WE'RE TALKING LIKE WE ALWAYS DO.
BUT IT'S NOT THE SAME.
BUT...

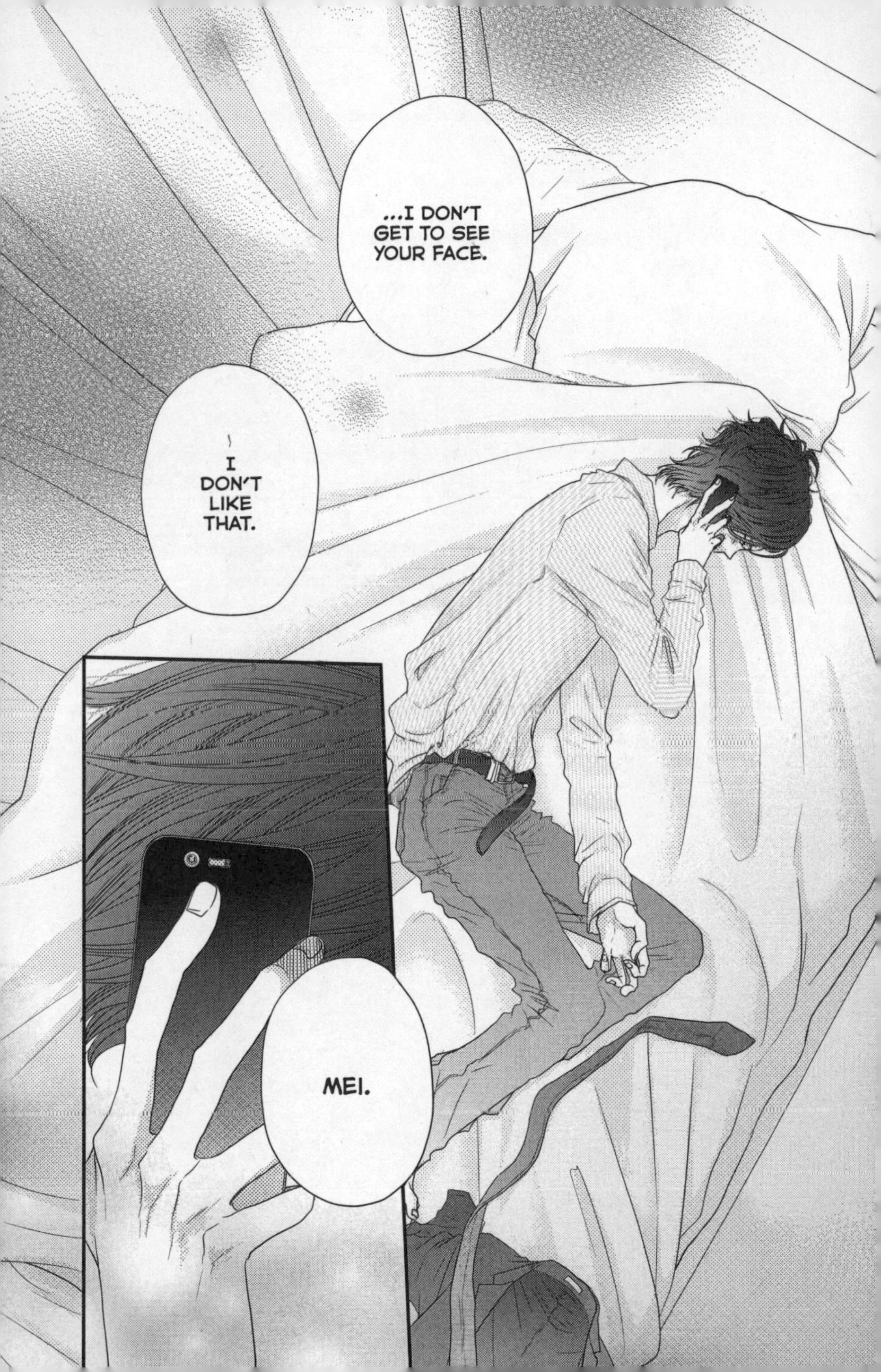
...I DON'T GET TO SEE YOUR FACE.
I DON'T LIKE THAT.
MEI.

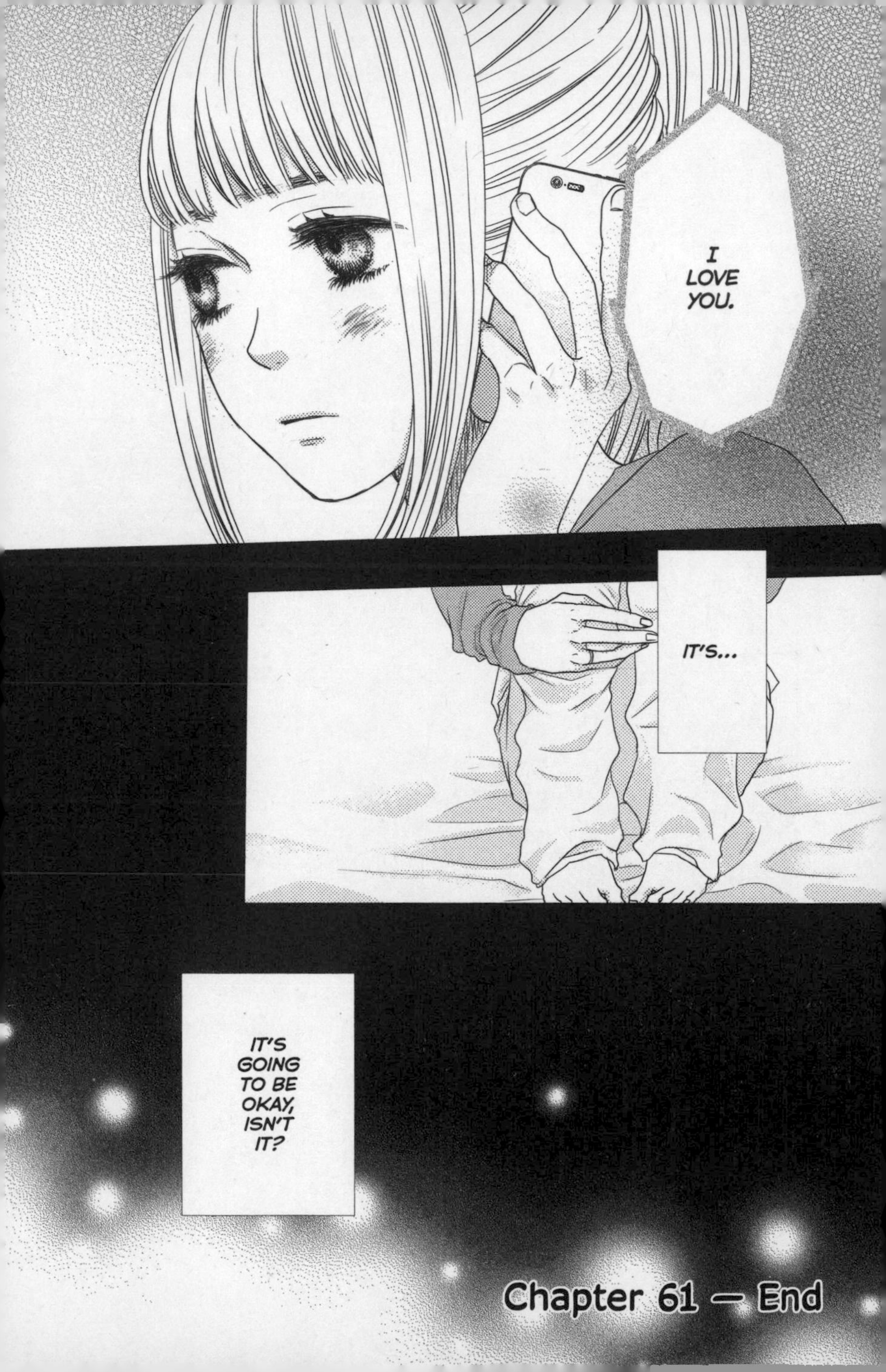
I LOVE YOU.
IT'S...
IT'S GOING TO BE OKAY, ISN'T IT?
Chapter 61 — End

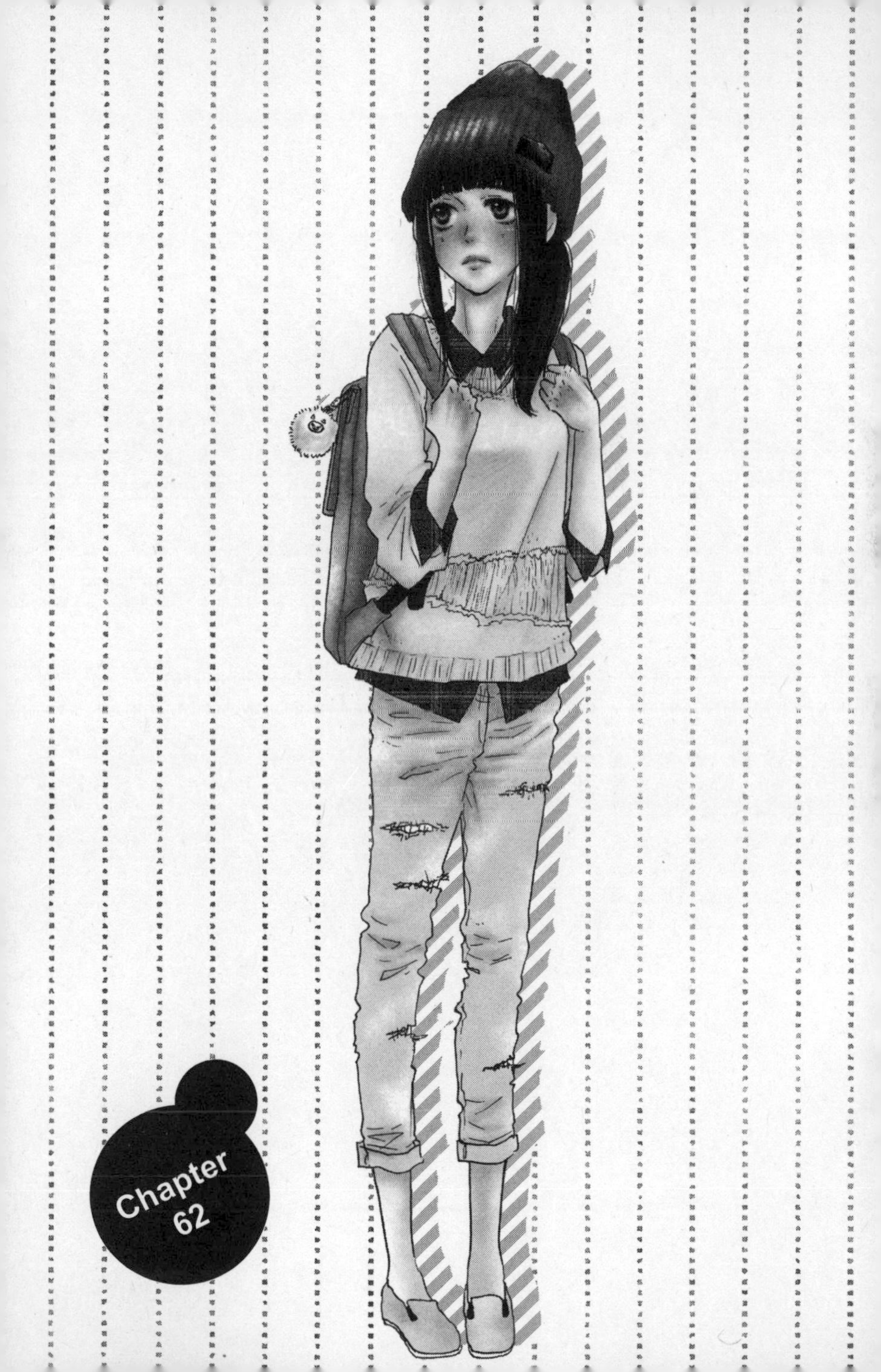
Chapter
62

Say "I love you".

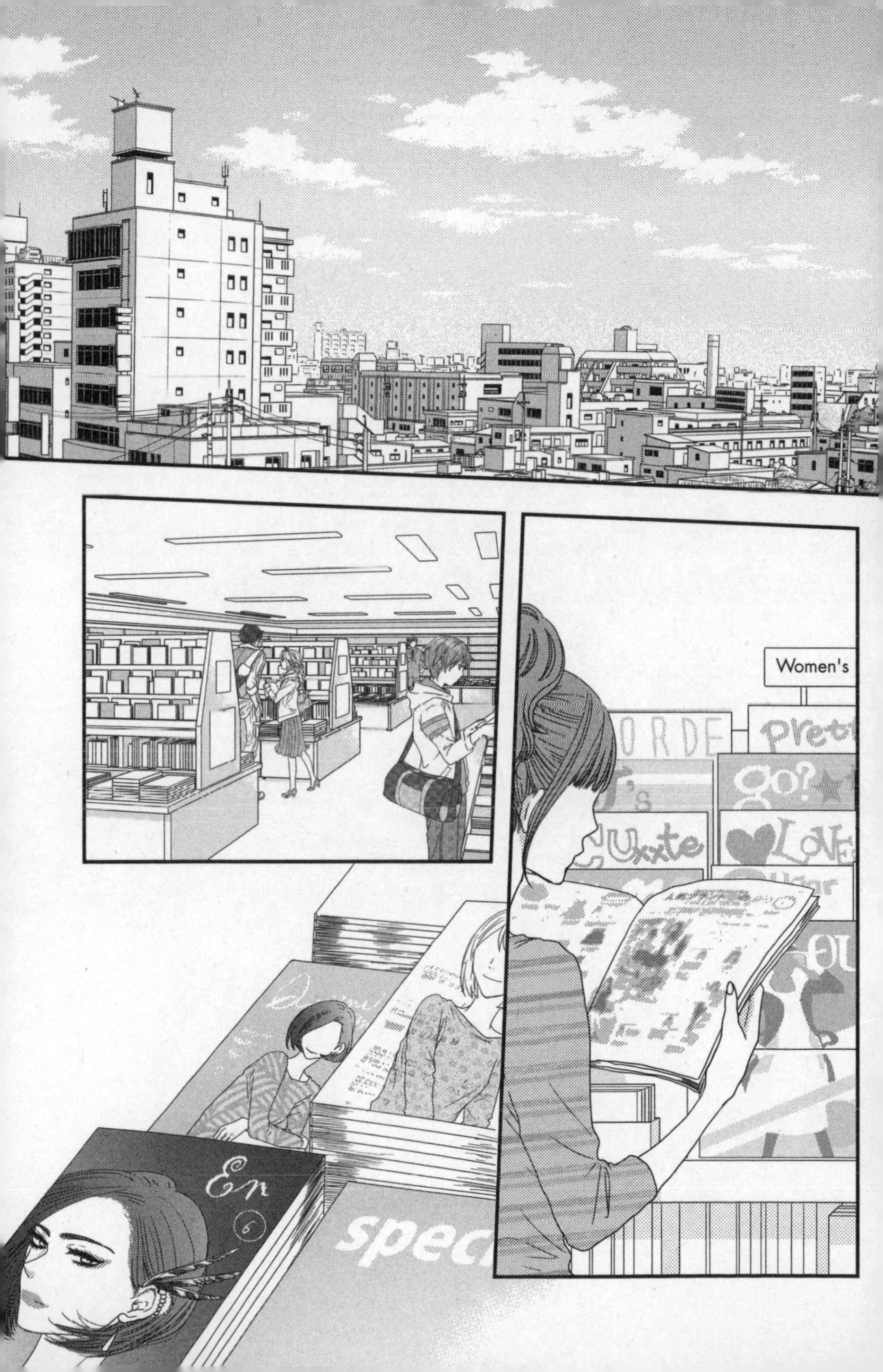
Women's

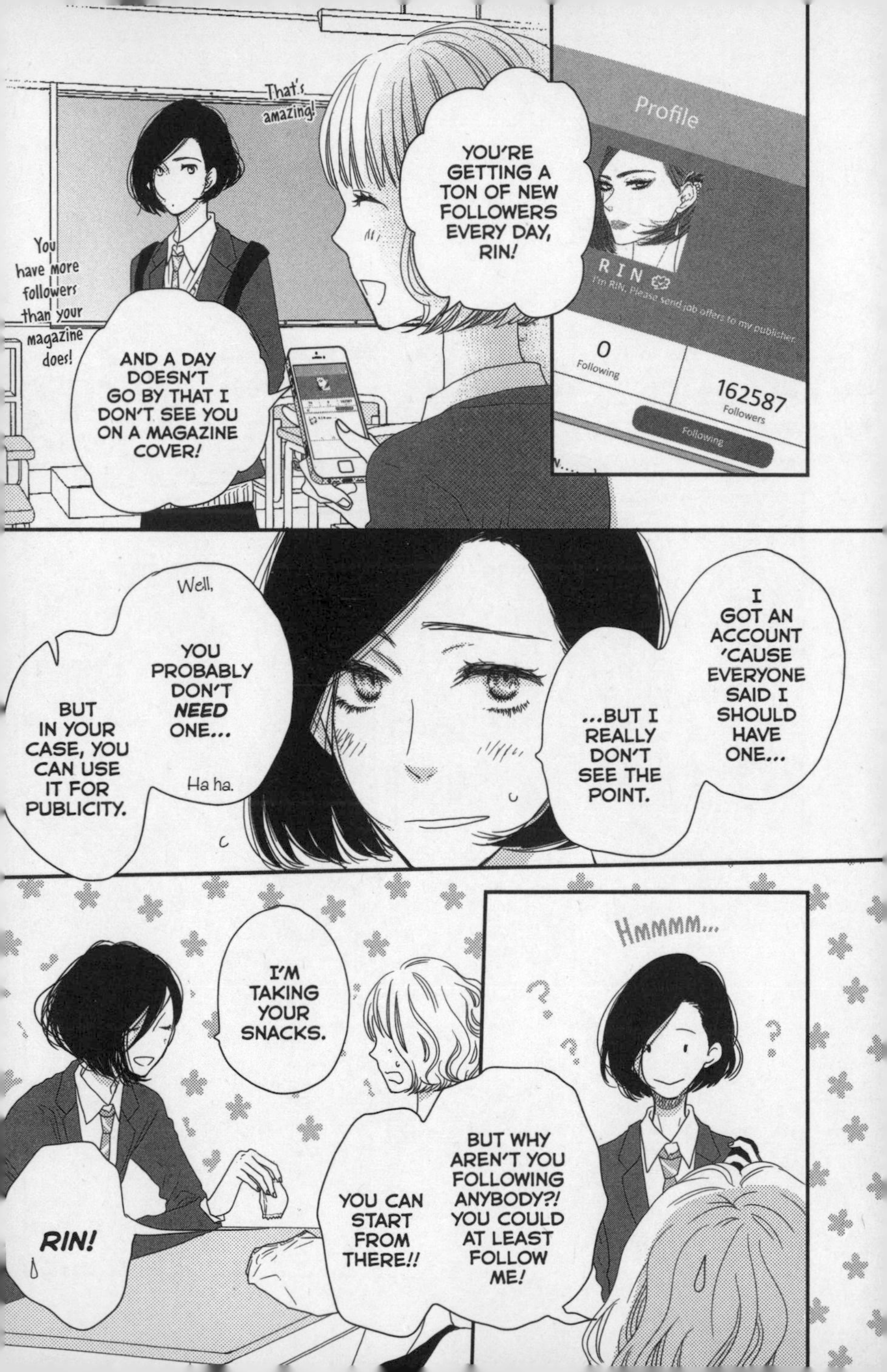
Profile
RIN
I'm RIN. Please send job offers to my publisher.
0
Following
162587
Followers
Following
YOU'RE GETTING A TON OF NEW FOLLOWERS EVERY DAY, RIN!
That's amazing!
You have more followers than your magazine does!
AND A DAY DOESN'T GO BY THAT I DON'T SEE YOU ON A MAGAZINE COVER!
I GOT AN ACCOUNT 'CAUSE EVERYONE SAID I SHOULD HAVE ONE...
...BUT I REALLY DON'T SEE THE POINT.
Well,
YOU PROBABLY DON'T *NEED* ONE...
Ha ha.
BUT IN YOUR CASE, YOU CAN USE IT FOR PUBLICITY.
Hmmmm...
BUT WHY AREN'T YOU FOLLOWING ANYBODY?! YOU COULD AT LEAST FOLLOW ME!
YOU CAN START FROM THERE!!
I'M TAKING YOUR SNACKS.
RIN!

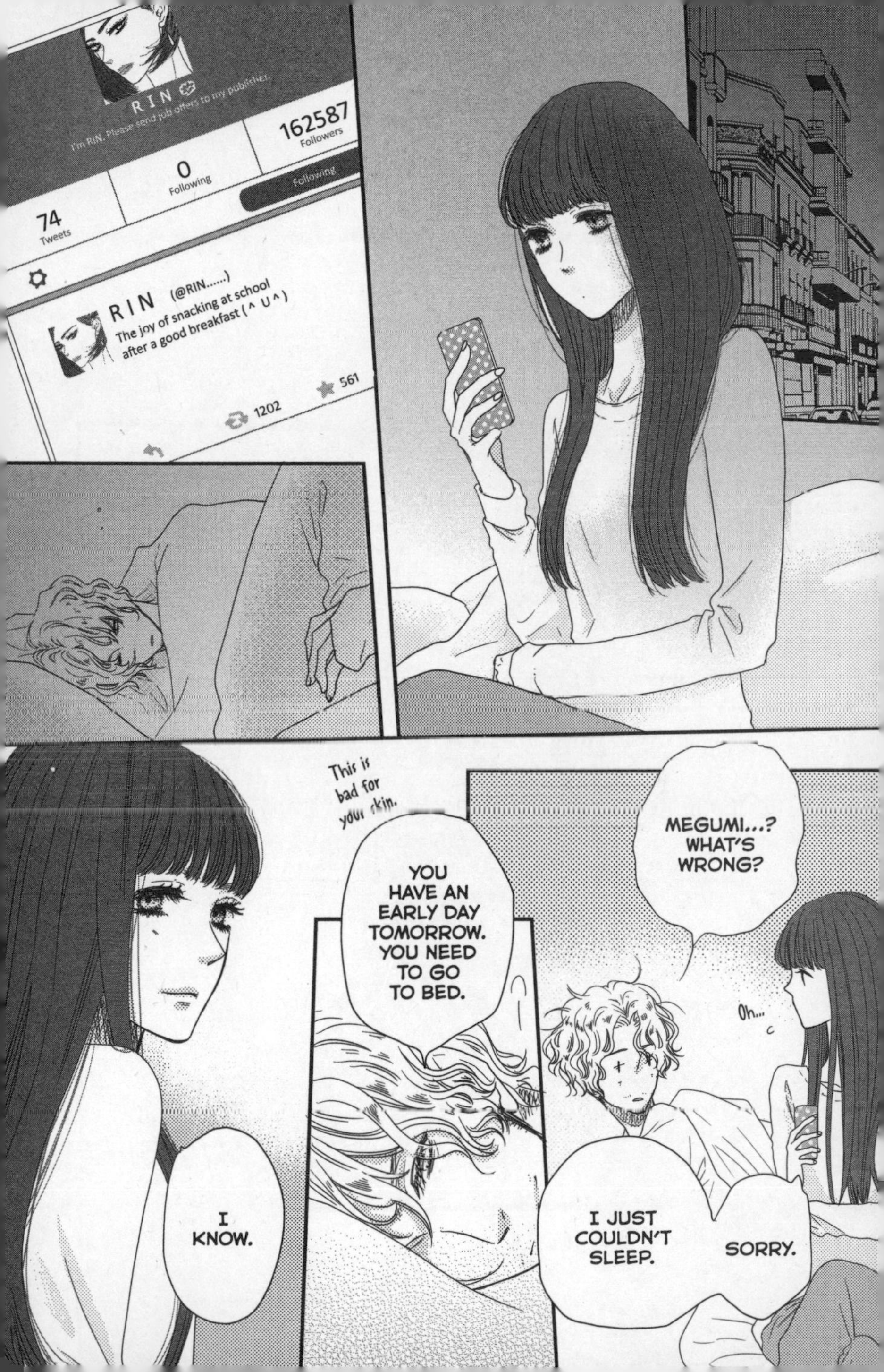
RIN
I'm RIN. Please send job offers to my publisher.
162587
Followers
0
Following
Following
74
Tweets
RIN (@RIN......)
The joy of snacking at school after a good breakfast (^ U ^)
1202
561
MEGUMI...? WHAT'S WRONG?
Oh...
SORRY.
I JUST COULDN'T SLEEP.
This is bad for your skin.
YOU HAVE AN EARLY DAY TOMORROW. YOU NEED TO GO TO BED.
I KNOW.

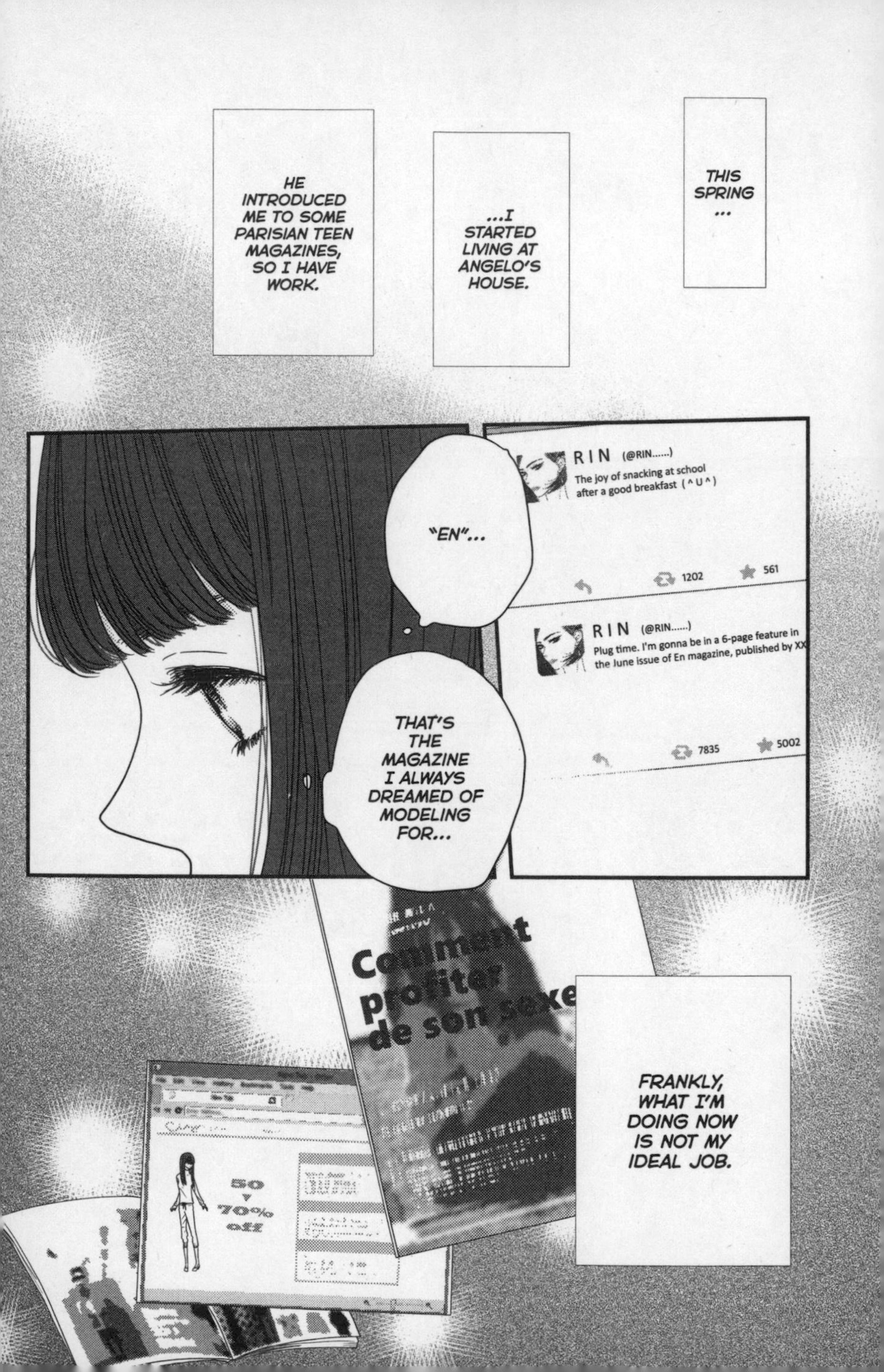
THIS SPRING...
...I STARTED LIVING AT ANGELO'S HOUSE.
HE INTRODUCED ME TO SOME PARISIAN TEEN MAGAZINES, SO I HAVE WORK.
RIN (@RIN......)
The joy of snacking at school after a good breakfast (^U^)
1202
561
RIN (@RIN......)
Plug time. I'm gonna be in a 6-page feature in the June issue of En magazine, published by XX
7835
5002
"EN"...
THAT'S THE MAGAZINE I ALWAYS DREAMED OF MODELING FOR...
Comment profiter de son sexe
50 ▾ 70% off
FRANKLY, WHAT I'M DOING NOW IS NOT MY IDEAL JOB.

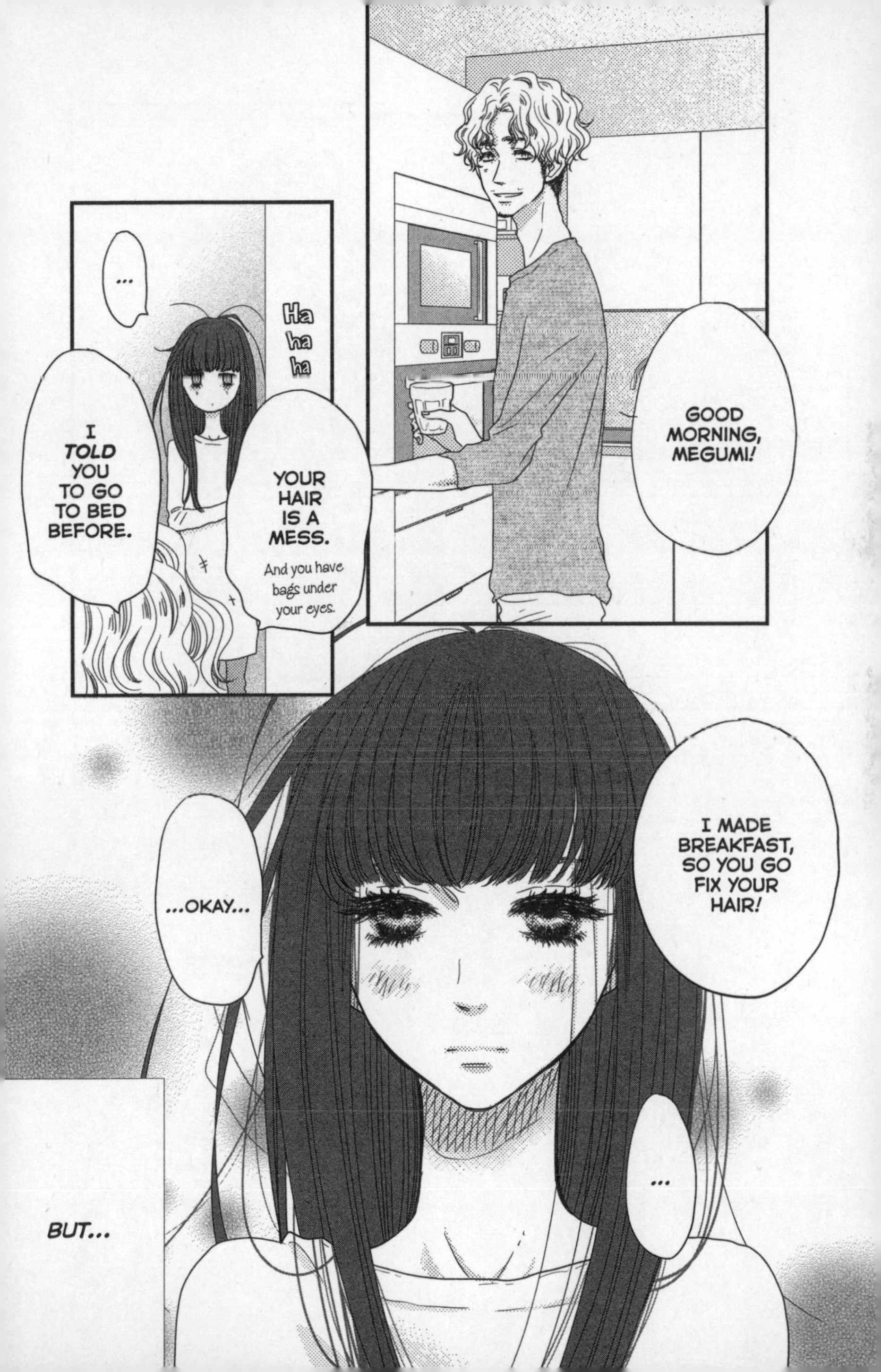
GOOD MORNING, MEGUMI!
Ha ha ha
YOUR HAIR IS A MESS.
And you have bags under your eyes.
I *TOLD* YOU TO GO TO BED BEFORE.
...
I MADE BREAKFAST, SO YOU GO FIX YOUR HAIR!
...OKAY...
...
BUT...

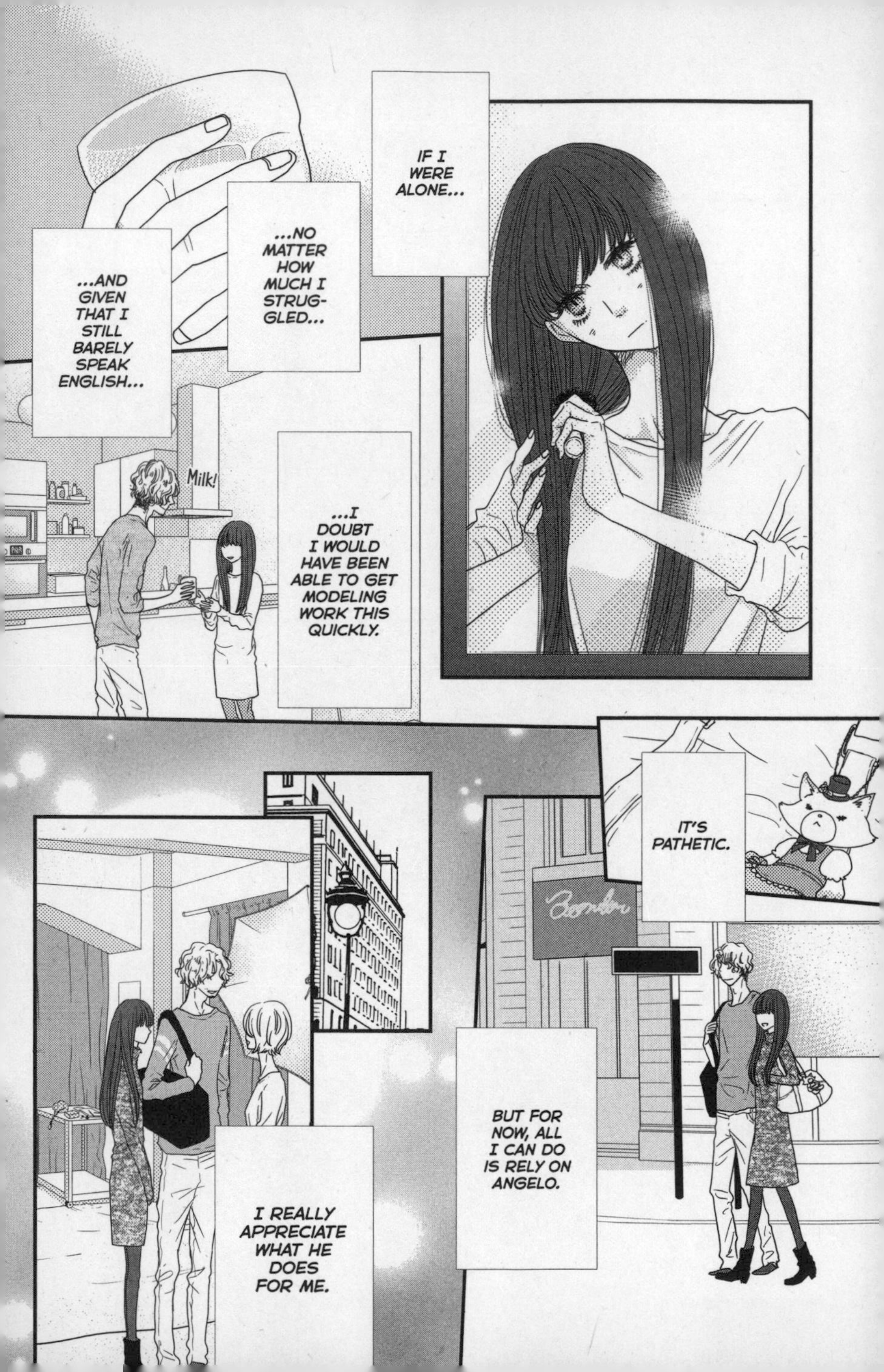
IF I WERE ALONE...
...NO MATTER HOW MUCH I STRUG-GLED...
...AND GIVEN THAT I STILL BARELY SPEAK ENGLISH...
...I DOUBT I WOULD HAVE BEEN ABLE TO GET MODELING WORK THIS QUICKLY.
Milk!
IT'S PATHETIC.
BUT FOR NOW, ALL I CAN DO IS RELY ON ANGELO.
I REALLY APPRECIATE WHAT HE DOES FOR ME.

SOMEDAY...
...I WANT TO GO FIND WORK WITHOUT ANY HELP.
IF THERE ARE SO MANY THINGS I LACK...
...THEN I'LL TAKE THE CONNECTIONS PEOPLE GIVE ME AND TIE THEM TO THE NEXT THING.
I HAVE NOTHING.
SO EVERYTHING I DO HERE IN PARIS COUNTS FOR SOMETHING.

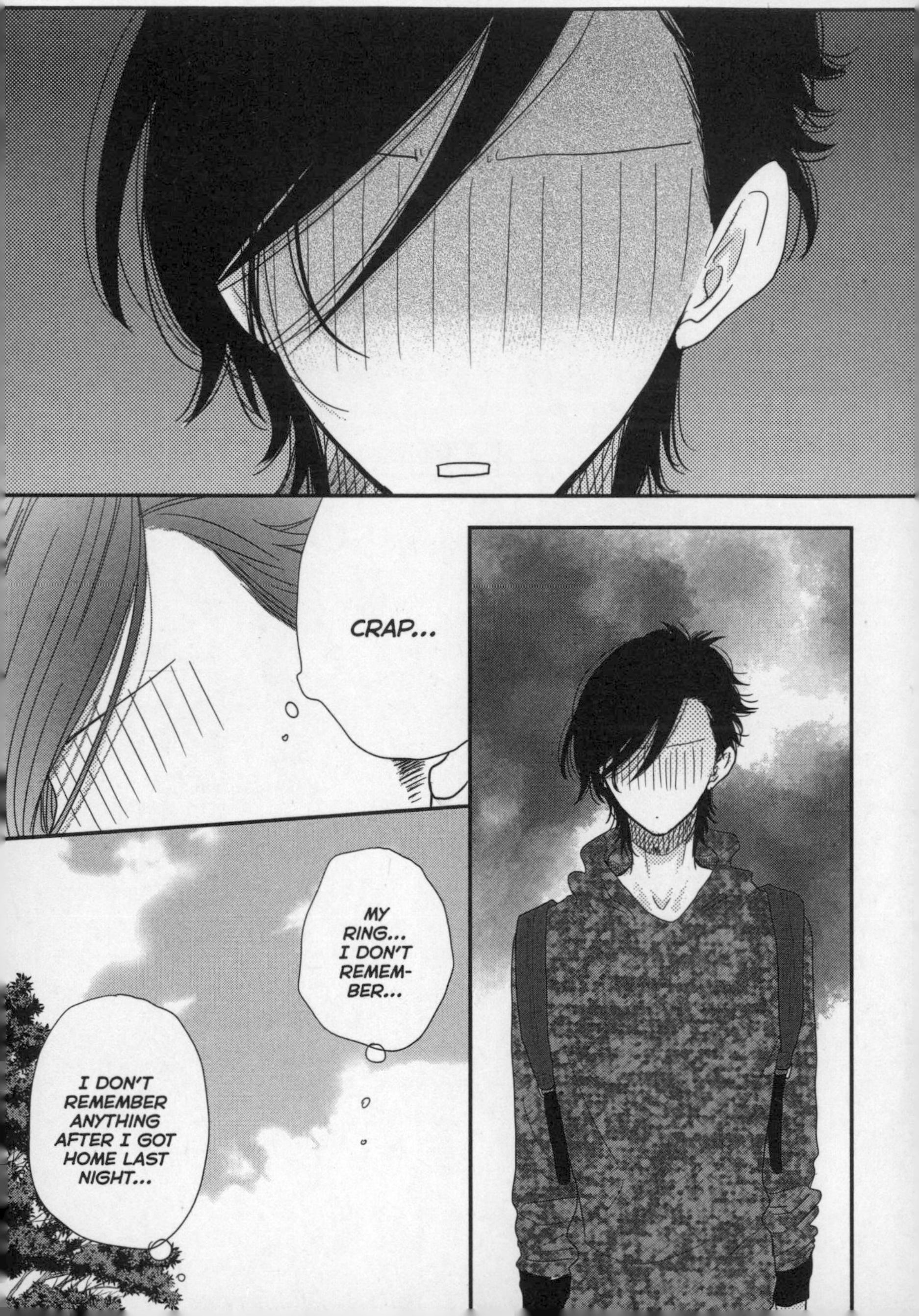
CRAP...
MY RING... I DON'T REMEMBER...
I DON'T REMEMBER ANYTHING AFTER I GOT HOME LAST NIGHT...

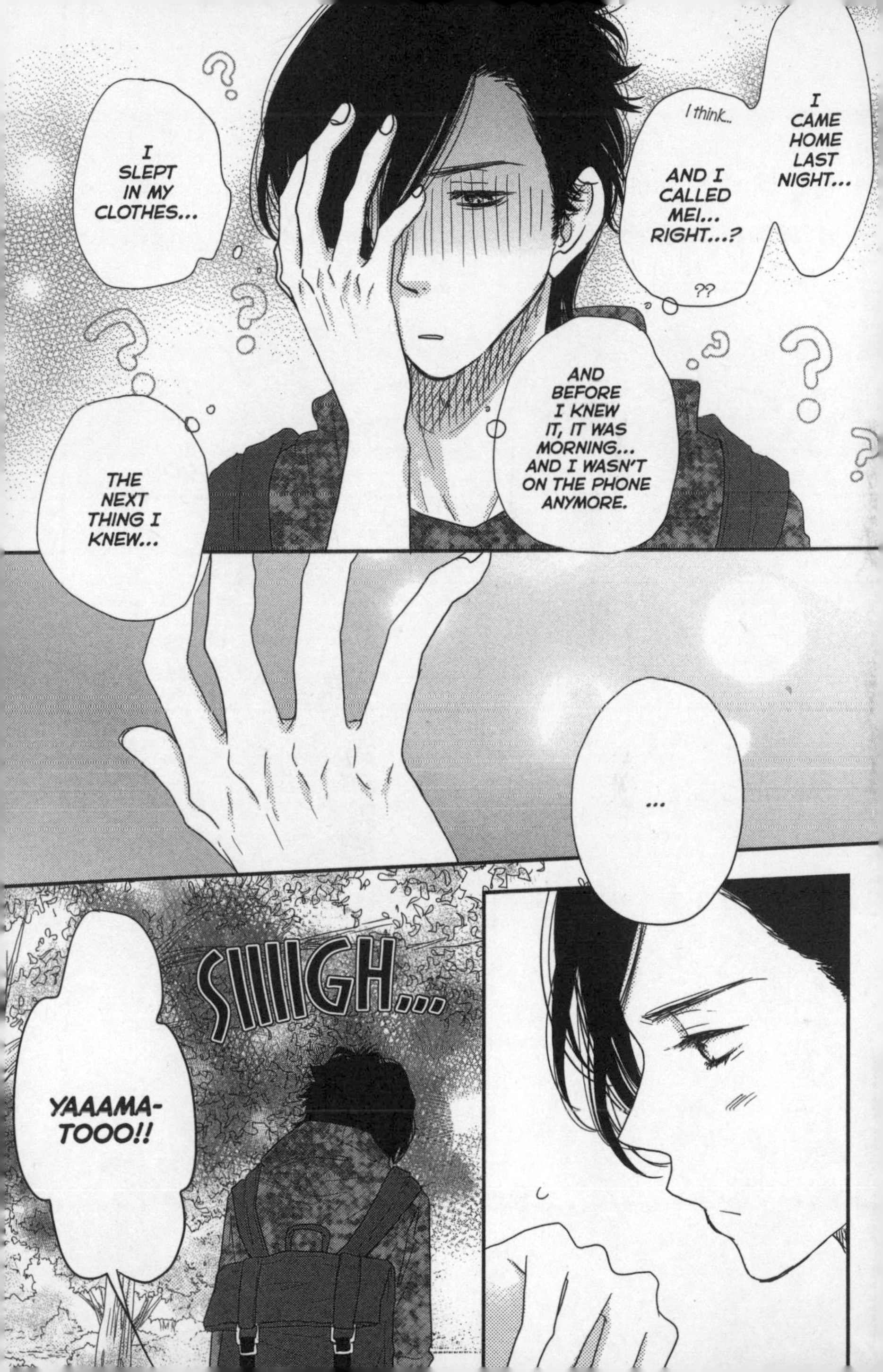
I CAME HOME LAST NIGHT...
I think...
AND I CALLED MEI... RIGHT...?
??
I SLEPT IN MY CLOTHES...
THE NEXT THING I KNEW...
AND BEFORE I KNEW IT, IT WAS MORNING... AND I WASN'T ON THE PHONE ANYMORE.
...
SIIIGH...
YAAAMA-TOOO!!

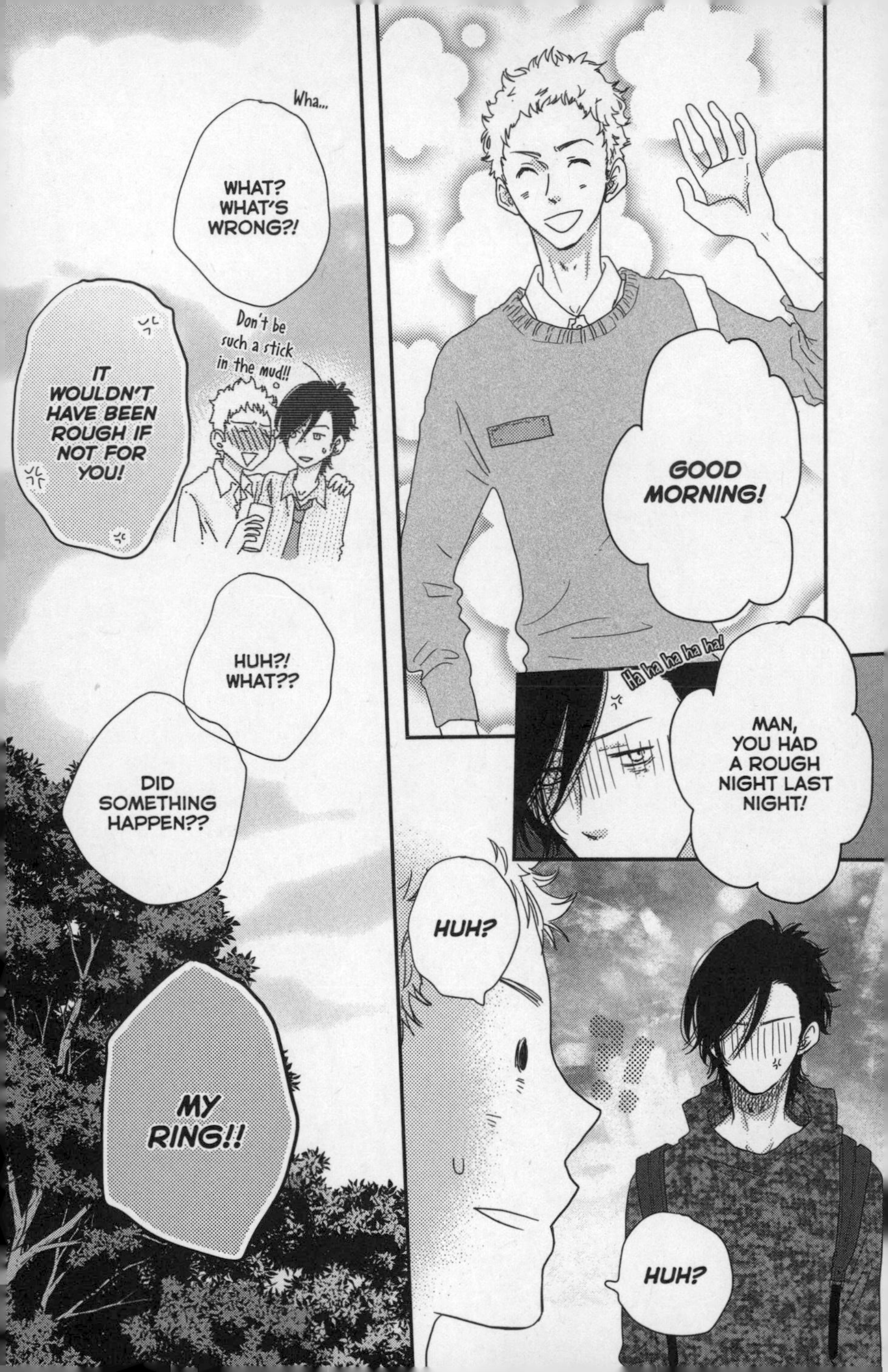
GOOD MORNING!
Ha ha ha ha ha!
MAN, YOU HAD A ROUGH NIGHT LAST NIGHT!
HUH?
HUH?
Wha...
WHAT? WHAT'S WRONG?!
Don't be such a stick in the mud!!
IT WOULDN'T HAVE BEEN ROUGH IF NOT FOR YOU!
HUH?! WHAT??
DID SOMETHING HAPPEN??
MY RING!!

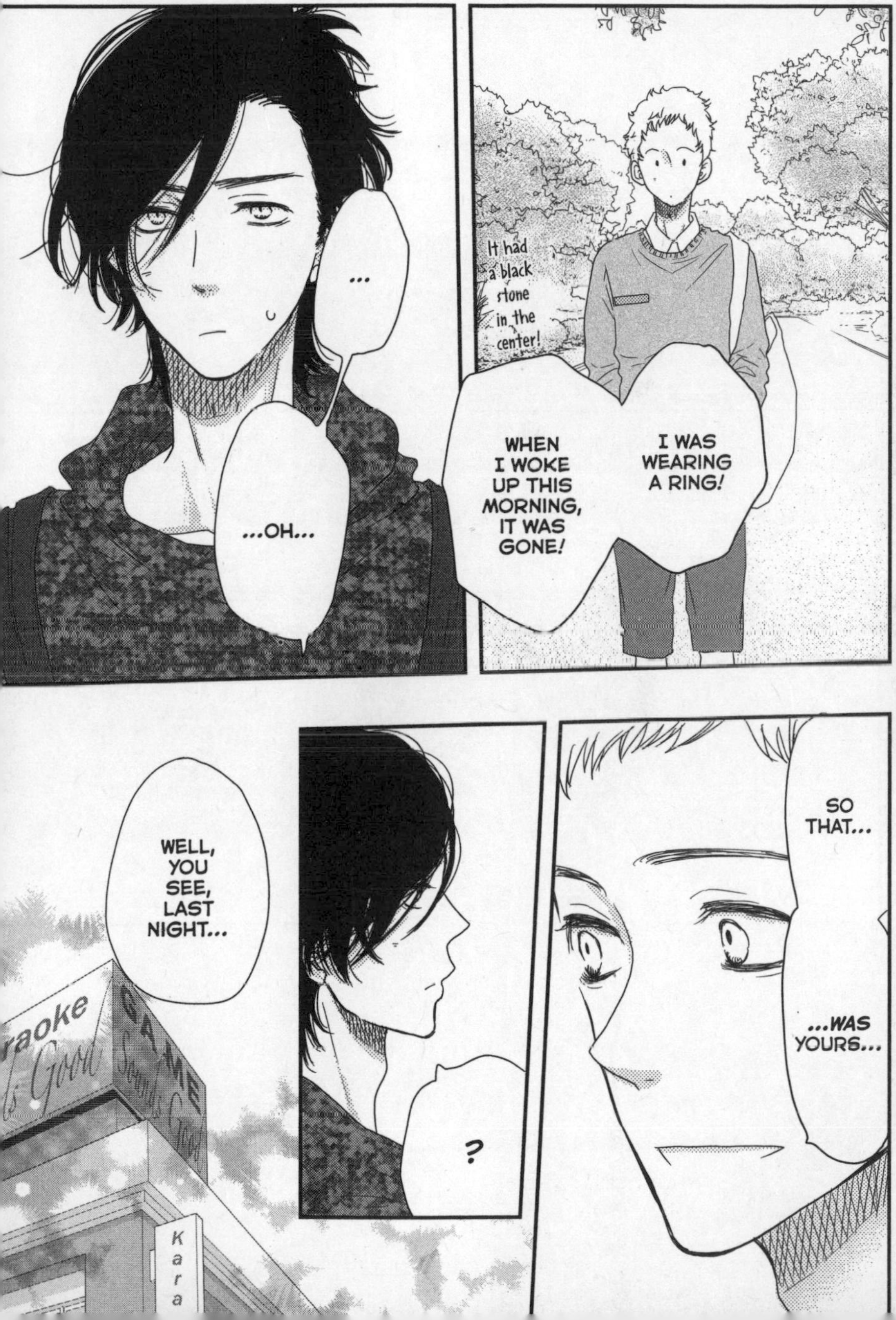
It had a black stone in the center!
I WAS WEARING A RING!
WHEN I WOKE UP THIS MORNING, IT WAS GONE!
...
...OH...
SO THAT...
...WAS YOURS...
?
WELL, YOU SEE, LAST NIGHT...
GAME
Kara

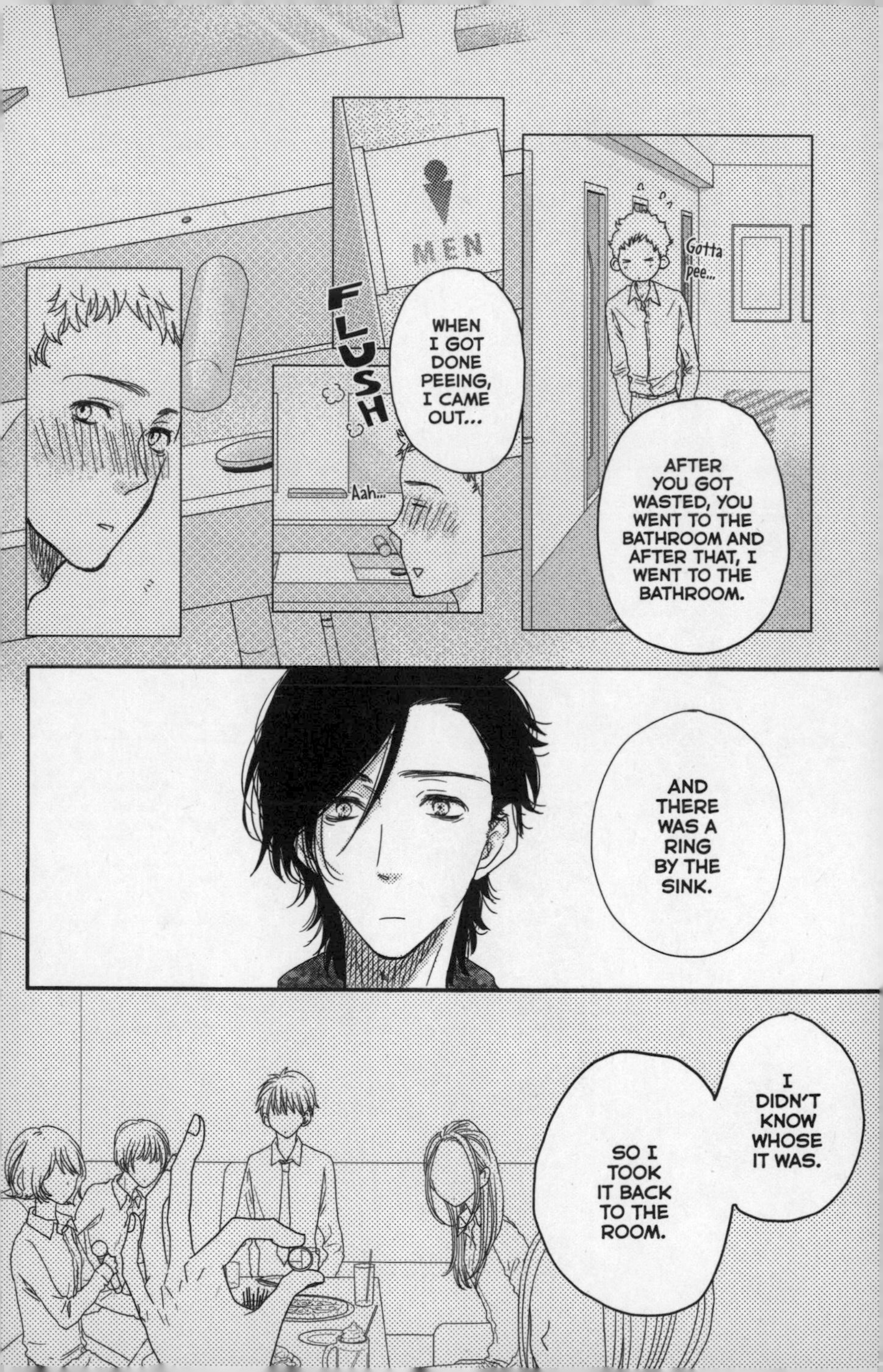
Gotta pee...
AFTER YOU GOT WASTED, YOU WENT TO THE BATHROOM AND AFTER THAT, I WENT TO THE BATHROOM.
MEN
FLUSH
WHEN I GOT DONE PEEING, I CAME OUT...
Aah...
AND THERE WAS A RING BY THE SINK.
I DIDN'T KNOW WHOSE IT WAS.
SO I TOOK IT BACK TO THE ROOM.

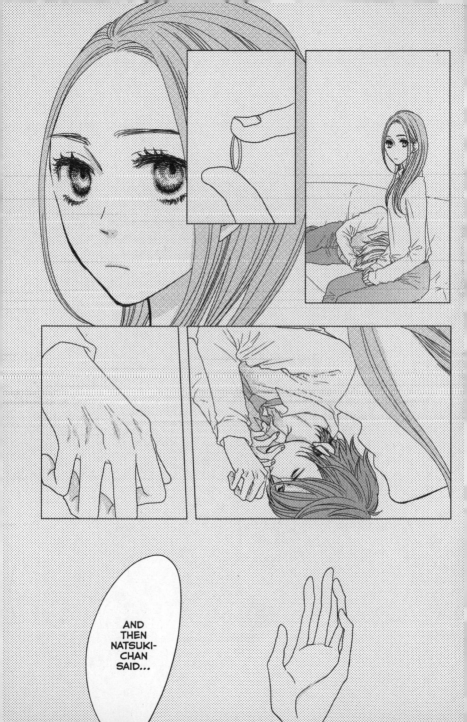

AND THEN
NATSUKI-
CHAN
SAID...

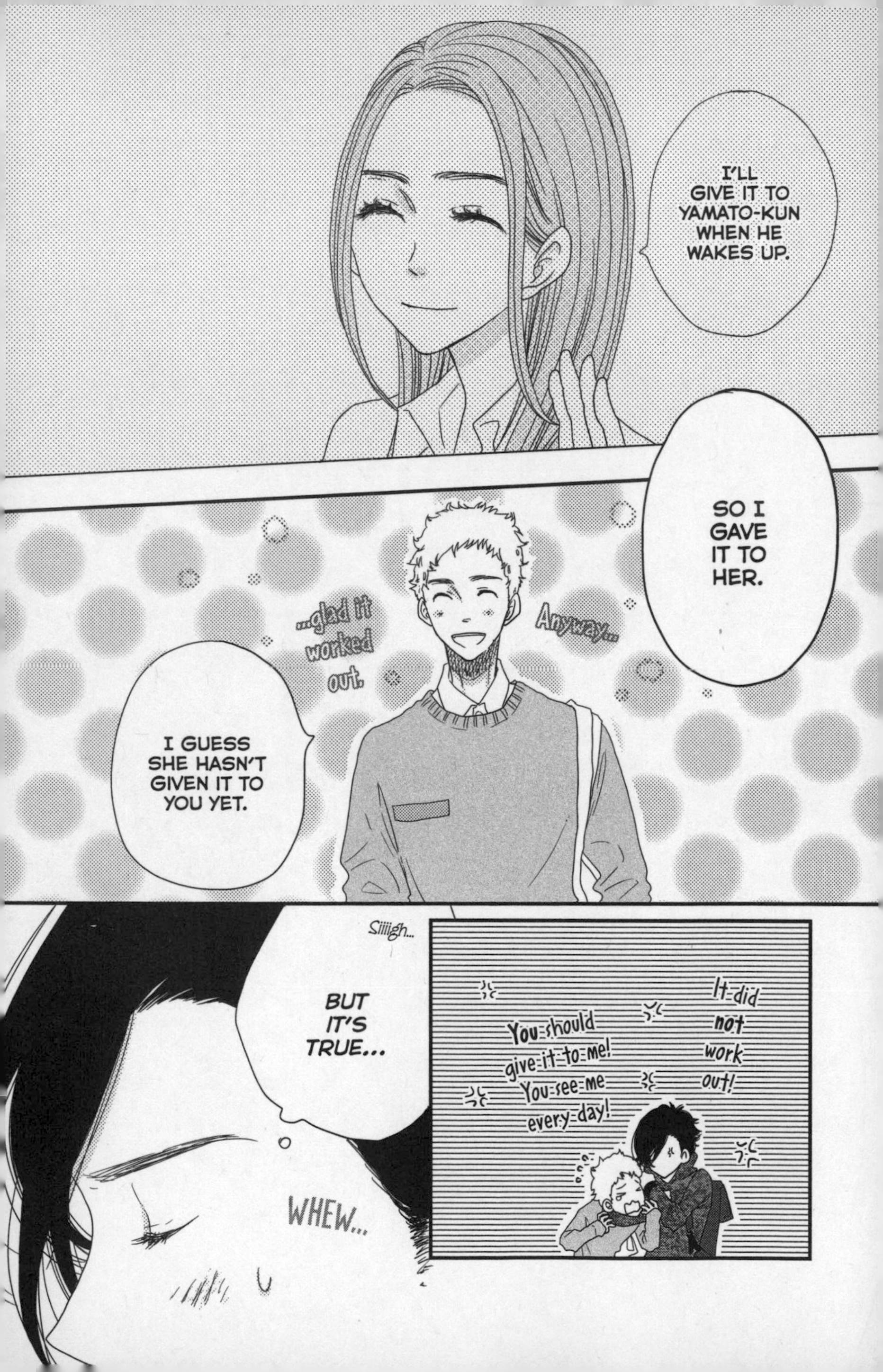
I'LL GIVE IT TO YAMATO-KUN WHEN HE WAKES UP.
SO I GAVE IT TO HER.
Anyway...
...glad it worked out.
I GUESS SHE HASN'T GIVEN IT TO YOU YET.
It did not work out!
You should give it to me! You see me every day!
Siiiigh...
BUT IT'S TRUE...
WHEW...

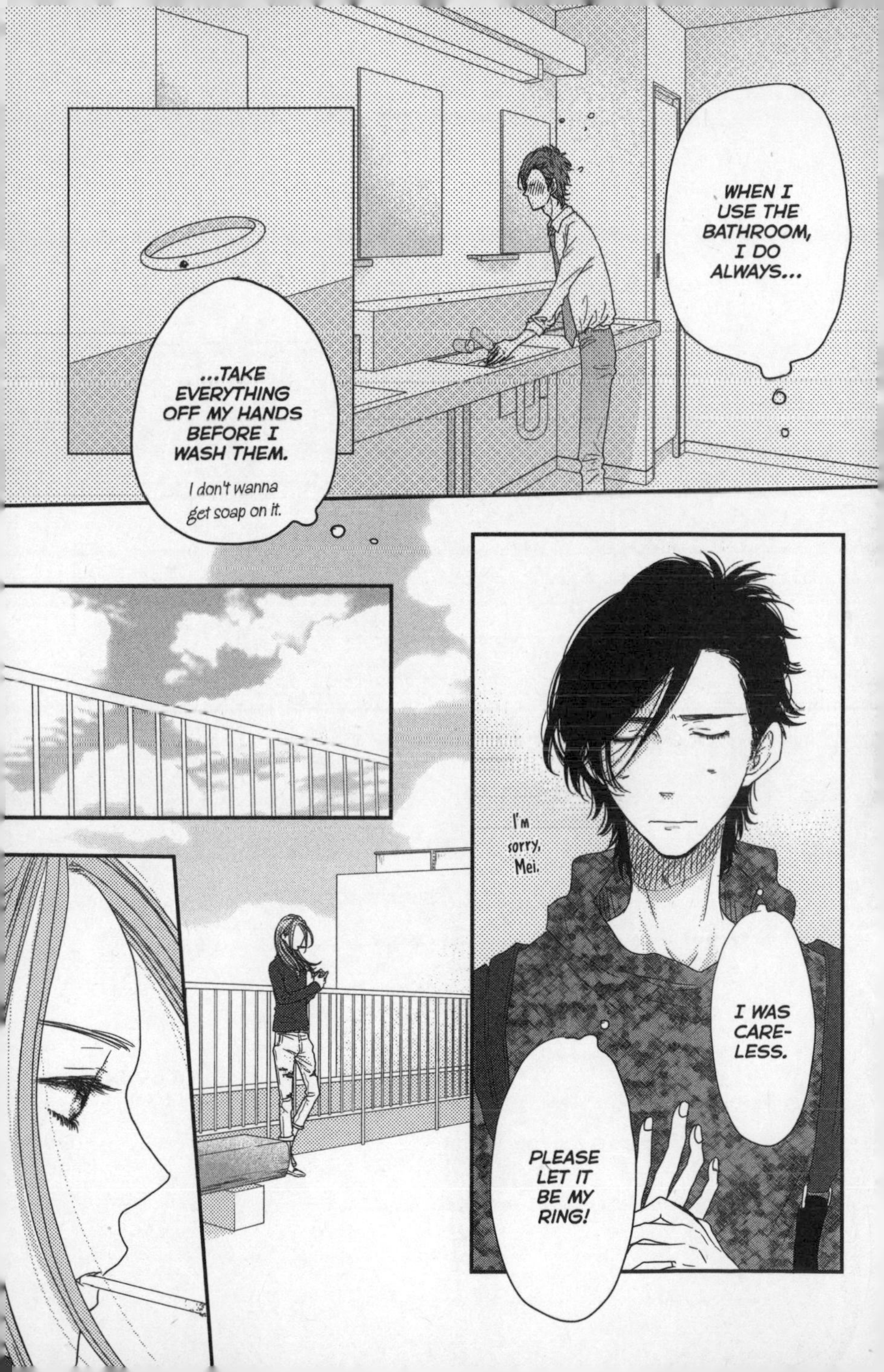
WHEN I USE THE BATHROOM, I DO ALWAYS...
...TAKE EVERYTHING OFF MY HANDS BEFORE I WASH THEM.
I don't wanna get soap on it.
I'm sorry, Mei.
I WAS CARE-LESS.
PLEASE LET IT BE MY RING!

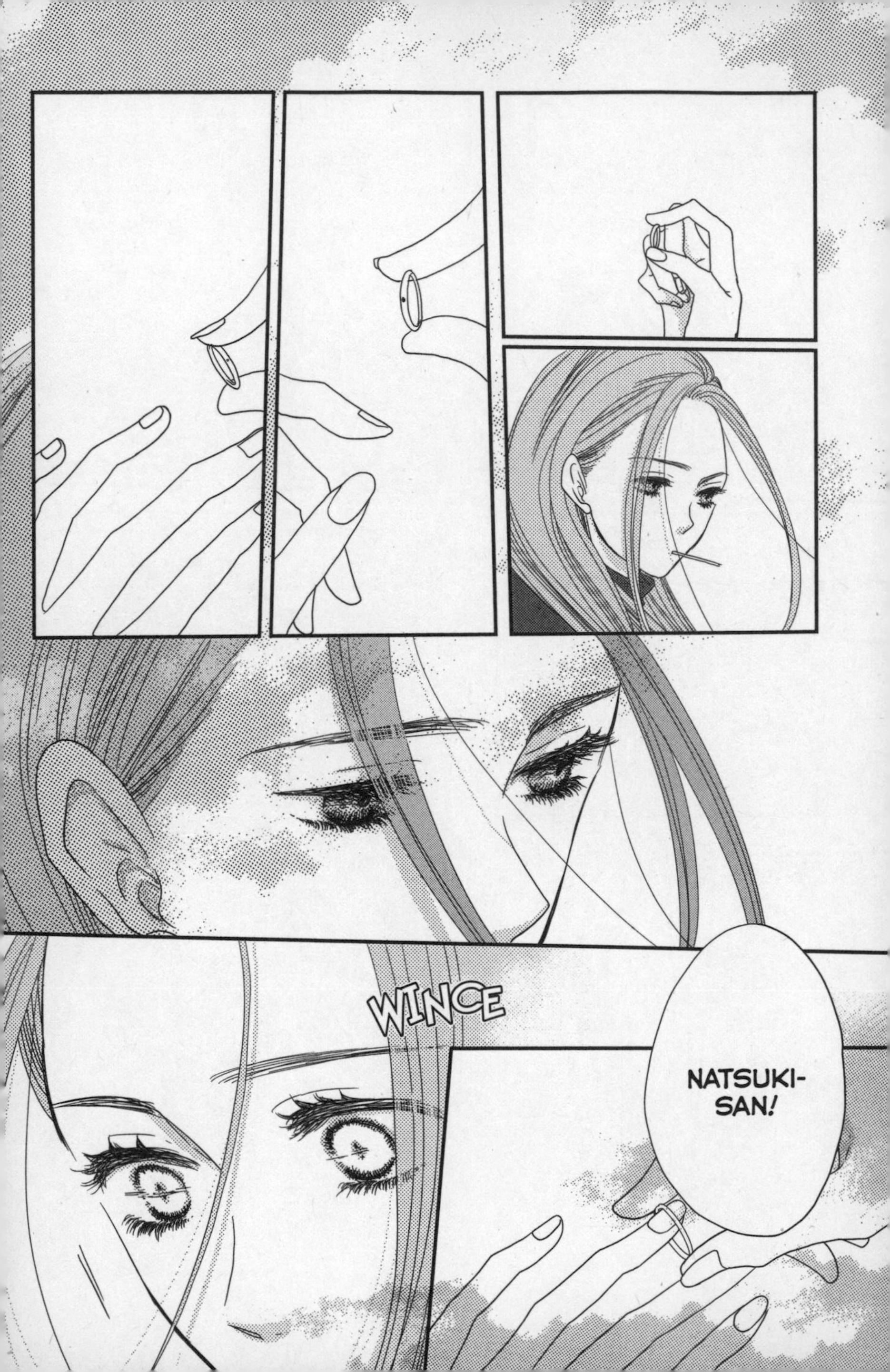
WINCE
NATSUKI-SAN!

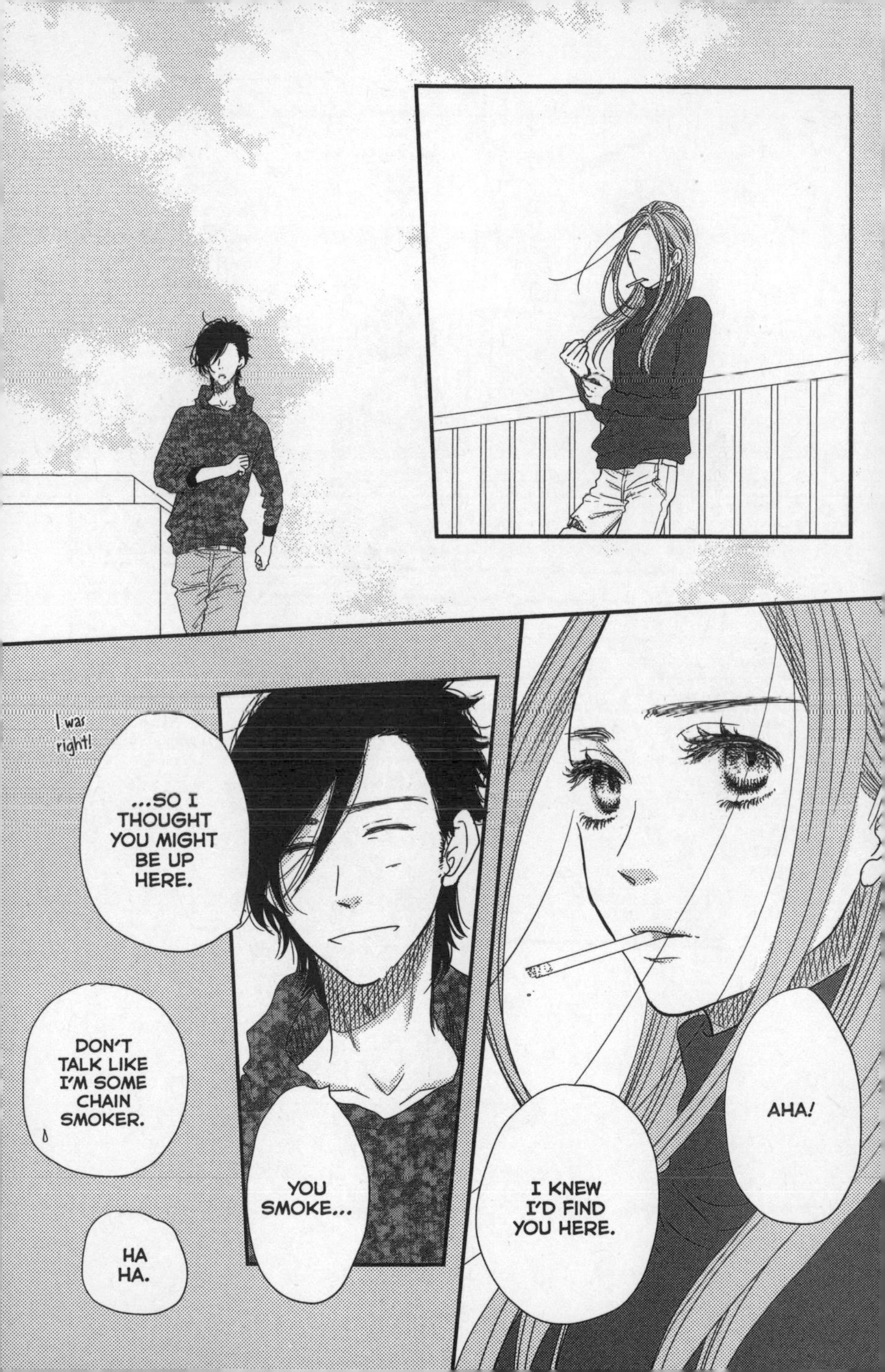
AHA!
I KNEW I'D FIND YOU HERE.
YOU SMOKE...
...SO I THOUGHT YOU MIGHT BE UP HERE.
I was right!
DON'T TALK LIKE I'M SOME CHAIN SMOKER.
HA HA.

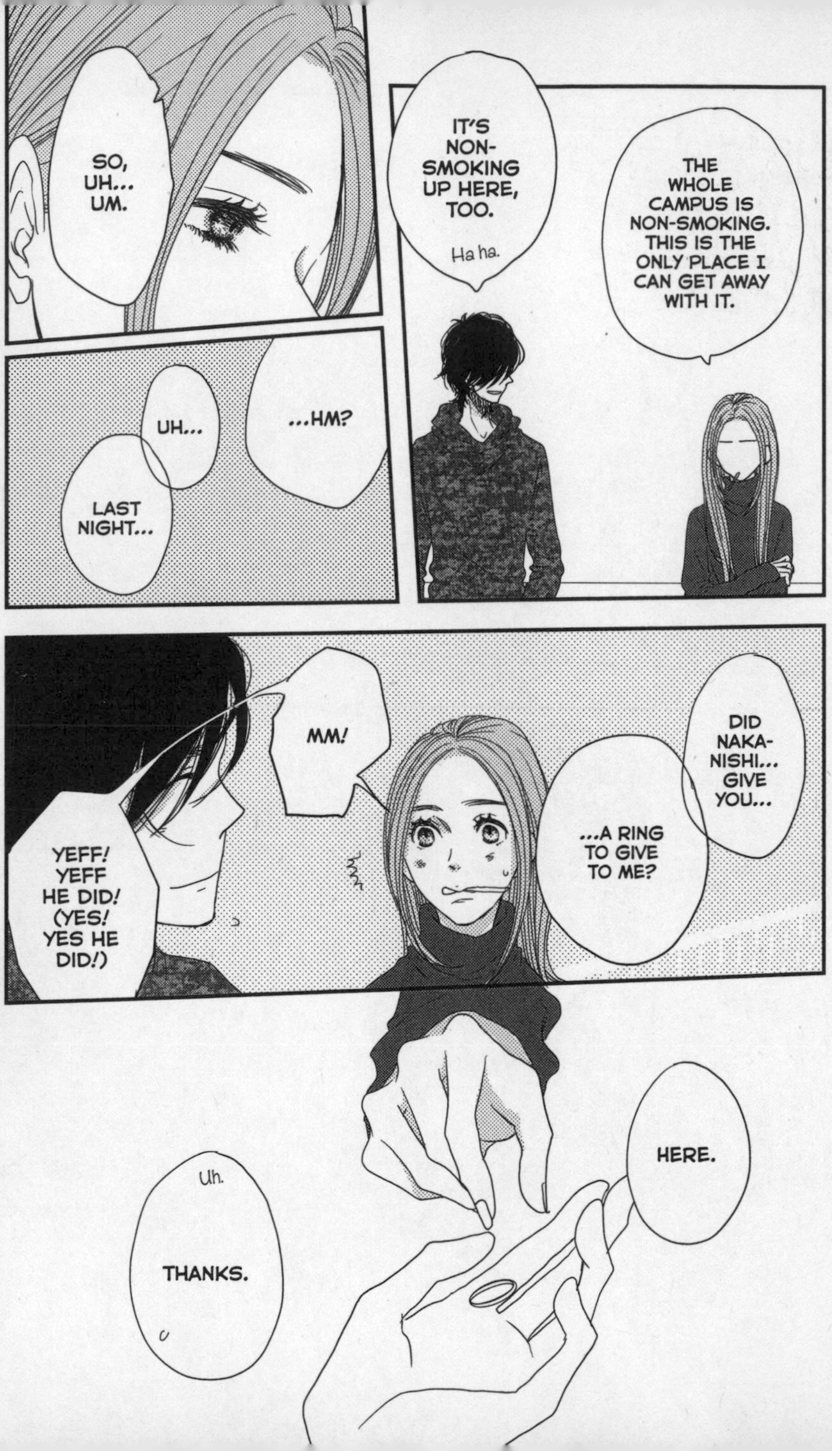
IT'S NON-SMOKING UP HERE, TOO.
Ha ha.
THE WHOLE CAMPUS IS NON-SMOKING. THIS IS THE ONLY PLACE I CAN GET AWAY WITH IT.
SO, UH... UM.
...HM?
UH...
LAST NIGHT...
DID NAKANISHI... GIVE YOU...
...A RING TO GIVE TO ME?
MM!
YEFF! YEFF HE DID! (YES! YES HE DID!)
HERE.
Uh.
THANKS.

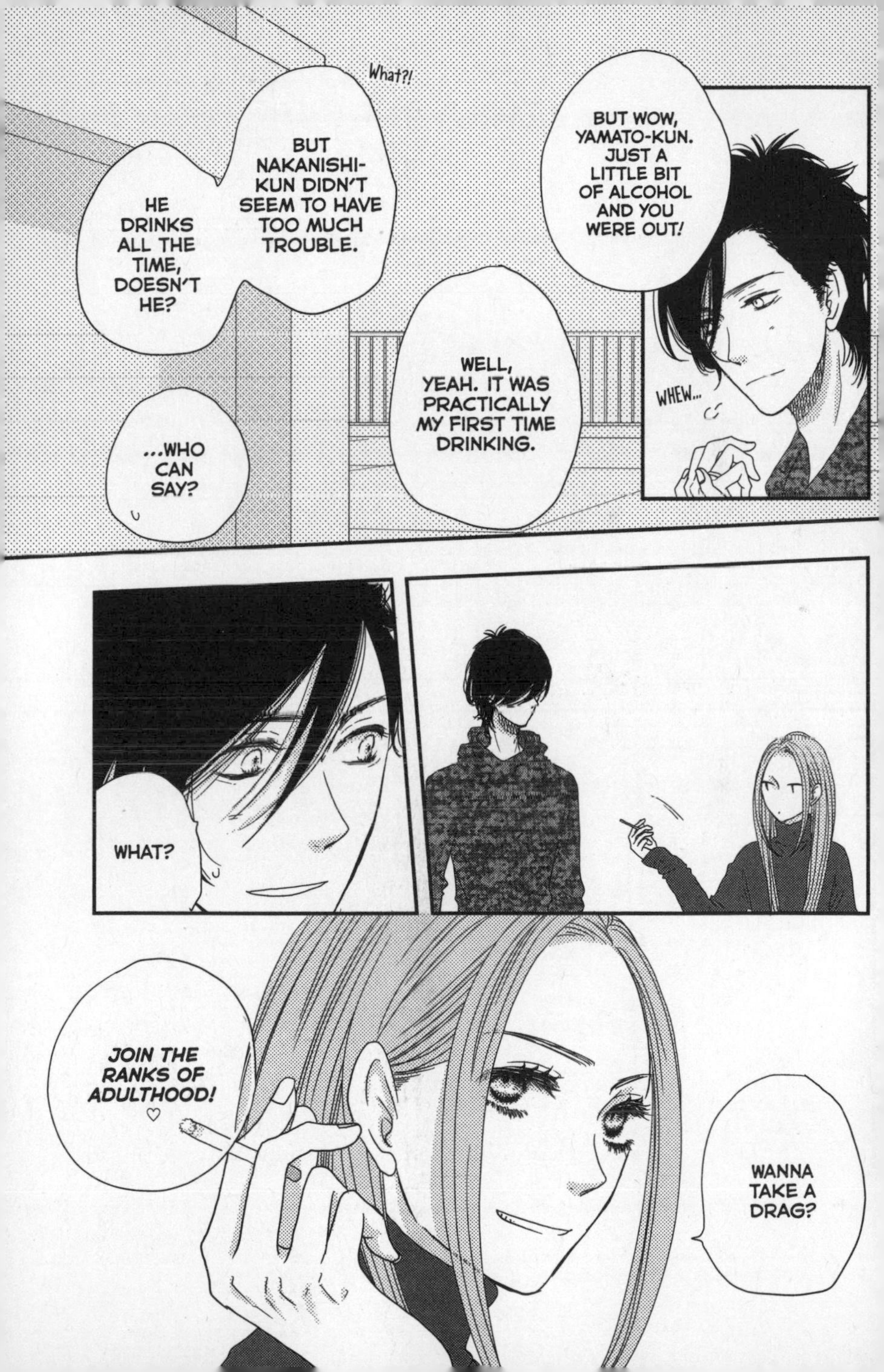
BUT WOW, YAMATO-KUN. JUST A LITTLE BIT OF ALCOHOL AND YOU WERE OUT!
WHEW...
WELL, YEAH. IT WAS PRACTICALLY MY FIRST TIME DRINKING.
What?!
BUT NAKANISHI-KUN DIDN'T SEEM TO HAVE TOO MUCH TROUBLE.
HE DRINKS ALL THE TIME, DOESN'T HE?
...WHO CAN SAY?
WHAT?
WANNA TAKE A DRAG?
JOIN THE RANKS OF ADULTHOOD! ♡

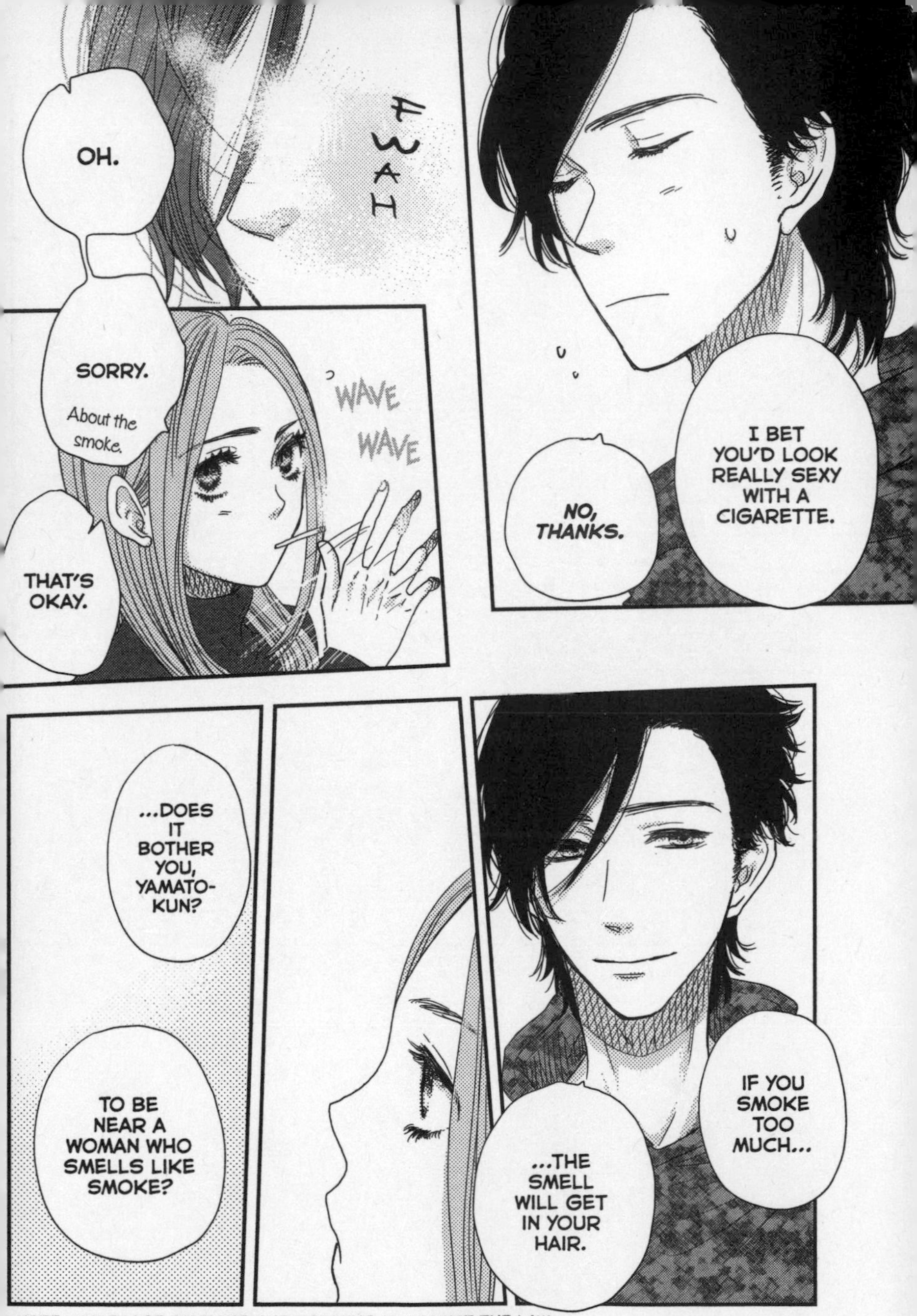
I BET YOU'D LOOK REALLY SEXY WITH A CIGARETTE.
NO, THANKS.
OH.
FWAH
SORRY.
About the smoke.
WAVE WAVE
THAT'S OKAY.
IF YOU SMOKE TOO MUCH...
...THE SMELL WILL GET IN YOUR HAIR.
...DOES IT BOTHER YOU, YAMATO-KUN?
TO BE NEAR A WOMAN WHO SMELLS LIKE SMOKE?

NOTE: UNDERAGE SMOKING AND DRINKING IS AGAINST THE LAW.

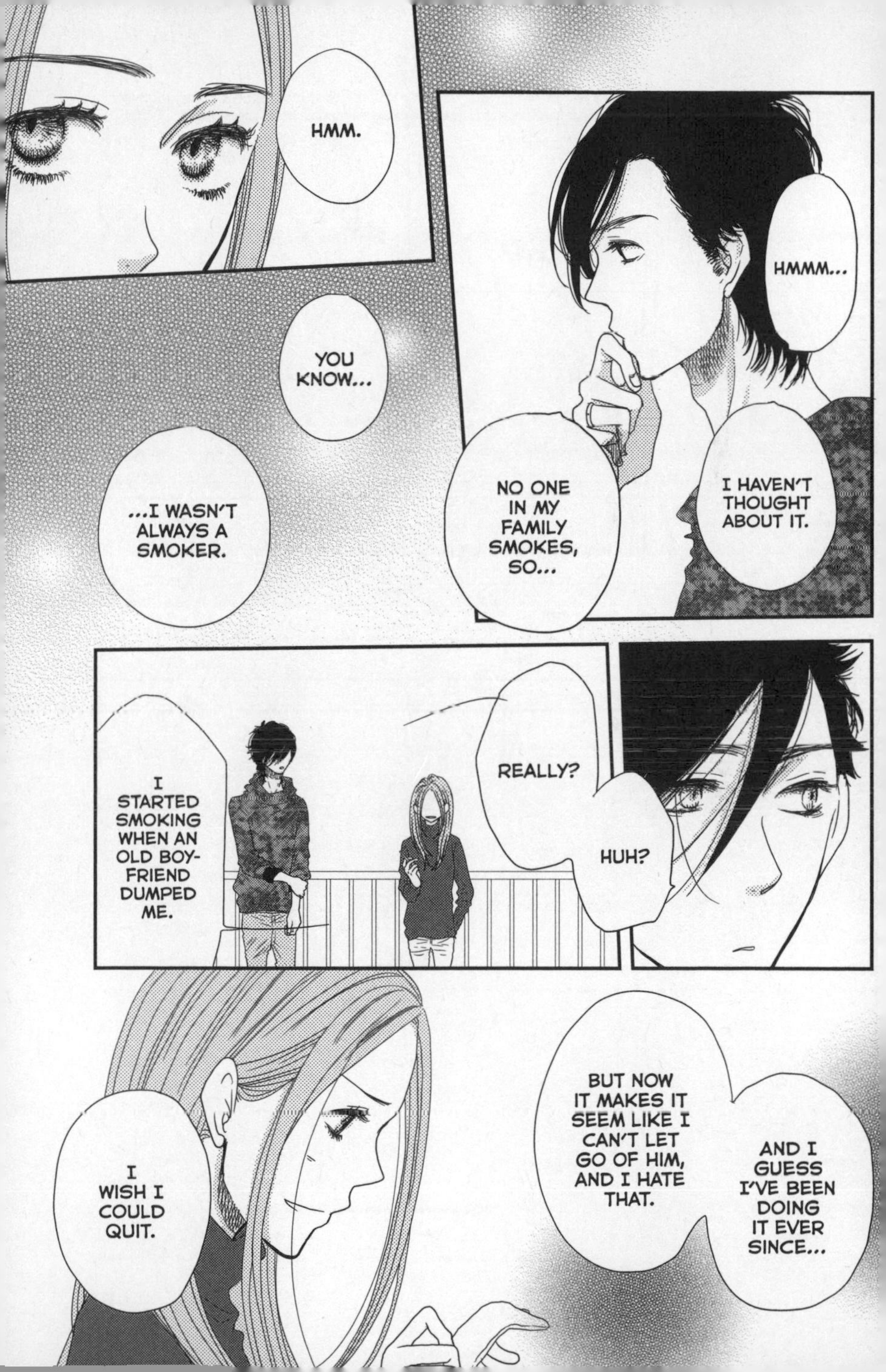
HMMM...
I HAVEN'T THOUGHT ABOUT IT.
NO ONE IN MY FAMILY SMOKES, SO...
HMM.
YOU KNOW...
...I WASN'T ALWAYS A SMOKER.
HUH?
REALLY?
I STARTED SMOKING WHEN AN OLD BOY-FRIEND DUMPED ME.
AND I GUESS I'VE BEEN DOING IT EVER SINCE...
BUT NOW IT MAKES IT SEEM LIKE I CAN'T LET GO OF HIM, AND I HATE THAT.
I WISH I COULD QUIT.

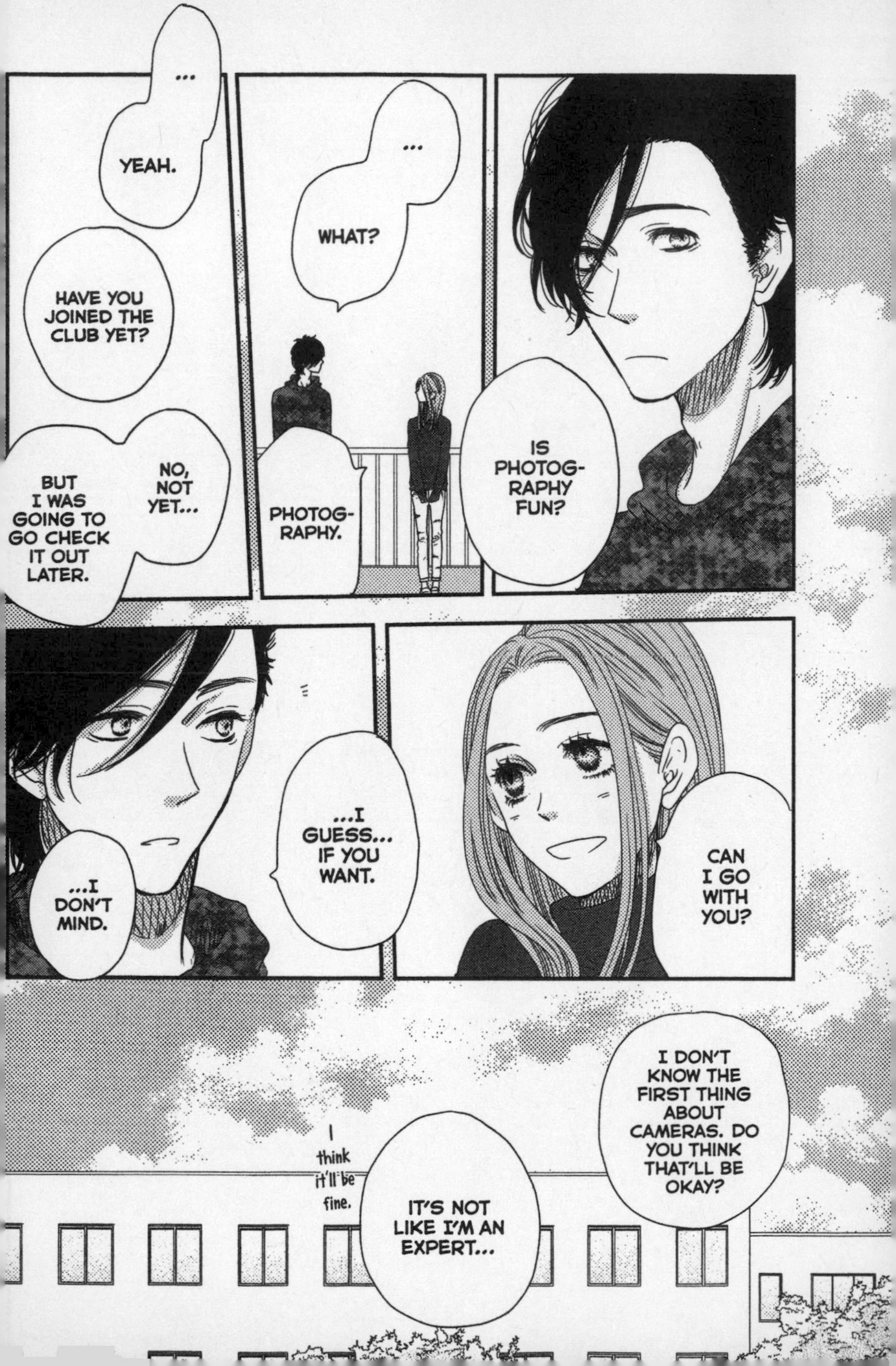
IS PHOTOGRAPHY FUN?
...
WHAT?
PHOTOGRAPHY.
...
YEAH.
HAVE YOU JOINED THE CLUB YET?
NO, NOT YET...
BUT I WAS GOING TO GO CHECK IT OUT LATER.
CAN I GO WITH YOU?
...I GUESS... IF YOU WANT.
...I DON'T MIND.
I DON'T KNOW THE FIRST THING ABOUT CAMERAS. DO YOU THINK THAT'LL BE OKAY?
IT'S NOT LIKE I'M AN EXPERT...
I think it'll be fine.

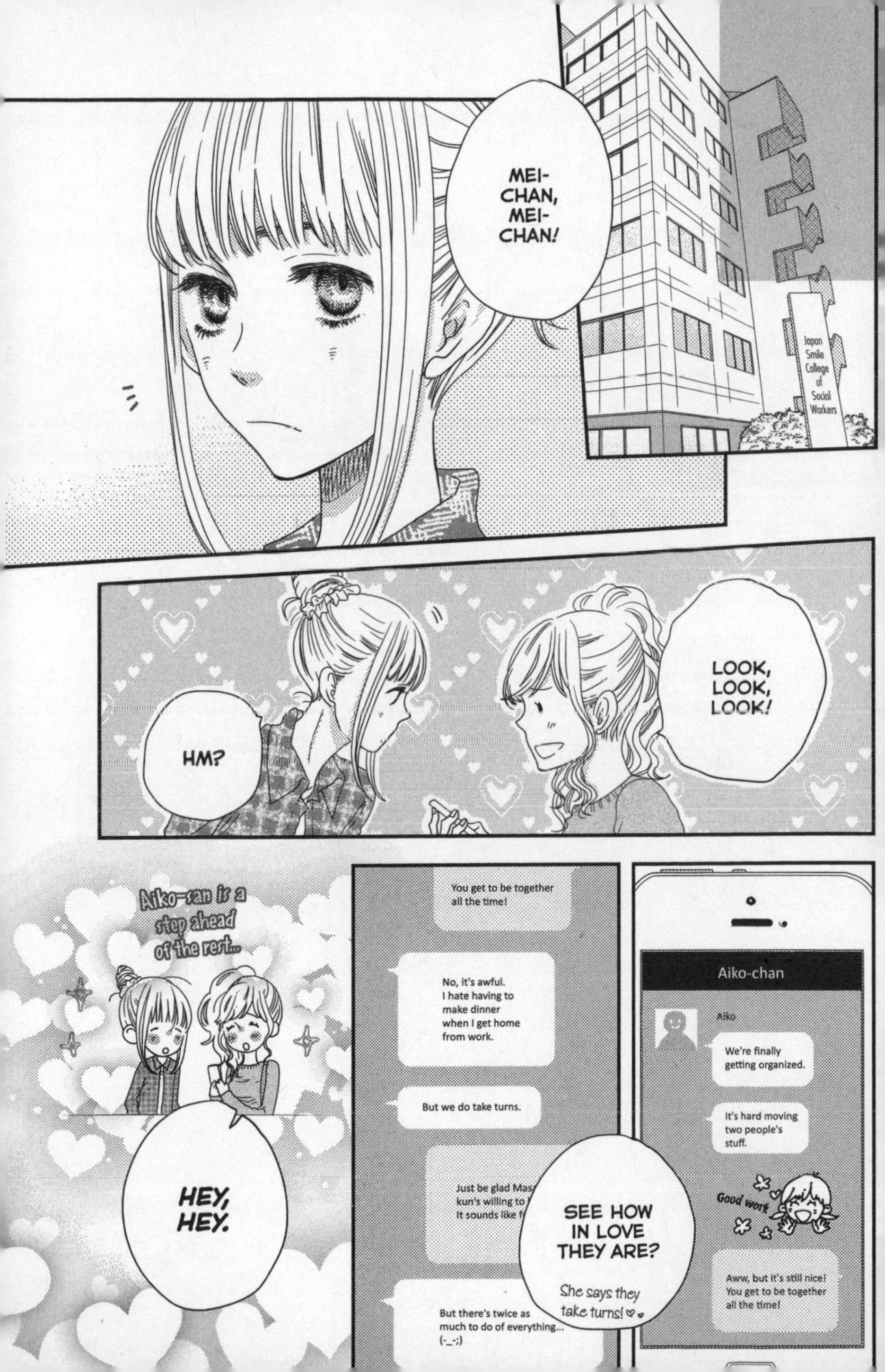
MEI-CHAN, MEI-CHAN!
Japan Smile College of Social Workers
LOOK, LOOK, LOOK!
HM?
Aiko-chan
Aiko
We're finally getting organized.
It's hard moving two people's stuff.
Good work
Aww, but it's still nice! You get to be together all the time!
SEE HOW IN LOVE THEY ARE?
She says they take turns!
You get to be together all the time!
No, it's awful. I hate having to make dinner when I get home from work.
But we do take turns.
But there's twice as much to do of everything... (-_-;)
Aiko-san is a step ahead of the rest...
HEY, HEY.

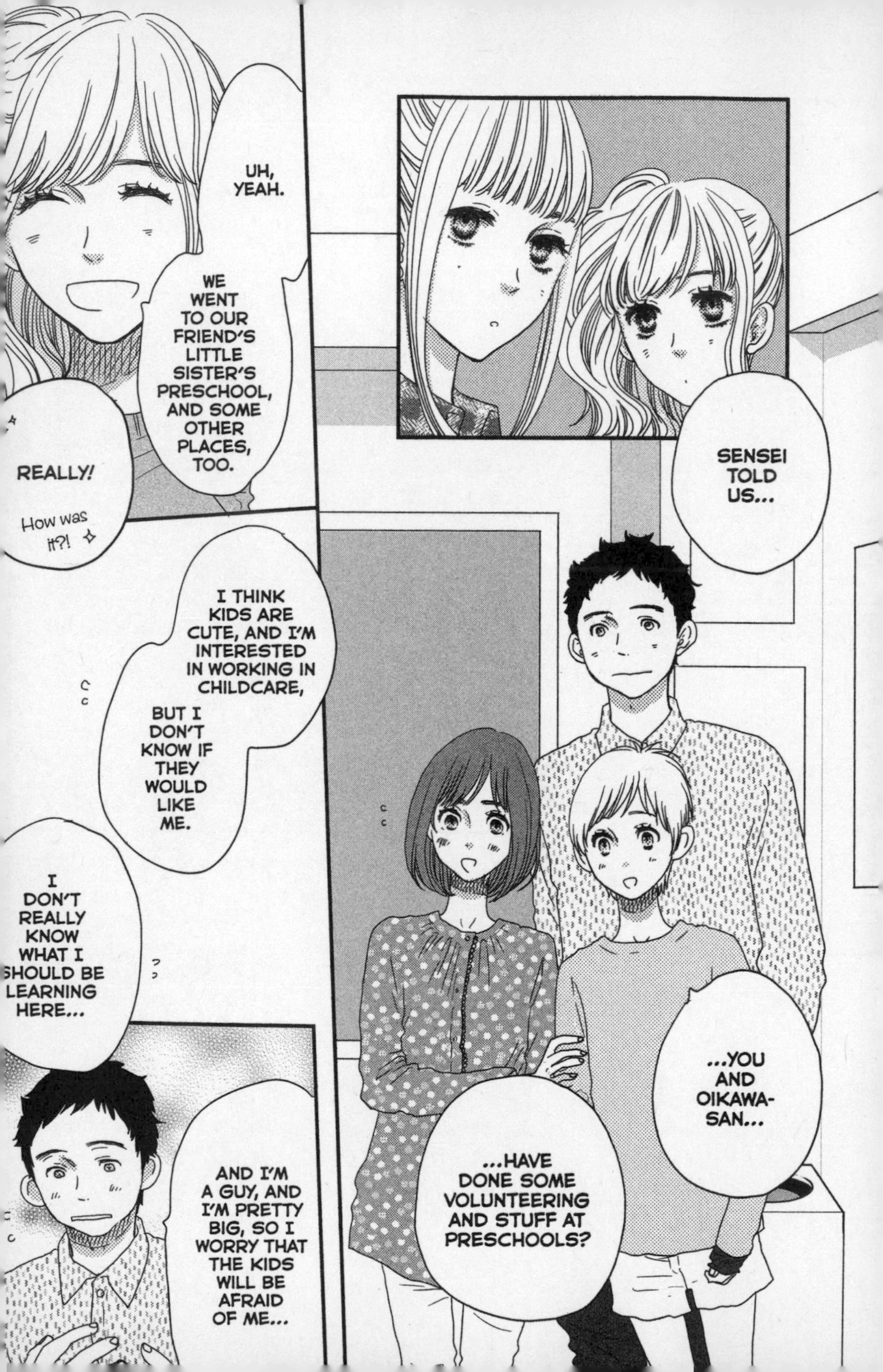
SENSEI TOLD US...
...YOU AND OIKAWA-SAN...
...HAVE DONE SOME VOLUNTEERING AND STUFF AT PRESCHOOLS?
UH, YEAH.
WE WENT TO OUR FRIEND'S LITTLE SISTER'S PRESCHOOL, AND SOME OTHER PLACES, TOO.
REALLY!
How was it?!
I THINK KIDS ARE CUTE, AND I'M INTERESTED IN WORKING IN CHILDCARE,
BUT I DON'T KNOW IF THEY WOULD LIKE ME.
I DON'T REALLY KNOW WHAT I SHOULD BE LEARNING HERE...
AND I'M A GUY, AND I'M PRETTY BIG, SO I WORRY THAT THE KIDS WILL BE AFRAID OF ME...

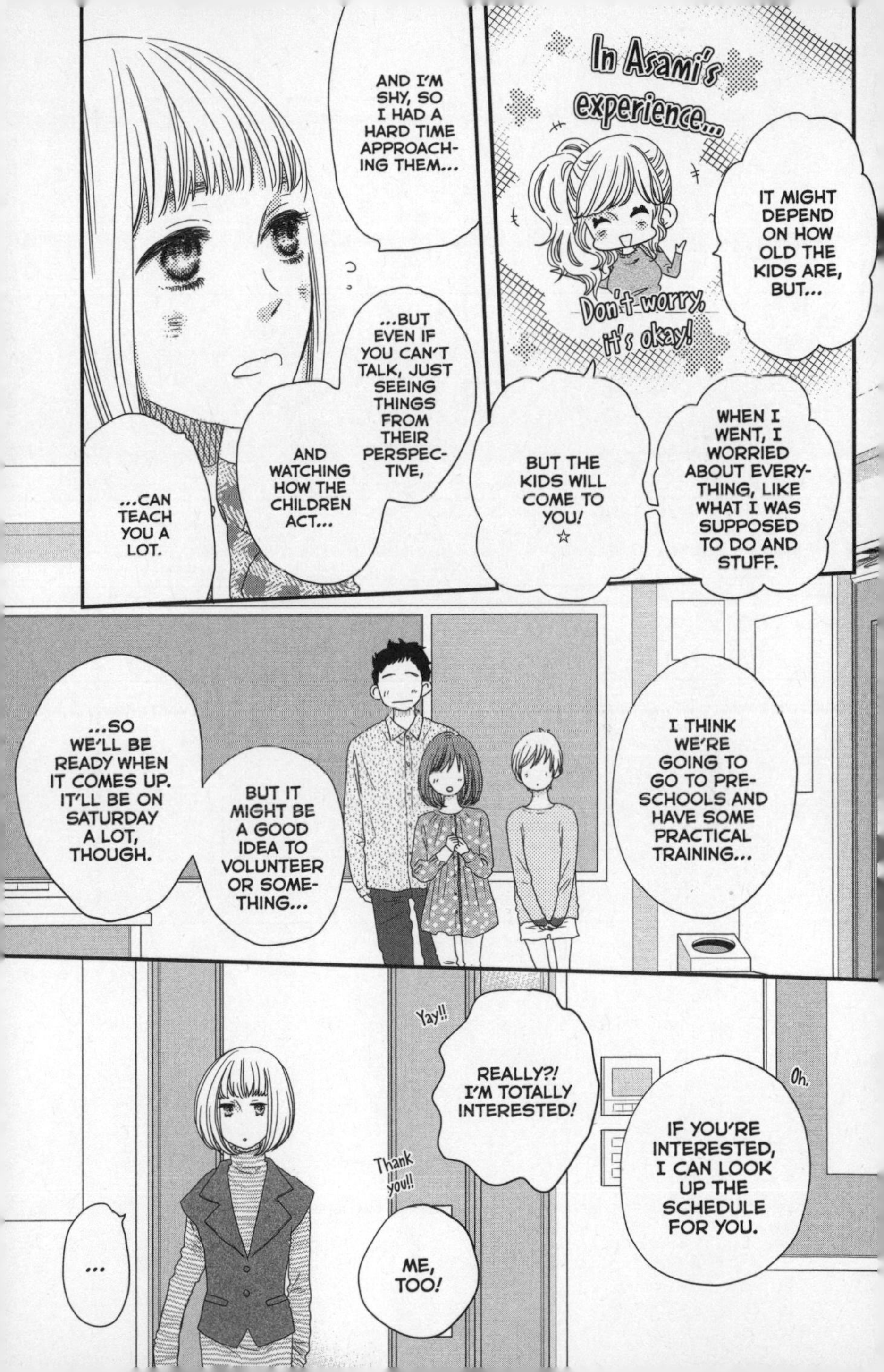
IT MIGHT DEPEND ON HOW OLD THE KIDS ARE, BUT...
In Asami's experience...
Don't worry, it's okay!
WHEN I WENT, I WORRIED ABOUT EVERY-THING, LIKE WHAT I WAS SUPPOSED TO DO AND STUFF.
BUT THE KIDS WILL COME TO YOU! ☆
AND I'M SHY, SO I HAD A HARD TIME APPROACH-ING THEM...
...BUT EVEN IF YOU CAN'T TALK, JUST SEEING THINGS FROM THEIR PERSPEC-TIVE,
AND WATCHING HOW THE CHILDREN ACT...
...CAN TEACH YOU A LOT.
I THINK WE'RE GOING TO GO TO PRE-SCHOOLS AND HAVE SOME PRACTICAL TRAINING...
...SO WE'LL BE READY WHEN IT COMES UP. IT'LL BE ON SATURDAY A LOT, THOUGH.
BUT IT MIGHT BE A GOOD IDEA TO VOLUNTEER OR SOME-THING...
Oh.
IF YOU'RE INTERESTED, I CAN LOOK UP THE SCHEDULE FOR YOU.
REALLY?! I'M TOTALLY INTERESTED!
Yay!!
Thank you!!
ME, TOO!
...

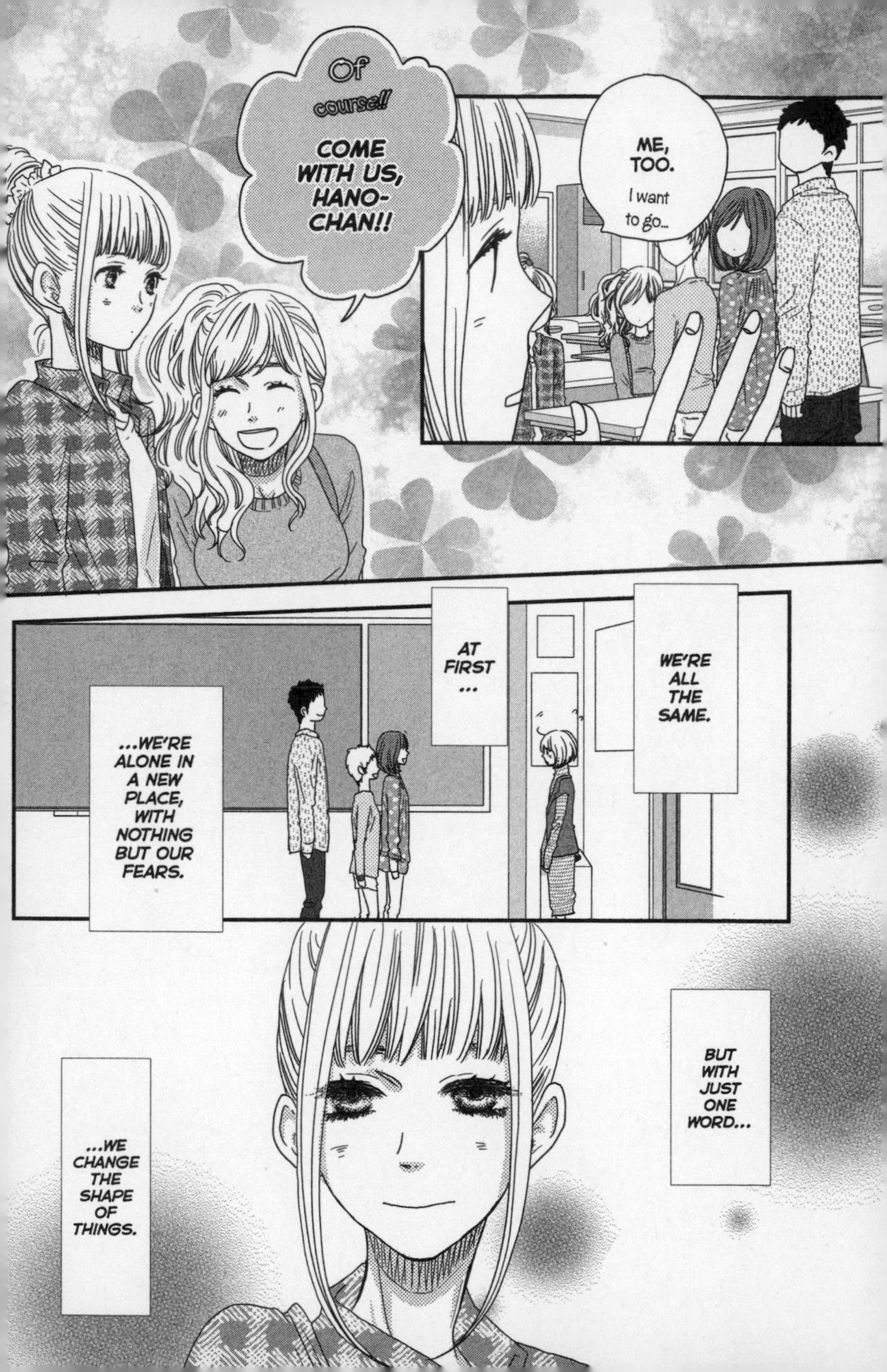
ME, TOO. I want to go...
Of course!! COME WITH US, HANO-CHAN!!
WE'RE ALL THE SAME.
AT FIRST...
...WE'RE ALONE IN A NEW PLACE, WITH NOTHING BUT OUR FEARS.
BUT WITH JUST ONE WORD...
...WE CHANGE THE SHAPE OF THINGS.

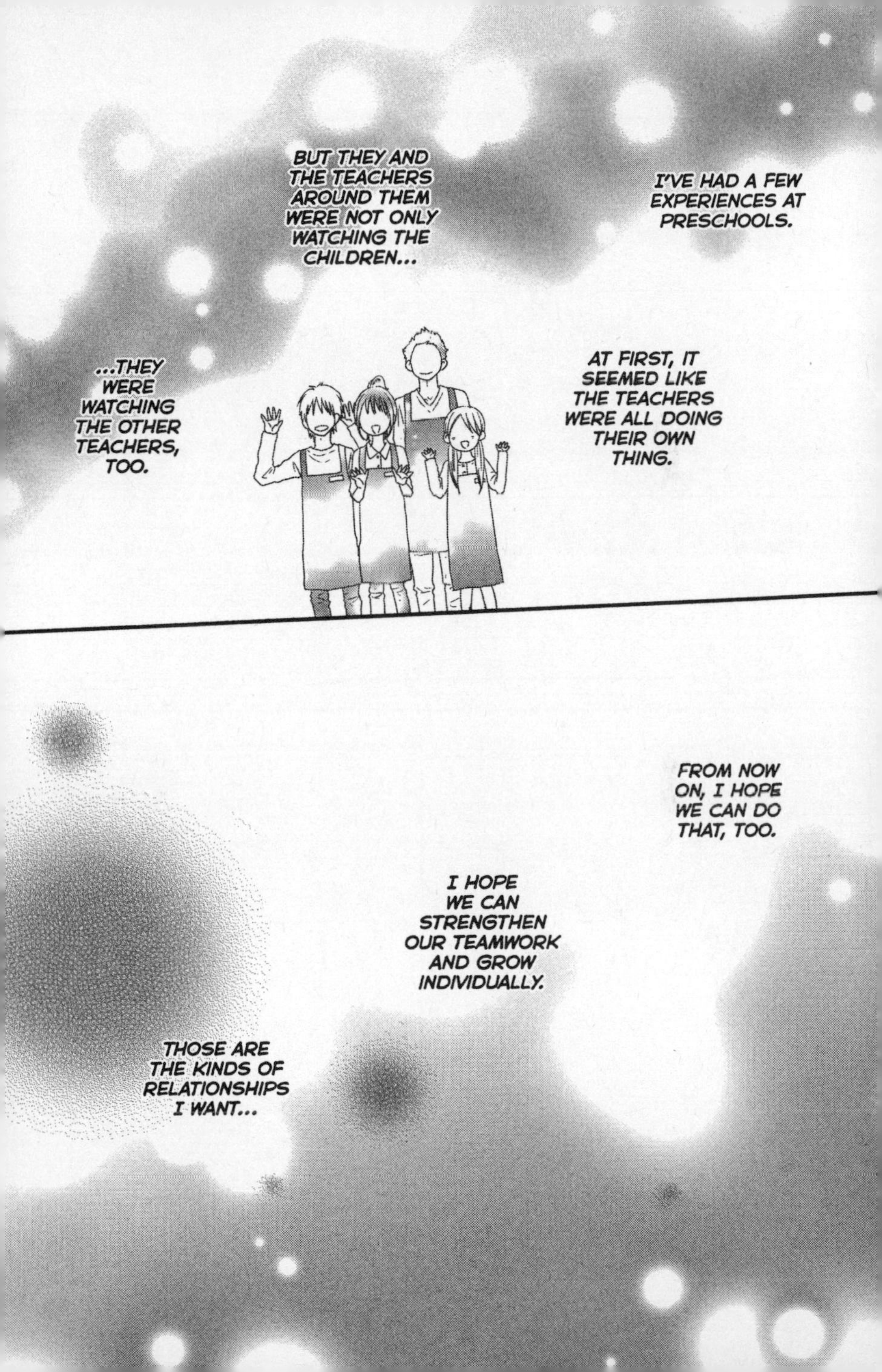
I'VE HAD A FEW EXPERIENCES AT PRESCHOOLS.
AT FIRST, IT SEEMED LIKE THE TEACHERS WERE ALL DOING THEIR OWN THING.
BUT THEY AND THE TEACHERS AROUND THEM WERE NOT ONLY WATCHING THE CHILDREN...
...THEY WERE WATCHING THE OTHER TEACHERS, TOO.
FROM NOW ON, I HOPE WE CAN DO THAT, TOO.
I HOPE WE CAN STRENGTHEN OUR TEAMWORK AND GROW INDIVIDUALLY.
THOSE ARE THE KINDS OF RELATIONSHIPS I WANT...

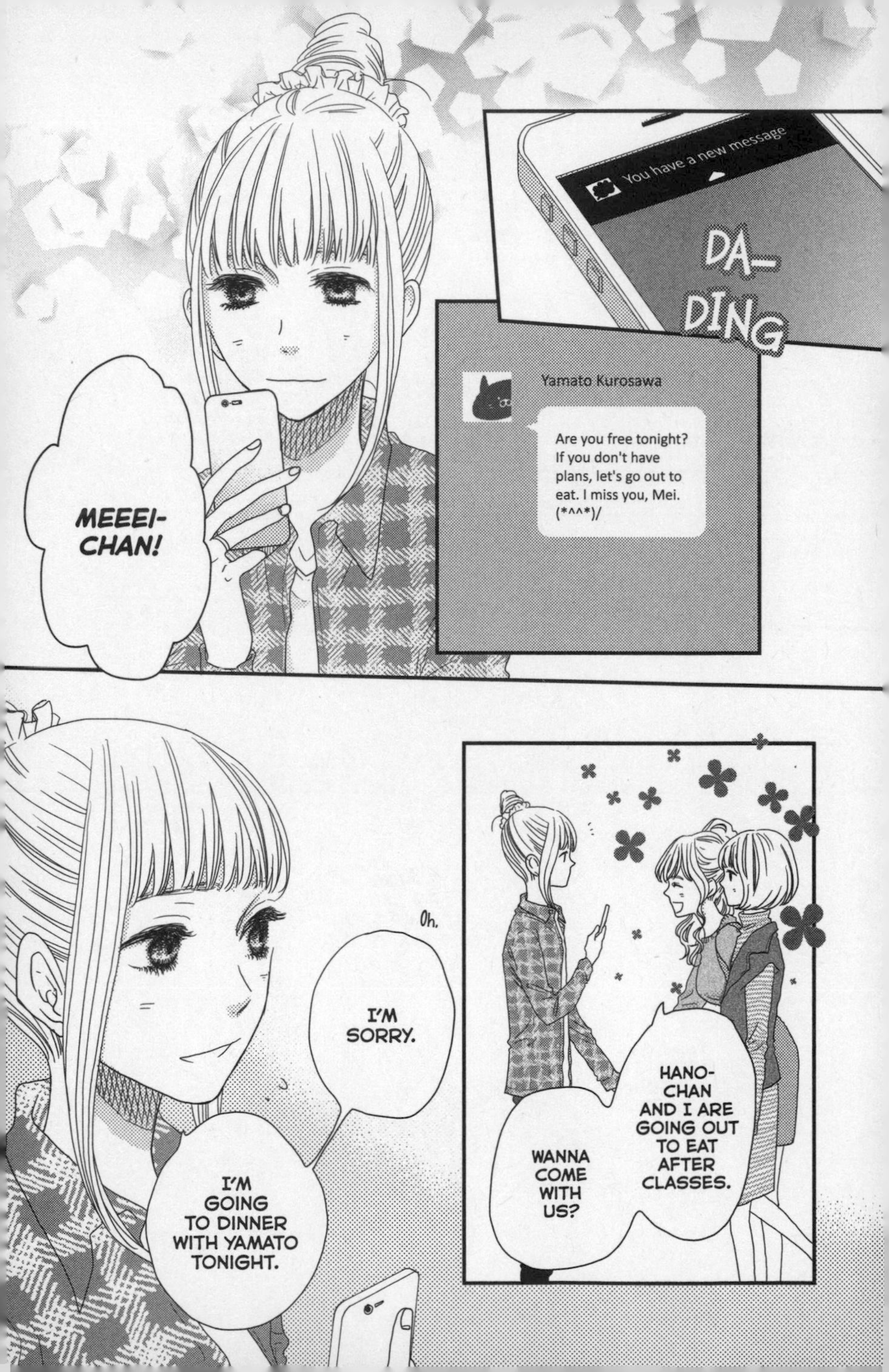
You have a new message
DA-DING
Yamato Kurosawa
Are you free tonight? If you don't have plans, let's go out to eat. I miss you, Mei. (*^^*)/
MEEEI-CHAN!
HANO-CHAN AND I ARE GOING OUT TO EAT AFTER CLASSES.
WANNA COME WITH US?
Oh.
I'M SORRY.
I'M GOING TO DINNER WITH YAMATO TONIGHT.

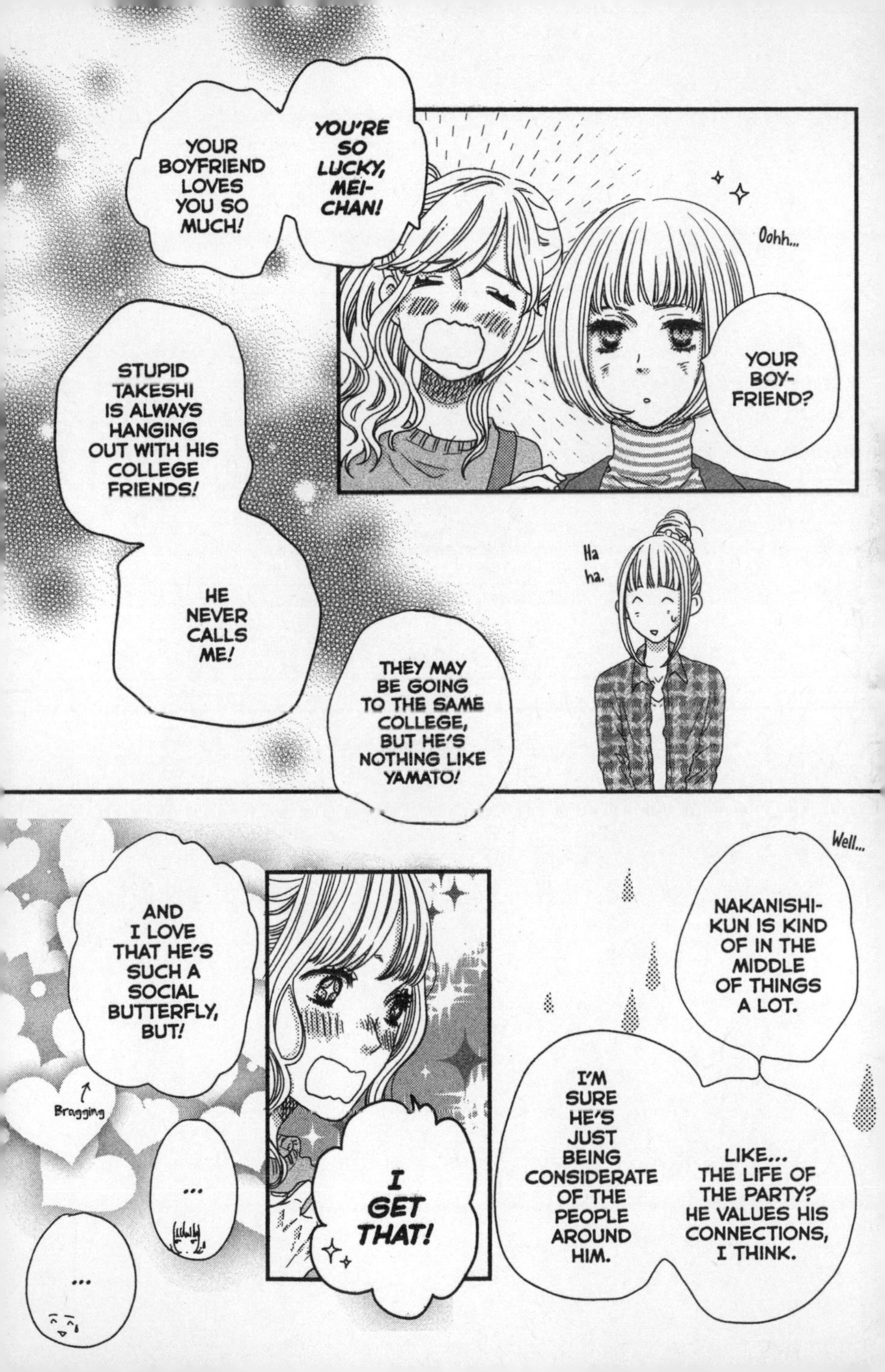
YOU'RE SO LUCKY, MEI-CHAN!
YOUR BOYFRIEND LOVES YOU SO MUCH!
Oohh...
YOUR BOY-FRIEND?
STUPID TAKESHI IS ALWAYS HANGING OUT WITH HIS COLLEGE FRIENDS!
HE NEVER CALLS ME!
Ha ha.
THEY MAY BE GOING TO THE SAME COLLEGE, BUT HE'S NOTHING LIKE YAMATO!
Well...
NAKANISHI-KUN IS KIND OF IN THE MIDDLE OF THINGS A LOT.
LIKE... THE LIFE OF THE PARTY? HE VALUES HIS CONNECTIONS, I THINK.
I'M SURE HE'S JUST BEING CONSIDERATE OF THE PEOPLE AROUND HIM.
I GET THAT!
AND I LOVE THAT HE'S SUCH A SOCIAL BUTTERFLY, BUT!
Bragging
...
...

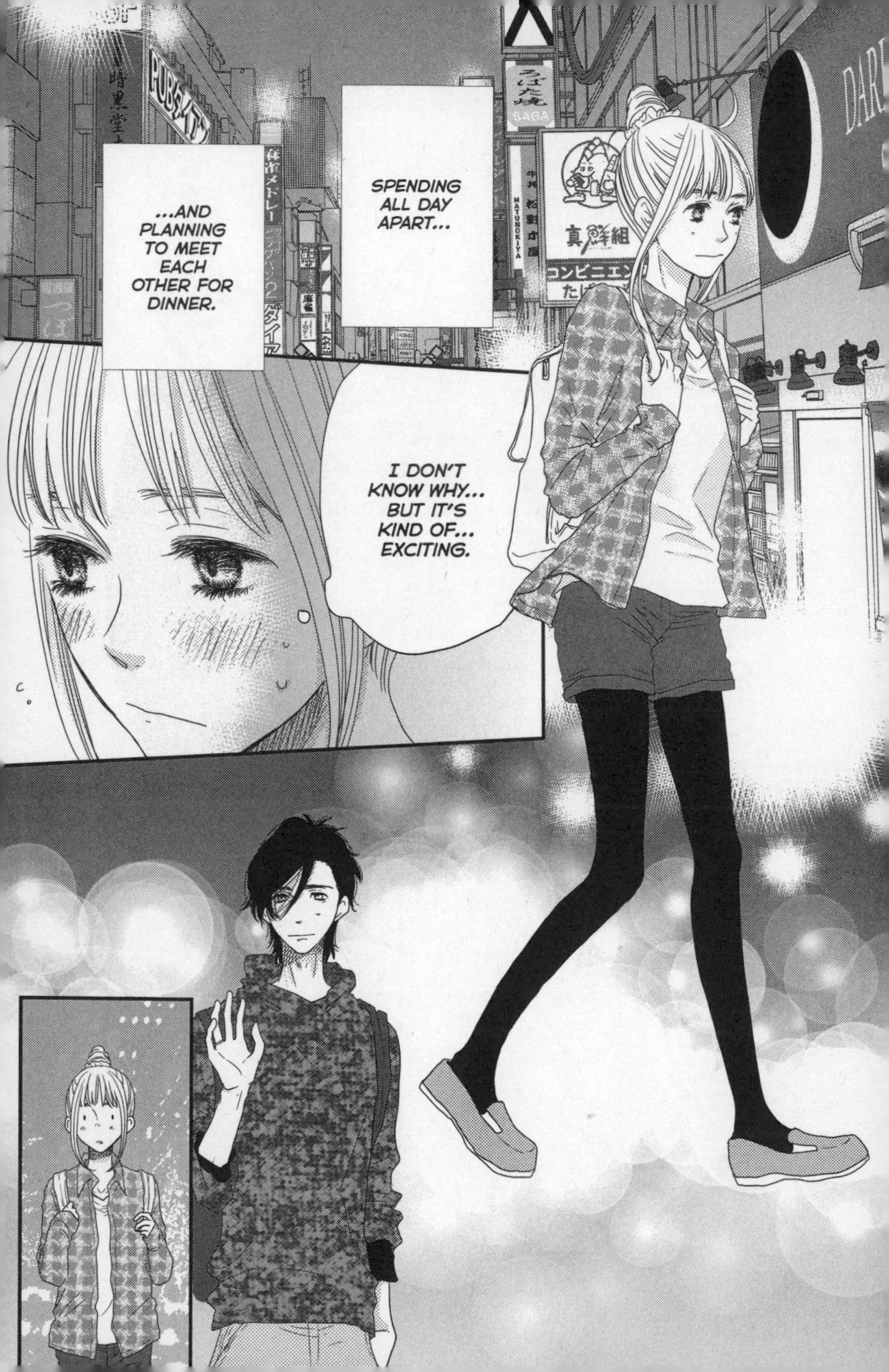
SPENDING ALL DAY APART...
...AND PLANNING TO MEET EACH OTHER FOR DINNER.
I DON'T KNOW WHY... BUT IT'S KIND OF... EXCITING.

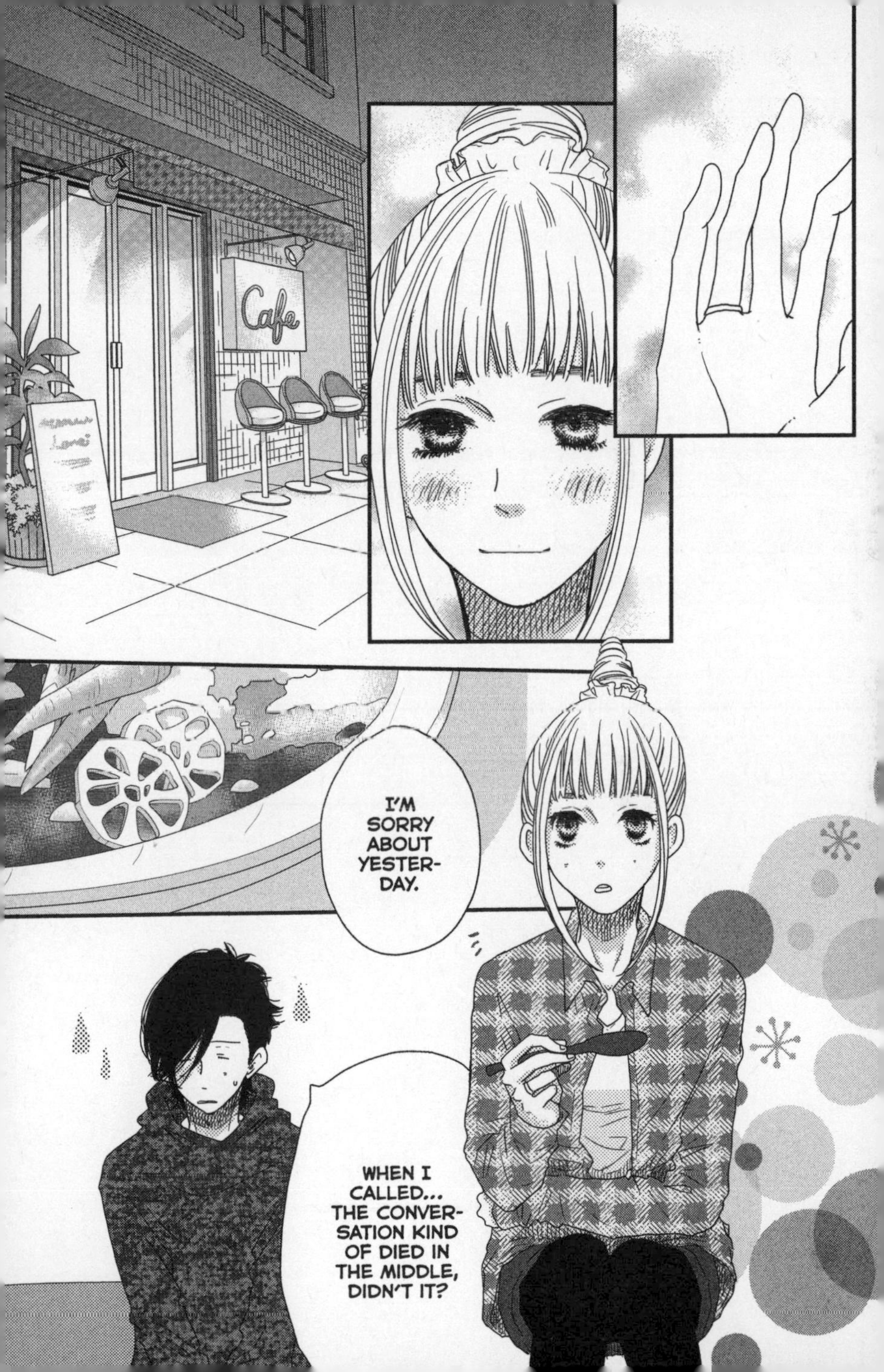
Cafe
I'M SORRY ABOUT YESTER-DAY.
WHEN I CALLED... THE CONVER-SATION KIND OF DIED IN THE MIDDLE, DIDN'T IT?

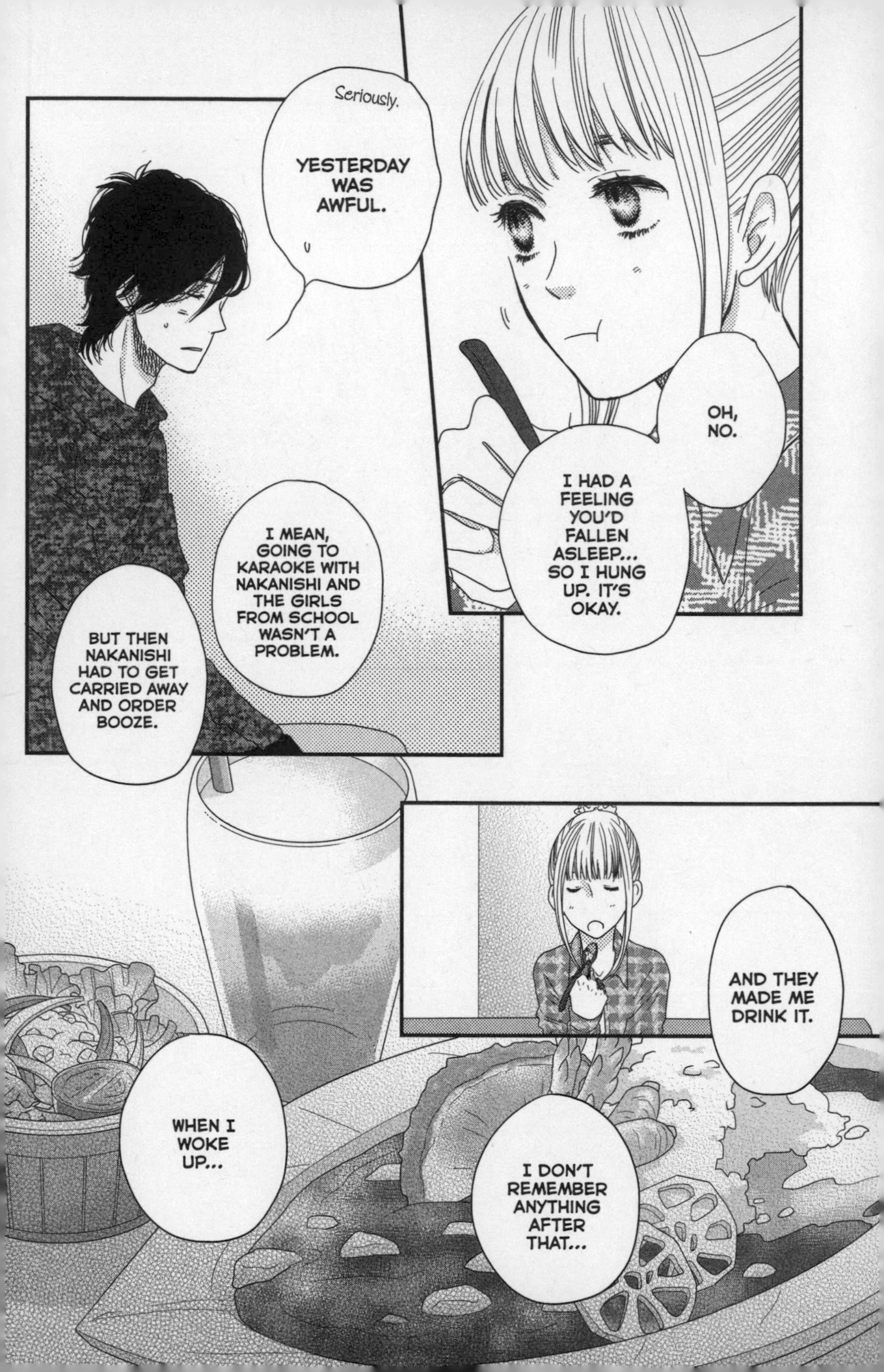
OH, NO.
I HAD A FEELING YOU'D FALLEN ASLEEP... SO I HUNG UP. IT'S OKAY.
Seriously.
YESTERDAY WAS AWFUL.
I MEAN, GOING TO KARAOKE WITH NAKANISHI AND THE GIRLS FROM SCHOOL WASN'T A PROBLEM.
BUT THEN NAKANISHI HAD TO GET CARRIED AWAY AND ORDER BOOZE.
AND THEY MADE ME DRINK IT.
I DON'T REMEMBER ANYTHING AFTER THAT...
WHEN I WOKE UP...

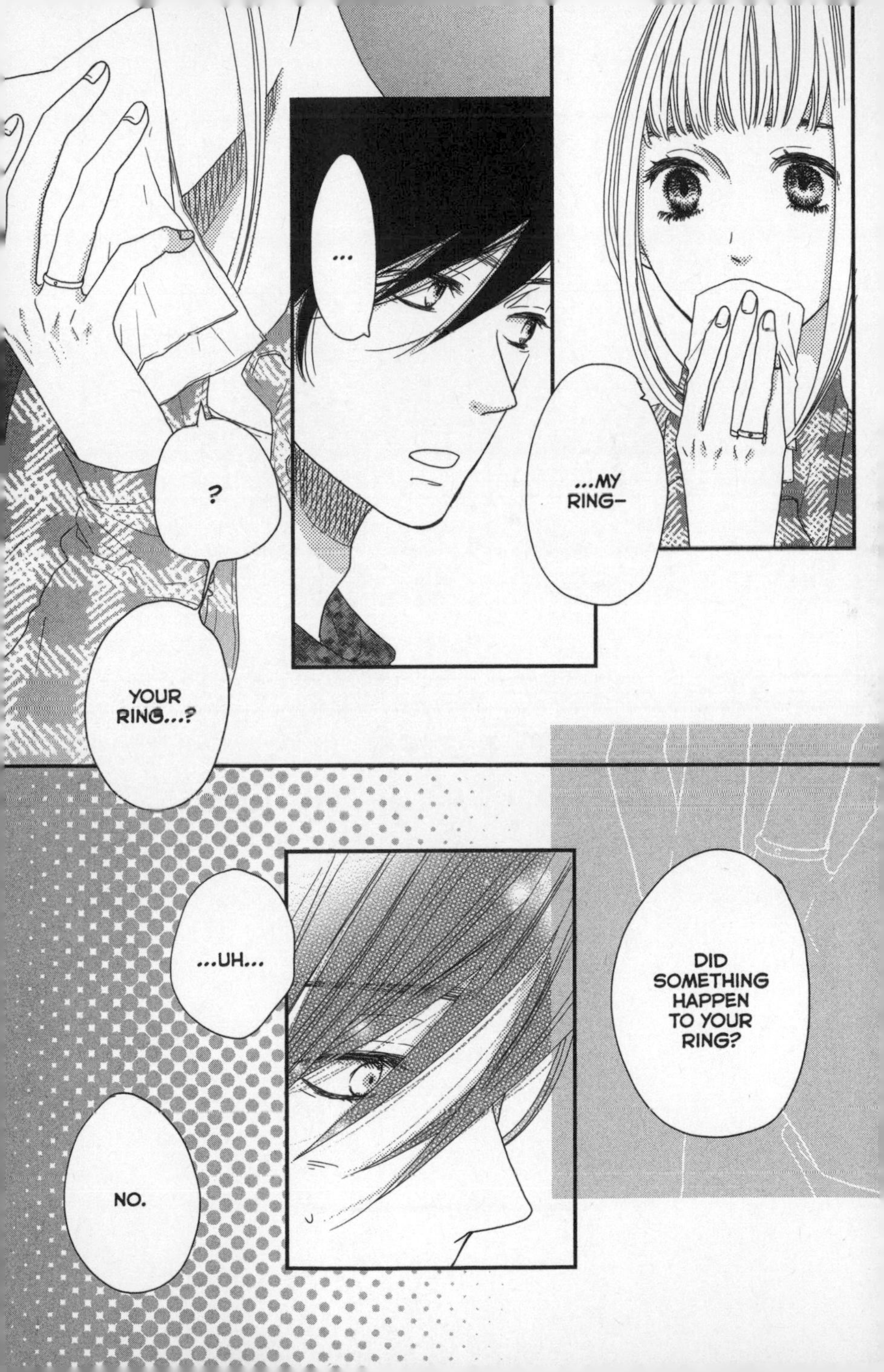
...MY RING–
...
?
YOUR RING...?
DID SOMETHING HAPPEN TO YOUR RING?
...UH...
NO.

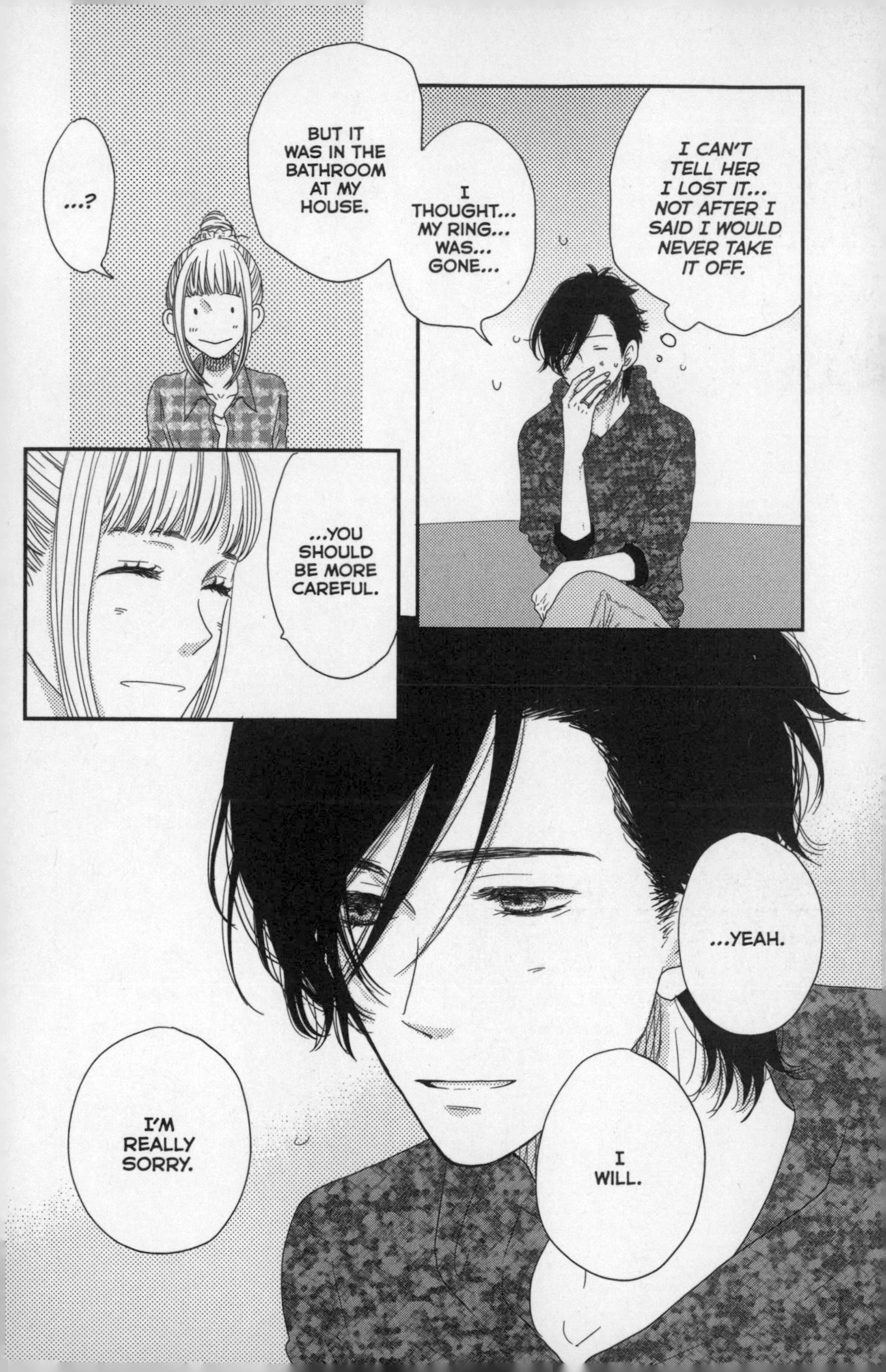
I CAN'T TELL HER I LOST IT... NOT AFTER I SAID I WOULD NEVER TAKE IT OFF.
I THOUGHT... MY RING... WAS... GONE...
BUT IT WAS IN THE BATHROOM AT MY HOUSE.
...?
...YOU SHOULD BE MORE CAREFUL.
...YEAH.
I WILL.
I'M REALLY SORRY.

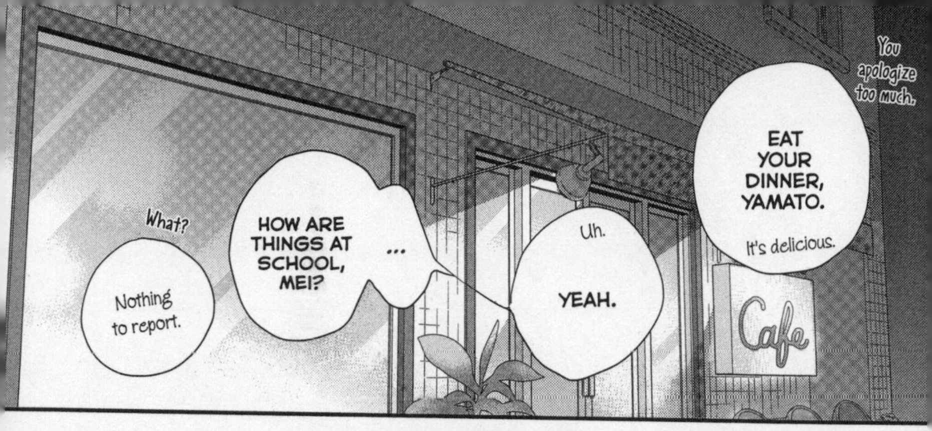
You apologize too much.
EAT YOUR DINNER, YAMATO.
It's delicious.
Cafe
Uh.
YEAH.
HOW ARE THINGS AT SCHOOL, MEI?
...
What?
Nothing to report.
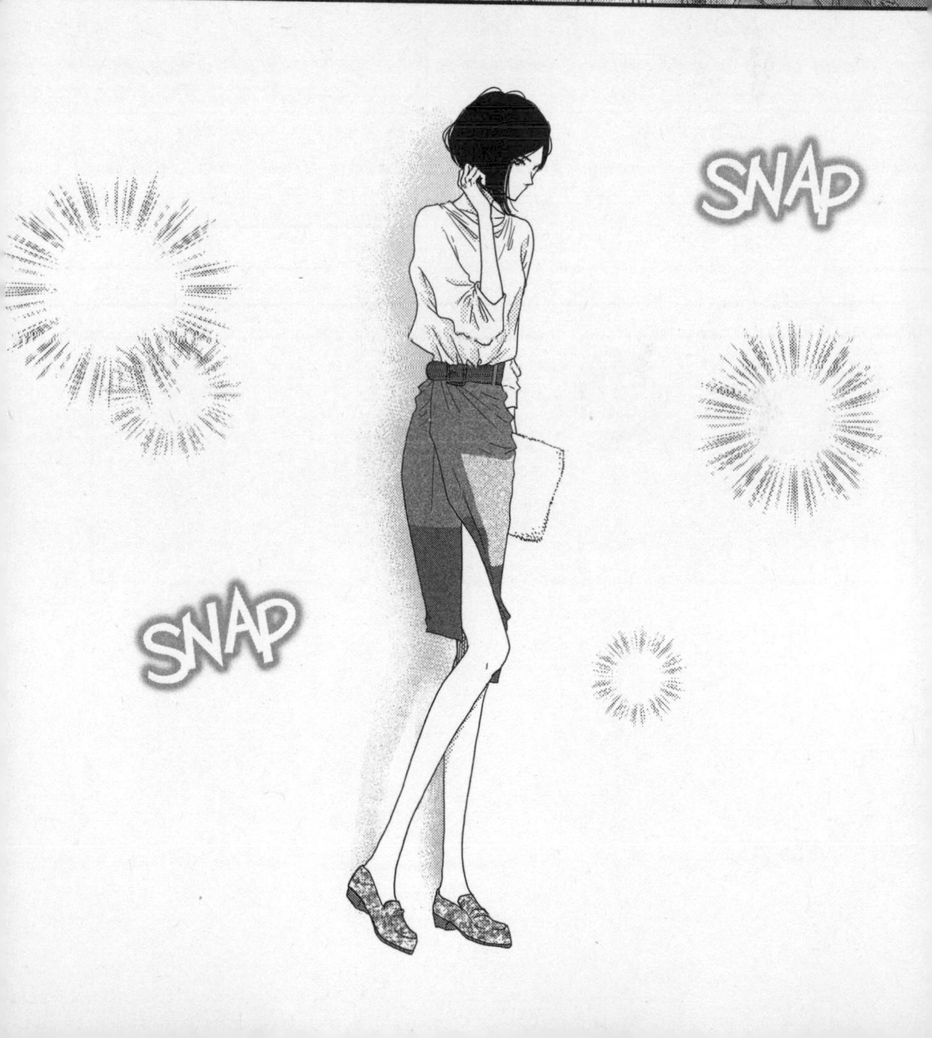
SNAP
SNAP

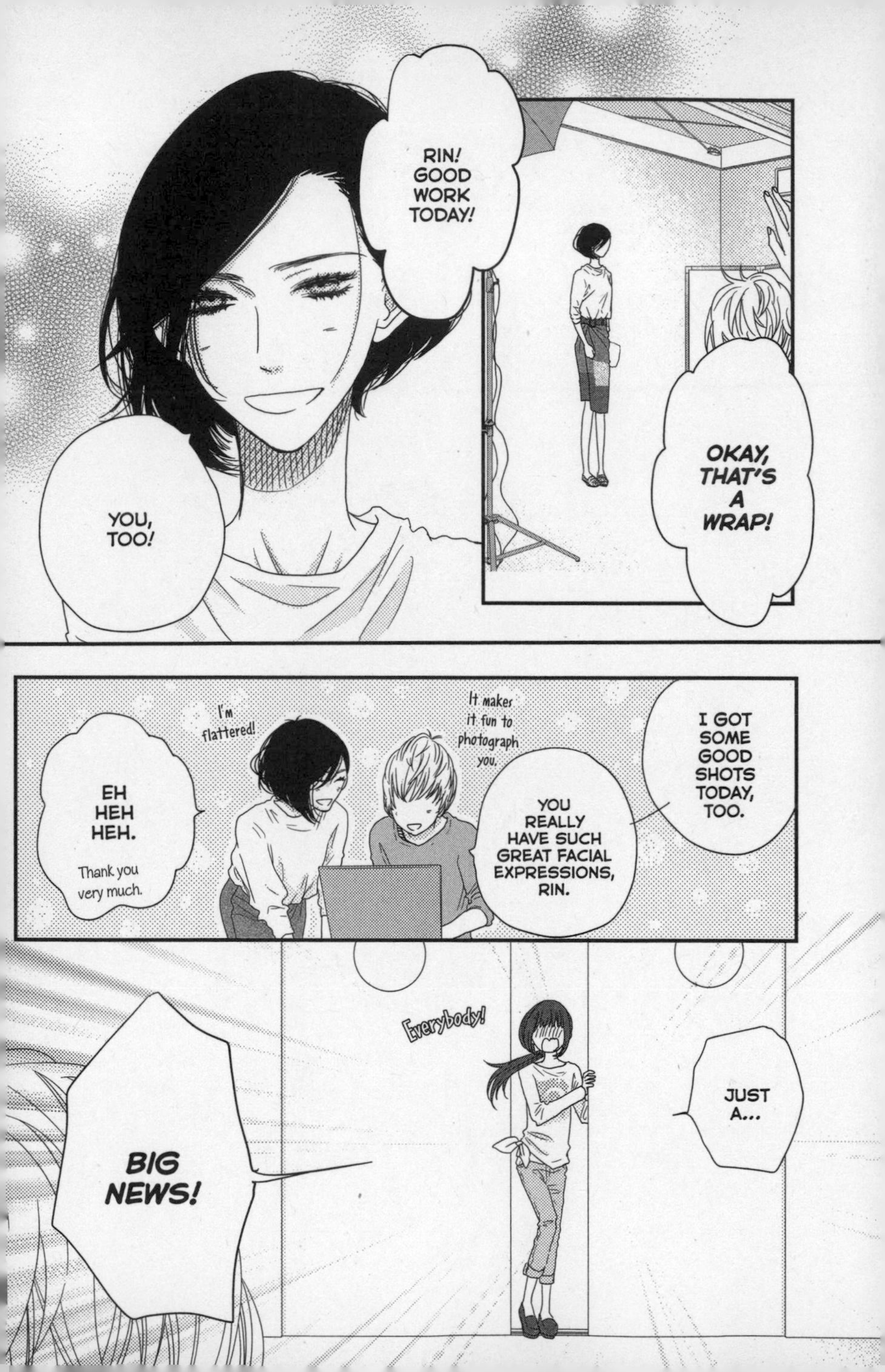
OKAY, THAT'S A WRAP!
RIN! GOOD WORK TODAY!
YOU, TOO!
I GOT SOME GOOD SHOTS TODAY, TOO.
YOU REALLY HAVE SUCH GREAT FACIAL EXPRESSIONS, RIN.
It makes it fun to photograph you.
I'm flattered!
EH HEH HEH.
Thank you very much.
Everybody!
JUST A...
BIG NEWS!

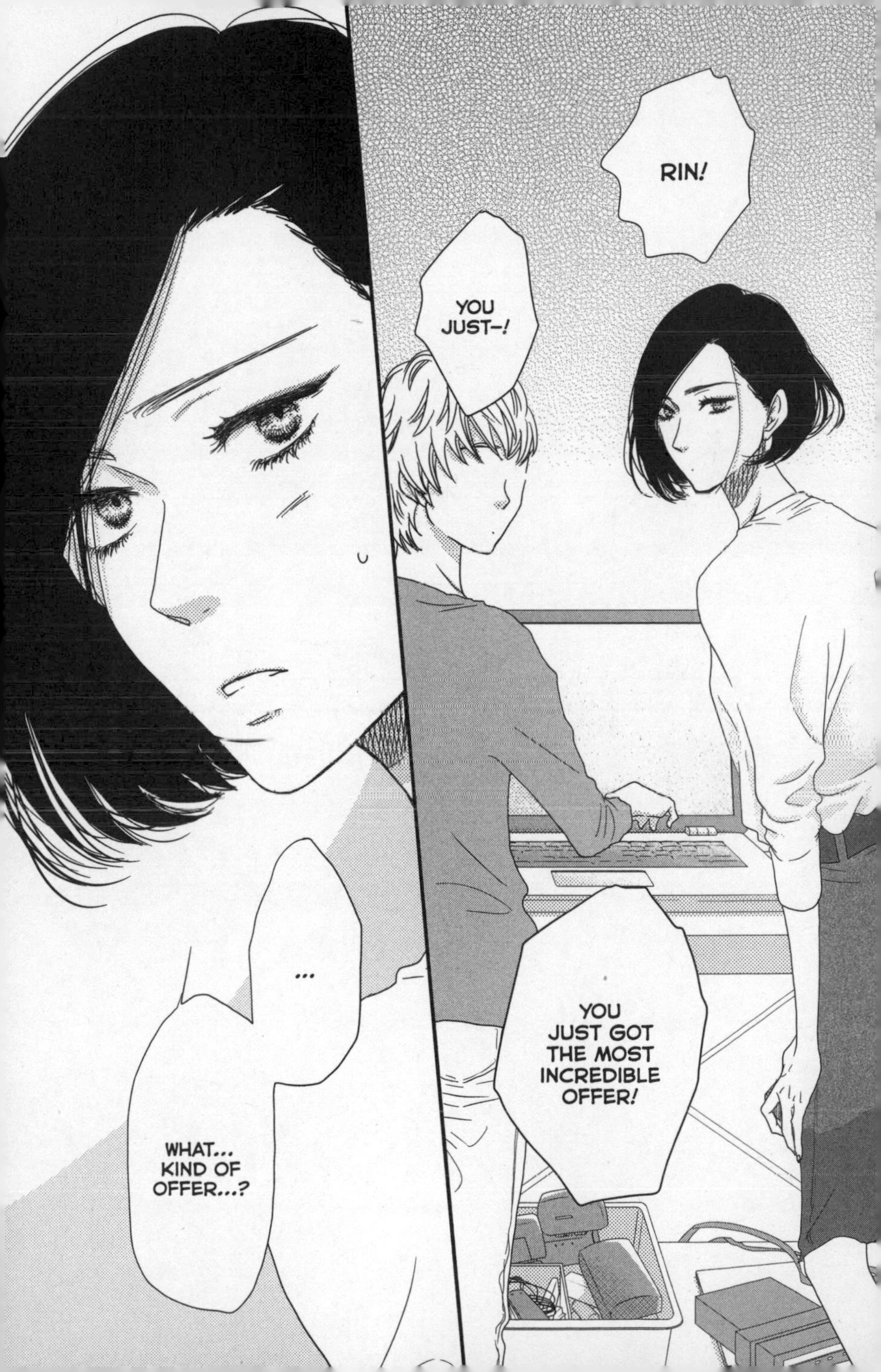
RIN!
YOU JUST–!
YOU JUST GOT THE MOST INCREDIBLE OFFER!
...
WHAT... KIND OF OFFER...?

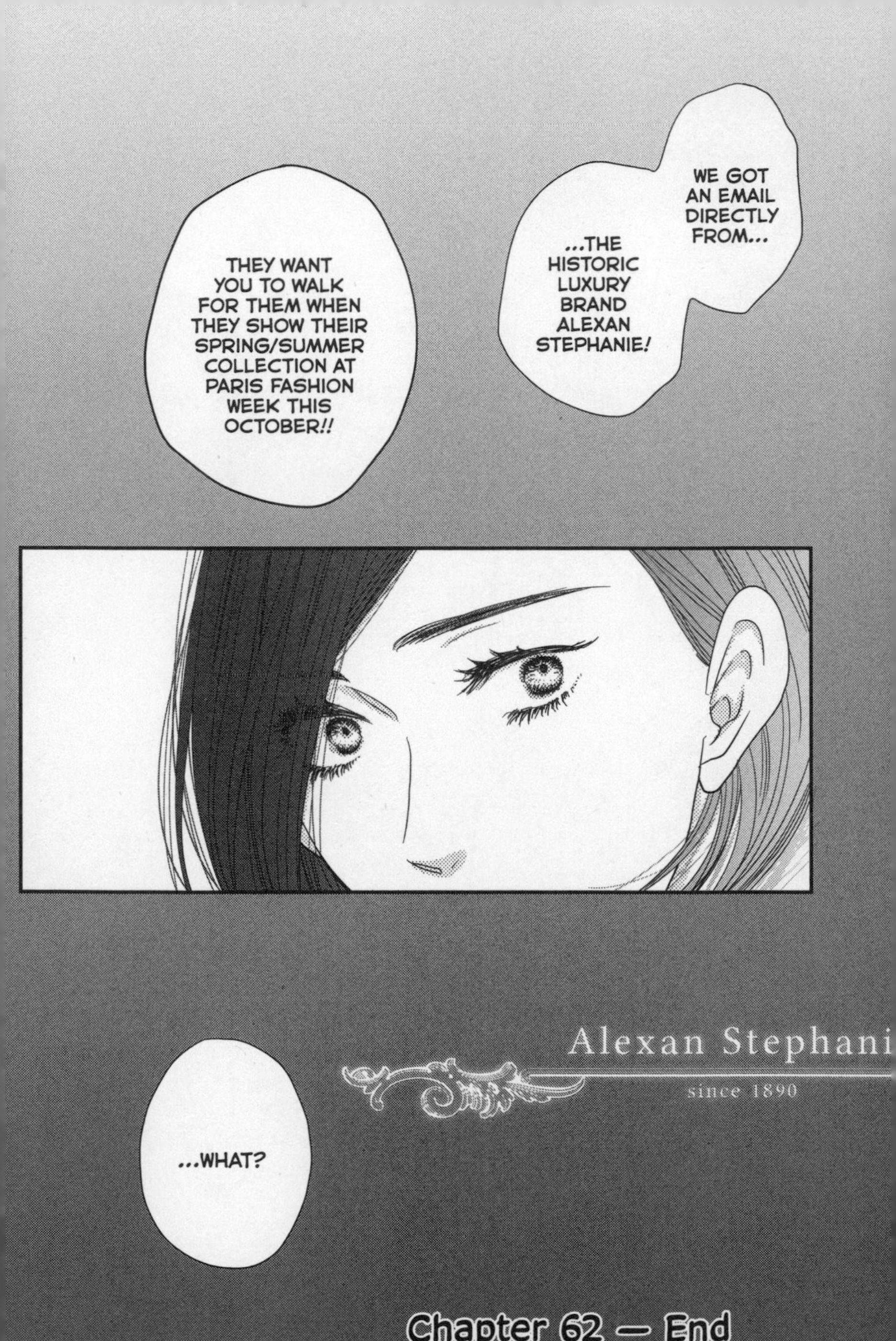
WE GOT AN EMAIL DIRECTLY FROM...
...THE HISTORIC LUXURY BRAND ALEXAN STEPHANIE!
THEY WANT YOU TO WALK FOR THEM WHEN THEY SHOW THEIR SPRING/SUMMER COLLECTION AT PARIS FASHION WEEK THIS OCTOBER!!
Alexan Stephani
since 1890
...WHAT?

Chapter 62 — End

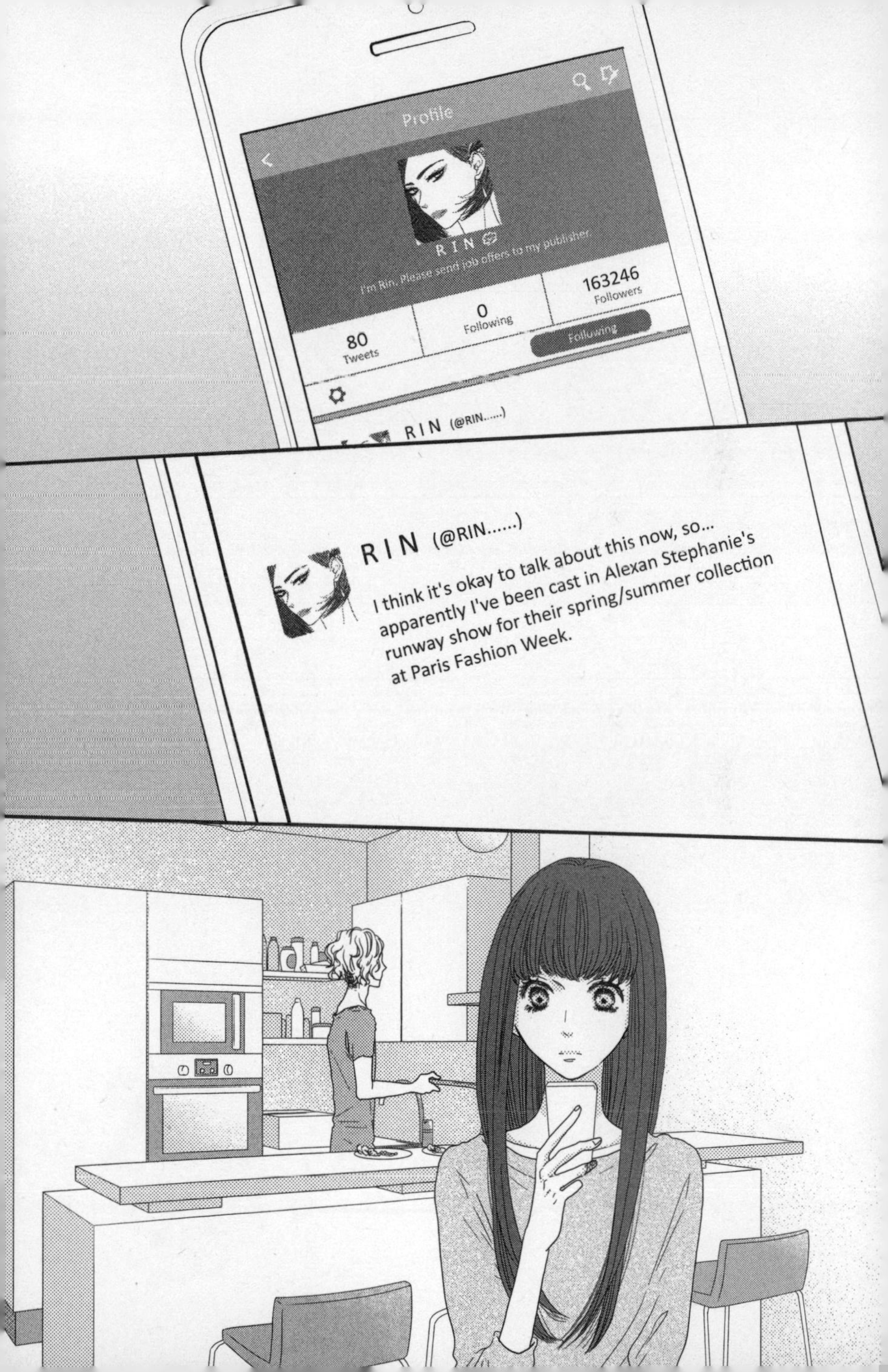
Profile
RIN
I'm Rin. Please send job offers to my publisher.
163246
Followers
0
Following
80
Tweets
Following
RIN (@RIN......)
RIN (@RIN......)
I think it's okay to talk about this now, so... apparently I've been cast in Alexan Stephanie's runway show for their spring/summer collection at Paris Fashion Week.

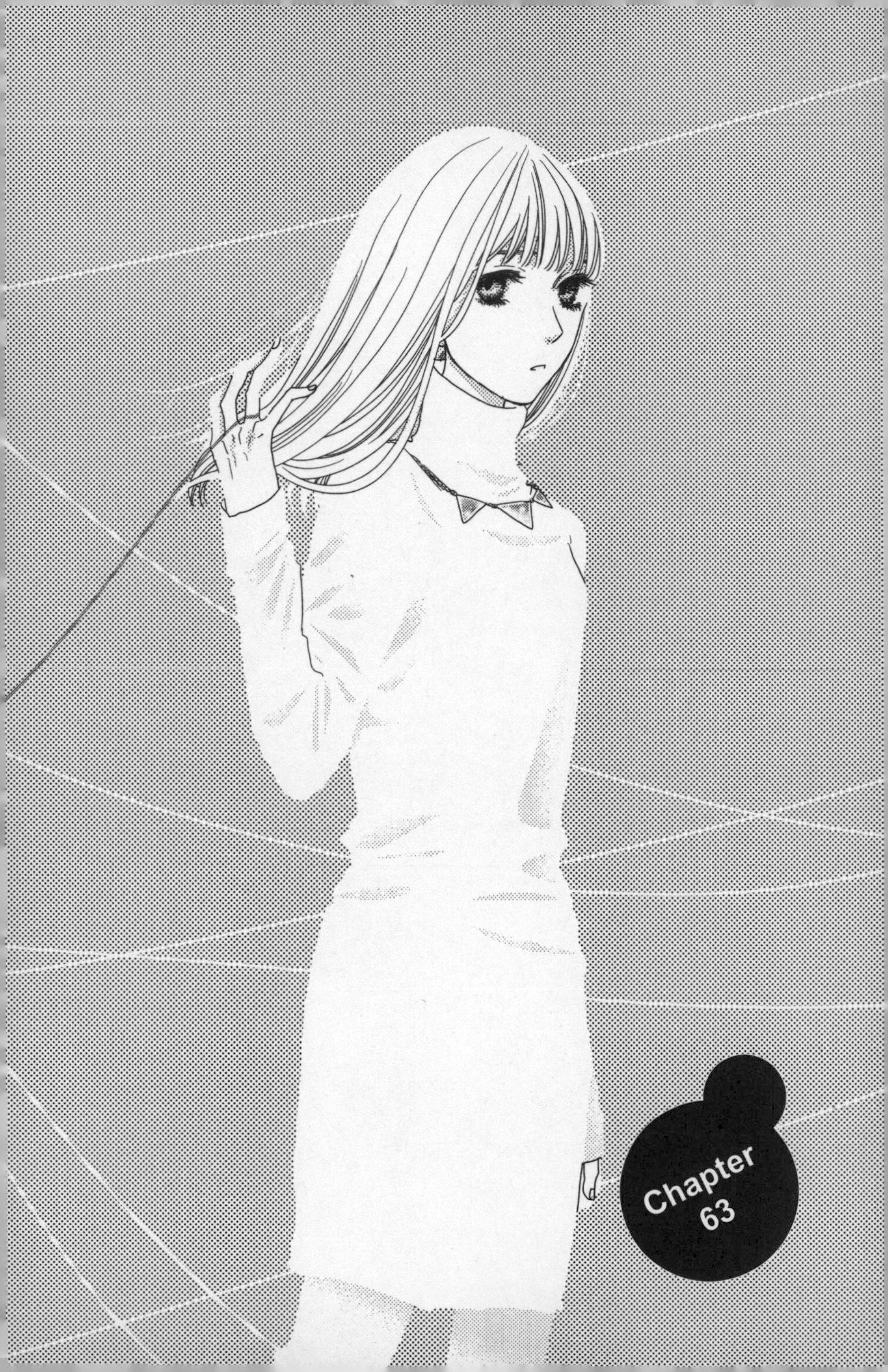
Chapter
63

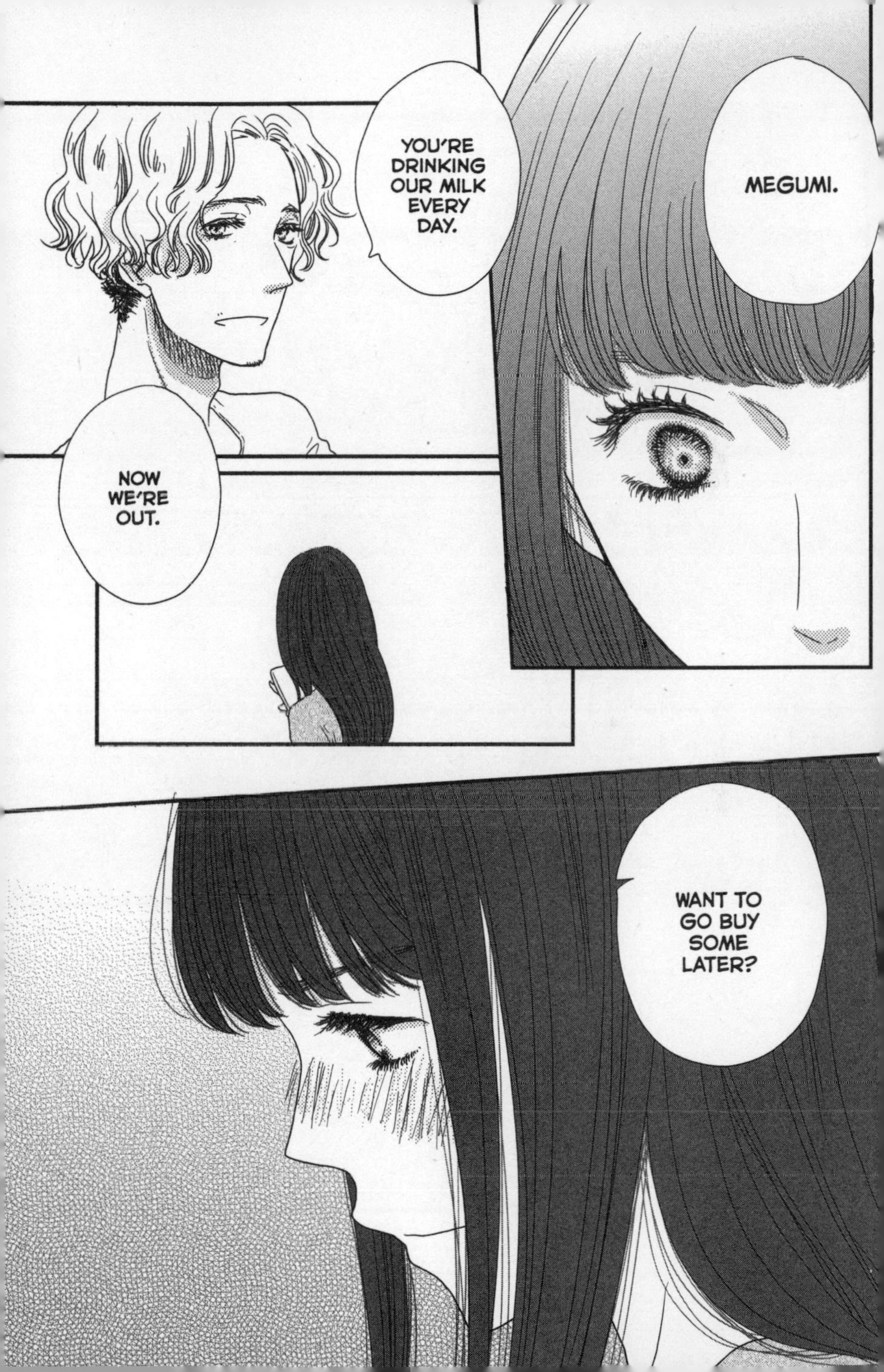
MEGUMI.
YOU'RE DRINKING OUR MILK EVERY DAY.
NOW WE'RE OUT.
WANT TO GO BUY SOME LATER?

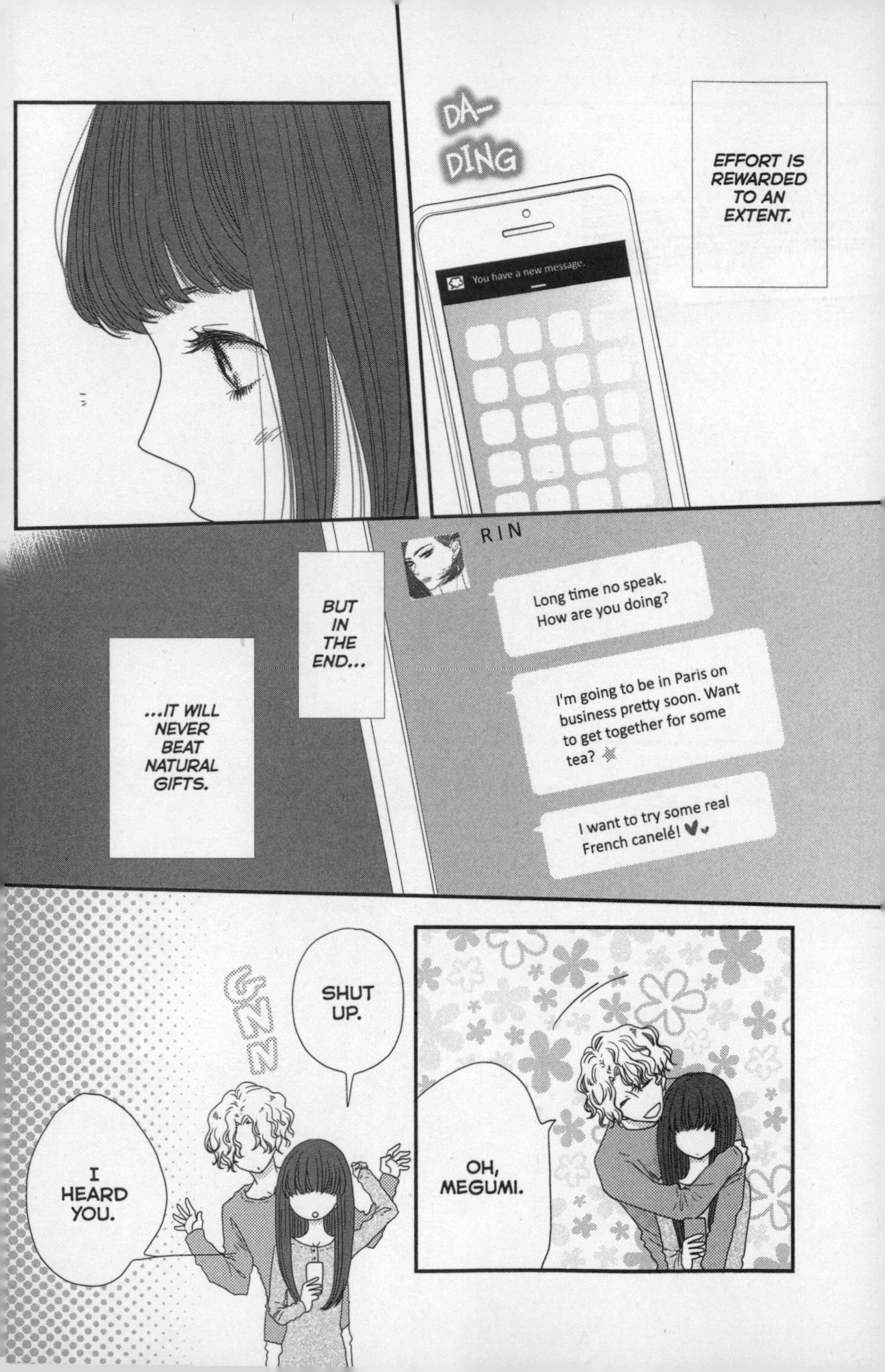
EFFORT IS REWARDED TO AN EXTENT.
DA-DING
You have a new message.
RIN
Long time no speak. How are you doing?
I'm going to be in Paris on business pretty soon. Want to get together for some tea?
I want to try some real French canelé!
BUT IN THE END...
...IT WILL NEVER BEAT NATURAL GIFTS.
OH, MEGUMI.
SHUT UP.
GNN
I HEARD YOU.

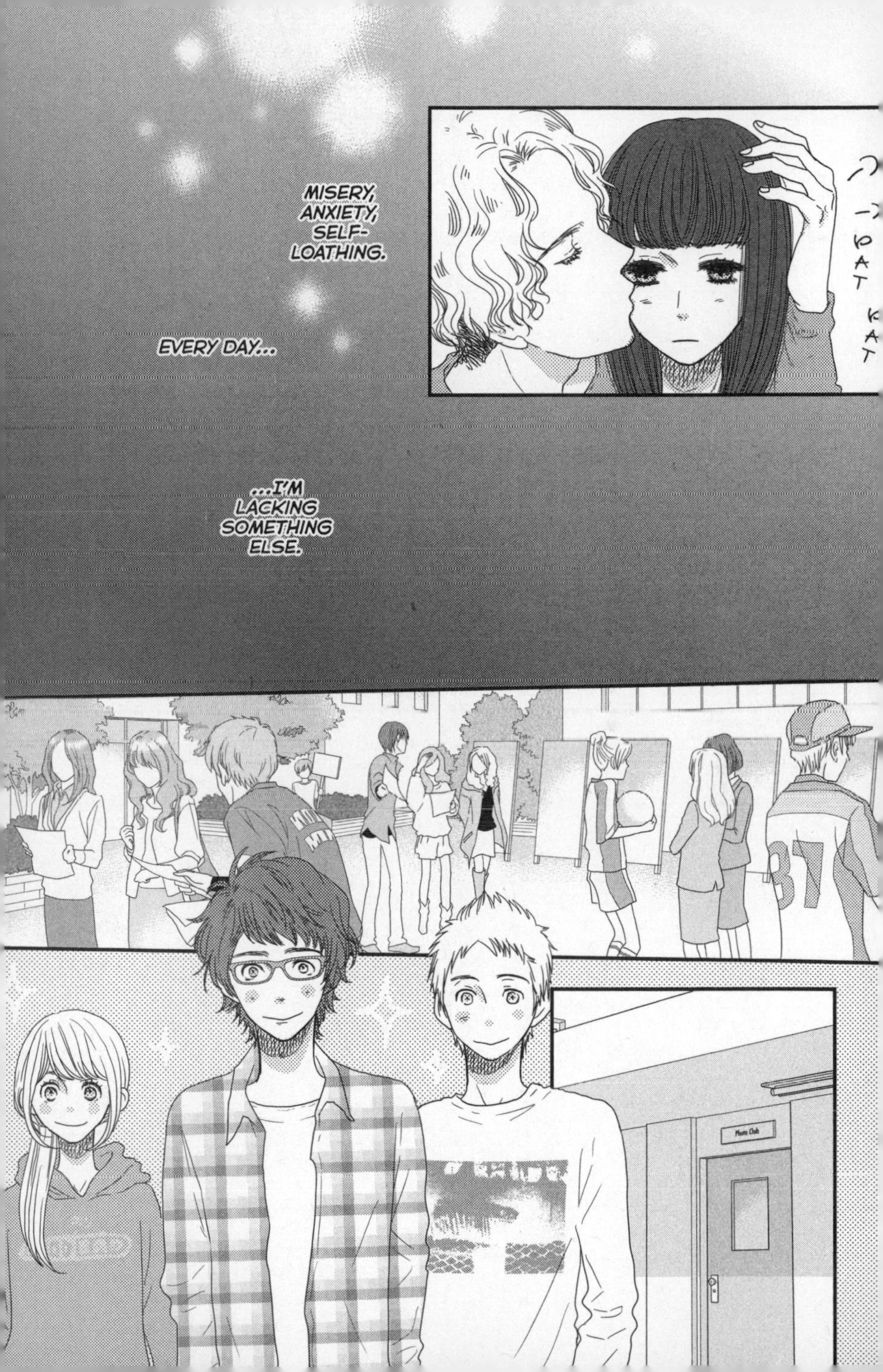
PAT PAT
MISERY, ANXIETY, SELF-LOATHING.
EVERY DAY...
...I'M LACKING SOMETHING ELSE.
Photo Club

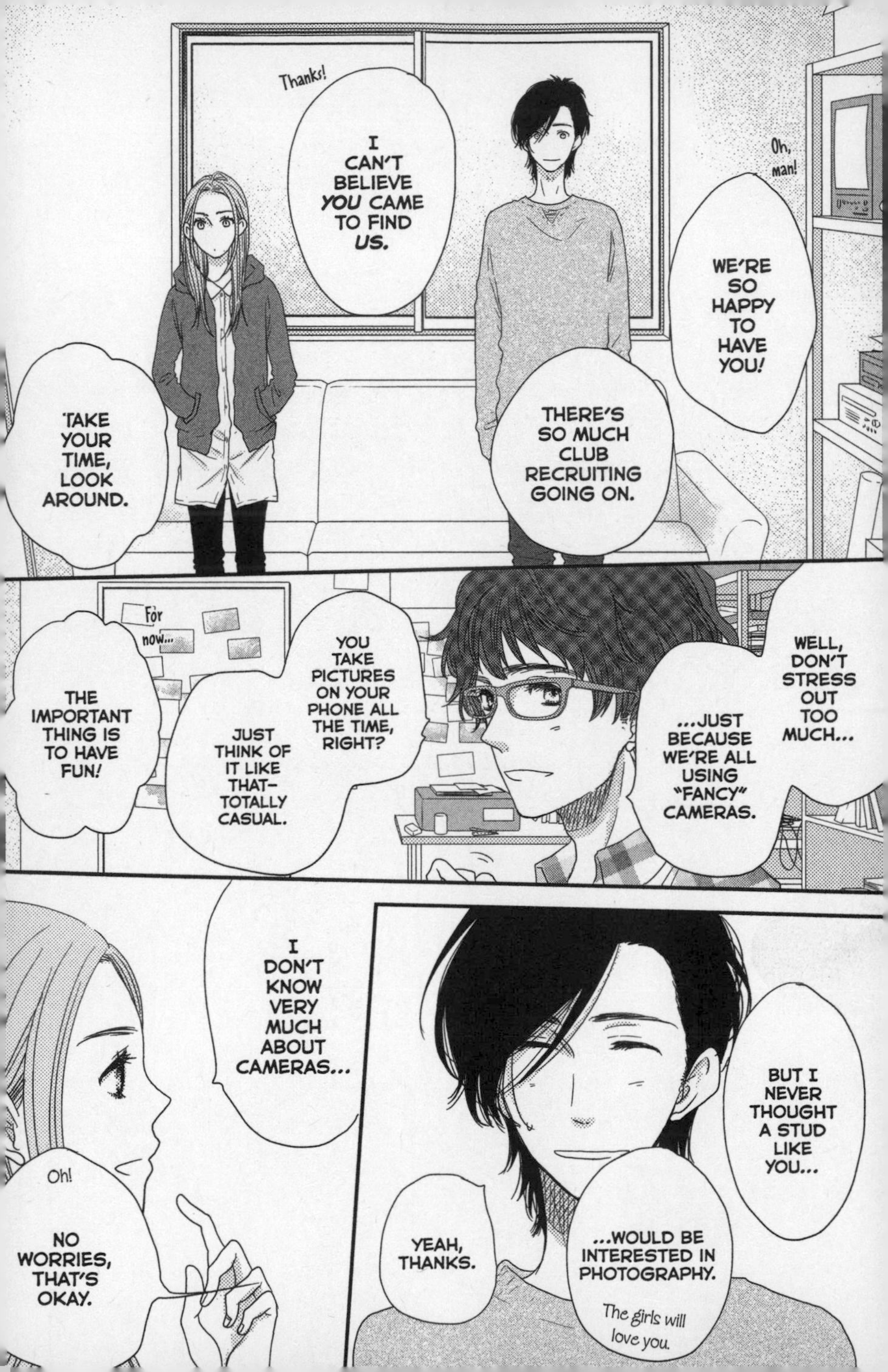
Oh, man!
WE'RE SO HAPPY TO HAVE YOU!
THERE'S SO MUCH CLUB RECRUITING GOING ON.
Thanks!
I CAN'T BELIEVE *YOU* CAME TO FIND *US*.
TAKE YOUR TIME, LOOK AROUND.
WELL, DON'T STRESS OUT TOO MUCH...
...JUST BECAUSE WE'RE ALL USING "FANCY" CAMERAS.
YOU TAKE PICTURES ON YOUR PHONE ALL THE TIME, RIGHT?
JUST THINK OF IT LIKE THAT—TOTALLY CASUAL.
For now...
THE IMPORTANT THING IS TO HAVE FUN!
BUT I NEVER THOUGHT A STUD LIKE YOU...
...WOULD BE INTERESTED IN PHOTOGRAPHY.
The girls will love you.
YEAH, THANKS.
I DON'T KNOW VERY MUCH ABOUT CAMERAS...
Oh!
NO WORRIES, THAT'S OKAY.

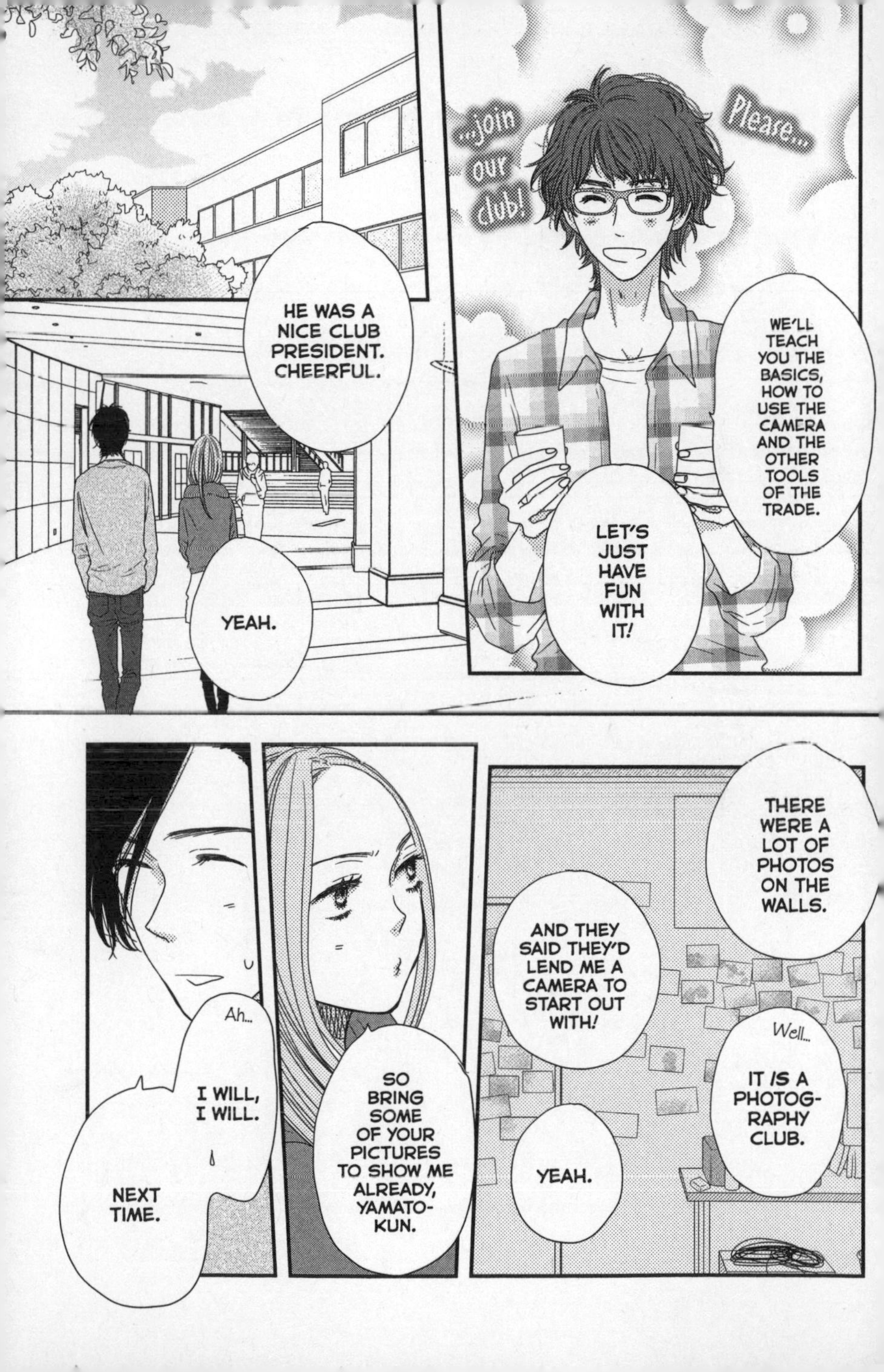
Please...
...join our club!
WE'LL TEACH YOU THE BASICS, HOW TO USE THE CAMERA AND THE OTHER TOOLS OF THE TRADE.
LET'S JUST HAVE FUN WITH IT!
HE WAS A NICE CLUB PRESIDENT. CHEERFUL.
YEAH.
THERE WERE A LOT OF PHOTOS ON THE WALLS.
AND THEY SAID THEY'D LEND ME A CAMERA TO START OUT WITH!
Well...
IT IS A PHOTOG-RAPHY CLUB.
YEAH.
SO BRING SOME OF YOUR PICTURES TO SHOW ME ALREADY, YAMATO-KUN.
Ah...
I WILL, I WILL.
NEXT TIME.

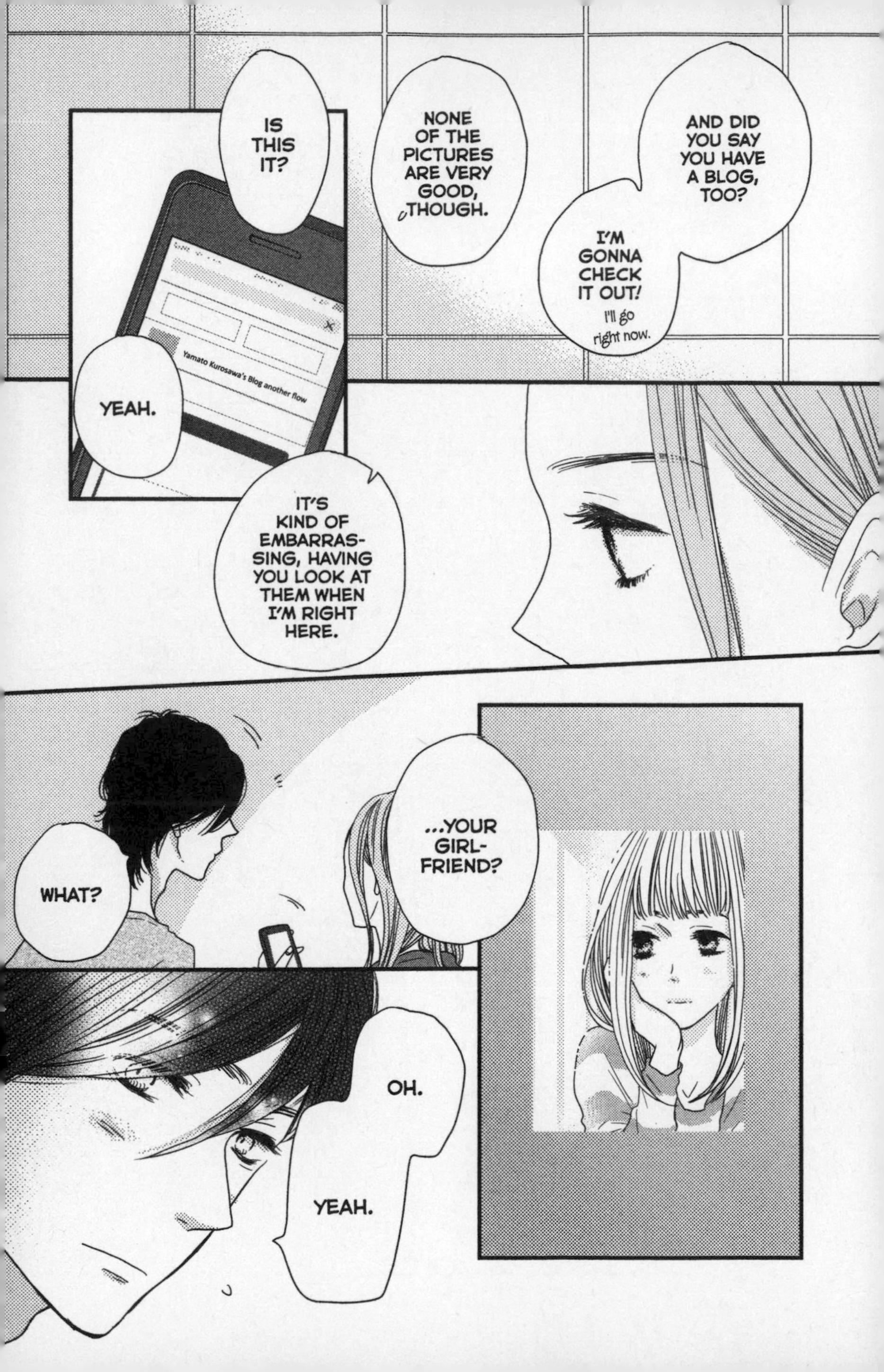
AND DID YOU SAY YOU HAVE A BLOG, TOO?
I'M GONNA CHECK IT OUT!
I'll go right now.
NONE OF THE PICTURES ARE VERY GOOD, THOUGH.
IS THIS IT?
Yamato Kurosawa's Blog another flow
YEAH.
IT'S KIND OF EMBARRAS-SING, HAVING YOU LOOK AT THEM WHEN I'M RIGHT HERE.
...YOUR GIRL-FRIEND?
WHAT?
OH.
YEAH.

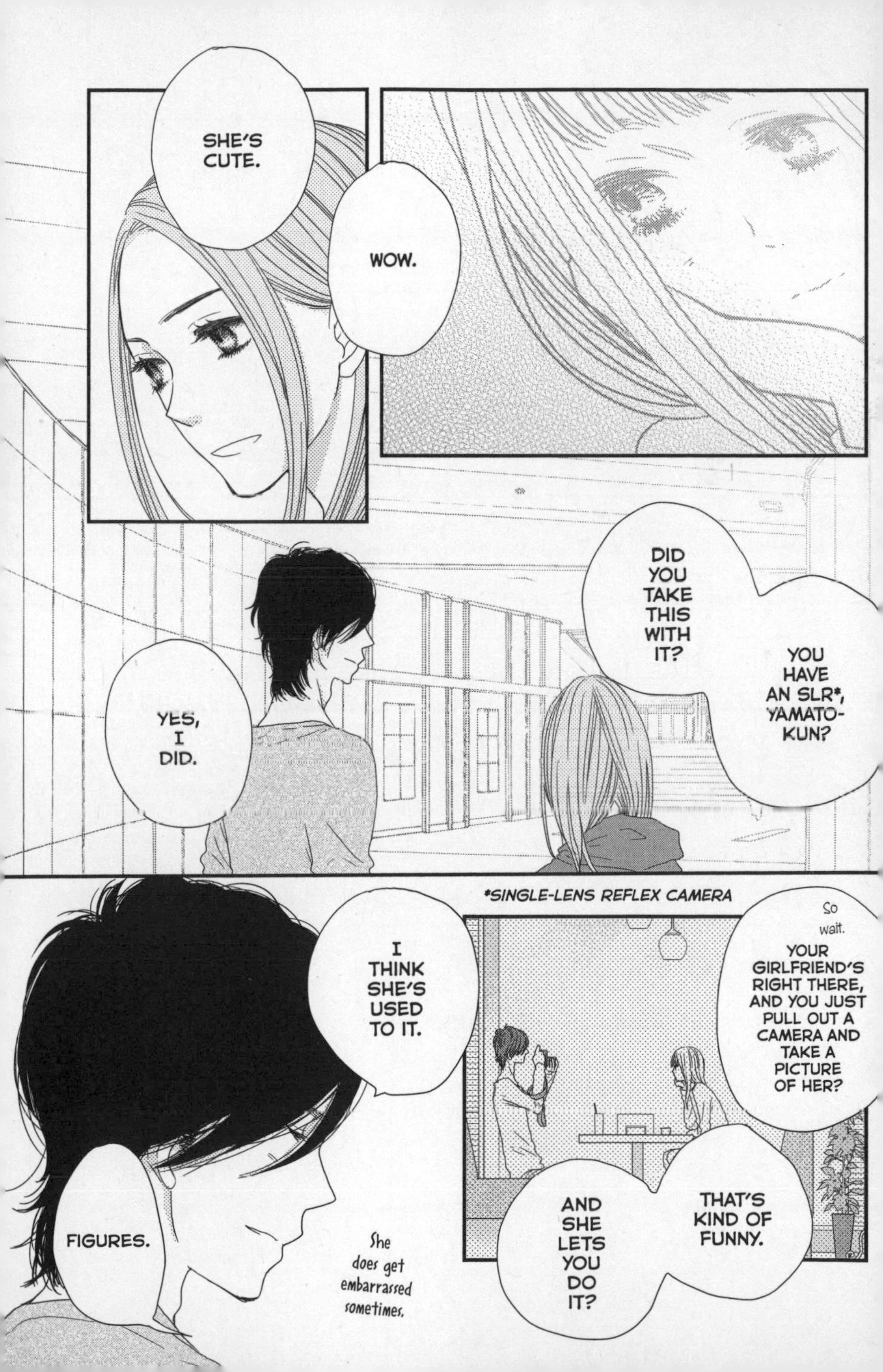
WOW.
SHE'S CUTE.
YOU HAVE AN SLR*, YAMATO-KUN?
DID YOU TAKE THIS WITH IT?
YES, I DID.
*SINGLE-LENS REFLEX CAMERA
So wait.
YOUR GIRLFRIEND'S RIGHT THERE, AND YOU JUST PULL OUT A CAMERA AND TAKE A PICTURE OF HER?
THAT'S KIND OF FUNNY.
AND SHE LETS YOU DO IT?
I THINK SHE'S USED TO IT.
FIGURES.
She does get embarrassed sometimes.

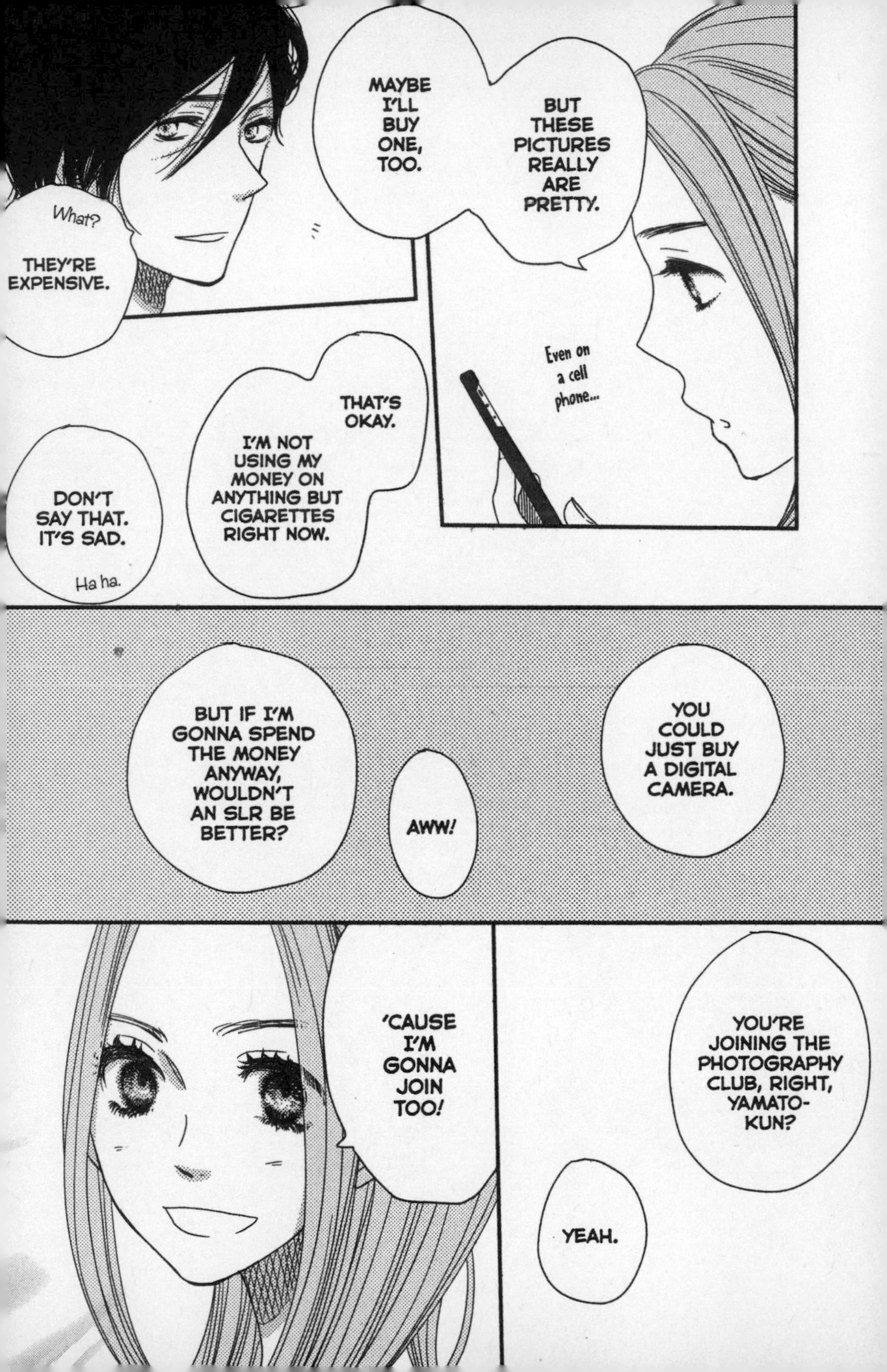
BUT THESE PICTURES REALLY ARE PRETTY.
Even on a cell phone...
MAYBE I'LL BUY ONE, TOO.
What?
THEY'RE EXPENSIVE.
THAT'S OKAY.
I'M NOT USING MY MONEY ON ANYTHING BUT CIGARETTES RIGHT NOW.
DON'T SAY THAT. IT'S SAD.
Ha ha.
YOU COULD JUST BUY A DIGITAL CAMERA.
AWW!
BUT IF I'M GONNA SPEND THE MONEY ANYWAY, WOULDN'T AN SLR BE BETTER?
YOU'RE JOINING THE PHOTOGRAPHY CLUB, RIGHT, YAMATO-KUN?
YEAH.
'CAUSE I'M GONNA JOIN TOO!

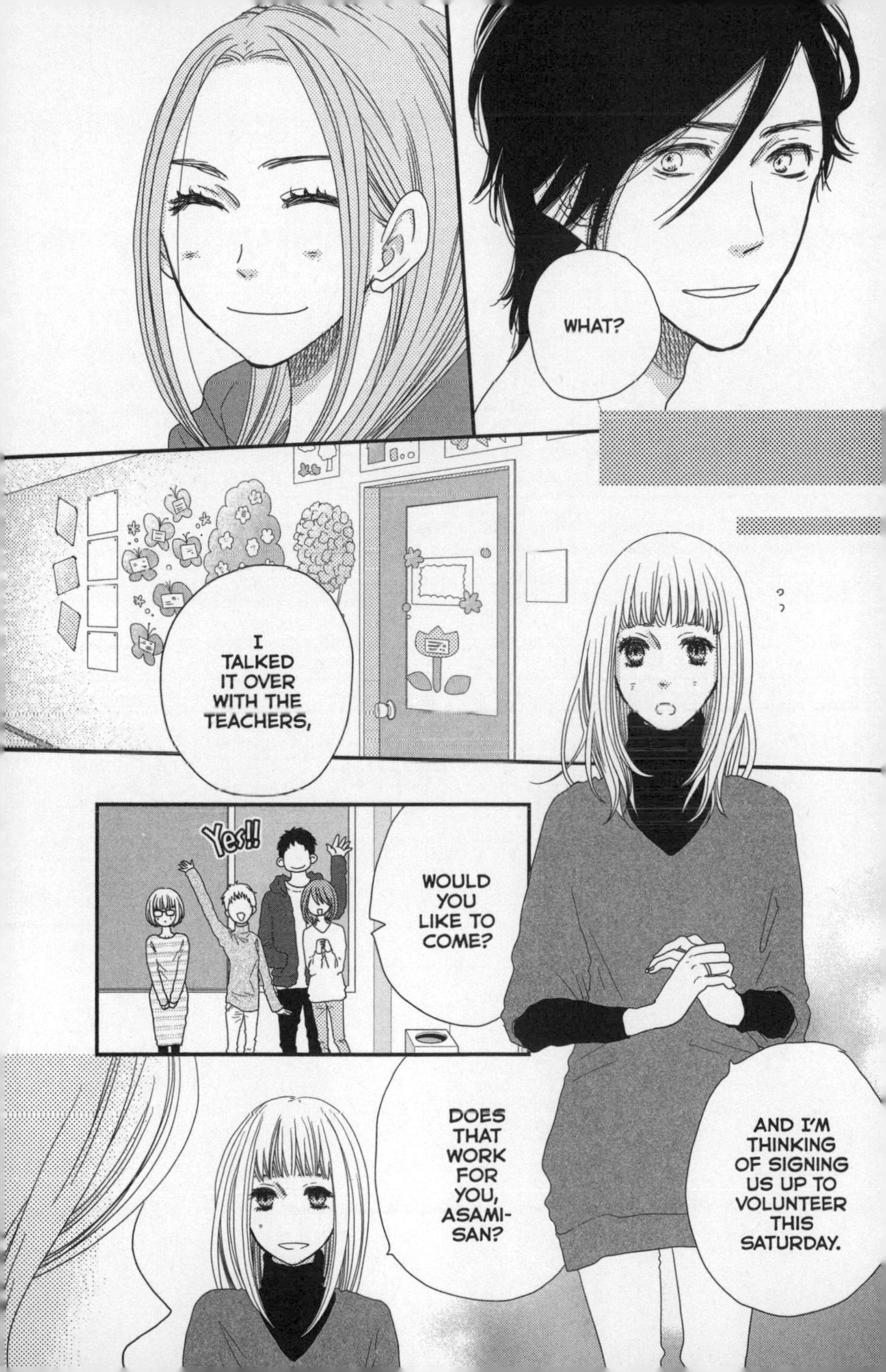
WHAT?
I TALKED IT OVER WITH THE TEACHERS,
AND I'M THINKING OF SIGNING US UP TO VOLUNTEER THIS SATURDAY.
WOULD YOU LIKE TO COME?
Yes!!
DOES THAT WORK FOR YOU, ASAMI-SAN?

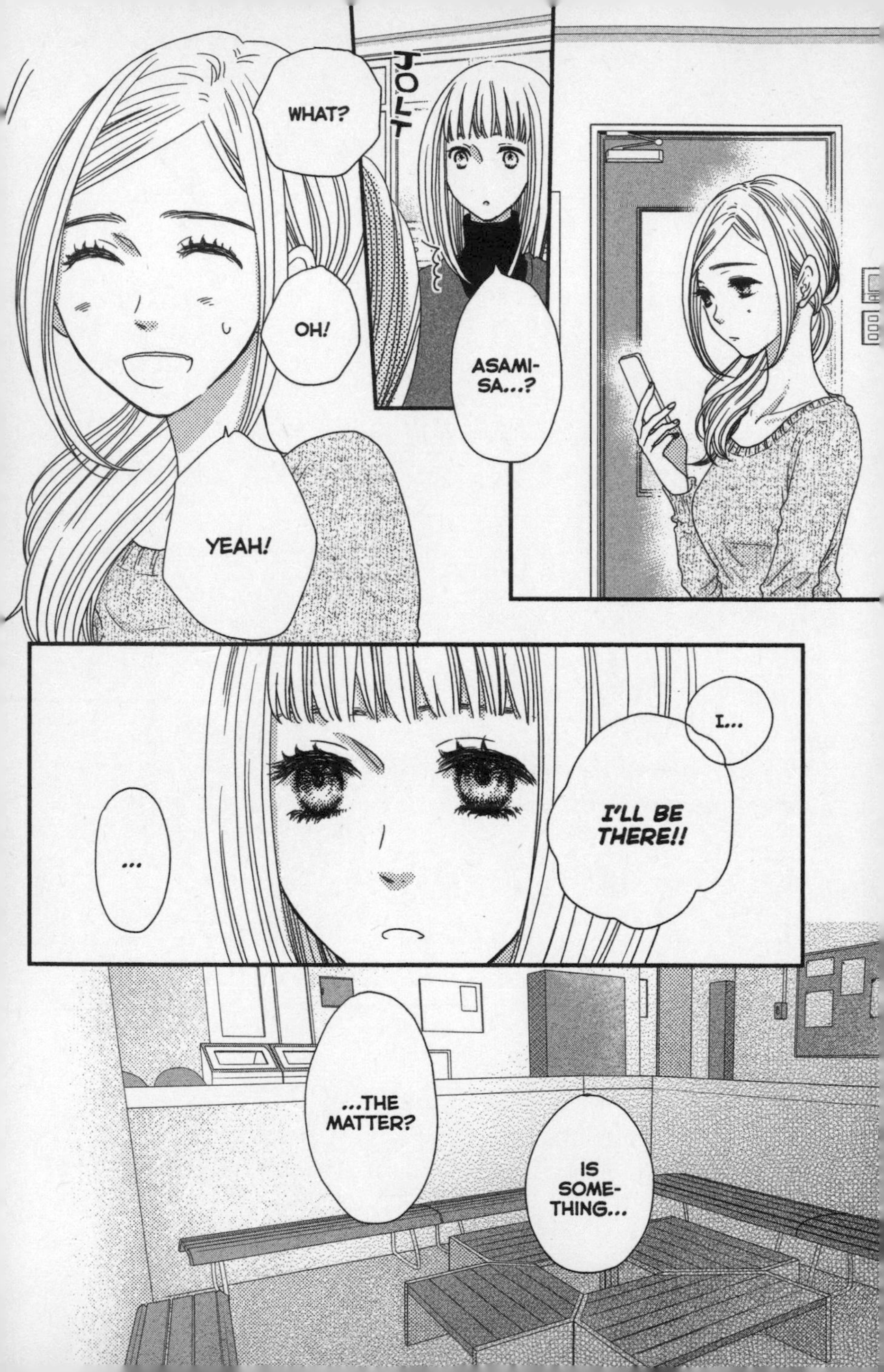
JOLT
ASAMI-SA...?
WHAT?
OH!
YEAH!
I...
I'LL BE THERE!!
...
IS SOMETHING...
...THE MATTER?

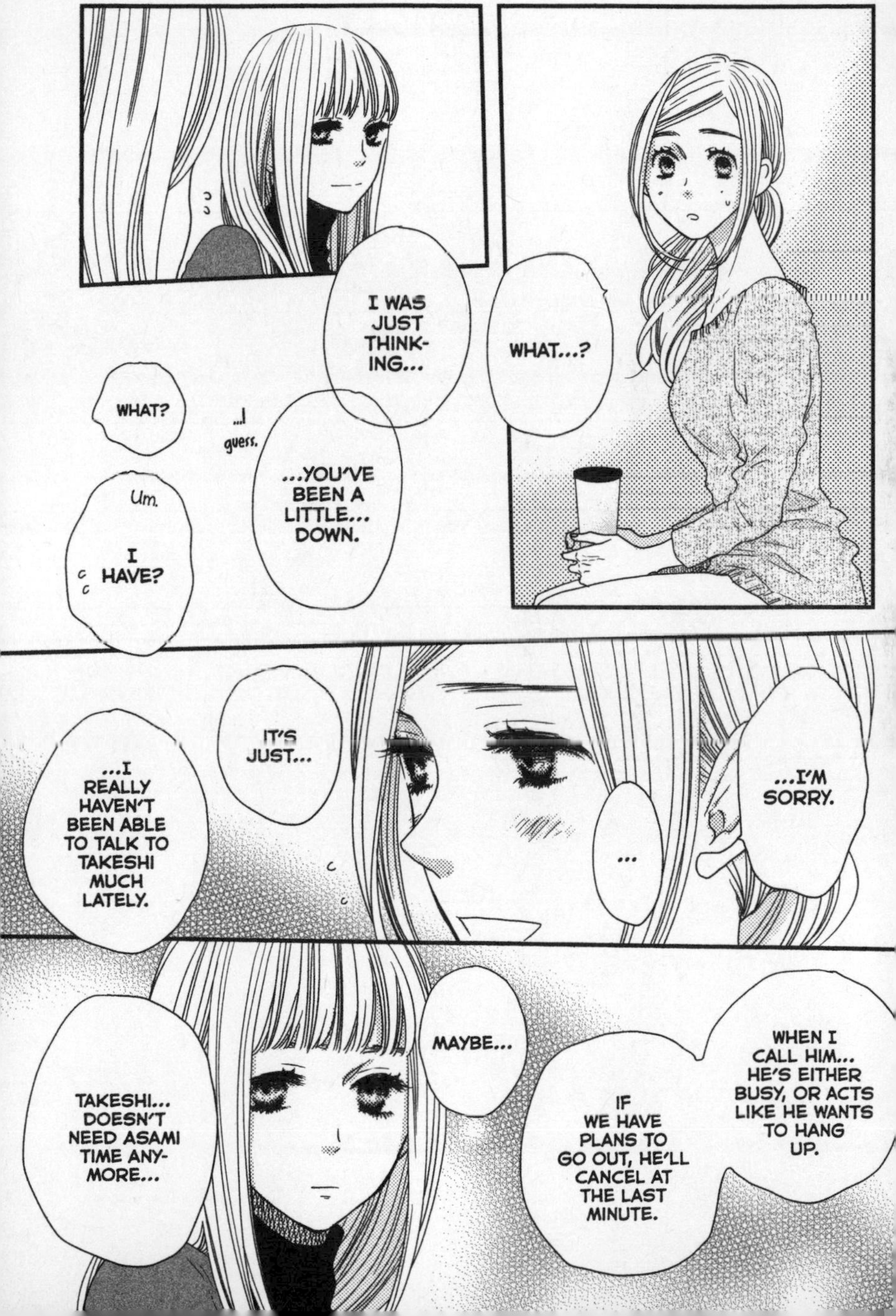
WHAT...?
I WAS JUST THINKING...
...YOU'VE BEEN A LITTLE... DOWN.
...I guess.
WHAT?
Um.
I HAVE?
...I'M SORRY.
...
IT'S JUST...
...I REALLY HAVEN'T BEEN ABLE TO TALK TO TAKESHI MUCH LATELY.
WHEN I CALL HIM... HE'S EITHER BUSY, OR ACTS LIKE HE WANTS TO HANG UP.
IF WE HAVE PLANS TO GO OUT, HE'LL CANCEL AT THE LAST MINUTE.
MAYBE...
TAKESHI... DOESN'T NEED ASAMI TIME ANYMORE...

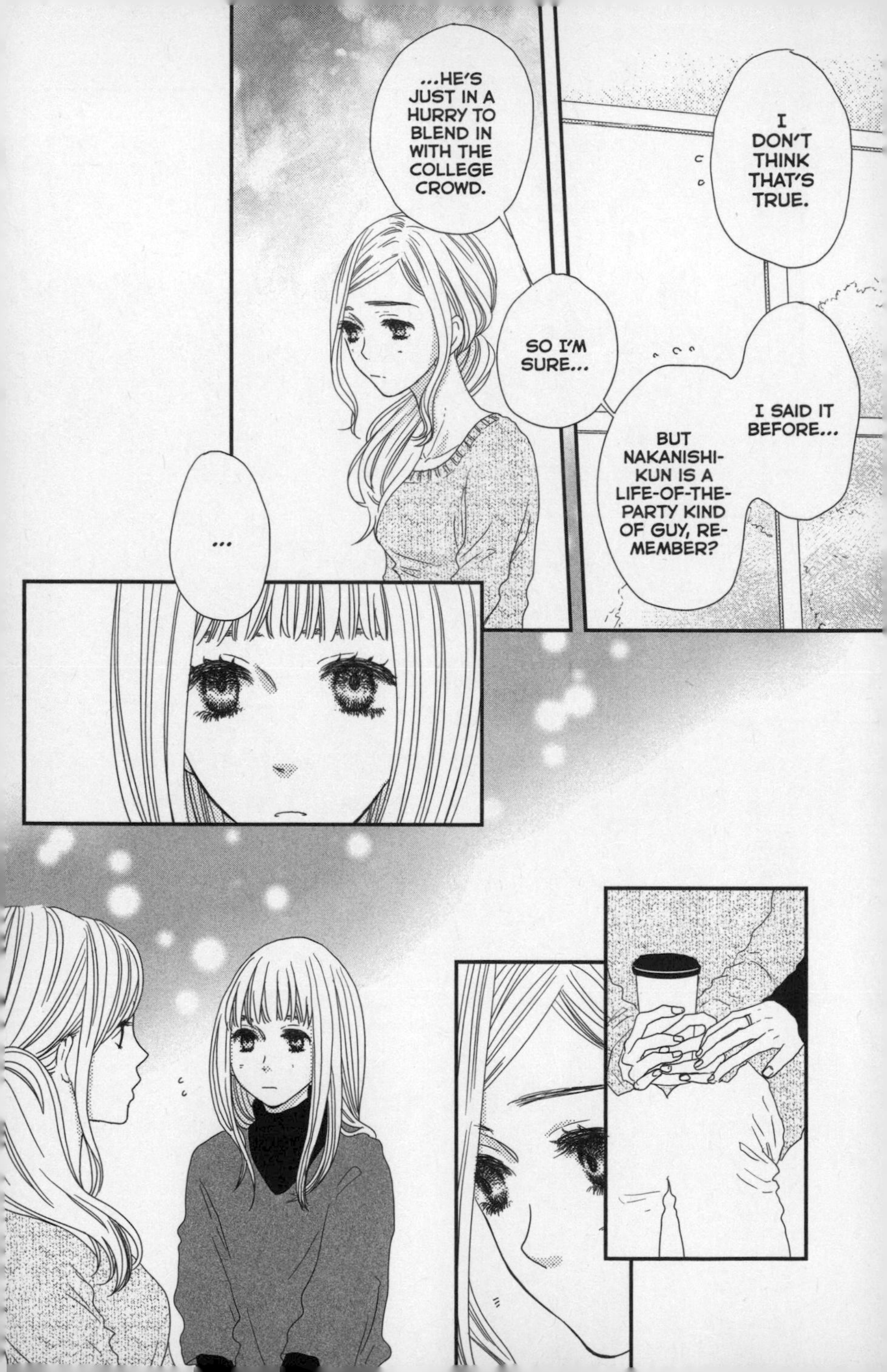
I DON'T THINK THAT'S TRUE.
I SAID IT BEFORE...
BUT NAKANISHI-KUN IS A LIFE-OF-THE-PARTY KIND OF GUY, REMEMBER?
SO I'M SURE...
...HE'S JUST IN A HURRY TO BLEND IN WITH THE COLLEGE CROWD.
...

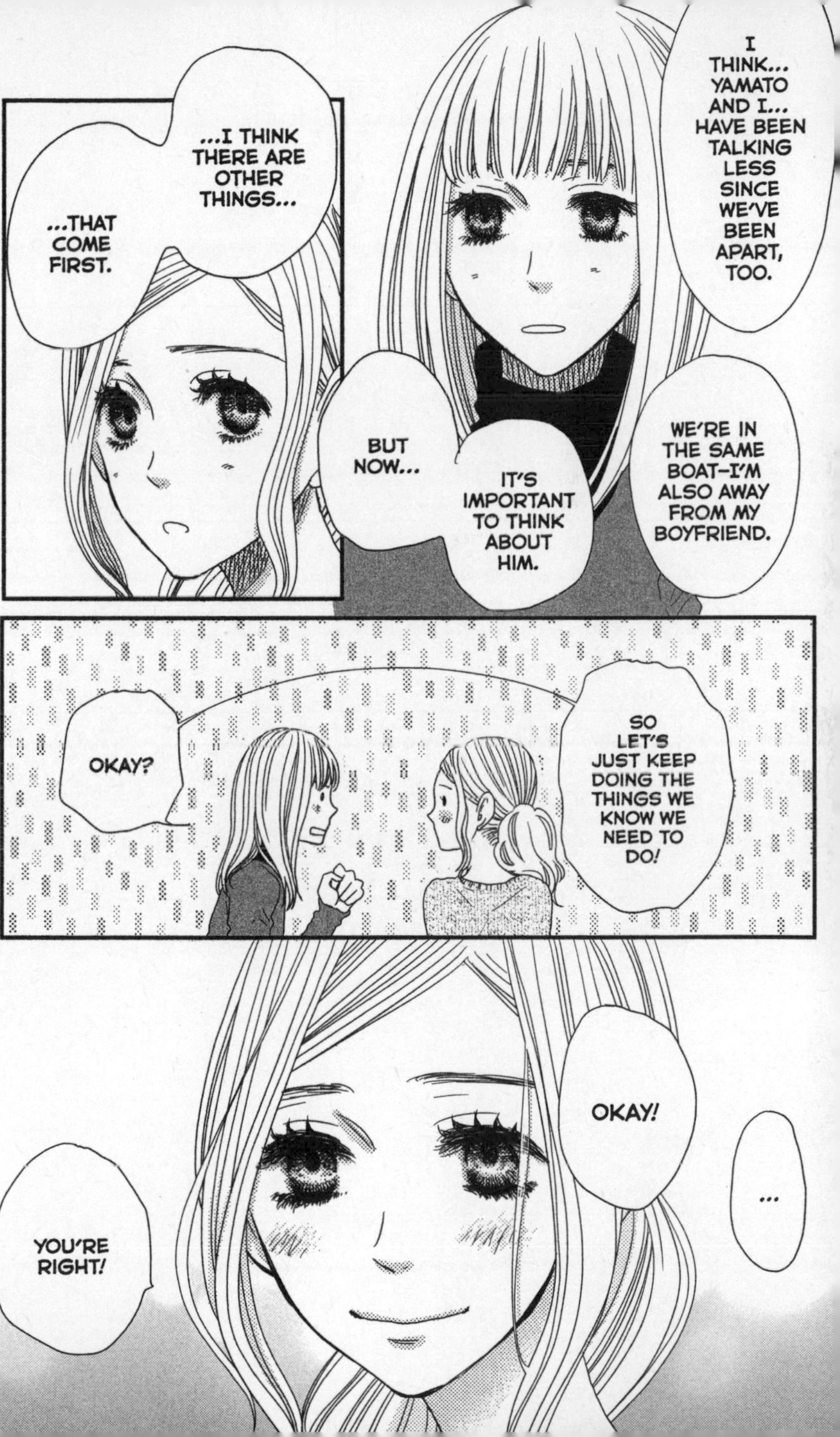
I THINK... YAMATO AND I... HAVE BEEN TALKING LESS SINCE WE'VE BEEN APART, TOO.
WE'RE IN THE SAME BOAT—I'M ALSO AWAY FROM MY BOYFRIEND.
BUT NOW...
IT'S IMPORTANT TO THINK ABOUT HIM.
...I THINK THERE ARE OTHER THINGS...
...THAT COME FIRST.
SO LET'S JUST KEEP DOING THE THINGS WE KNOW WE NEED TO DO!
OKAY?
OKAY!
...
YOU'RE RIGHT!

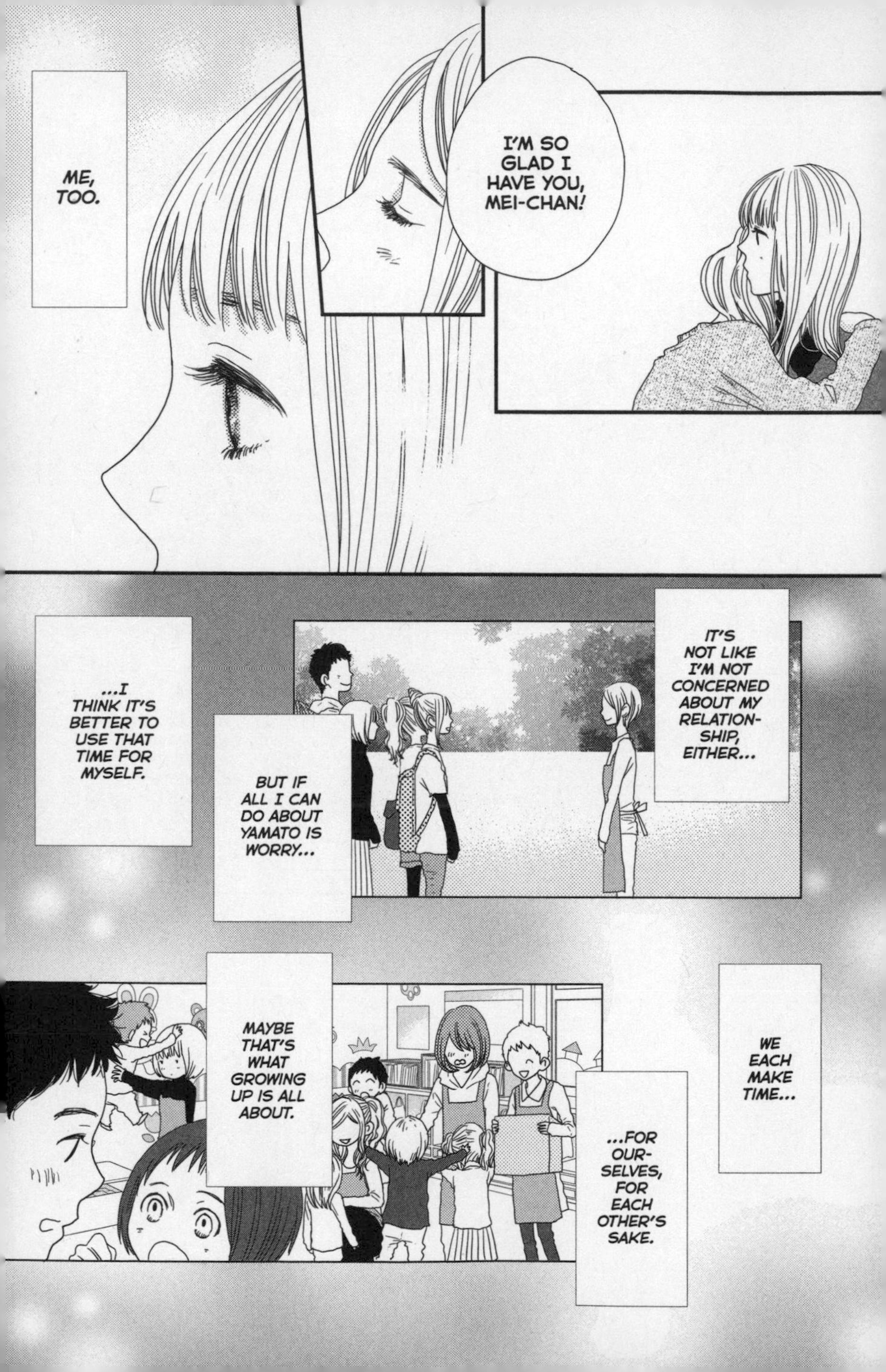
I'M SO GLAD I HAVE YOU, MEI-CHAN!
ME, TOO.
IT'S NOT LIKE I'M NOT CONCERNED ABOUT MY RELATION-SHIP, EITHER...
BUT IF ALL I CAN DO ABOUT YAMATO IS WORRY...
...I THINK IT'S BETTER TO USE THAT TIME FOR MYSELF.
WE EACH MAKE TIME...
...FOR OUR-SELVES, FOR EACH OTHER'S SAKE.
MAYBE THAT'S WHAT GROWING UP IS ALL ABOUT.

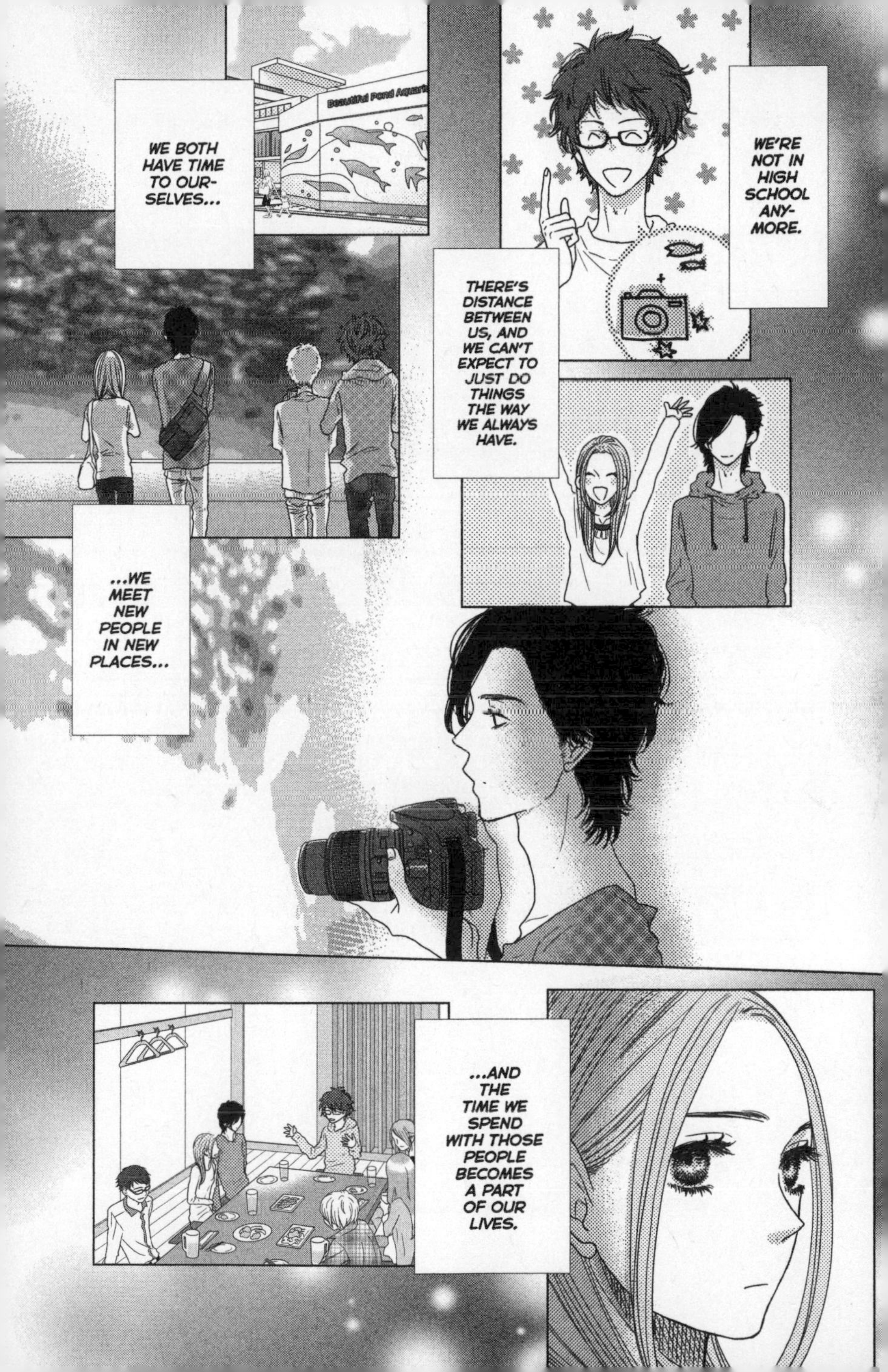
WE'RE NOT IN HIGH SCHOOL ANYMORE.
THERE'S DISTANCE BETWEEN US, AND WE CAN'T EXPECT TO JUST DO THINGS THE WAY WE ALWAYS HAVE.
WE BOTH HAVE TIME TO OURSELVES...
...WE MEET NEW PEOPLE IN NEW PLACES...
...AND THE TIME WE SPEND WITH THOSE PEOPLE BECOMES A PART OF OUR LIVES.

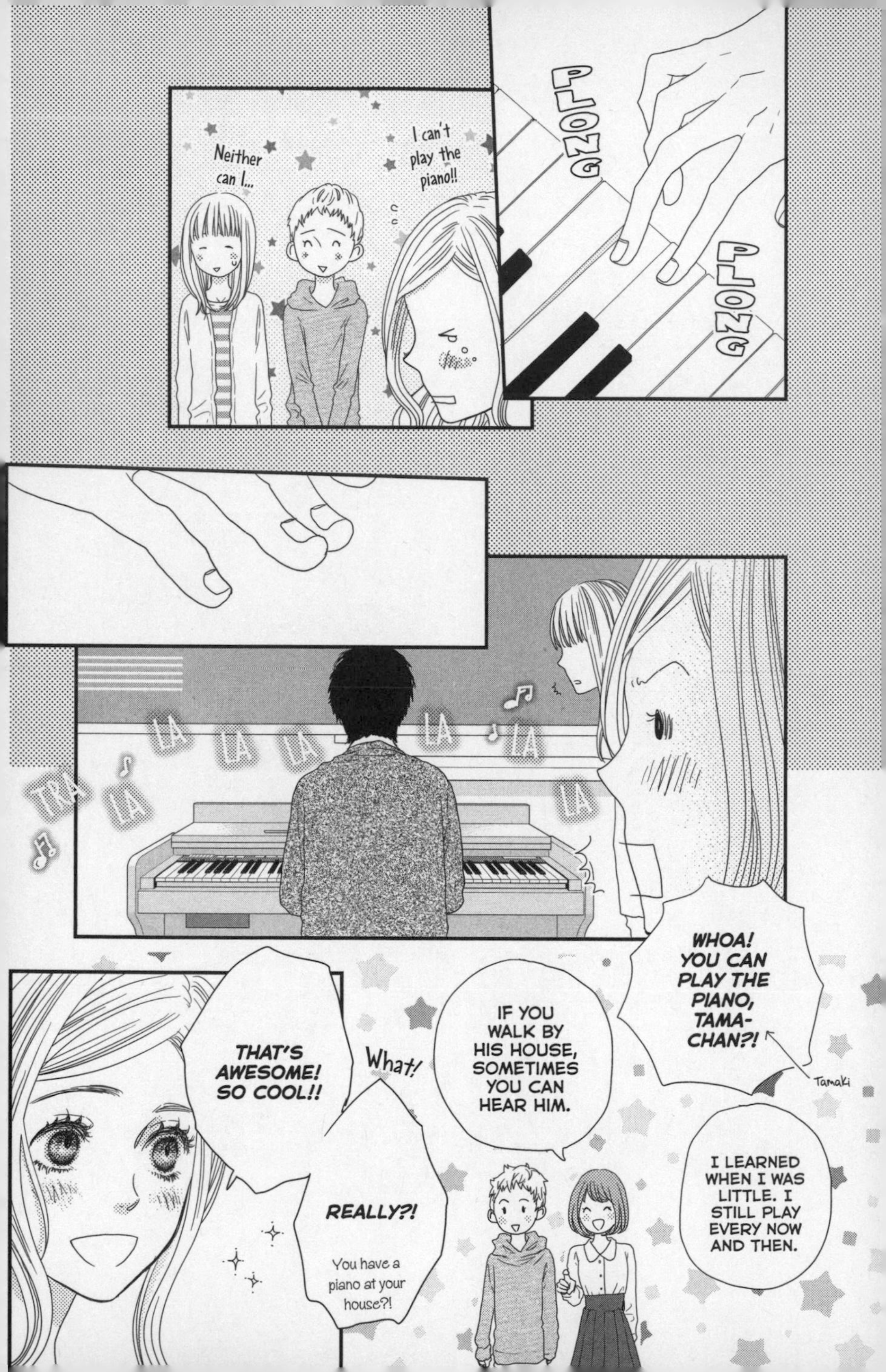
PLONG
PLONG
I can't play the piano!!
Neither can I...
TRA LA LA LA LA LA LA LA
WHOA! YOU CAN PLAY THE PIANO, TAMA-CHAN?!
Tamaki
I LEARNED WHEN I WAS LITTLE. I STILL PLAY EVERY NOW AND THEN.
IF YOU WALK BY HIS HOUSE, SOMETIMES YOU CAN HEAR HIM.
What!
REALLY?!
You have a piano at your house?!
THAT'S AWESOME! SO COOL!!

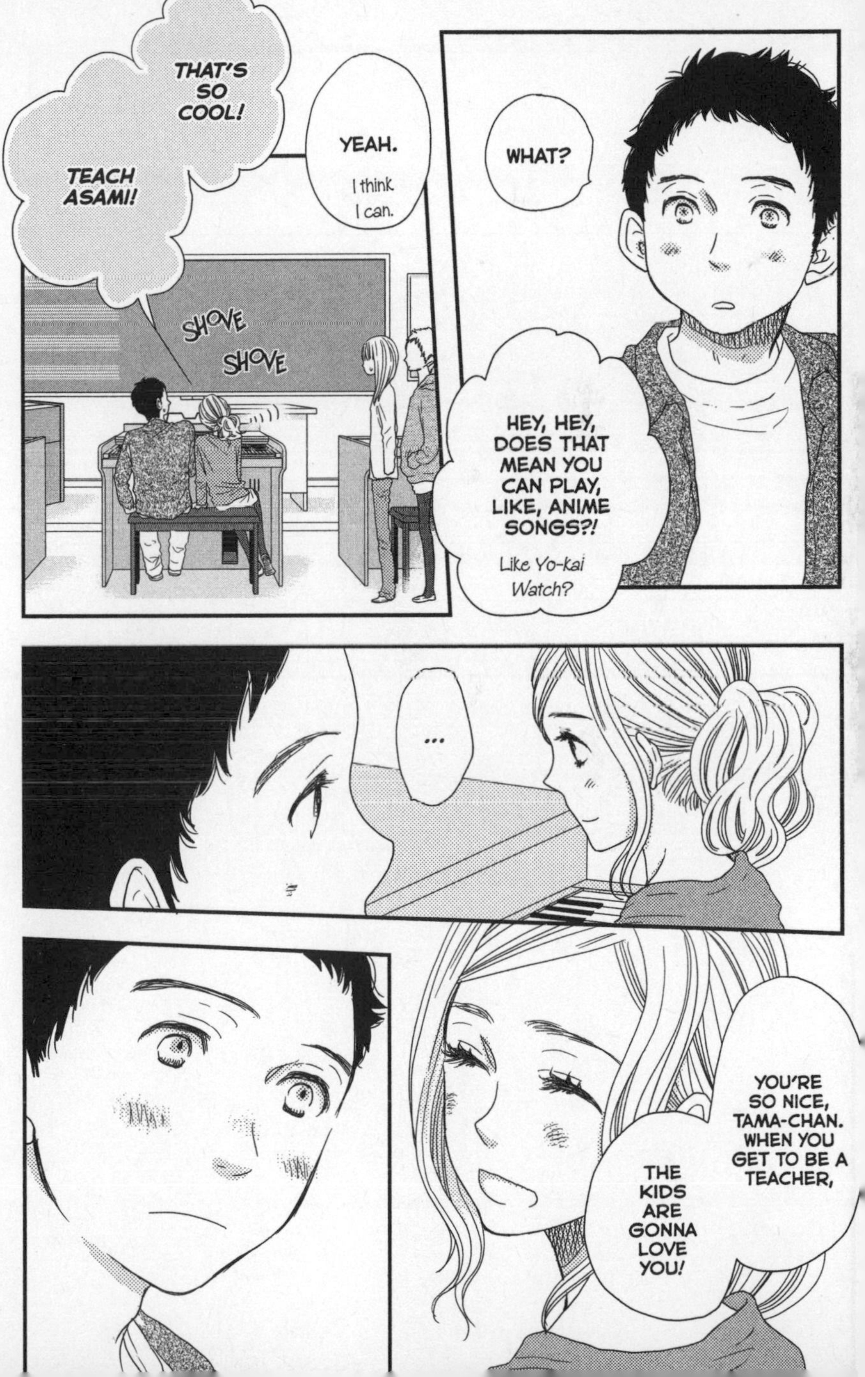
WHAT?
HEY, HEY, DOES THAT MEAN YOU CAN PLAY, LIKE, ANIME SONGS?!
Like Yo-kai Watch?
YEAH.
I think I can.
THAT'S SO COOL!
TEACH ASAMI!
SHOVE
SHOVE
...
YOU'RE SO NICE, TAMA-CHAN. WHEN YOU GET TO BE A TEACHER,
THE KIDS ARE GONNA LOVE YOU!

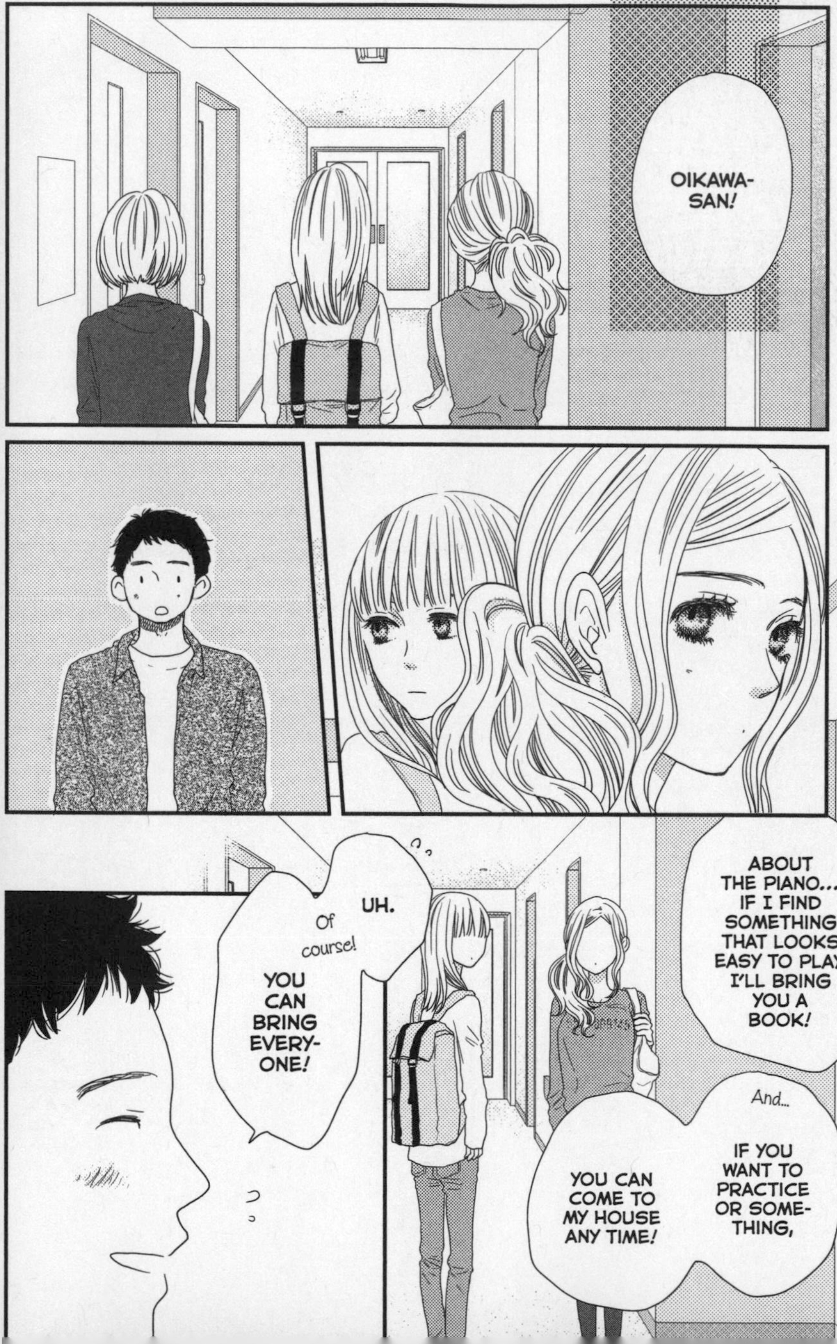
OIKAWA-SAN!
ABOUT THE PIANO... IF I FIND SOMETHING THAT LOOKS EASY TO PLAY, I'LL BRING YOU A BOOK!
And...
IF YOU WANT TO PRACTICE OR SOMETHING,
YOU CAN COME TO MY HOUSE ANY TIME!
UH.
Of course!
YOU CAN BRING EVERYONE!

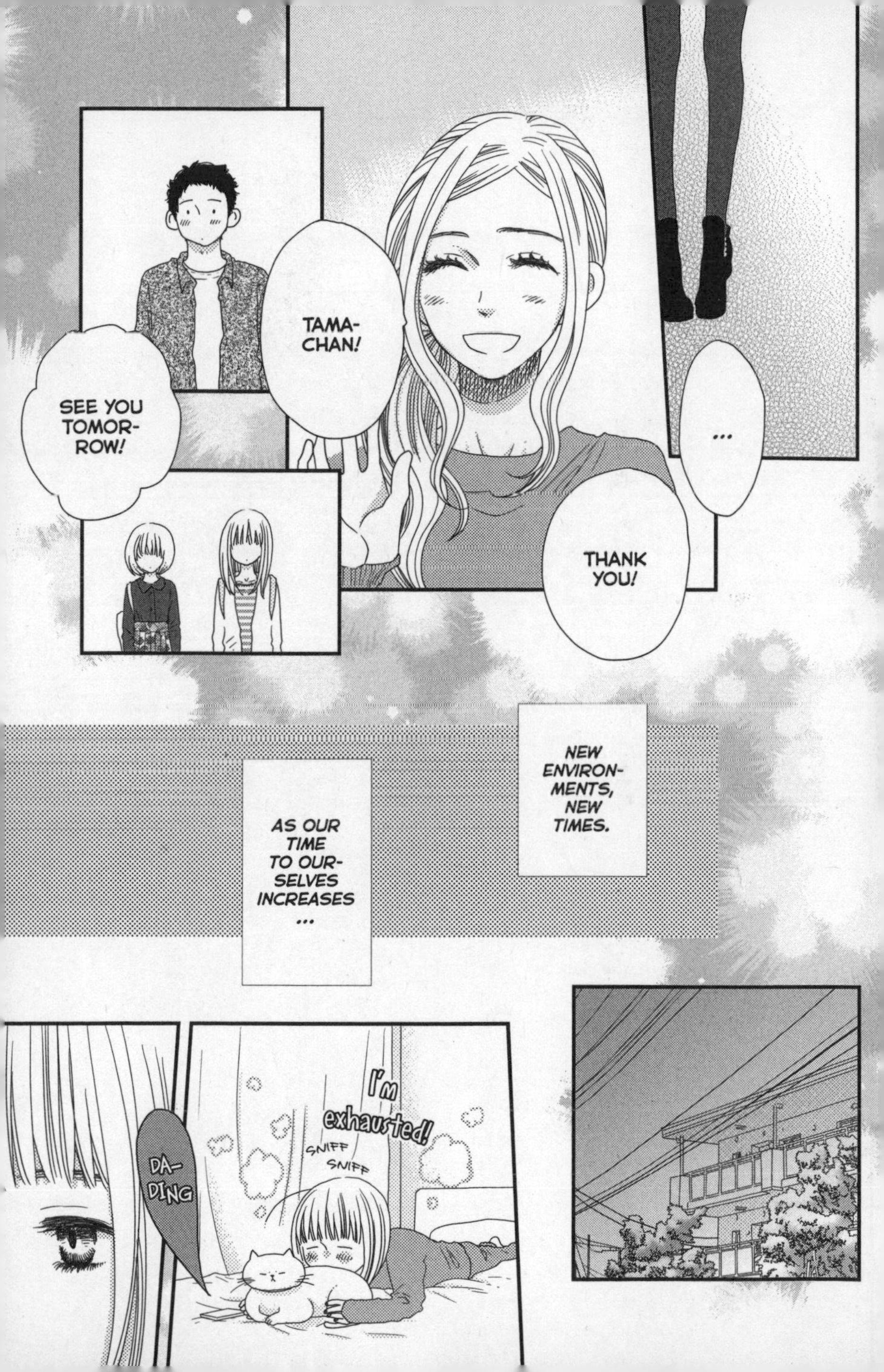
...
TAMA-CHAN!
THANK YOU!
SEE YOU TOMORROW!
NEW ENVIRONMENTS, NEW TIMES.
AS OUR TIME TO OURSELVES INCREASES...
I'm exhausted!
SNIFF SNIFF
DA-DING

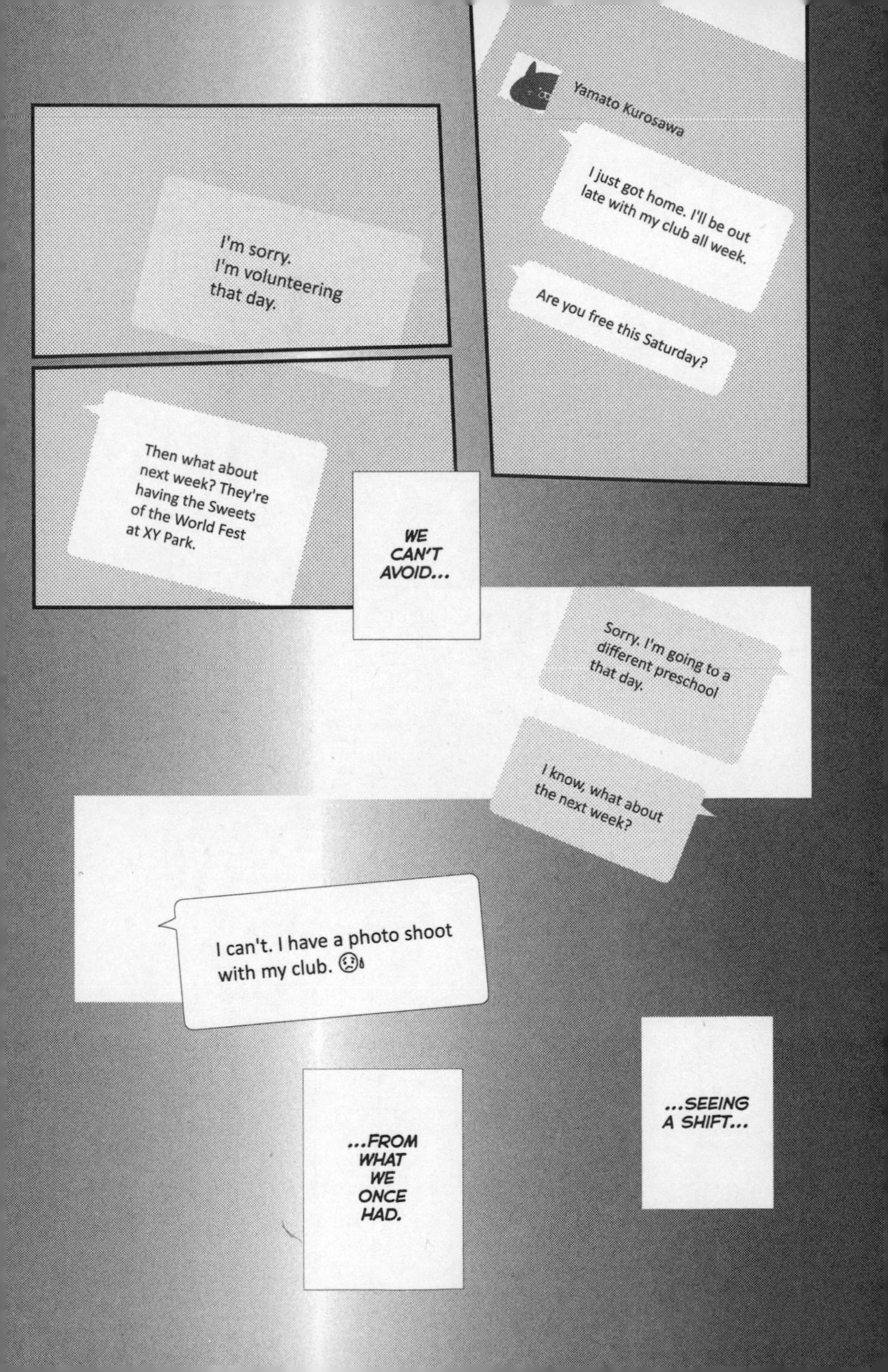
Yamato Kurosawa
I just got home. I'll be out late with my club all week.
Are you free this Saturday?
I'm sorry. I'm volunteering that day.
Then what about next week? They're having the Sweets of the World Fest at XY Park.
WE CAN'T AVOID...
Sorry. I'm going to a different preschool that day.
I know, what about the next week?
I can't. I have a photo shoot with my club.
...SEEING A SHIFT...
...FROM WHAT WE ONCE HAD.

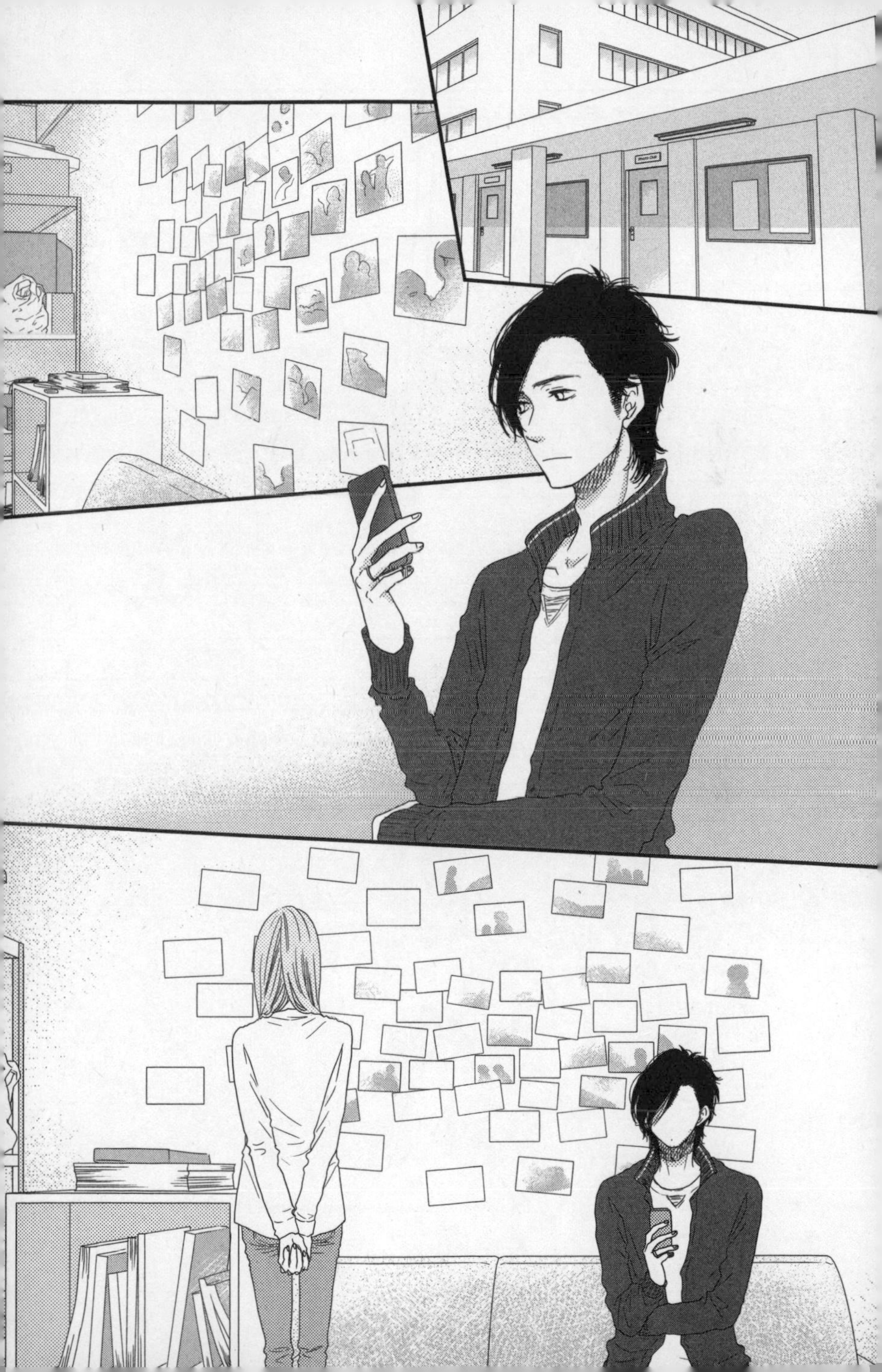

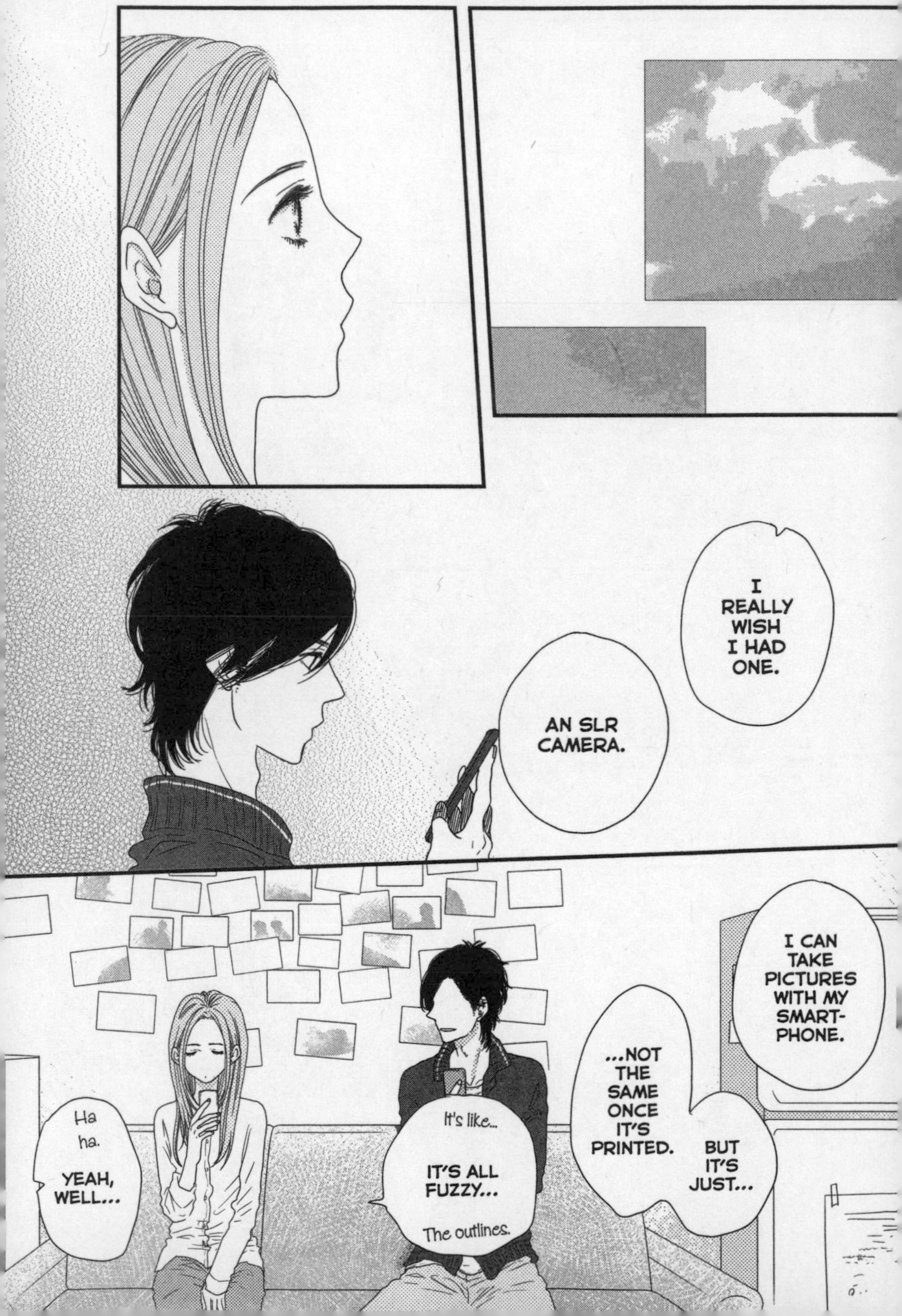
I REALLY WISH I HAD ONE.
AN SLR CAMERA.
I CAN TAKE PICTURES WITH MY SMARTPHONE.
BUT IT'S JUST...
...NOT THE SAME ONCE IT'S PRINTED.
It's like...
IT'S ALL FUZZY...
The outlines.
Ha ha.
YEAH, WELL...

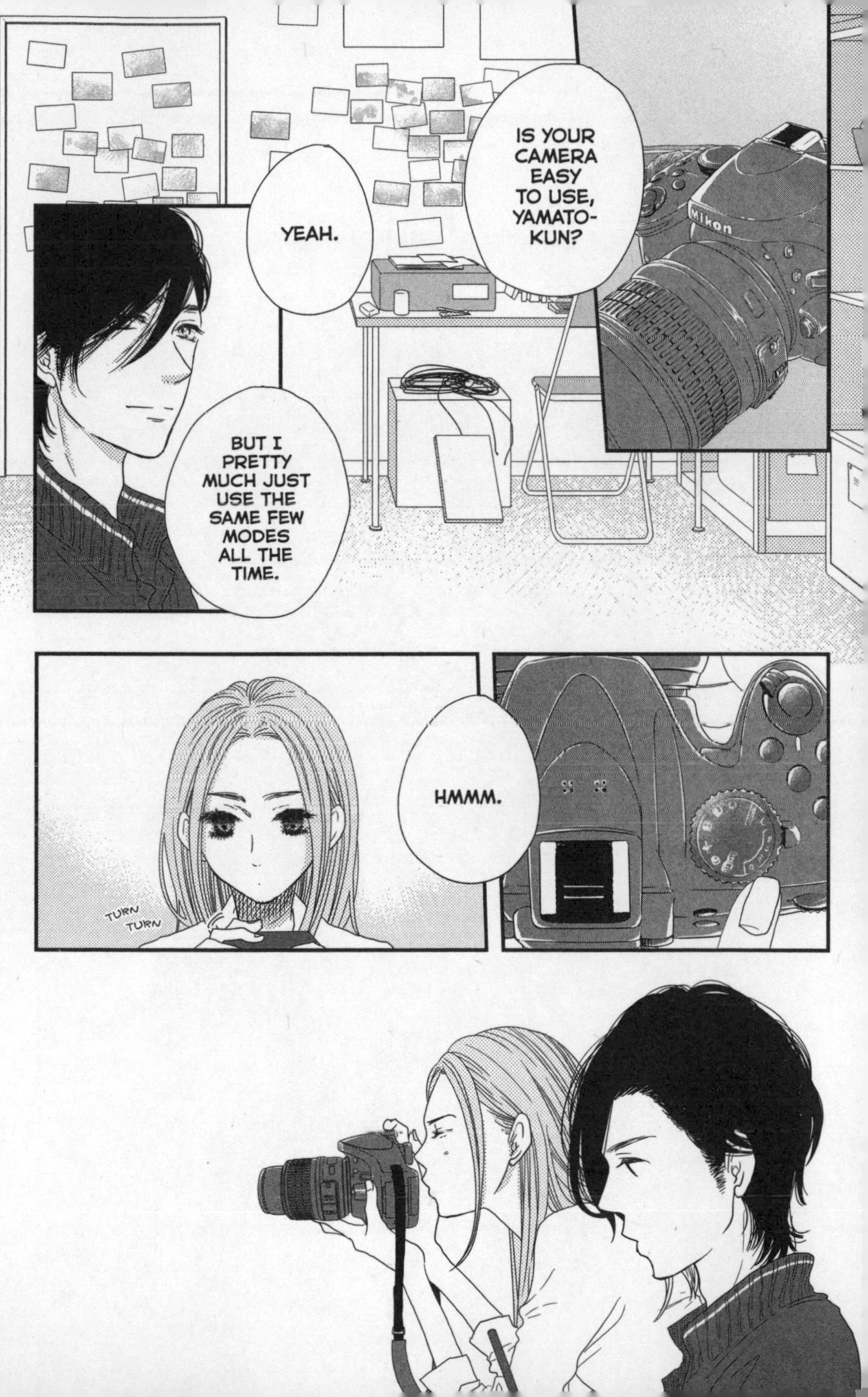
IS YOUR CAMERA EASY TO USE, YAMATO-KUN?
YEAH.
BUT I PRETTY MUCH JUST USE THE SAME FEW MODES ALL THE TIME.
HMMM.
TURN TURN

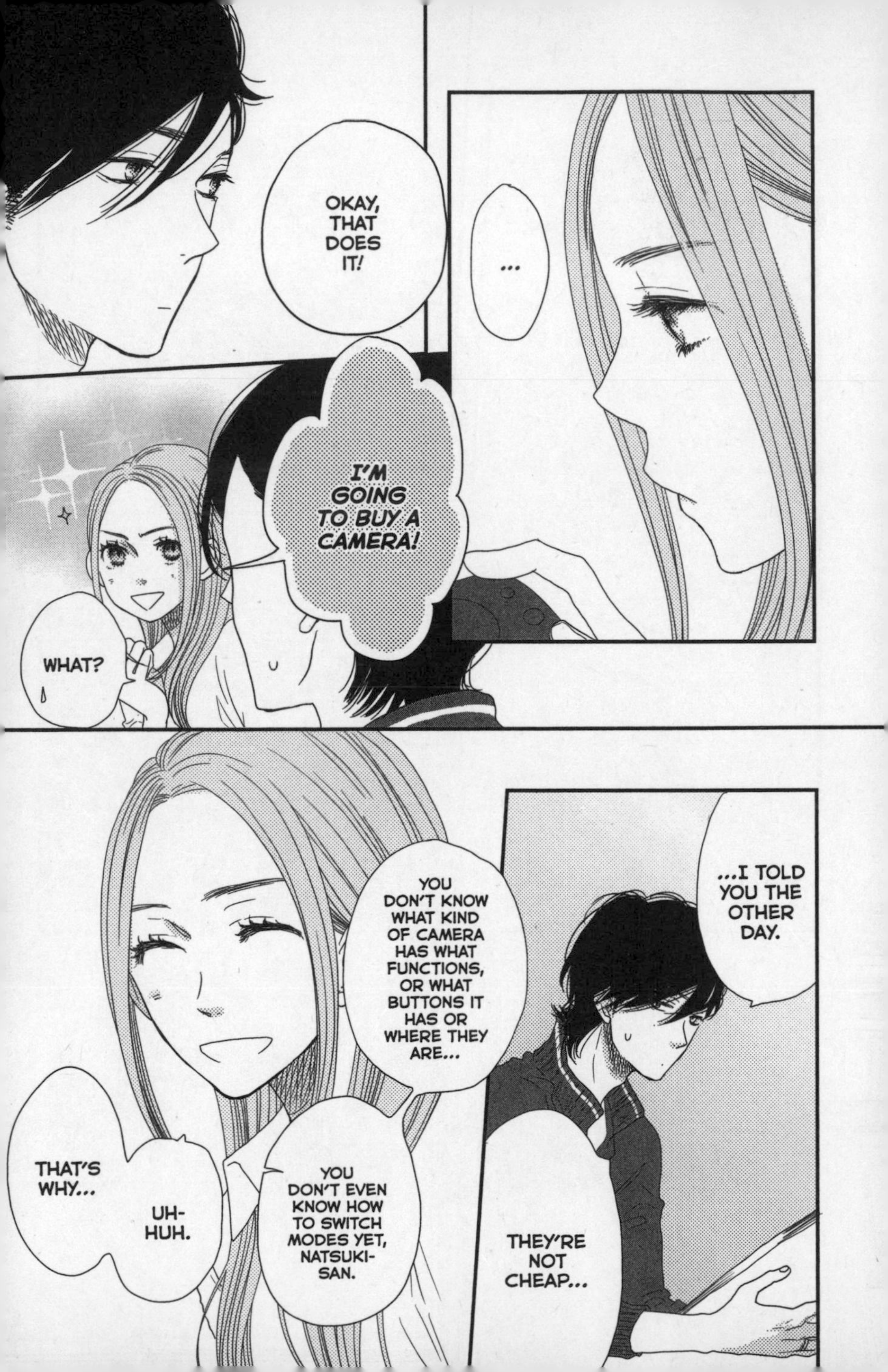
...
OKAY, THAT DOES IT!
I'M GOING TO BUY A CAMERA!
WHAT?
...I TOLD YOU THE OTHER DAY.
THEY'RE NOT CHEAP...
YOU DON'T KNOW WHAT KIND OF CAMERA HAS WHAT FUNCTIONS, OR WHAT BUTTONS IT HAS OR WHERE THEY ARE...
YOU DON'T EVEN KNOW HOW TO SWITCH MODES YET, NATSUKI-SAN.
UH-HUH.
THAT'S WHY...

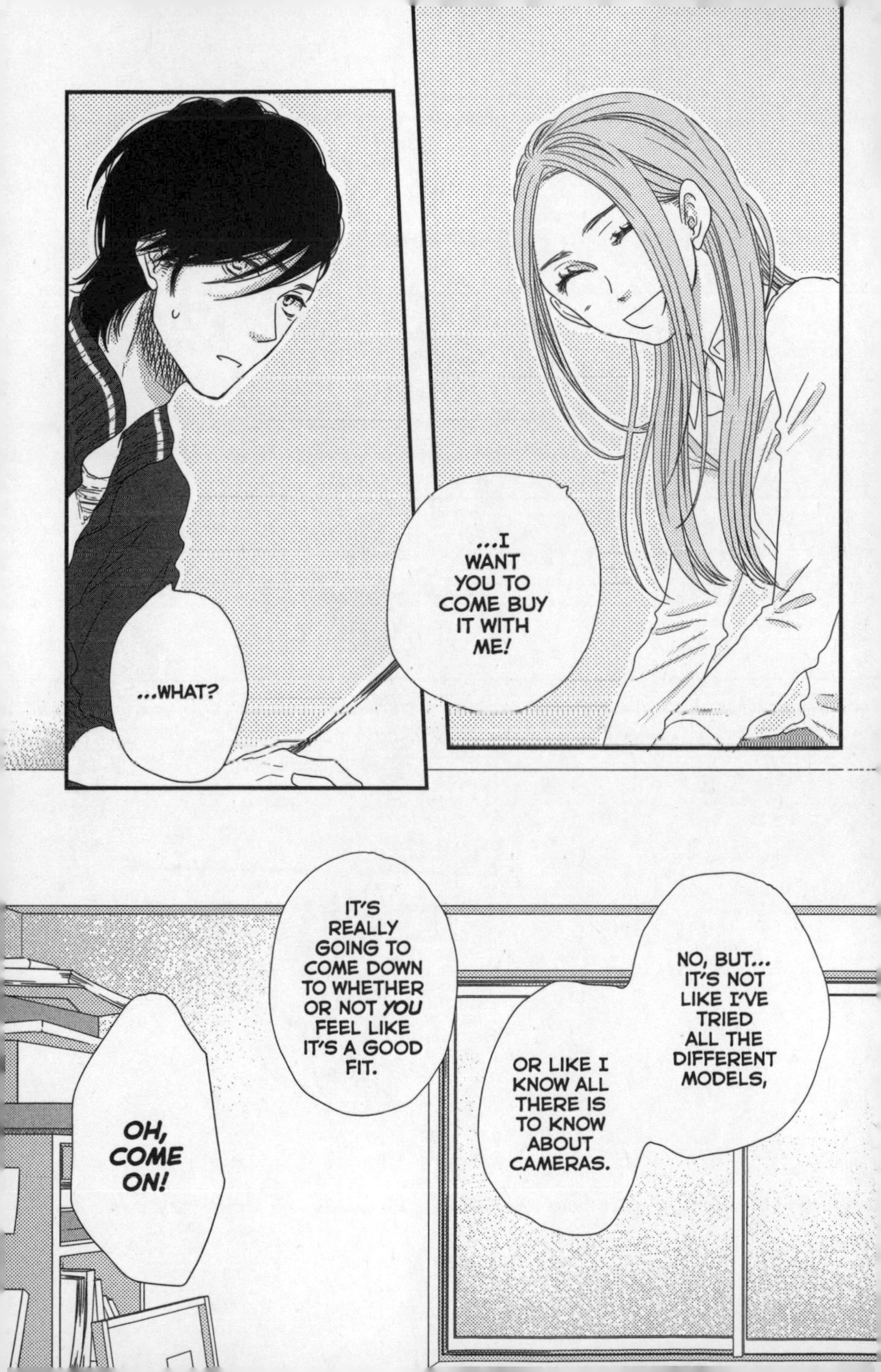
...I WANT YOU TO COME BUY IT WITH ME!
...WHAT?
NO, BUT... IT'S NOT LIKE I'VE TRIED ALL THE DIFFERENT MODELS,
OR LIKE I KNOW ALL THERE IS TO KNOW ABOUT CAMERAS.
IT'S REALLY GOING TO COME DOWN TO WHETHER OR NOT *YOU* FEEL LIKE IT'S A GOOD FIT.
OH, COME ON!

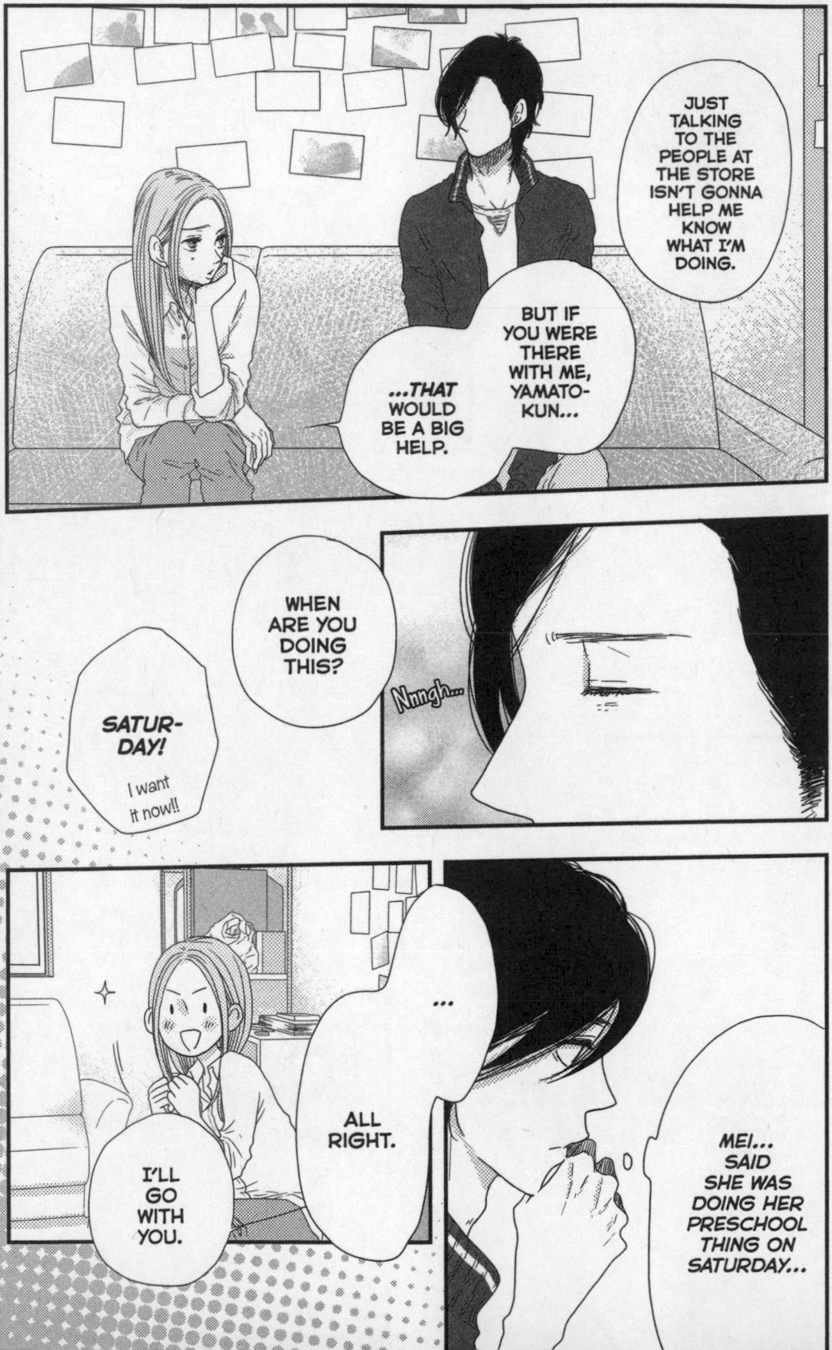
JUST TALKING TO THE PEOPLE AT THE STORE ISN'T GONNA HELP ME KNOW WHAT I'M DOING.
BUT IF YOU WERE THERE WITH ME, YAMATO-KUN...
...THAT WOULD BE A BIG HELP.
Nnngh...
WHEN ARE YOU DOING THIS?
SATUR-DAY!
I want it now!!
MEI... SAID SHE WAS DOING HER PRESCHOOL THING ON SATURDAY...
...
ALL RIGHT.
I'LL GO WITH YOU.

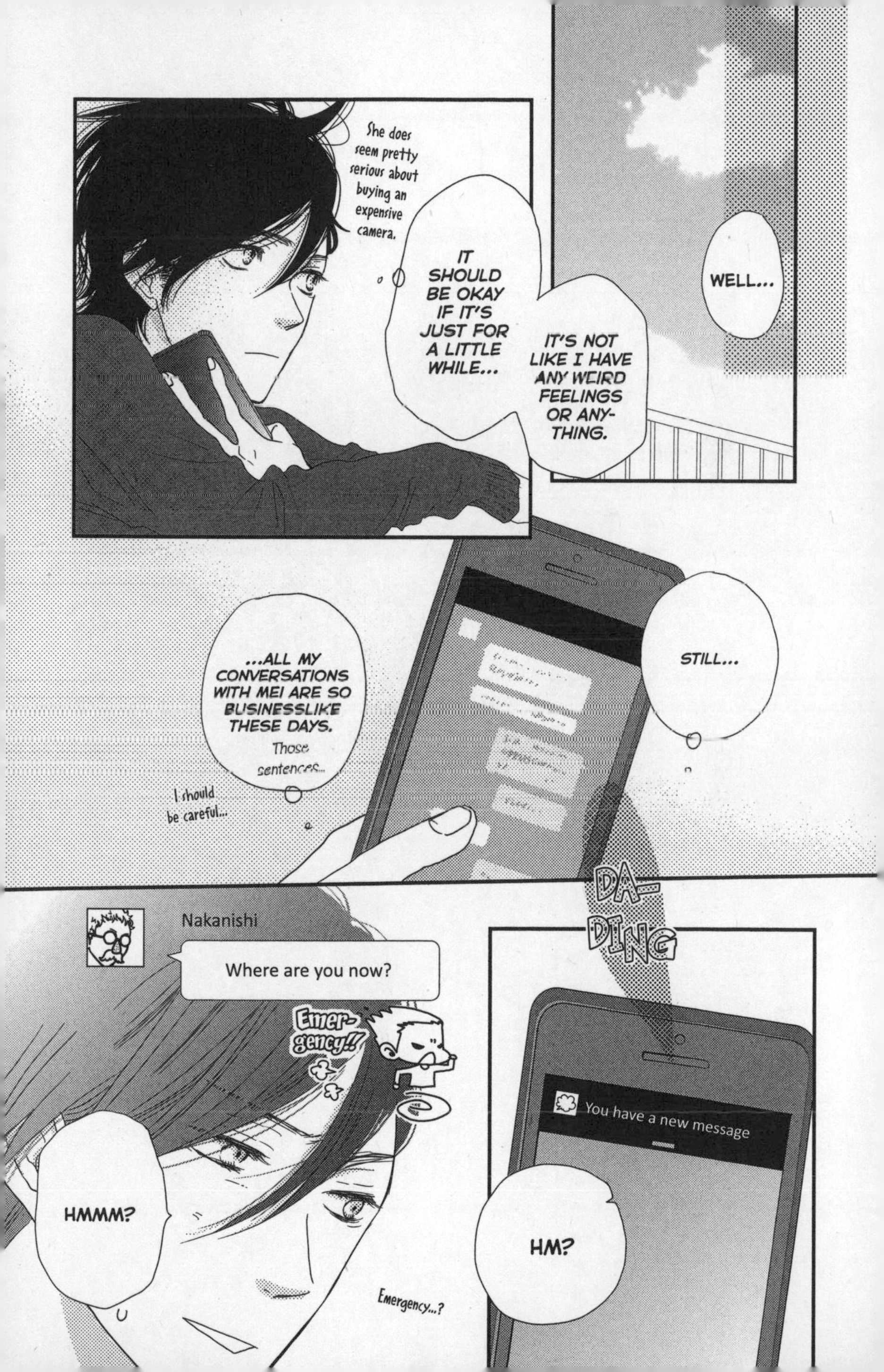
WELL...
IT'S NOT LIKE I HAVE ANY WEIRD FEELINGS OR ANYTHING.
She does seem pretty serious about buying an expensive camera.
IT SHOULD BE OKAY IF IT'S JUST FOR A LITTLE WHILE...
STILL...
...ALL MY CONVERSATIONS WITH MEI ARE SO BUSINESSLIKE THESE DAYS.
Those sentences...
I should be careful...
DA-DING
You have a new message
HM?
Nakanishi
Where are you now?
Emergency!!
HMMM?
Emergency...?

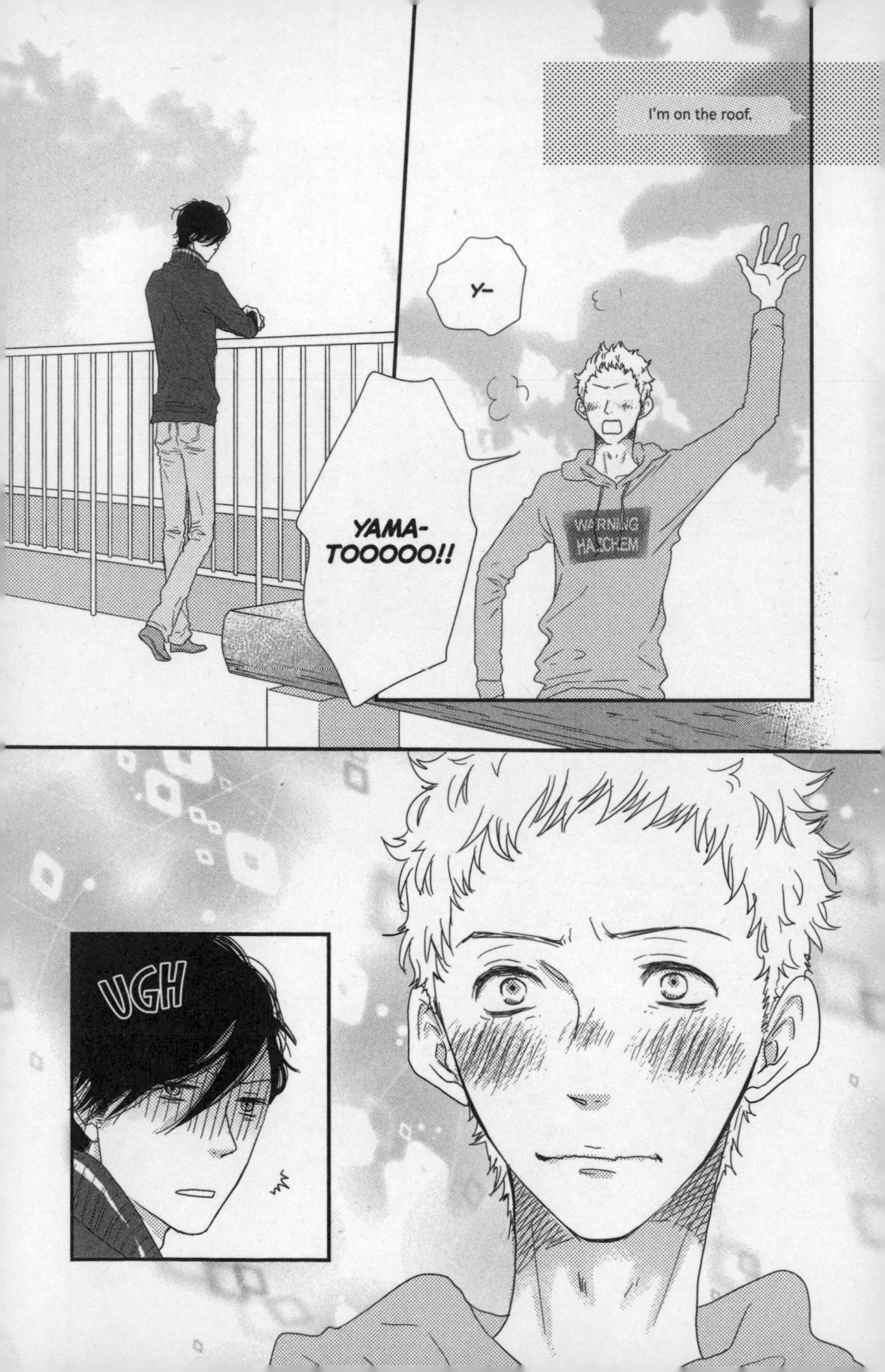

I'm on the roof.
Y-
YAMA-TOOOOO!!
UGH

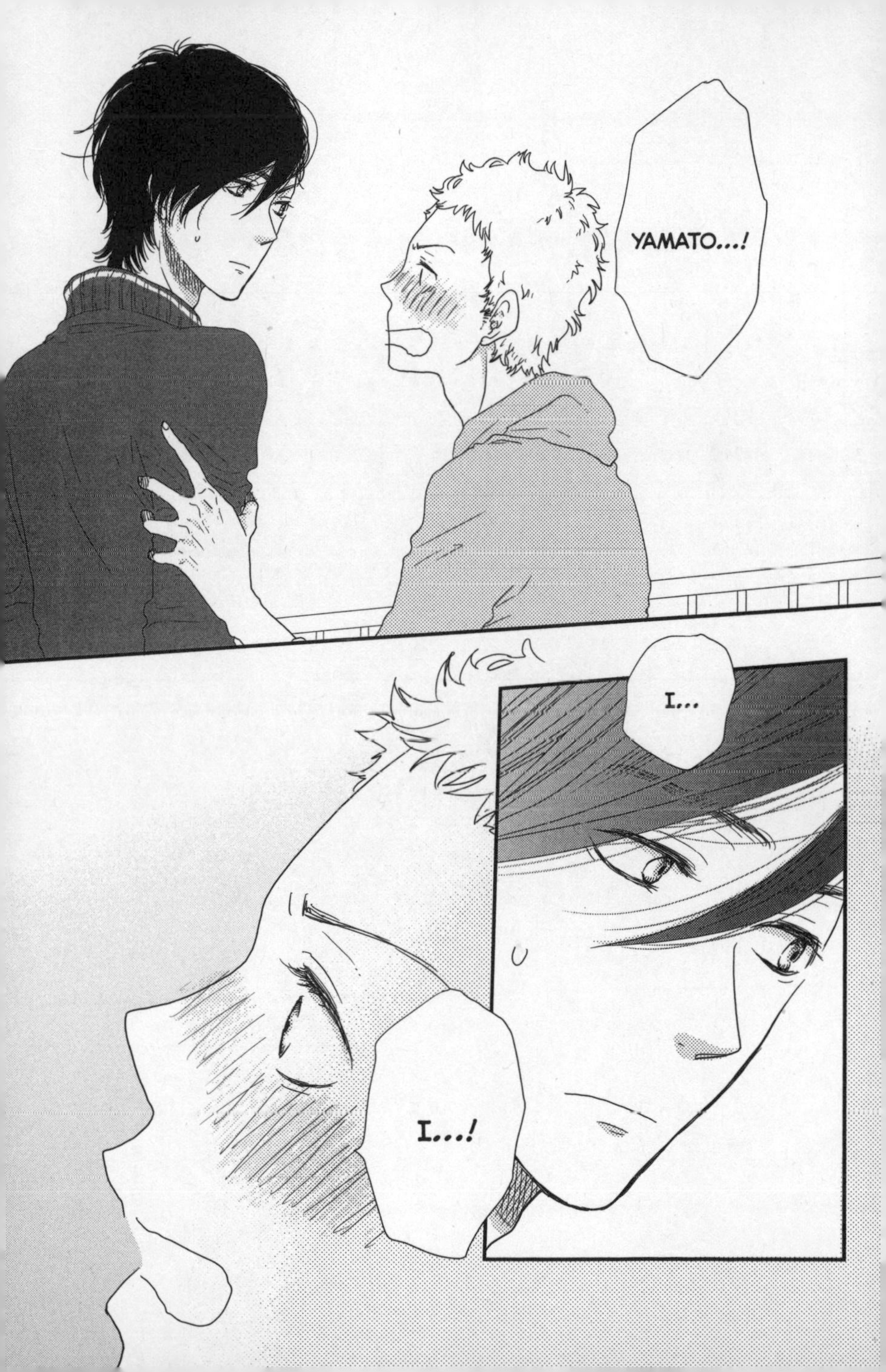
YAMATO...!
I...
I...!

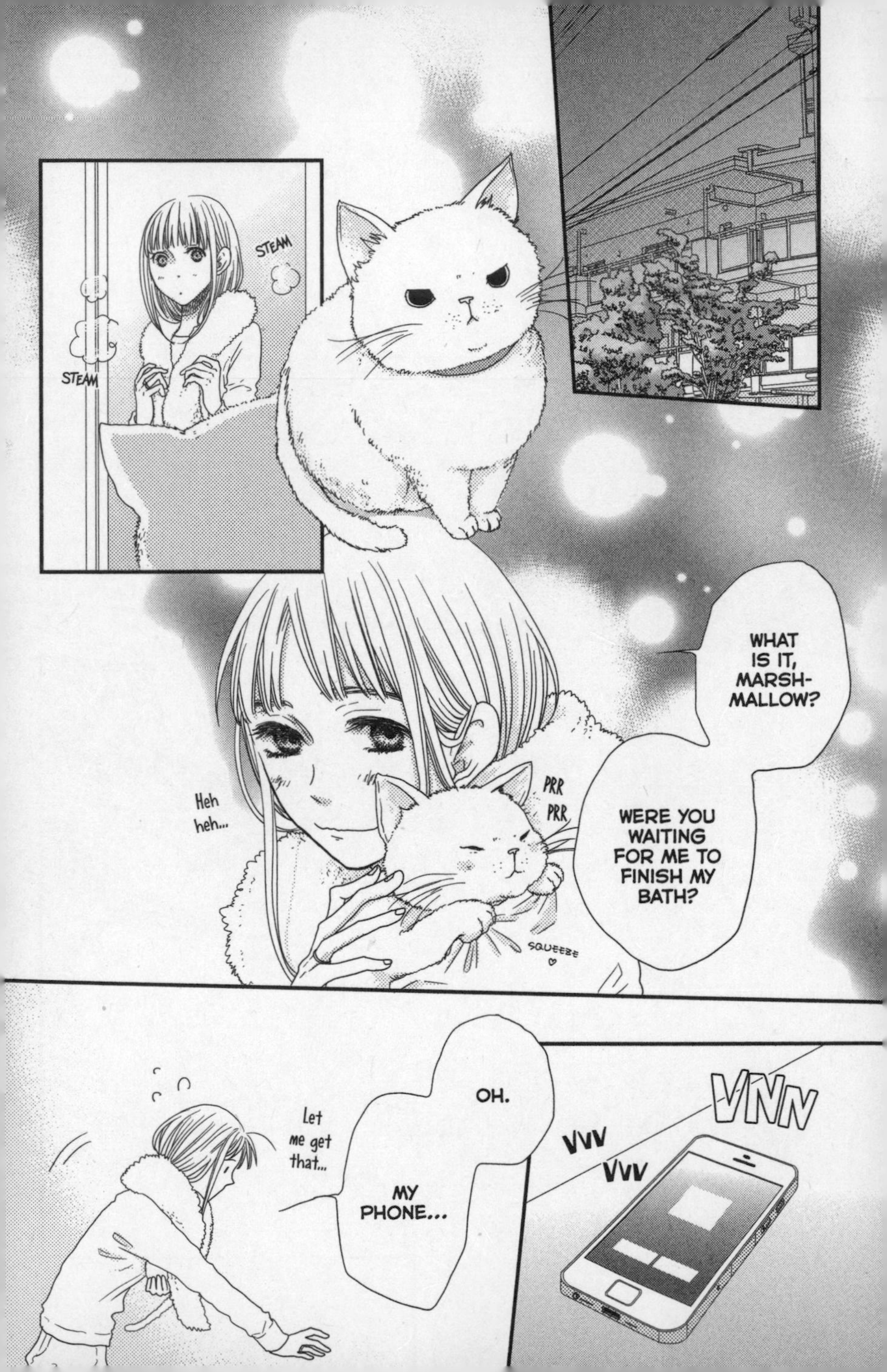
STEAM
STEAM
WHAT IS IT, MARSH-MALLOW?
WERE YOU WAITING FOR ME TO FINISH MY BATH?
PRR PRR
Heh heh...
SQUEEZE ♡
VNN
VVV VVV
OH.
MY PHONE...
Let me get that...

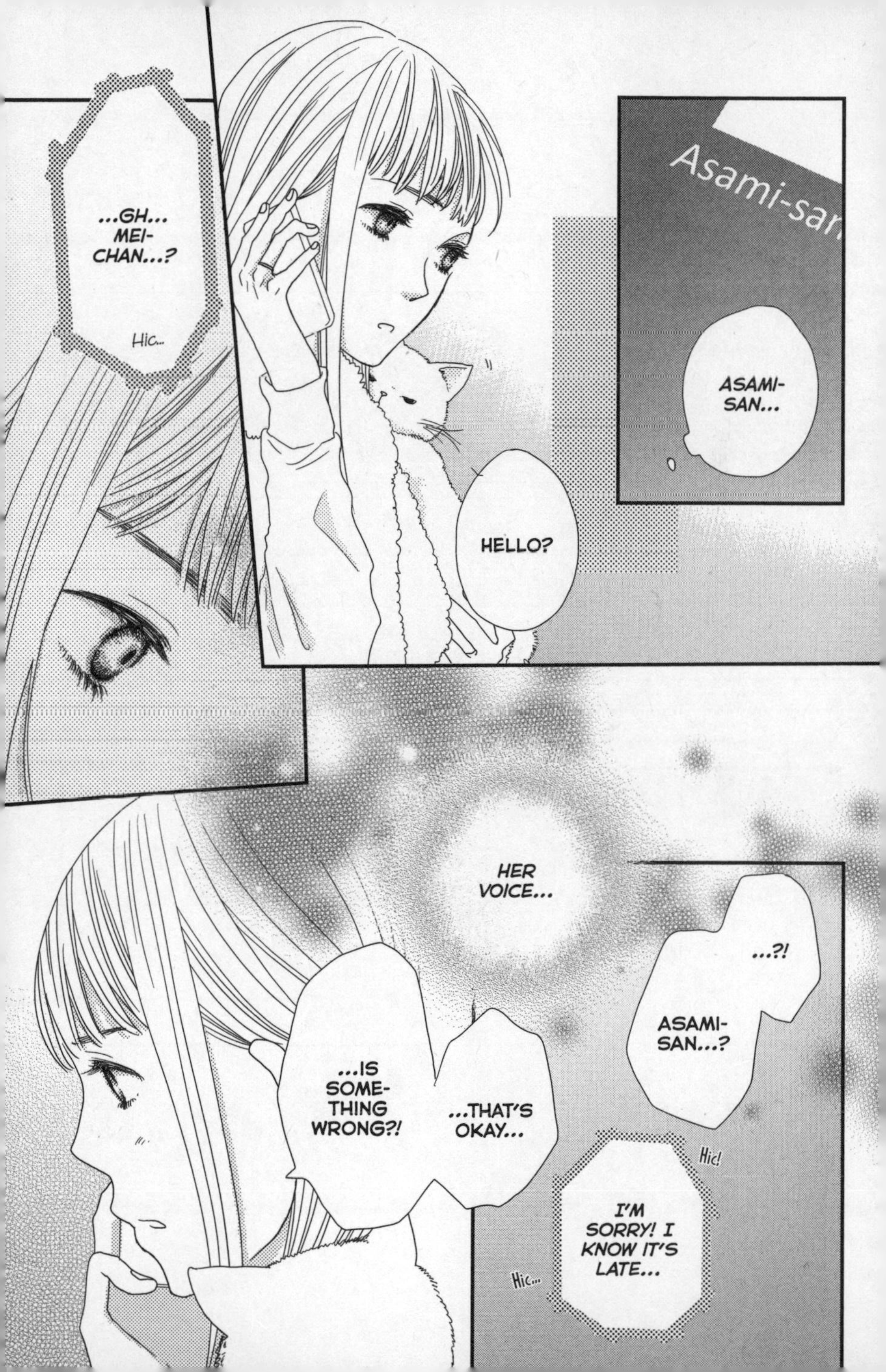
Asami-san
ASAMI-SAN...
HELLO?
...GH... MEI-CHAN...?
Hic...
...?!
ASAMI-SAN...?
HER VOICE...
Hic!
I'M SORRY! I KNOW IT'S LATE...
Hic...
...THAT'S OKAY...
...IS SOMETHING WRONG?!

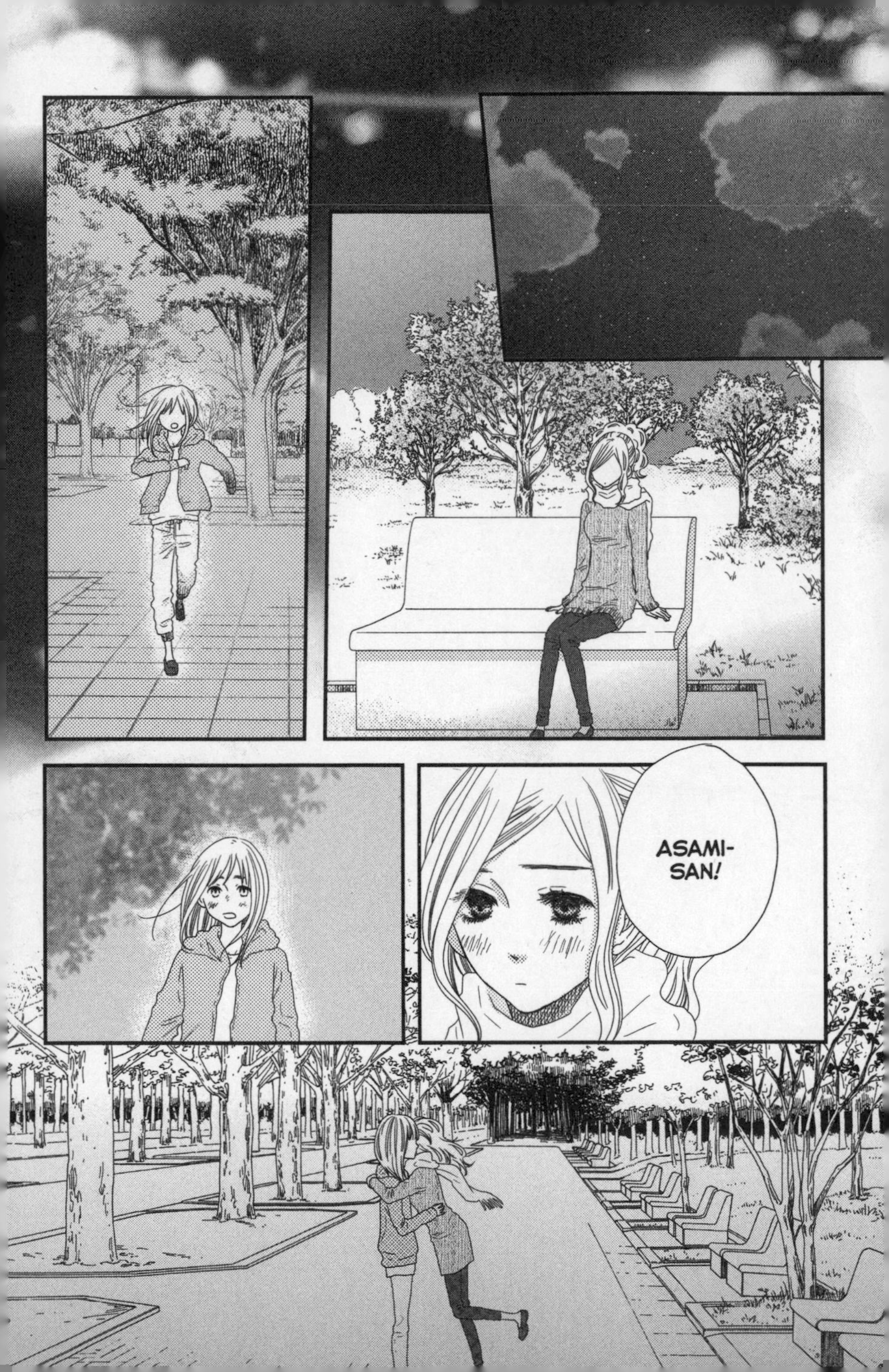
ASAMI-SAN!

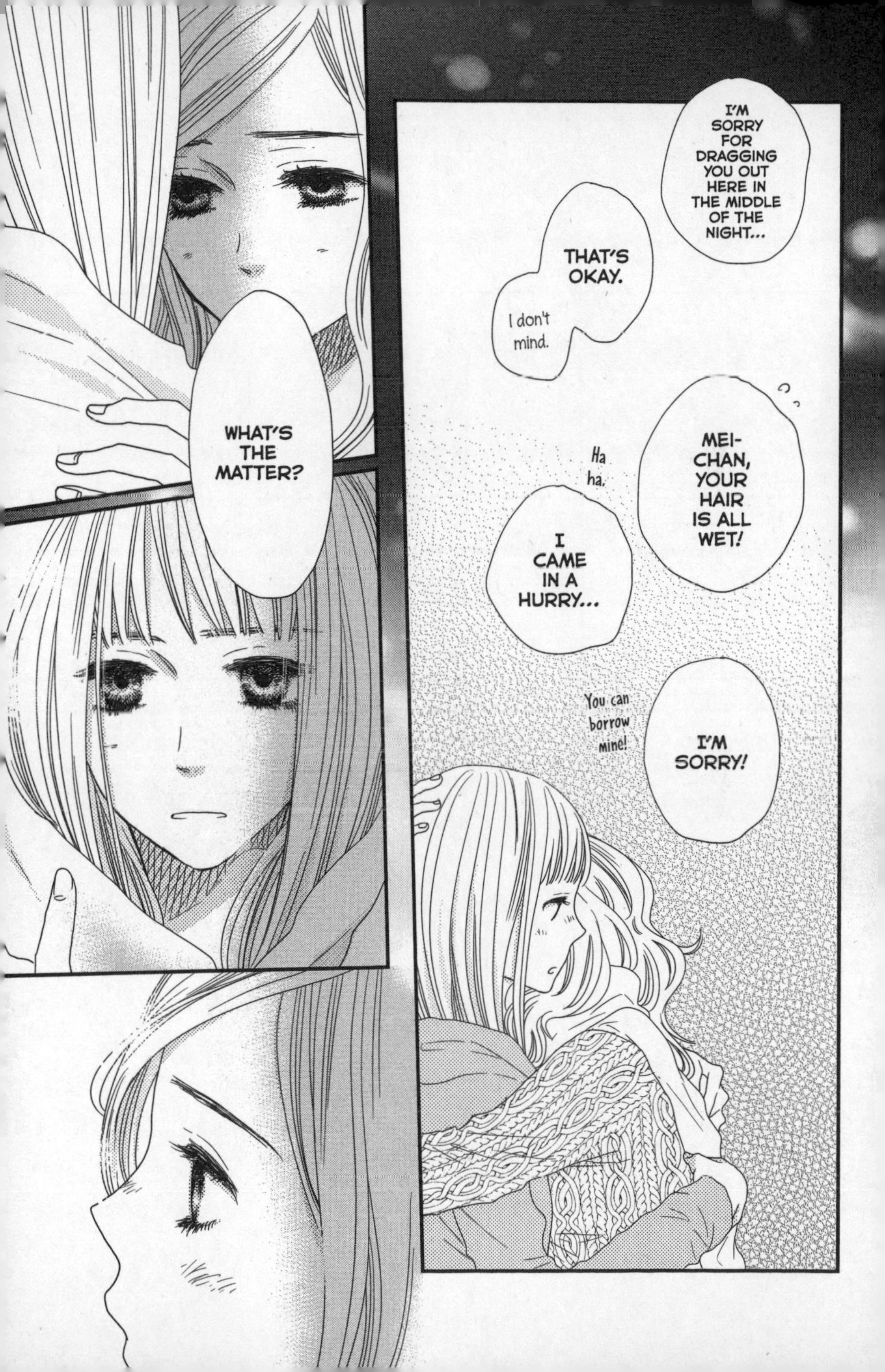
I'M SORRY FOR DRAGGING YOU OUT HERE IN THE MIDDLE OF THE NIGHT...
THAT'S OKAY.
I don't mind.
MEI-CHAN, YOUR HAIR IS ALL WET!
Ha ha.
I CAME IN A HURRY...
I'M SORRY!
You can borrow mine!
WHAT'S THE MATTER?

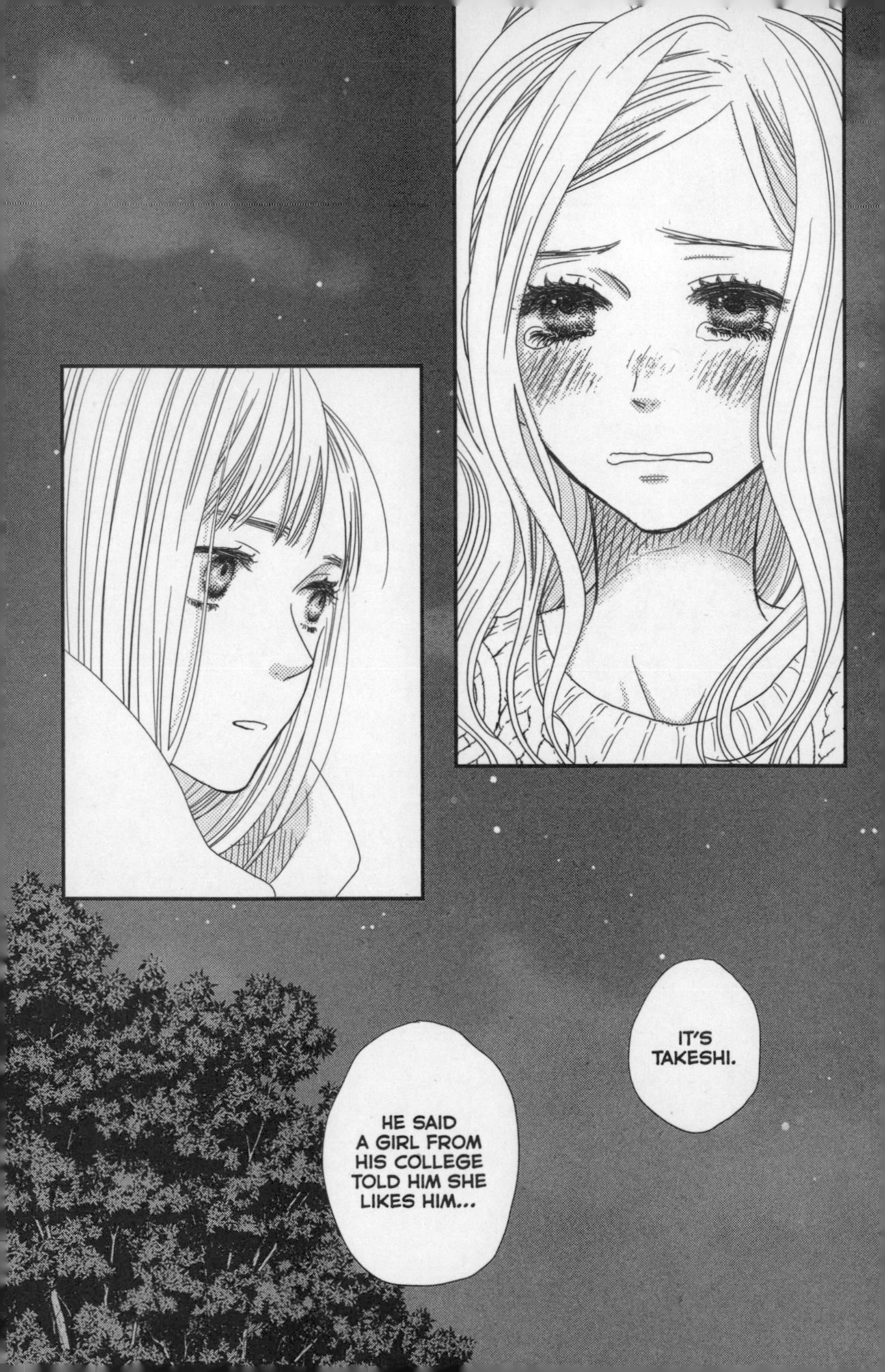
IT'S TAKESHI.
HE SAID A GIRL FROM HIS COLLEGE TOLD HIM SHE LIKES HIM...

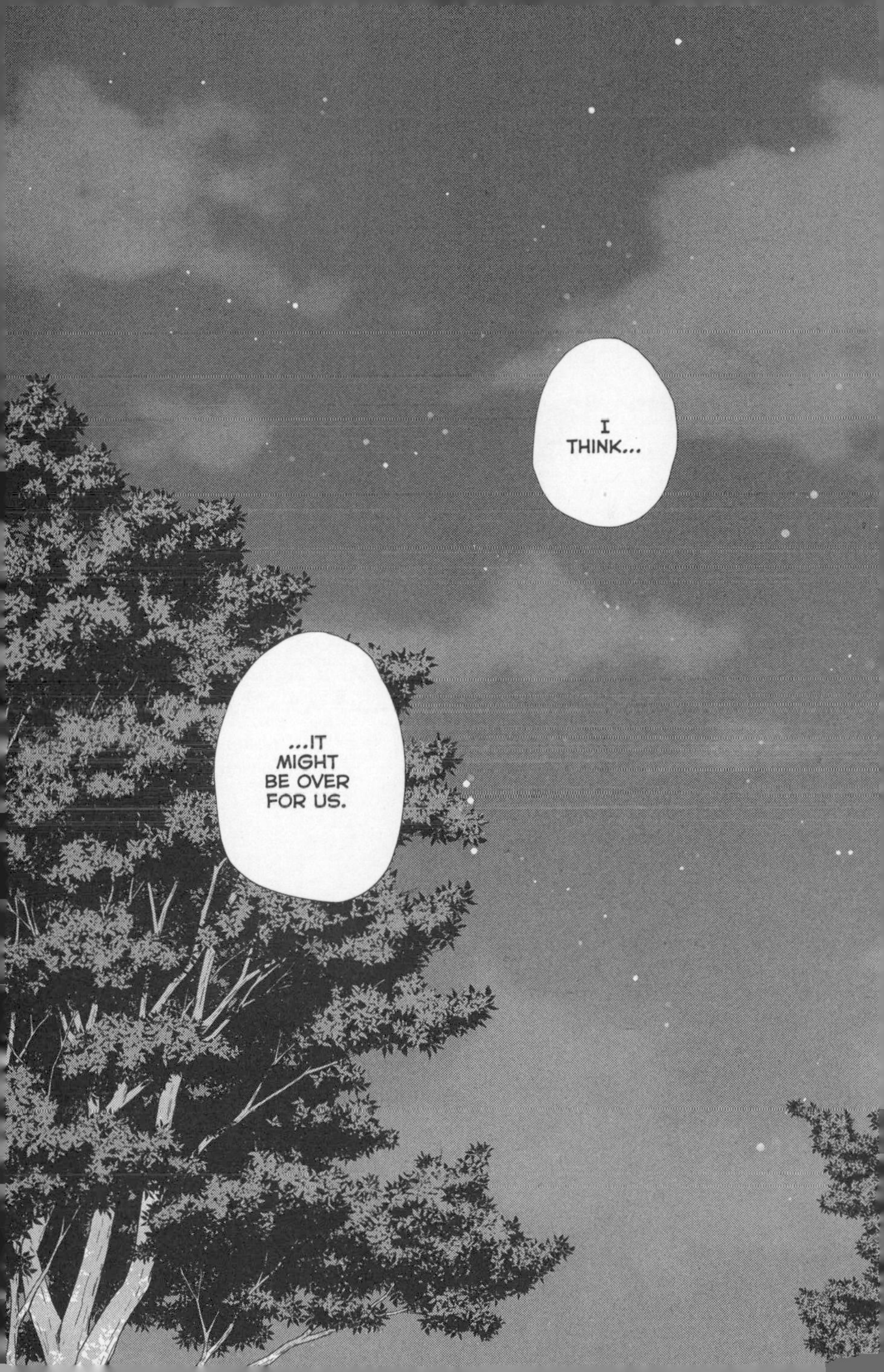
I THINK...
...IT MIGHT BE OVER FOR US.

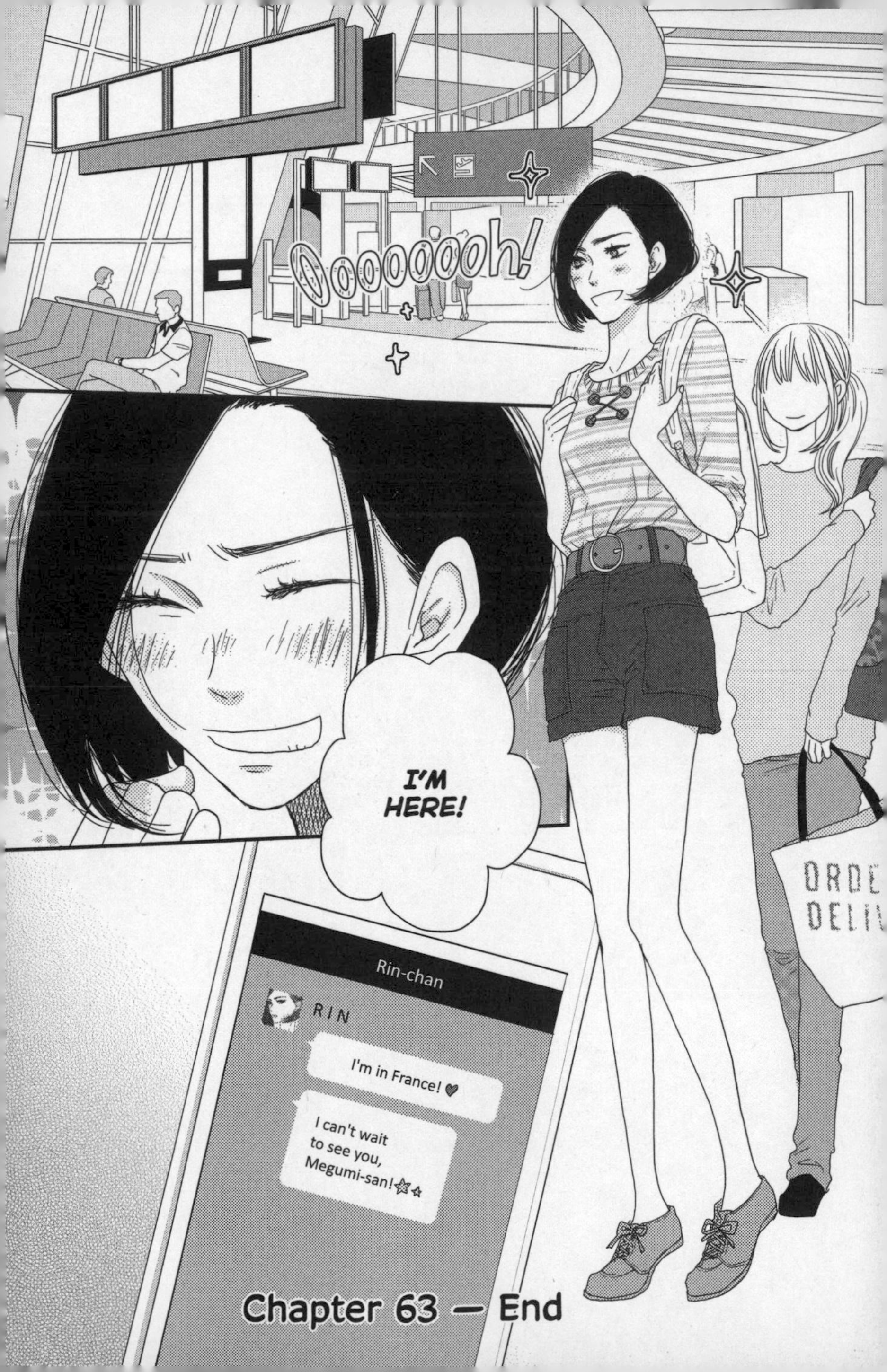
Oooooooh!
I'M HERE!
Rin-chan
RIN
I'm in France!
I can't wait to see you, Megumi-san!
Chapter 63 — End

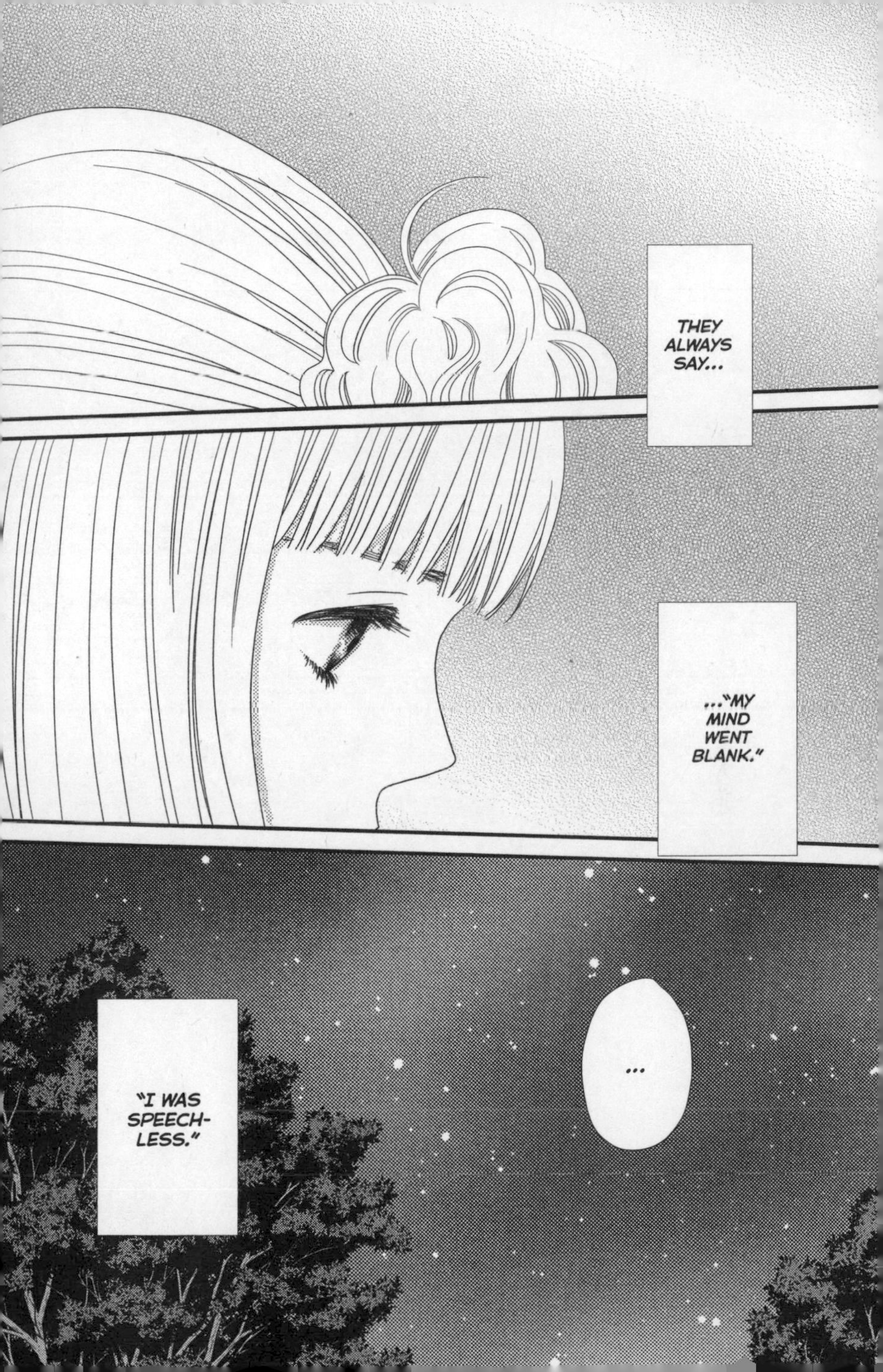
THEY ALWAYS SAY...
..."MY MIND WENT BLANK."
...
"I WAS SPEECH-LESS."

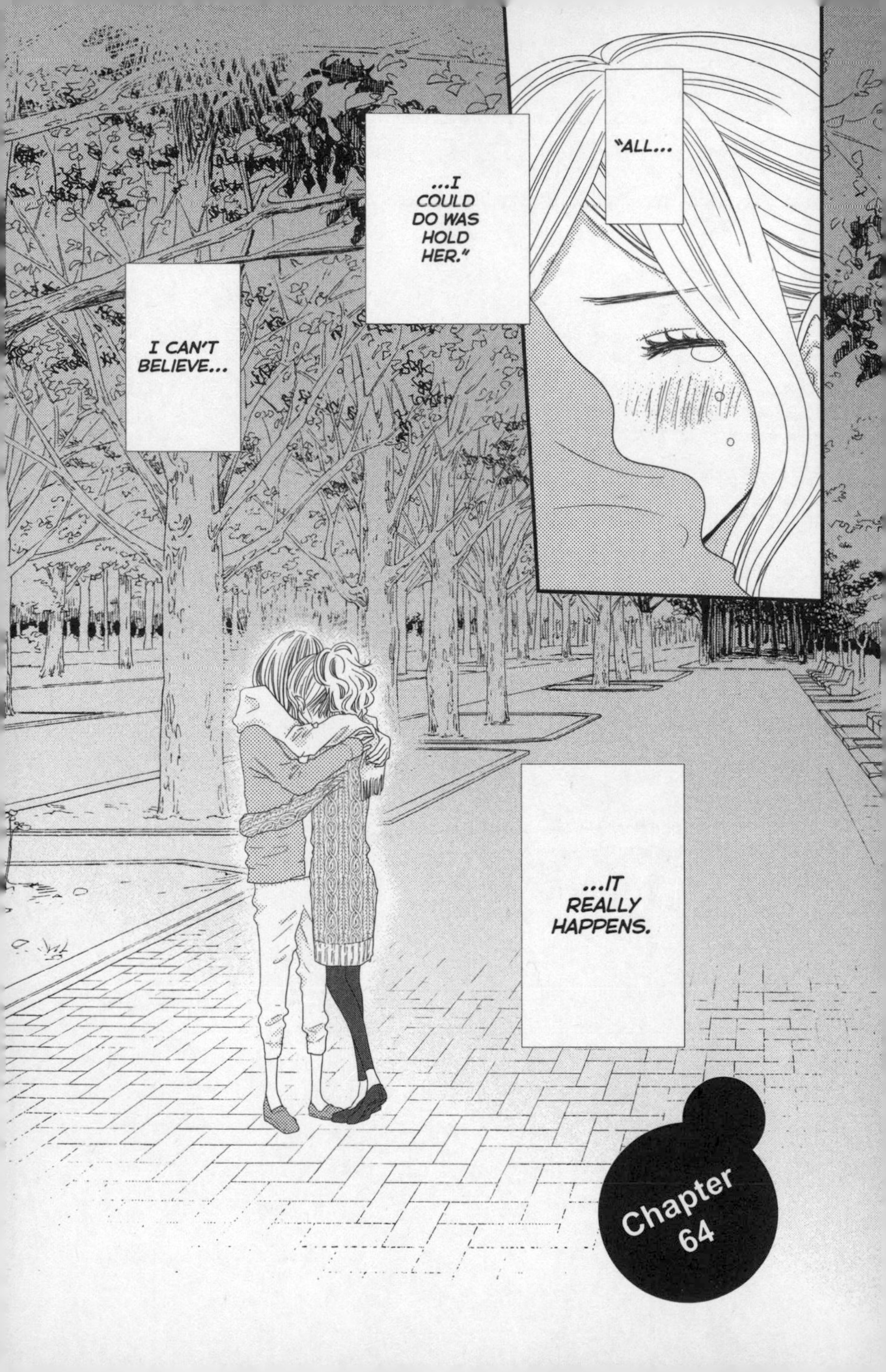
"ALL...
...I COULD DO WAS HOLD HER."
I CAN'T BELIEVE...
...IT REALLY HAPPENS.
Chapter 64

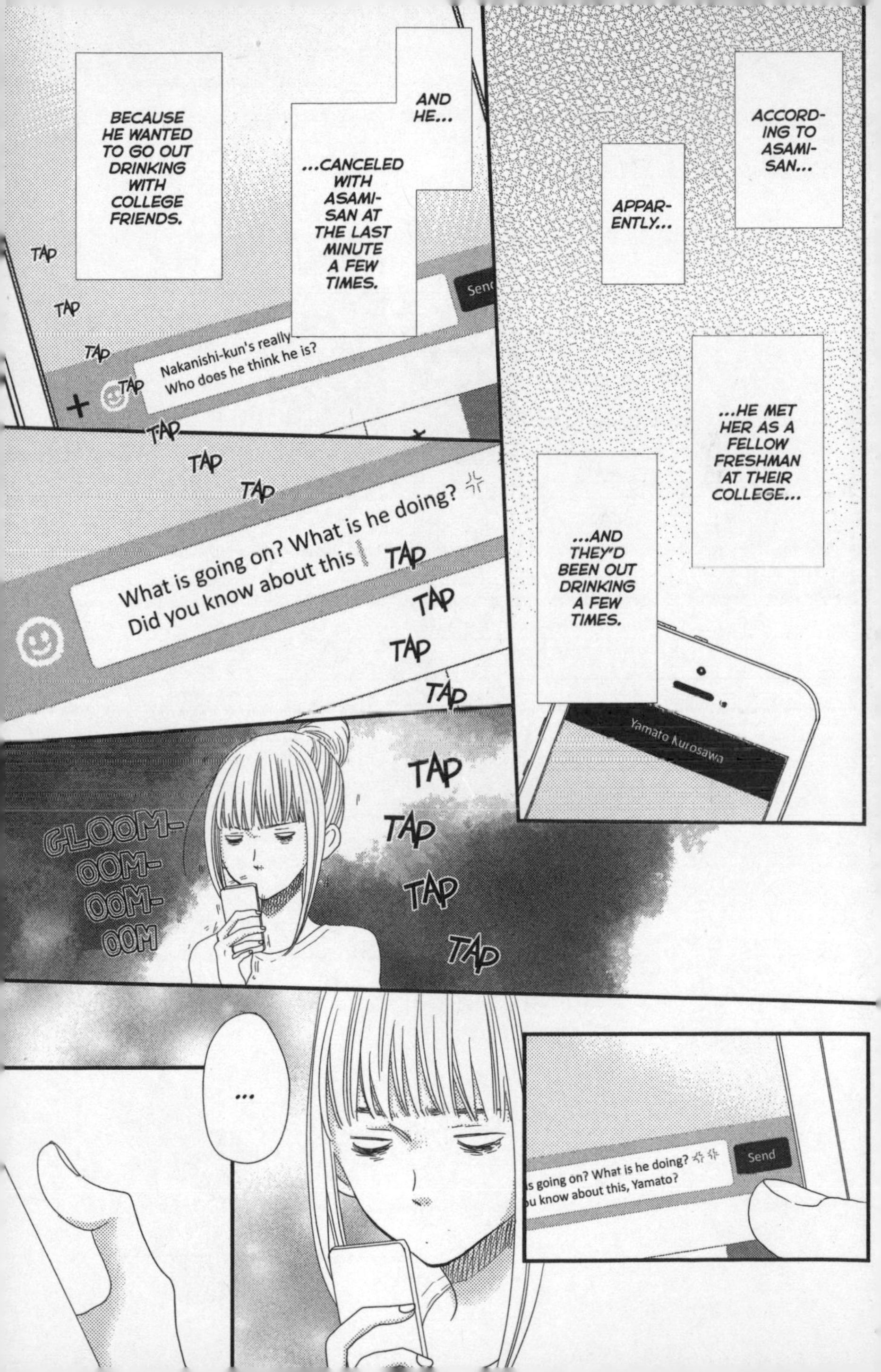
ACCORDING TO ASAMI-SAN...
APPARENTLY...
...HE MET HER AS A FELLOW FRESHMAN AT THEIR COLLEGE...
...AND THEY'D BEEN OUT DRINKING A FEW TIMES.
Yamato Kurosawa
AND HE...
...CANCELED WITH ASAMI-SAN AT THE LAST MINUTE A FEW TIMES.
BECAUSE HE WANTED TO GO OUT DRINKING WITH COLLEGE FRIENDS.
TAP
TAP
TAP
TAP
Nakanishi-kun's really
Who does he think he is?
TAP
TAP
TAP
What is going on? What is he doing?
Did you know about this
TAP
TAP
TAP
TAP
TAP
TAP
TAP
TAP
GLOOM-OOM-OOM-OOM
s going on? What is he doing?
u know about this, Yamato?
Send
...

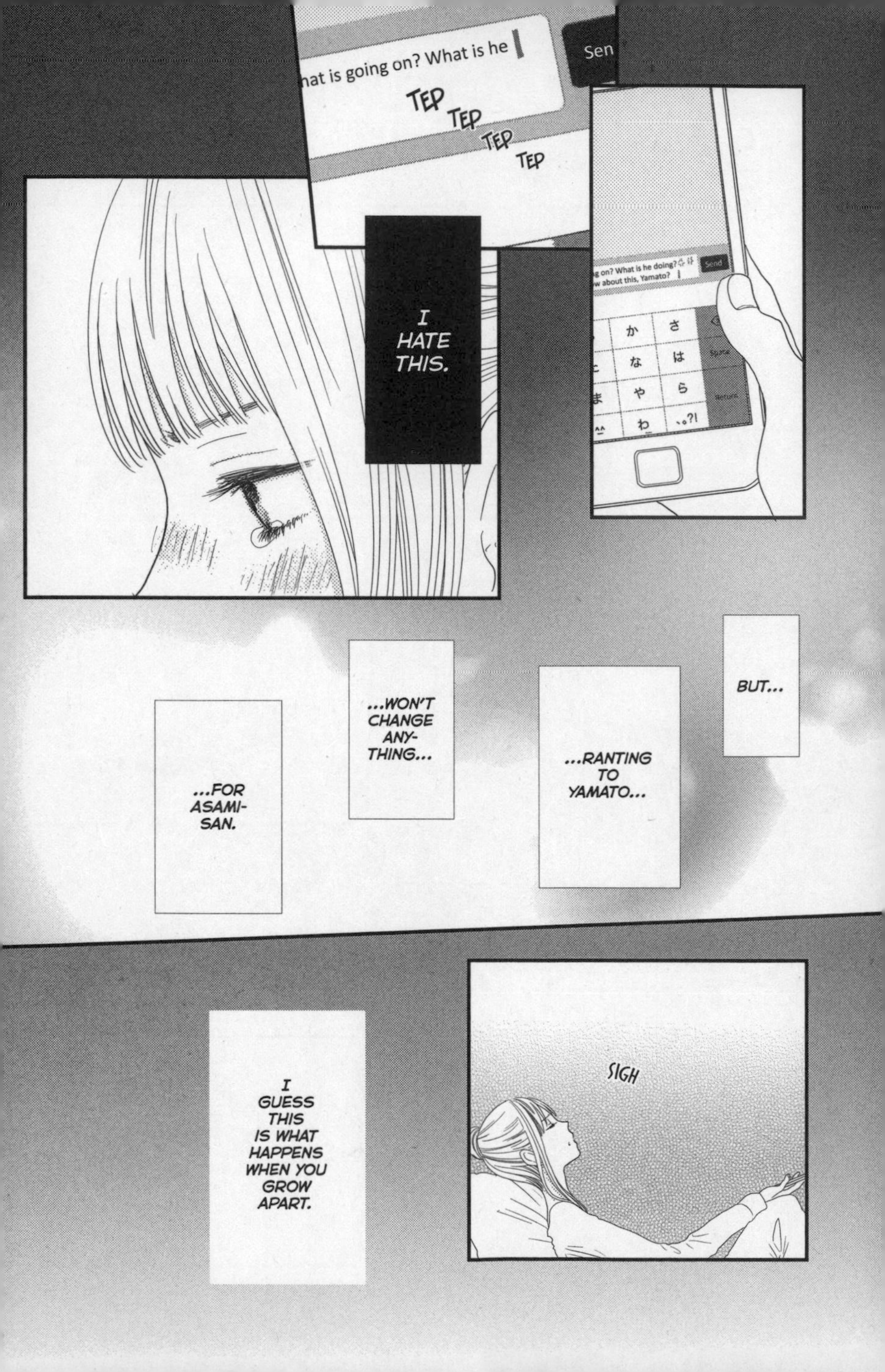
g on? What is he doing?
w about this, Yamato?
Send
hat is going on? What is he
Sen
TEP
TEP
TEP
TEP
I HATE THIS.
BUT...
...RANTING TO YAMATO...
...WON'T CHANGE ANYTHING...
...FOR ASAMI-SAN.
SIGH
I GUESS THIS IS WHAT HAPPENS WHEN YOU GROW APART.

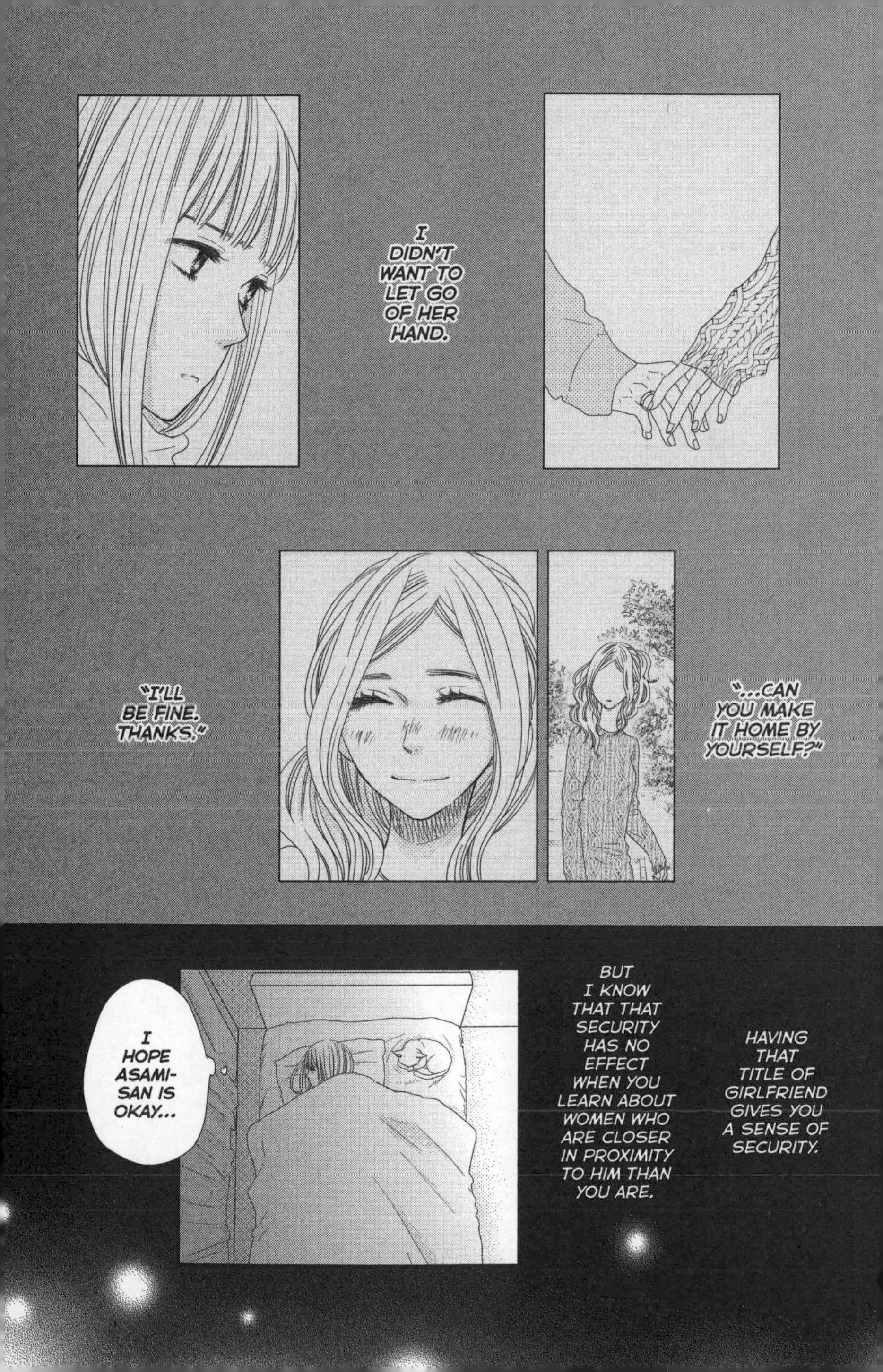
I DIDN'T WANT TO LET GO OF HER HAND.
"...CAN YOU MAKE IT HOME BY YOURSELF?"
"I'LL BE FINE. THANKS."
HAVING THAT TITLE OF GIRLFRIEND GIVES YOU A SENSE OF SECURITY.
BUT I KNOW THAT THAT SECURITY HAS NO EFFECT WHEN YOU LEARN ABOUT WOMEN WHO ARE CLOSER IN PROXIMITY TO HIM THAN YOU ARE.
I HOPE ASAMI-SAN IS OKAY...

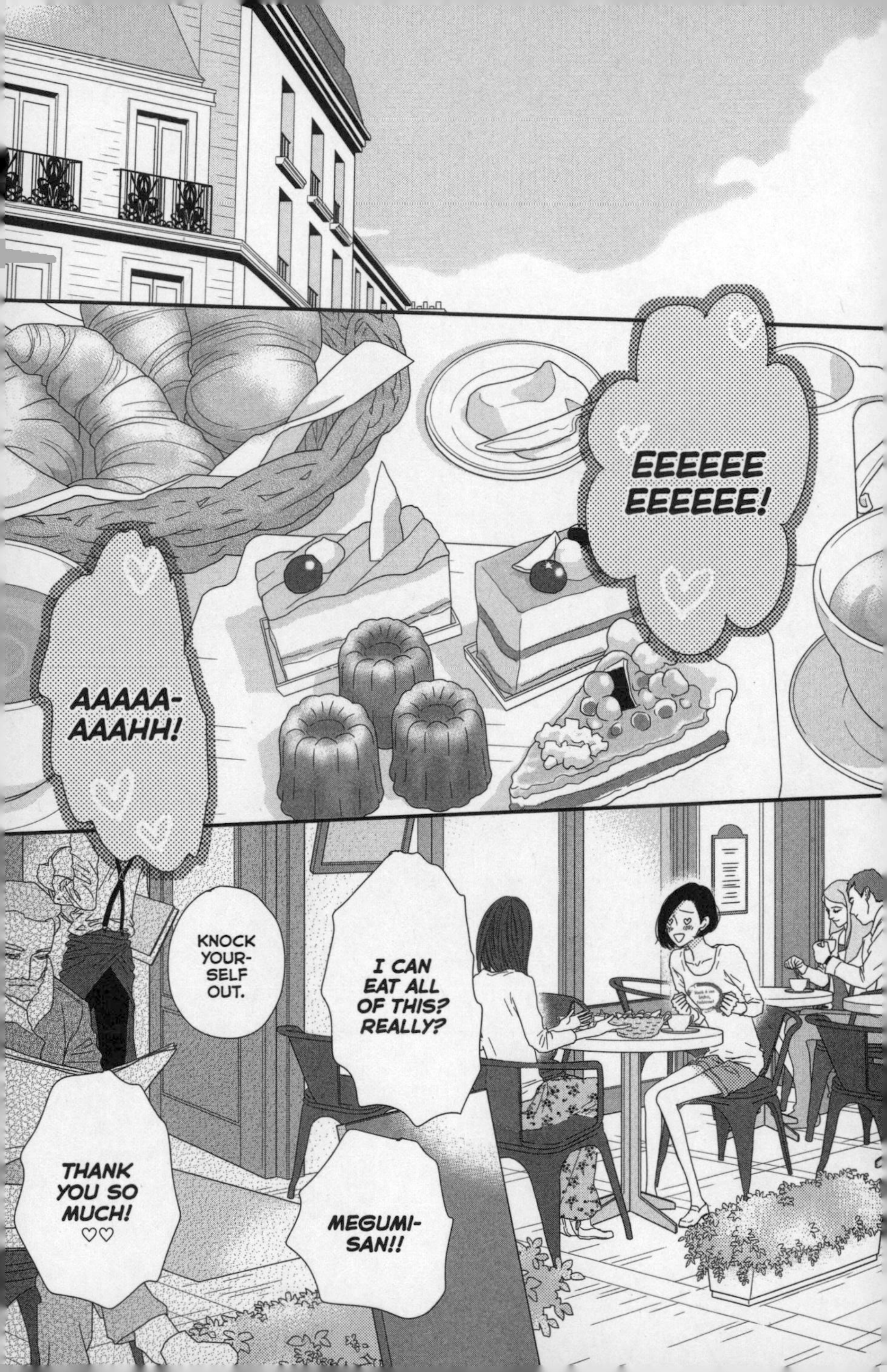
EEEEEE EEEEEE!
AAAAA-AAAHH!
I CAN EAT ALL OF THIS? REALLY?
KNOCK YOUR-SELF OUT.
MEGUMI-SAN!!
THANK YOU SO MUCH! ♡♡

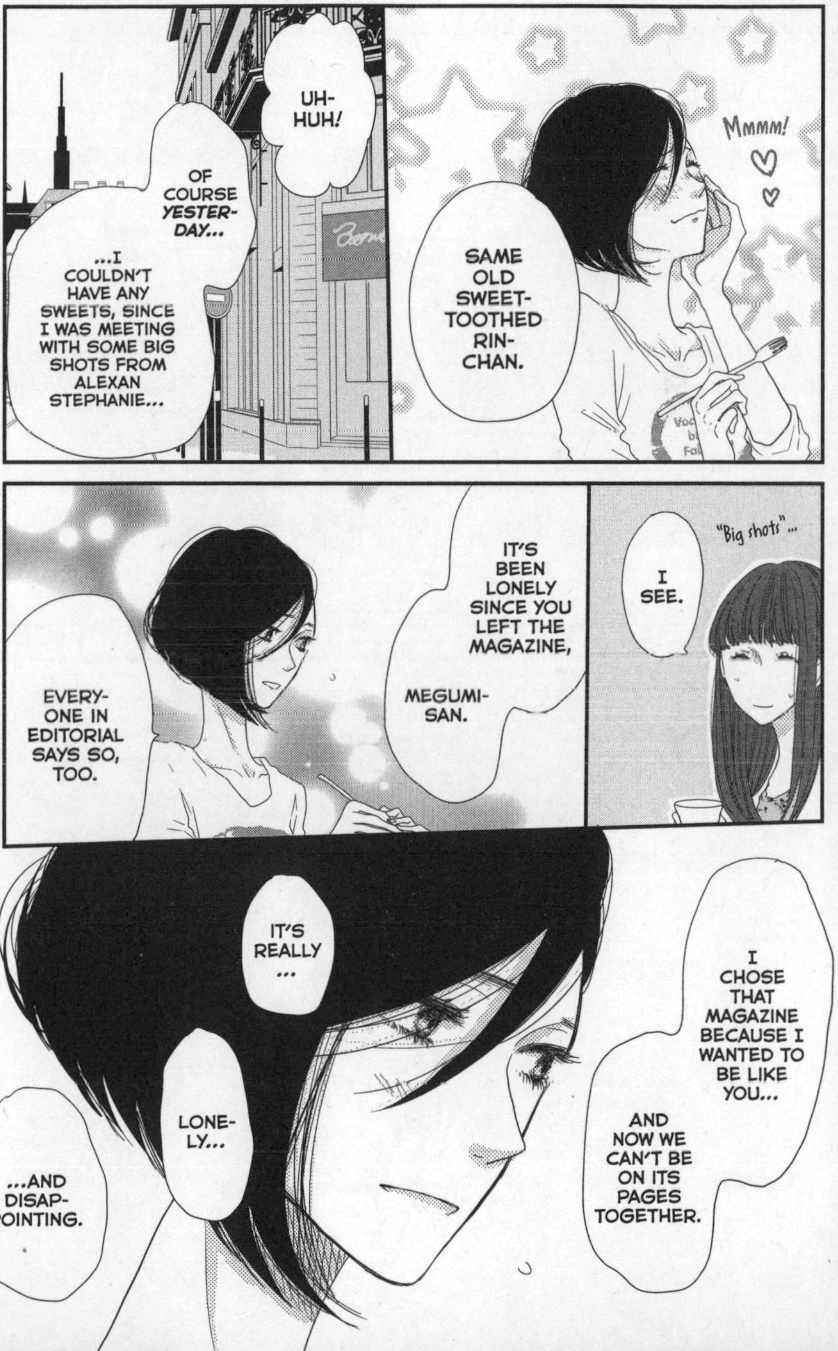
Mmmm!
SAME OLD SWEET-TOOTHED RIN-CHAN.
UH-HUH!
OF COURSE YESTERDAY...
...I COULDN'T HAVE ANY SWEETS, SINCE I WAS MEETING WITH SOME BIG SHOTS FROM ALEXAN STEPHANIE...
"Big shots"...
I SEE.
IT'S BEEN LONELY SINCE YOU LEFT THE MAGAZINE,
MEGUMI-SAN.
EVERYONE IN EDITORIAL SAYS SO, TOO.
I CHOSE THAT MAGAZINE BECAUSE I WANTED TO BE LIKE YOU...
AND NOW WE CAN'T BE ON ITS PAGES TOGETHER.
IT'S REALLY...
LONELY...
...AND DISAPPOINTING.

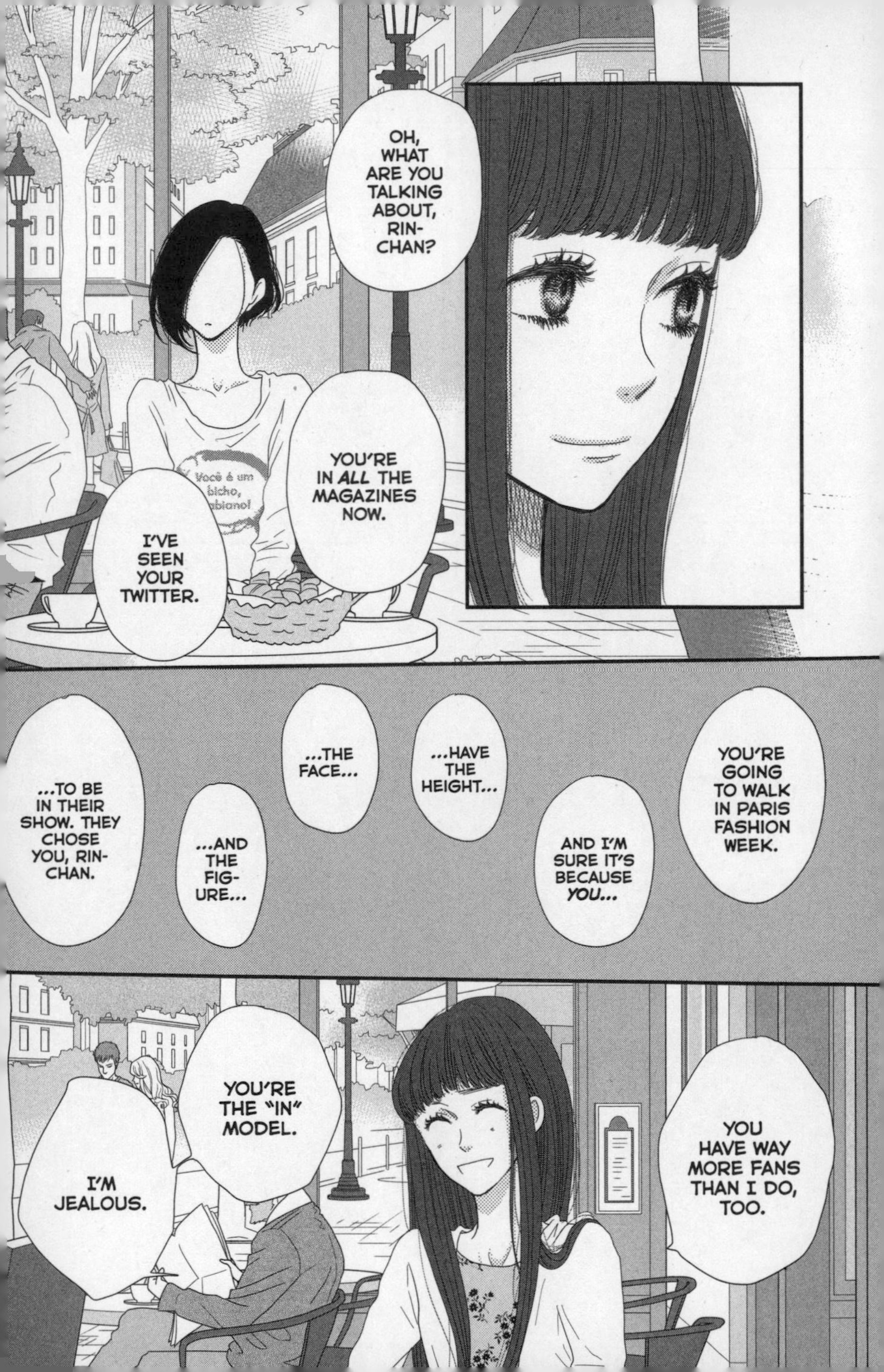
OH, WHAT ARE YOU TALKING ABOUT, RIN-CHAN?
YOU'RE IN *ALL* THE MAGAZINES NOW.
I'VE SEEN YOUR TWITTER.
YOU'RE GOING TO WALK IN PARIS FASHION WEEK.
AND I'M SURE IT'S BECAUSE *YOU*...
...HAVE THE HEIGHT...
...THE FACE...
...AND THE FIG-URE...
...TO BE IN THEIR SHOW. THEY CHOSE YOU, RIN-CHAN.
YOU HAVE WAY MORE FANS THAN I DO, TOO.
YOU'RE THE "IN" MODEL.
I'M JEALOUS.

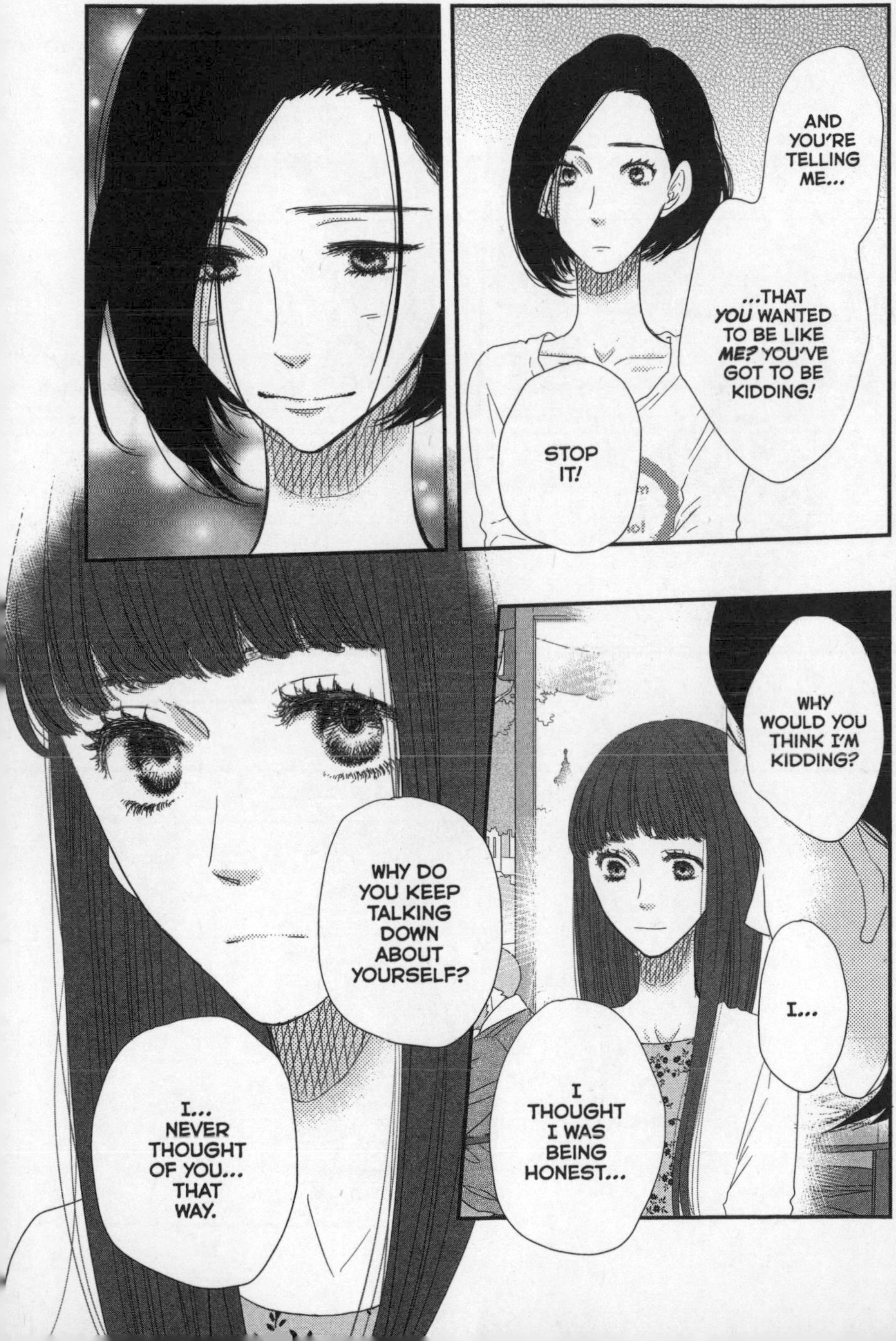
AND YOU'RE TELLING ME...
...THAT *YOU* WANTED TO BE LIKE *ME?* YOU'VE GOT TO BE KIDDING!
STOP IT!
WHY WOULD YOU THINK I'M KIDDING?
I...
I THOUGHT I WAS BEING HONEST...
WHY DO YOU KEEP TALKING DOWN ABOUT YOURSELF?
I... NEVER THOUGHT OF YOU... THAT WAY.

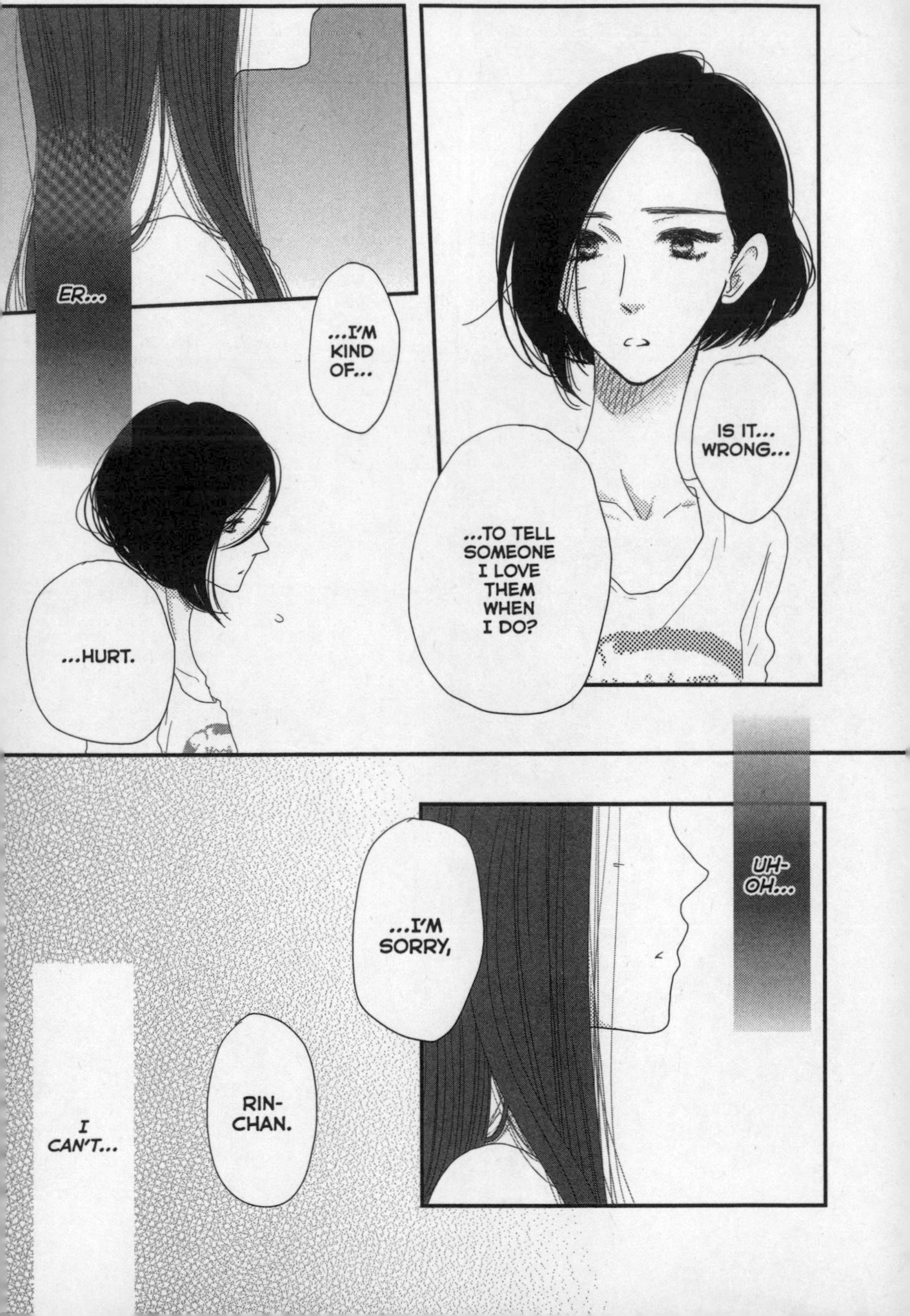
IS IT... WRONG...
...TO TELL SOMEONE I LOVE THEM WHEN I DO?
...I'M KIND OF...
ER...
...HURT.
UH-OH...
...I'M SORRY,
RIN-CHAN.
I CAN'T...

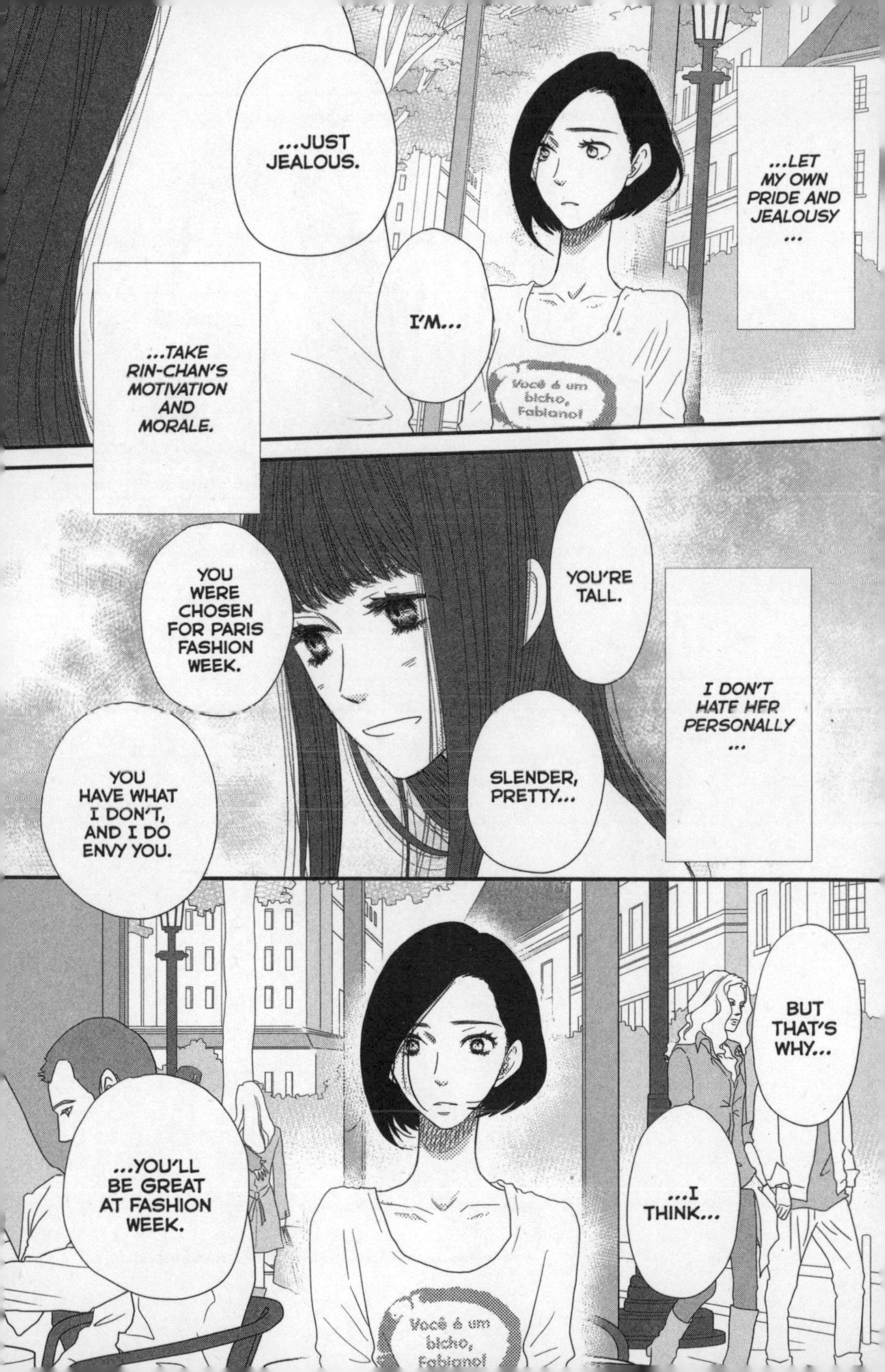
...LET MY OWN PRIDE AND JEALOUSY ...
I'M...
...JUST JEALOUS.
...TAKE RIN-CHAN'S MOTIVATION AND MORALE.
Você é um bicho, Fabiano!
I DON'T HATE HER PERSONALLY ...
YOU'RE TALL.
SLENDER, PRETTY...
YOU WERE CHOSEN FOR PARIS FASHION WEEK.
YOU HAVE WHAT I DON'T, AND I DO ENVY YOU.
BUT THAT'S WHY...
...I THINK...
...YOU'LL BE GREAT AT FASHION WEEK.
Você é um bicho, Fabiano!

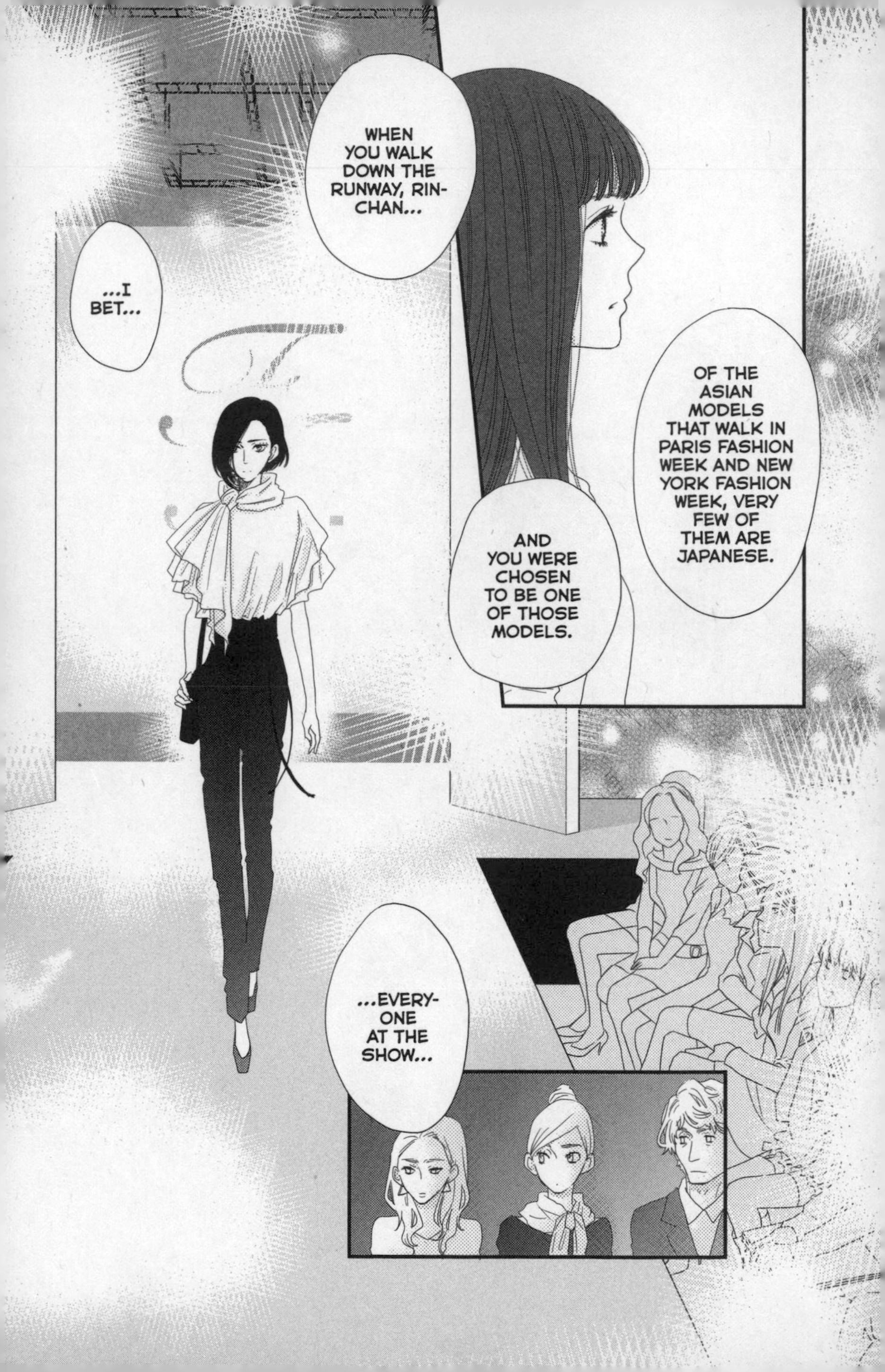
OF THE ASIAN MODELS THAT WALK IN PARIS FASHION WEEK AND NEW YORK FASHION WEEK, VERY FEW OF THEM ARE JAPANESE.
AND YOU WERE CHOSEN TO BE ONE OF THOSE MODELS.
WHEN YOU WALK DOWN THE RUNWAY, RIN-CHAN...
...I BET...
...EVERY-ONE AT THE SHOW...

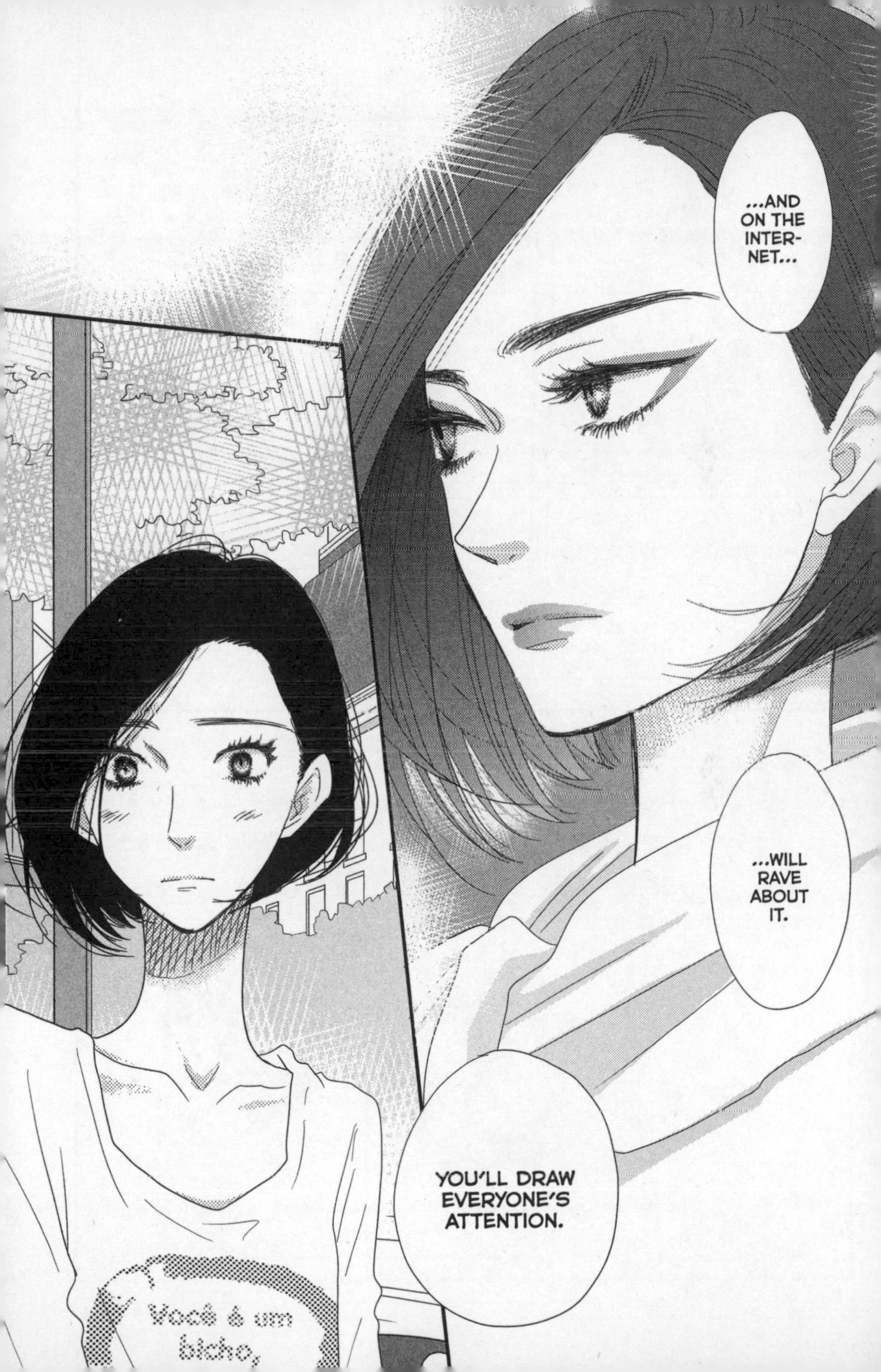
...AND ON THE INTER- NET...
...WILL RAVE ABOUT IT.
YOU'LL DRAW EVERYONE'S ATTENTION.
Você é um bicho,

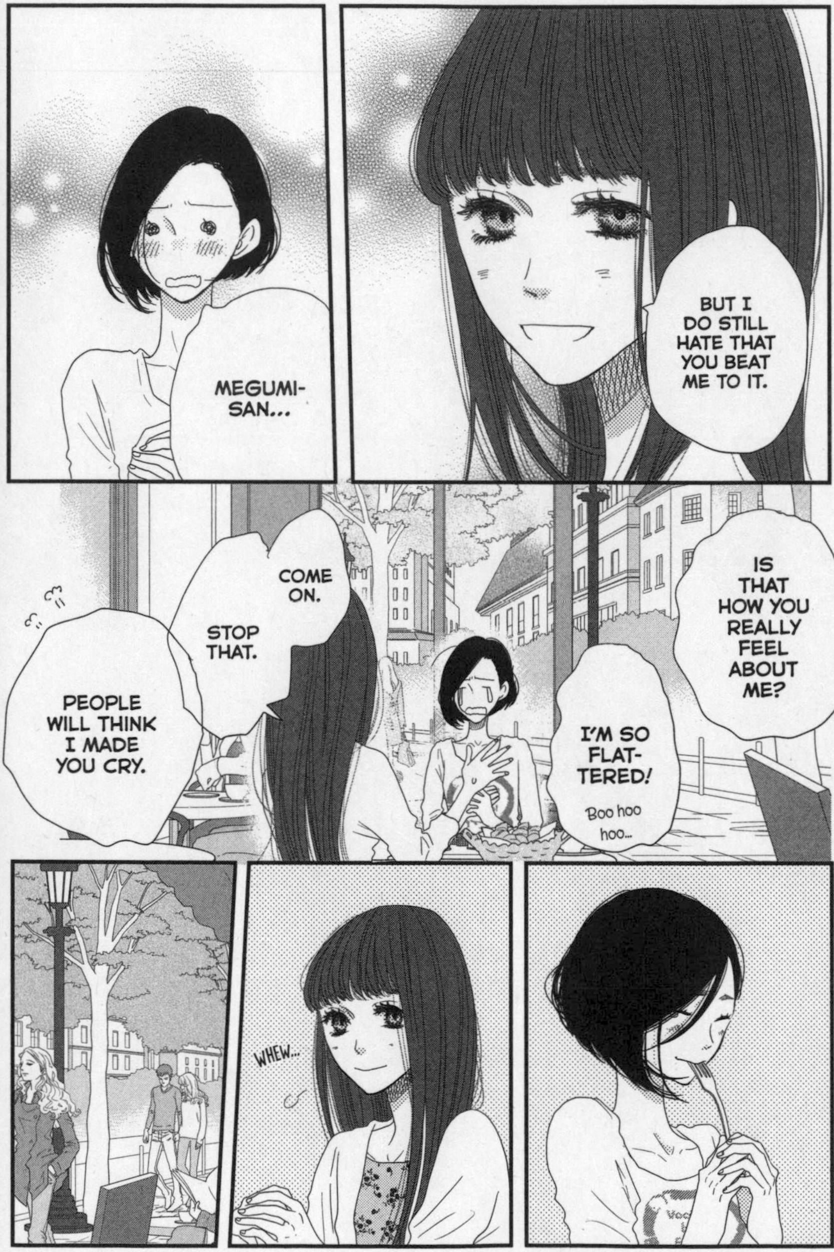
BUT I DO STILL HATE THAT YOU BEAT ME TO IT.
MEGUMI-SAN...
IS THAT HOW YOU REALLY FEEL ABOUT ME?
I'M SO FLATTERED!
Boo hoo hoo...
COME ON.
STOP THAT.
PEOPLE WILL THINK I MADE YOU CRY.
WHEW...

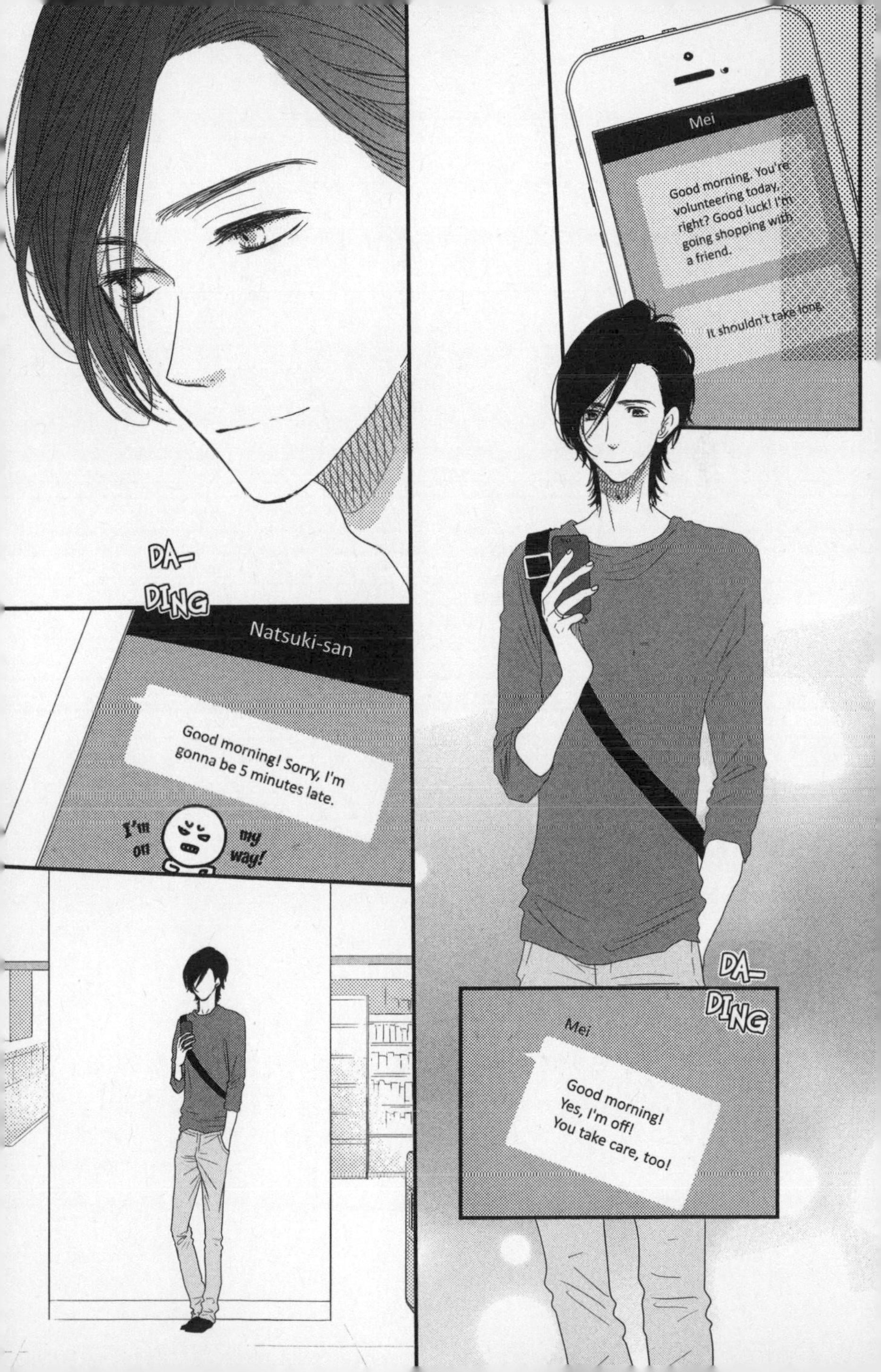
Mei
Good morning. You're volunteering today, right? Good luck! I'm going shopping with a friend.
It shouldn't take long.
DA-DING
Mei
Good morning! Yes, I'm off! You take care, too!
DA-DING
Natsuki-san
Good morning! Sorry, I'm gonna be 5 minutes late.
I'm on my way!

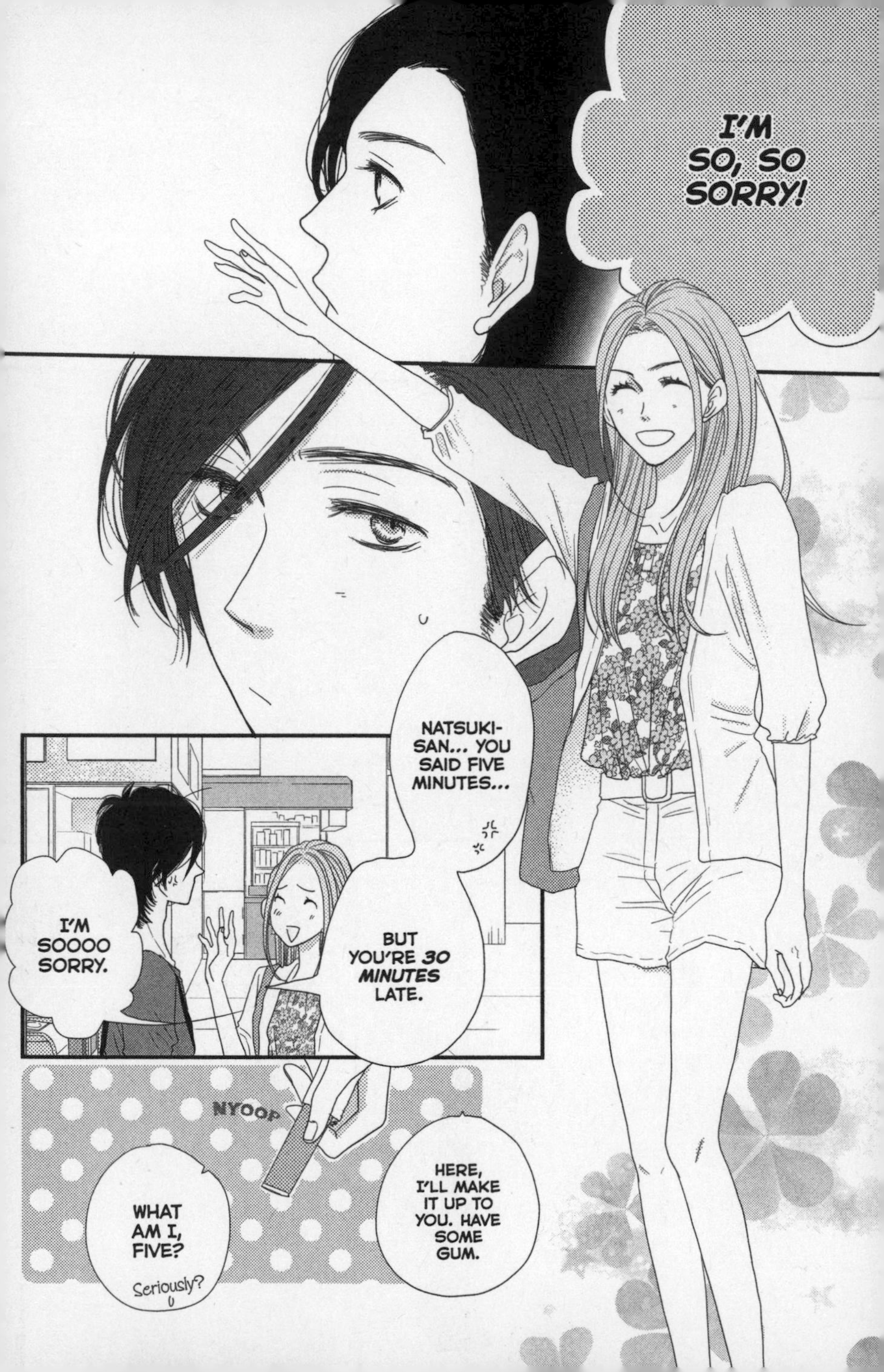
I'M SO, SO SORRY!
NATSUKI-SAN... YOU SAID FIVE MINUTES...
BUT YOU'RE *30 MINUTES* LATE.
I'M SOOOO SORRY.
NYOOP
HERE, I'LL MAKE IT UP TO YOU. HAVE SOME GUM.
WHAT AM I, FIVE?
Seriously?

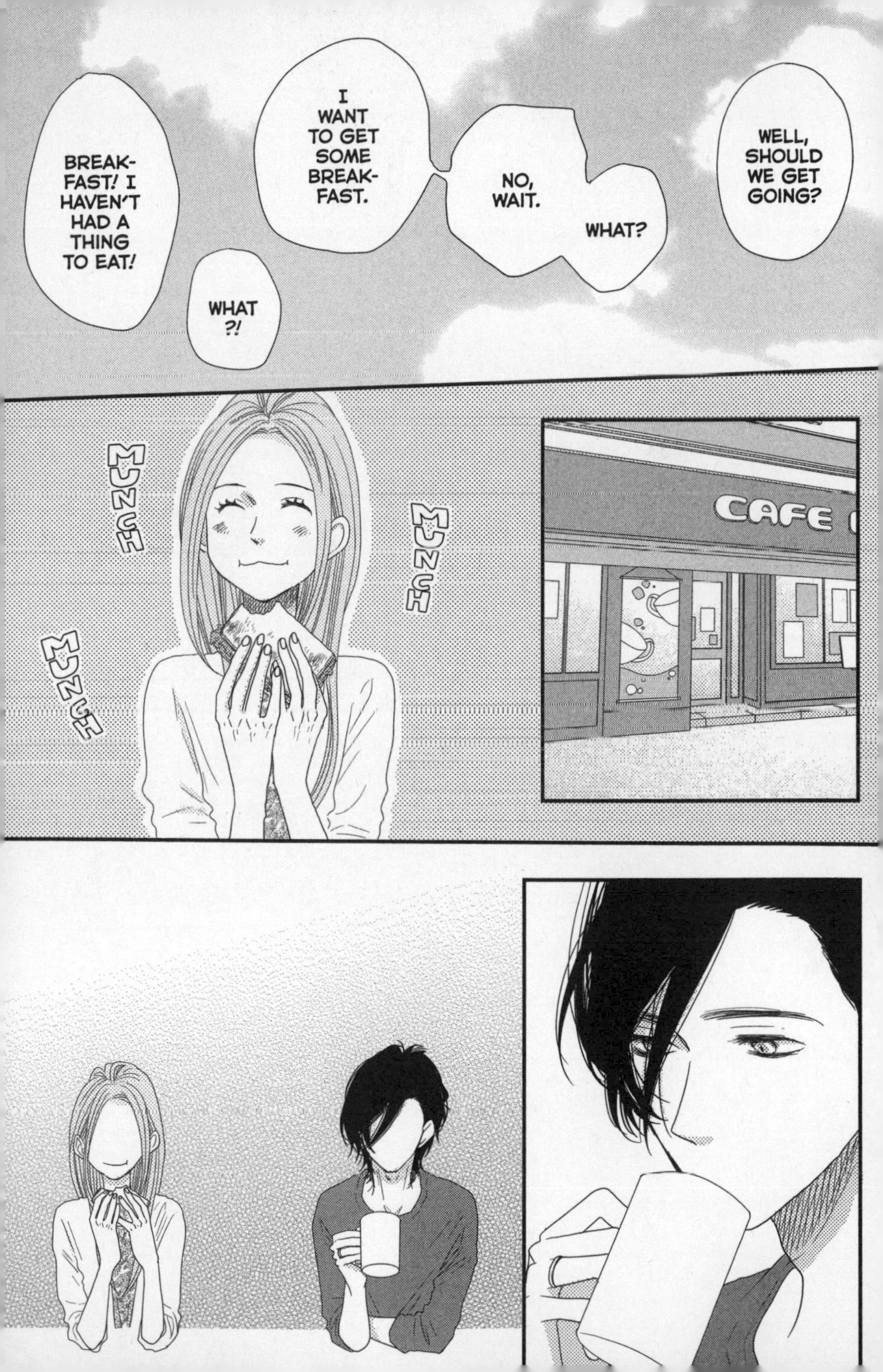
WELL, SHOULD WE GET GOING?
WHAT?
NO, WAIT.
I WANT TO GET SOME BREAK-FAST.
WHAT ?!
BREAK-FAST! I HAVEN'T HAD A THING TO EAT!
CAFE
MUNCH
MUNCH
MUNCH

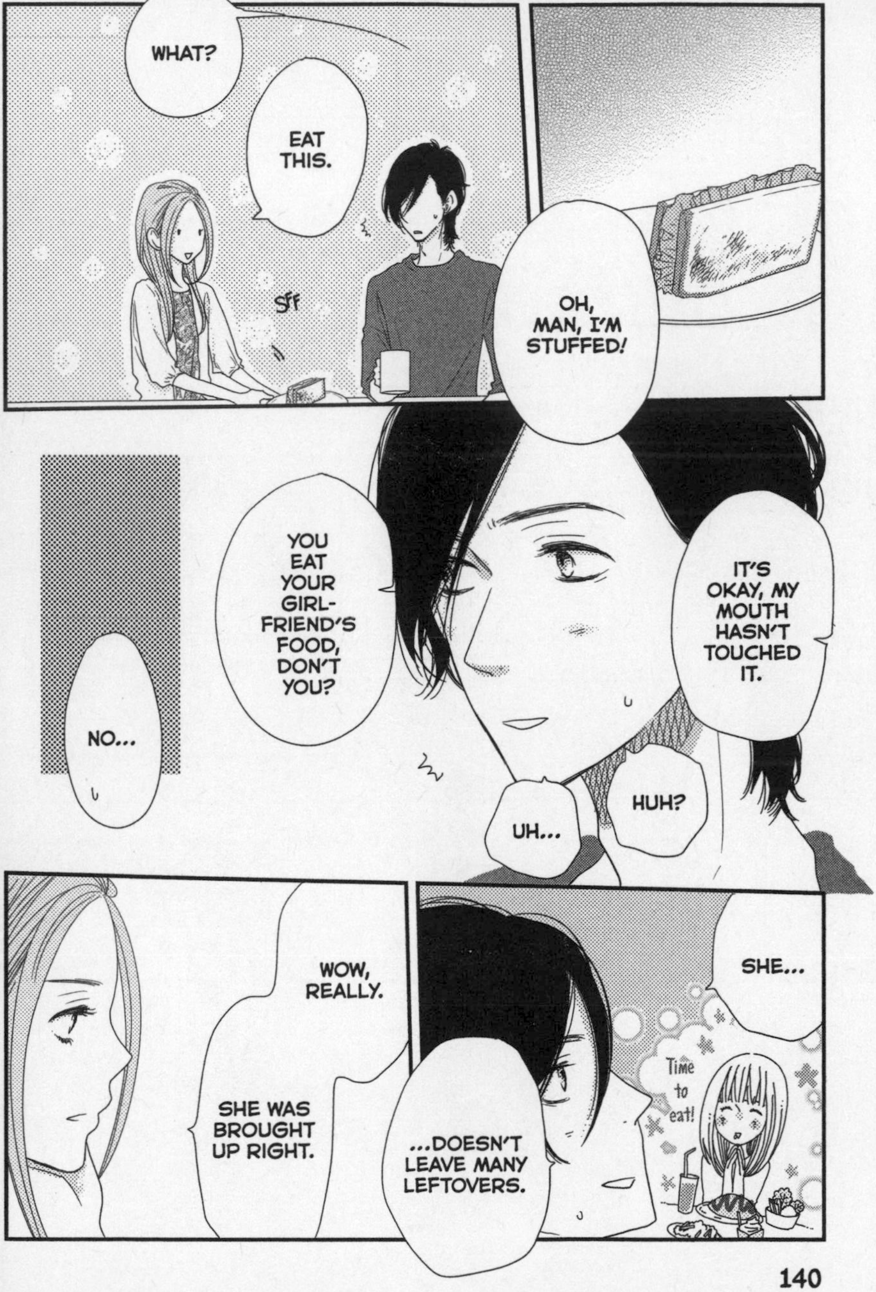
EAT THIS.
WHAT?
SFF
OH, MAN, I'M STUFFED!
IT'S OKAY, MY MOUTH HASN'T TOUCHED IT.
HUH?
UH...
YOU EAT YOUR GIRL-FRIEND'S FOOD, DON'T YOU?
NO...
SHE...
Time to eat!
...DOESN'T LEAVE MANY LEFTOVERS.
WOW, REALLY.
SHE WAS BROUGHT UP RIGHT.

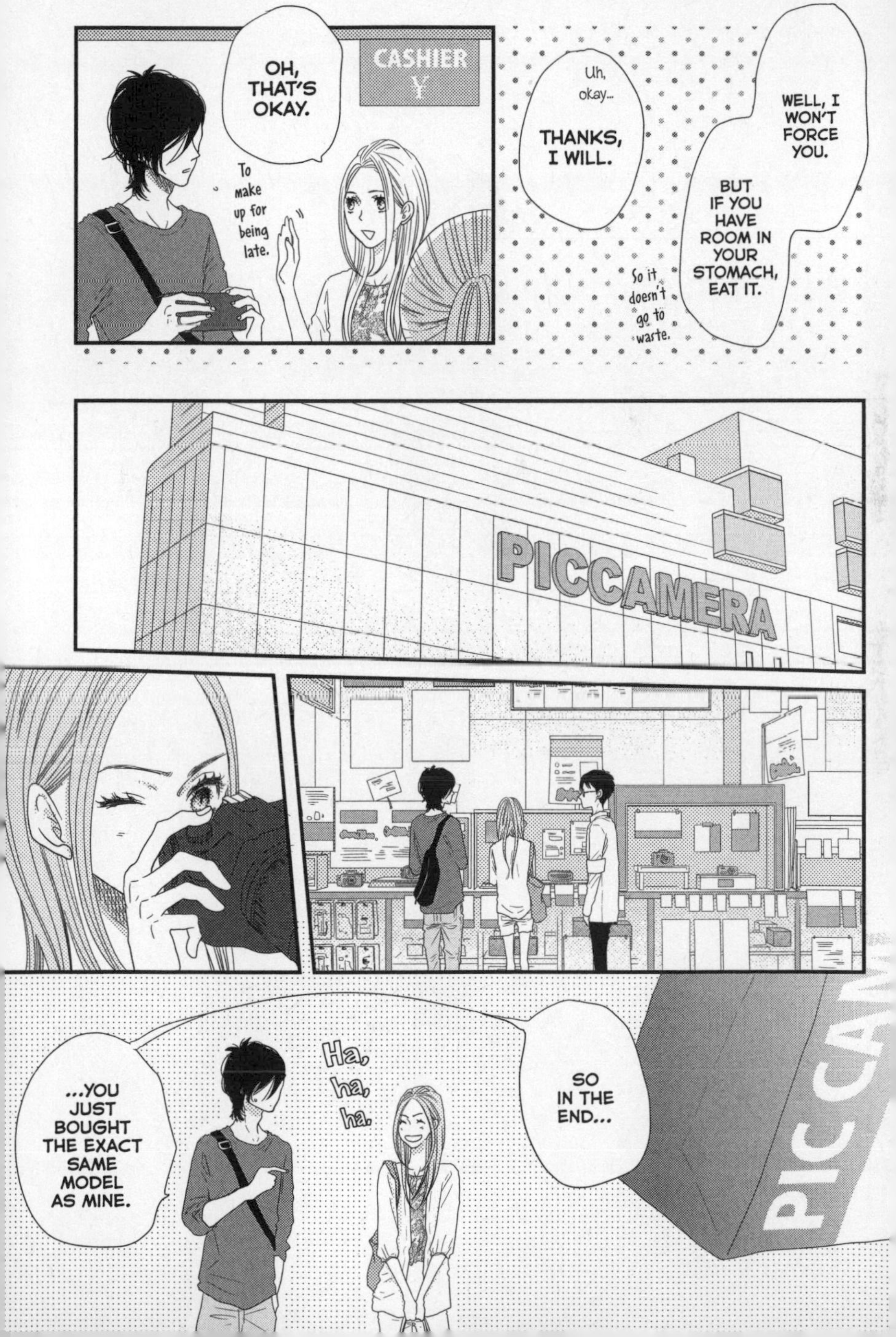
WELL, I WON'T FORCE YOU.
BUT IF YOU HAVE ROOM IN YOUR STOMACH, EAT IT.
So it doesn't go to waste.
Uh, okay...
THANKS, I WILL.
CASHIER ¥
OH, THAT'S OKAY.
To make up for being late.
PICCAMERA
SO IN THE END...
Ha, ha, ha.
...YOU JUST BOUGHT THE EXACT SAME MODEL AS MINE.

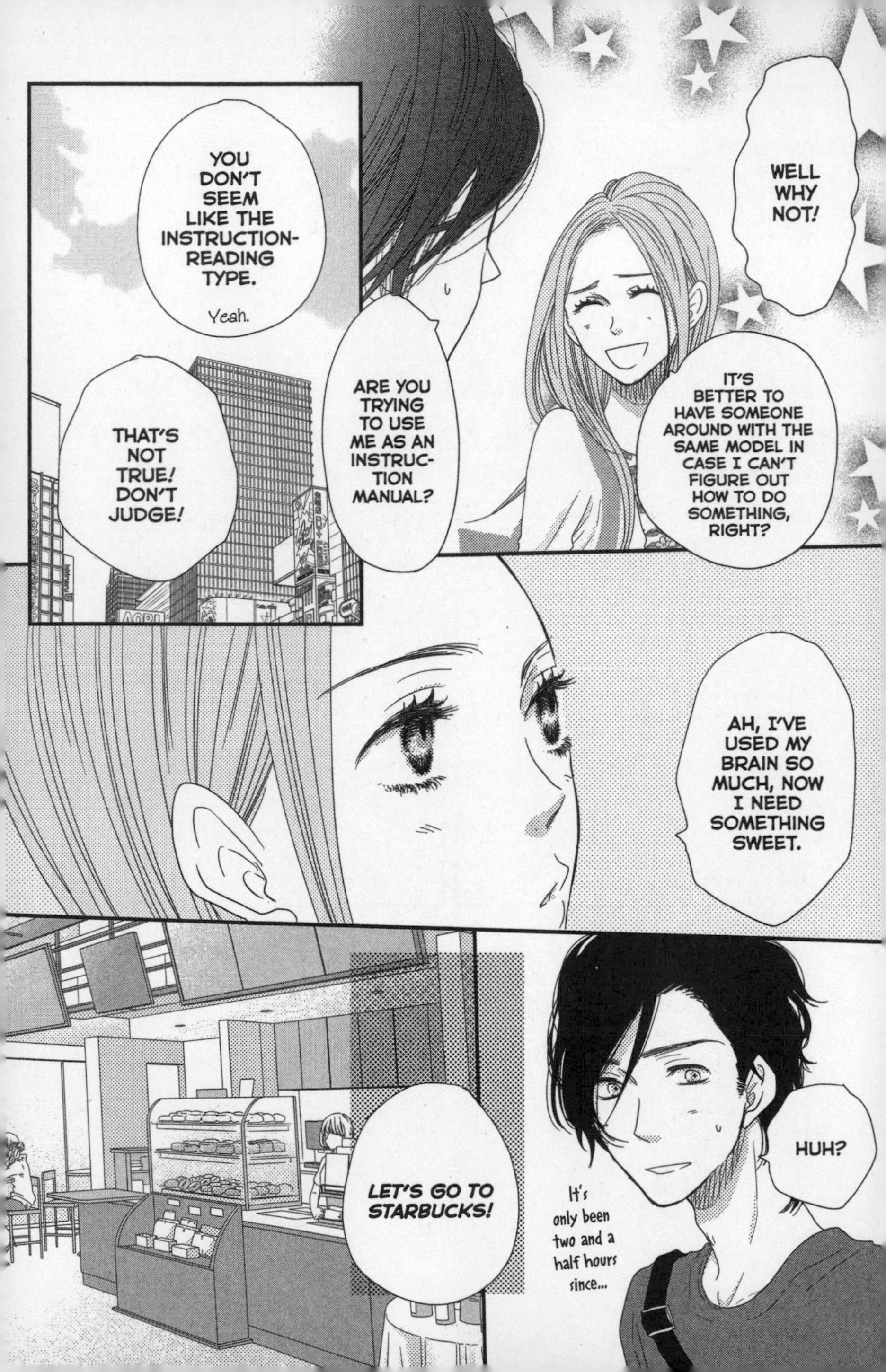
WELL WHY NOT!
IT'S BETTER TO HAVE SOMEONE AROUND WITH THE SAME MODEL IN CASE I CAN'T FIGURE OUT HOW TO DO SOMETHING, RIGHT?
ARE YOU TRYING TO USE ME AS AN INSTRUCTION MANUAL?
YOU DON'T SEEM LIKE THE INSTRUCTION-READING TYPE.
Yeah.
THAT'S NOT TRUE! DON'T JUDGE!
AH, I'VE USED MY BRAIN SO MUCH, NOW I NEED SOMETHING SWEET.
HUH?
It's only been two and a half hours since...
LET'S GO TO STARBUCKS!

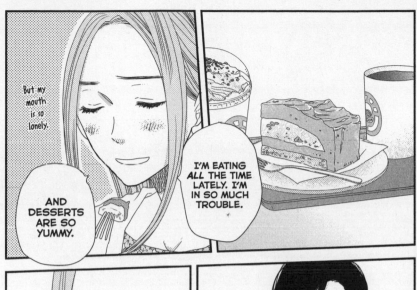

I'M EATING *ALL* THE TIME LATELY. I'M IN SO MUCH TROUBLE.
But my mouth is so lonely.
AND DESSERTS ARE SO YUMMY.
DID SOMETHING HAPPEN?
...
MM-HM.
I QUIT SMOKING.

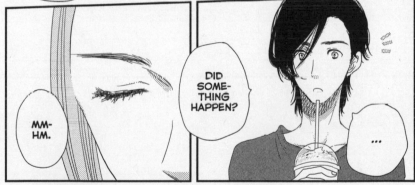

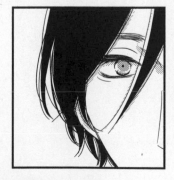

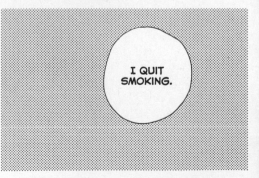

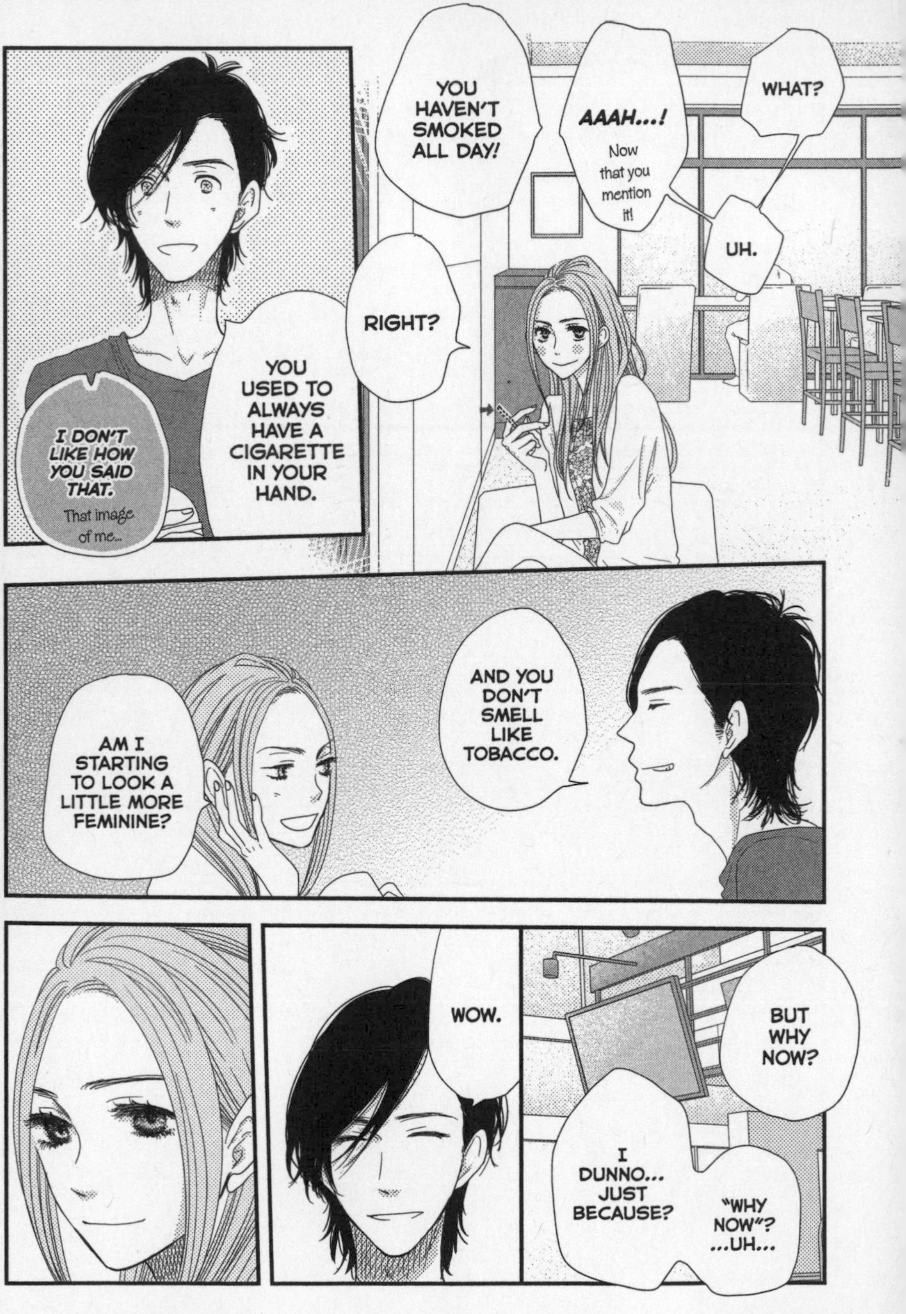
WHAT?
AAAH...! Now that you mention it!
YOU HAVEN'T SMOKED ALL DAY!
UH.
RIGHT?
YOU USED TO ALWAYS HAVE A CIGARETTE IN YOUR HAND.
I DON'T LIKE HOW YOU SAID THAT. That image of me...
AND YOU DON'T SMELL LIKE TOBACCO.
AM I STARTING TO LOOK A LITTLE MORE FEMININE?
BUT WHY NOW?
"WHY NOW"? ...UH...
I DUNNO... JUST BECAUSE?
WOW.

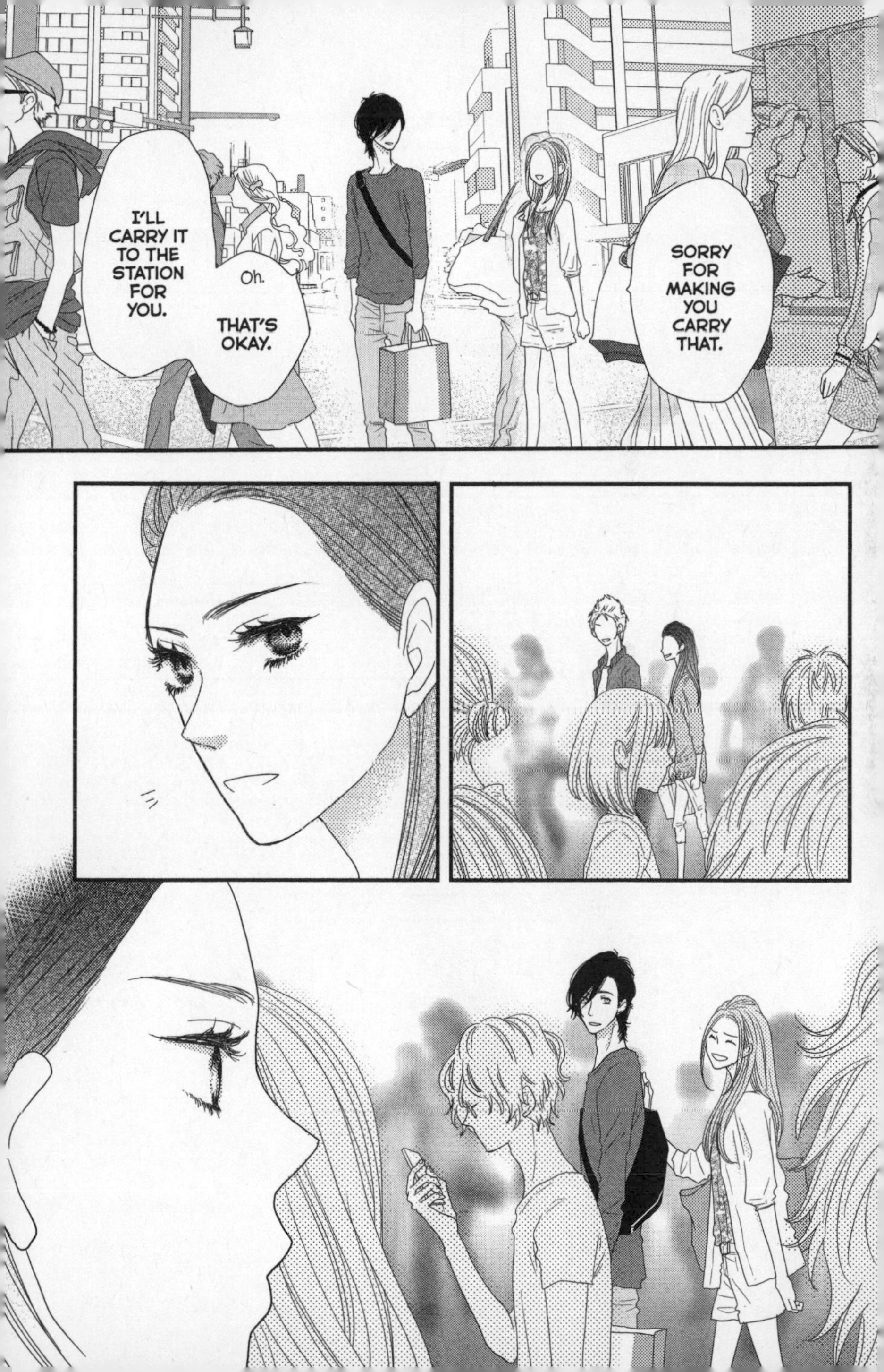
SORRY FOR MAKING YOU CARRY THAT.
Oh. THAT'S OKAY.
I'LL CARRY IT TO THE STATION FOR YOU.

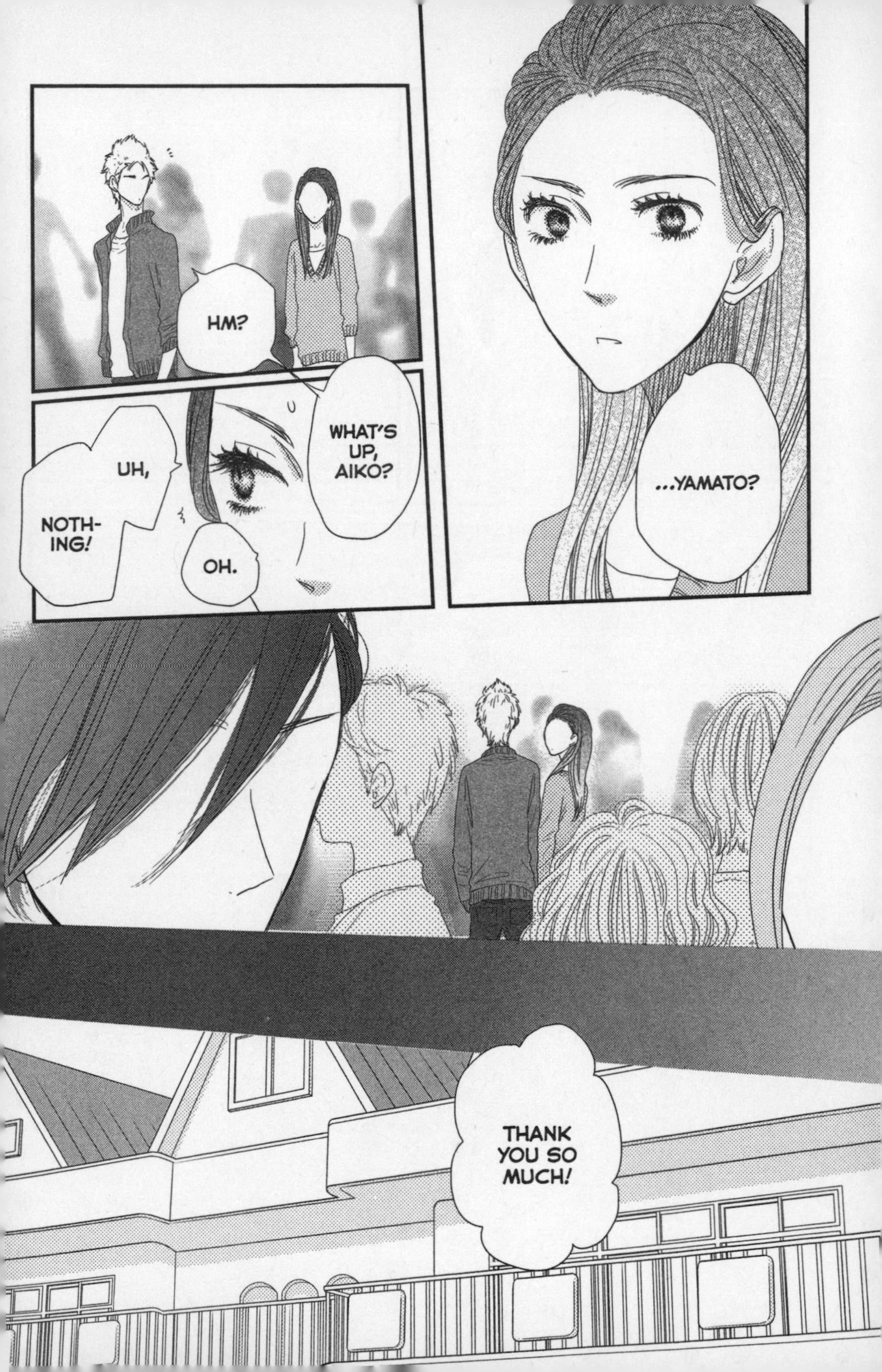
...YAMATO?
HM?
WHAT'S UP, AIKO?
OH.
UH, NOTHING!
THANK YOU SO MUCH!

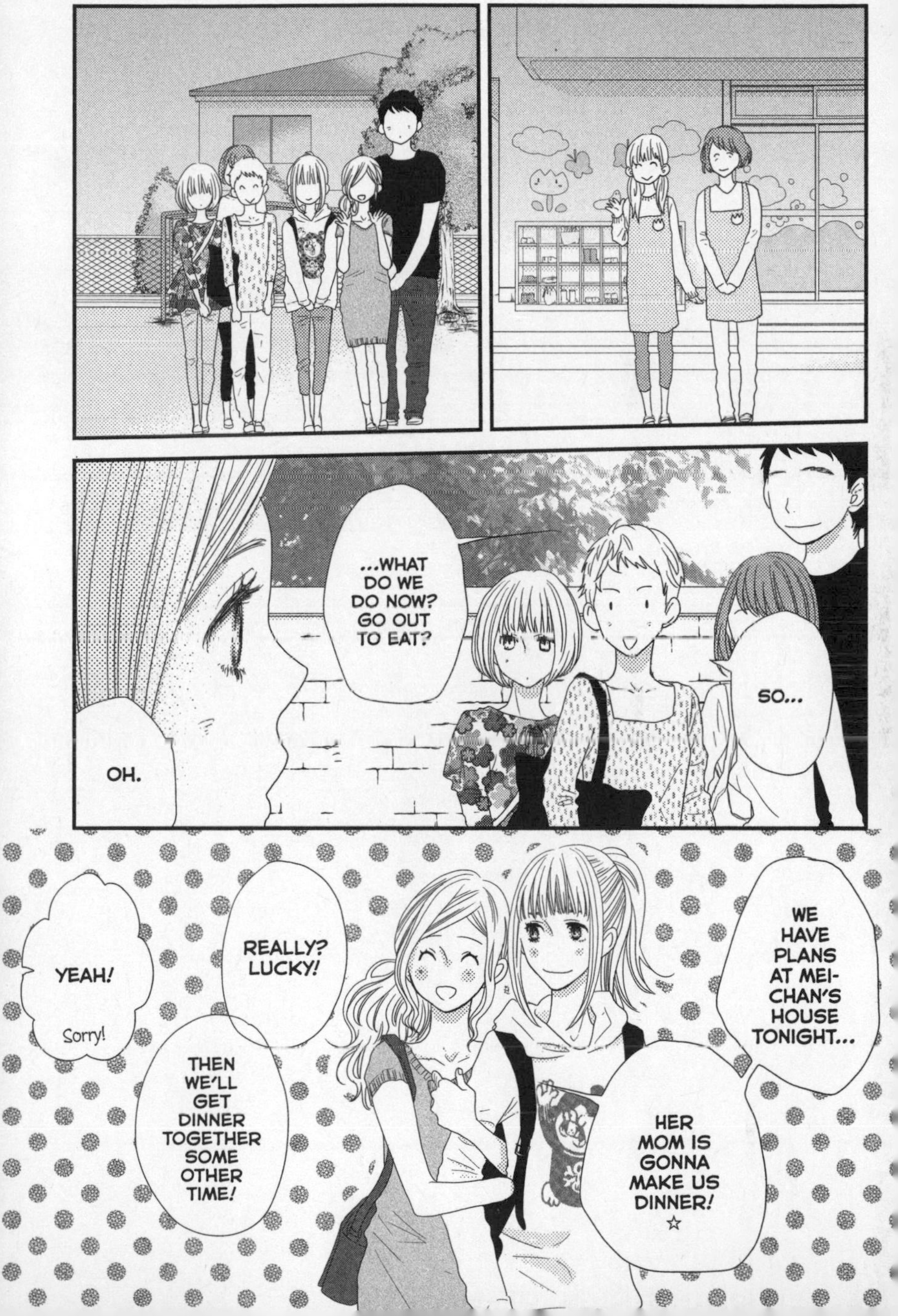
SO...
...WHAT DO WE DO NOW? GO OUT TO EAT?
OH.
WE HAVE PLANS AT MEI-CHAN'S HOUSE TONIGHT...
HER MOM IS GONNA MAKE US DINNER! ☆
REALLY? LUCKY!
THEN WE'LL GET DINNER TOGETHER SOME OTHER TIME!
YEAH!
Sorry!

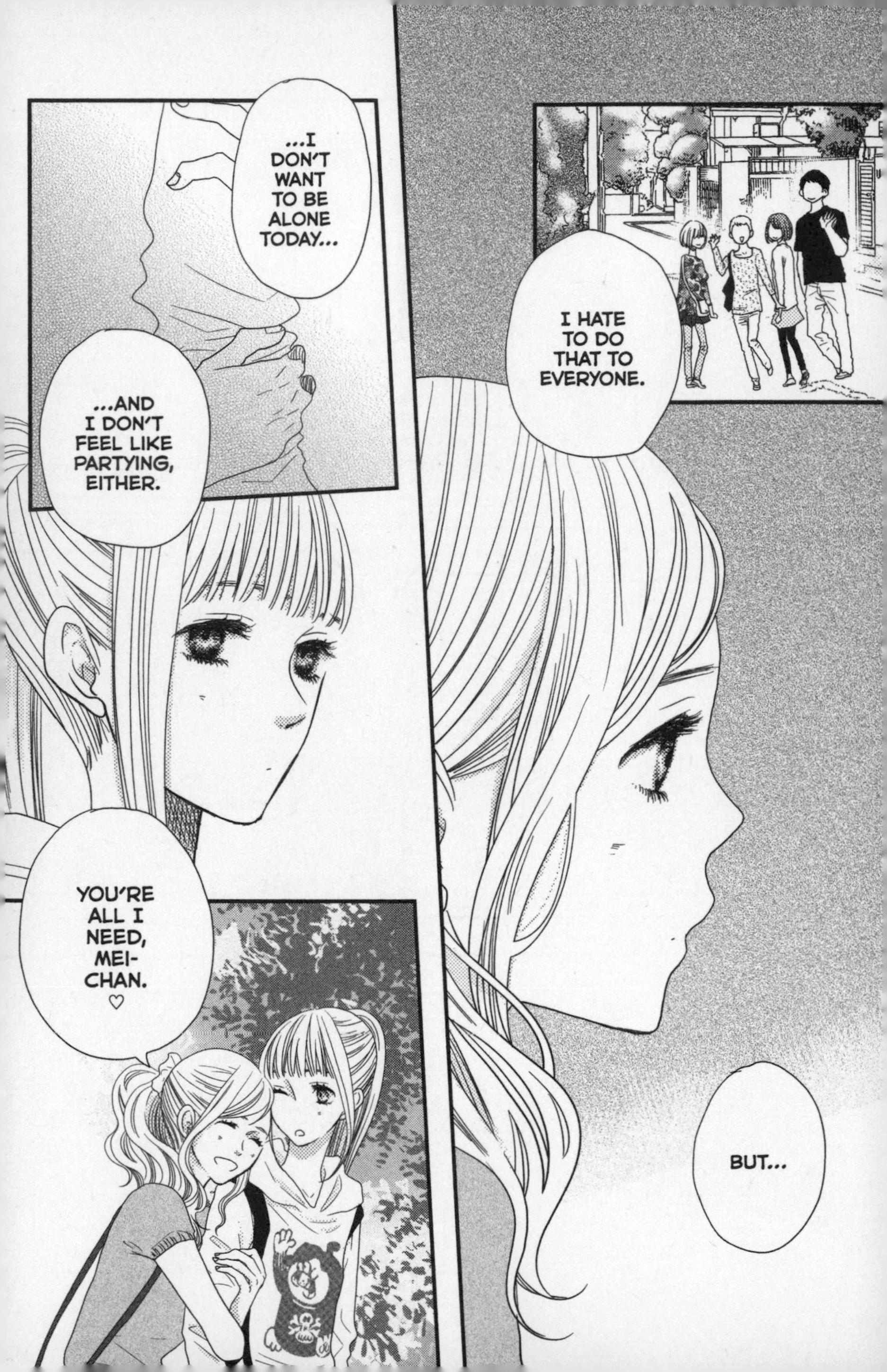
I HATE TO DO THAT TO EVERYONE.
BUT...
...I DON'T WANT TO BE ALONE TODAY...
...AND I DON'T FEEL LIKE PARTYING, EITHER.
YOU'RE ALL I NEED, MEI-CHAN. ♡

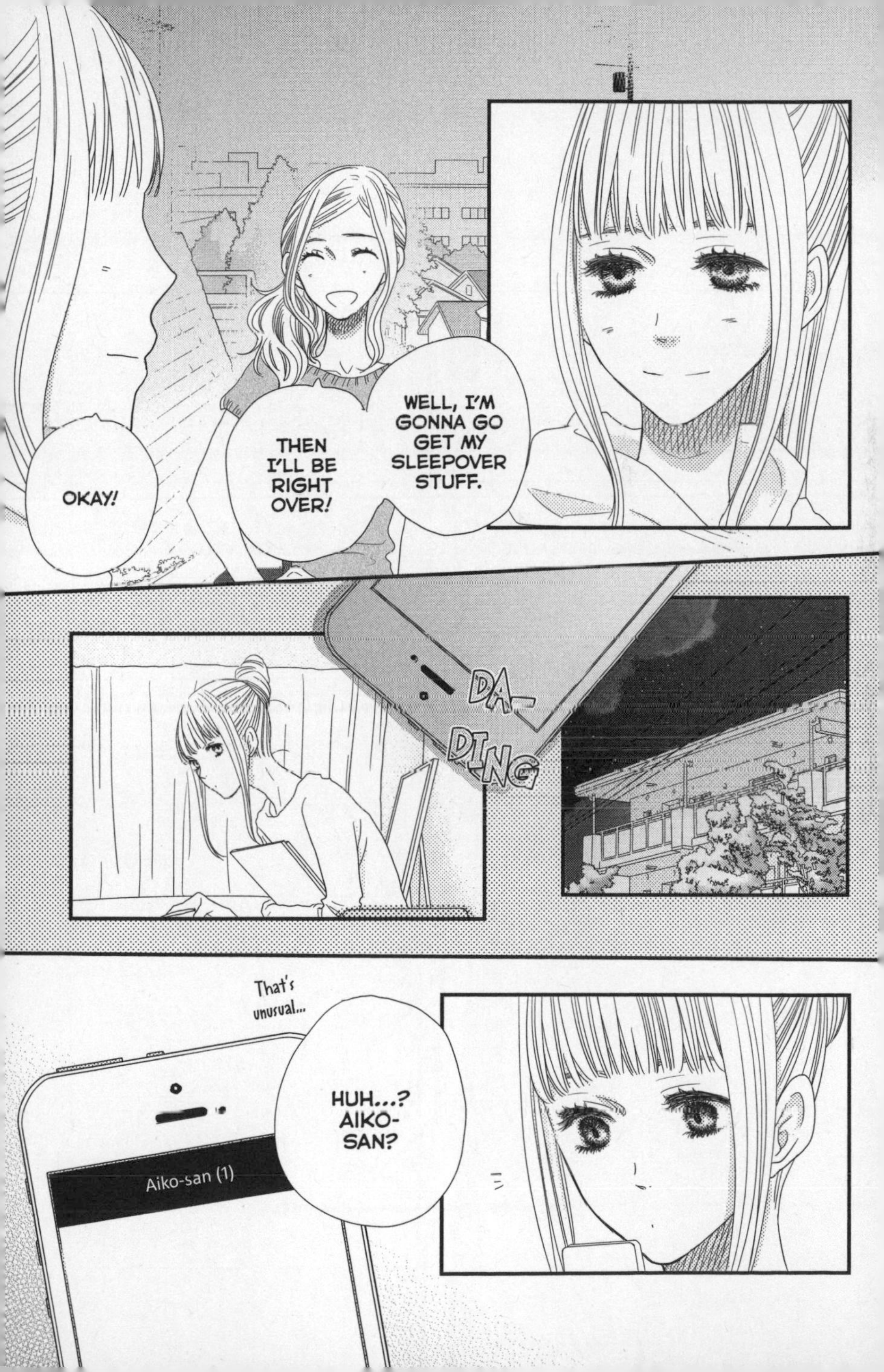
WELL, I'M GONNA GO GET MY SLEEPOVER STUFF.
THEN I'LL BE RIGHT OVER!
OKAY!
DA-DING
HUH...? AIKO-SAN?
That's unusual...
Aiko-san (1)

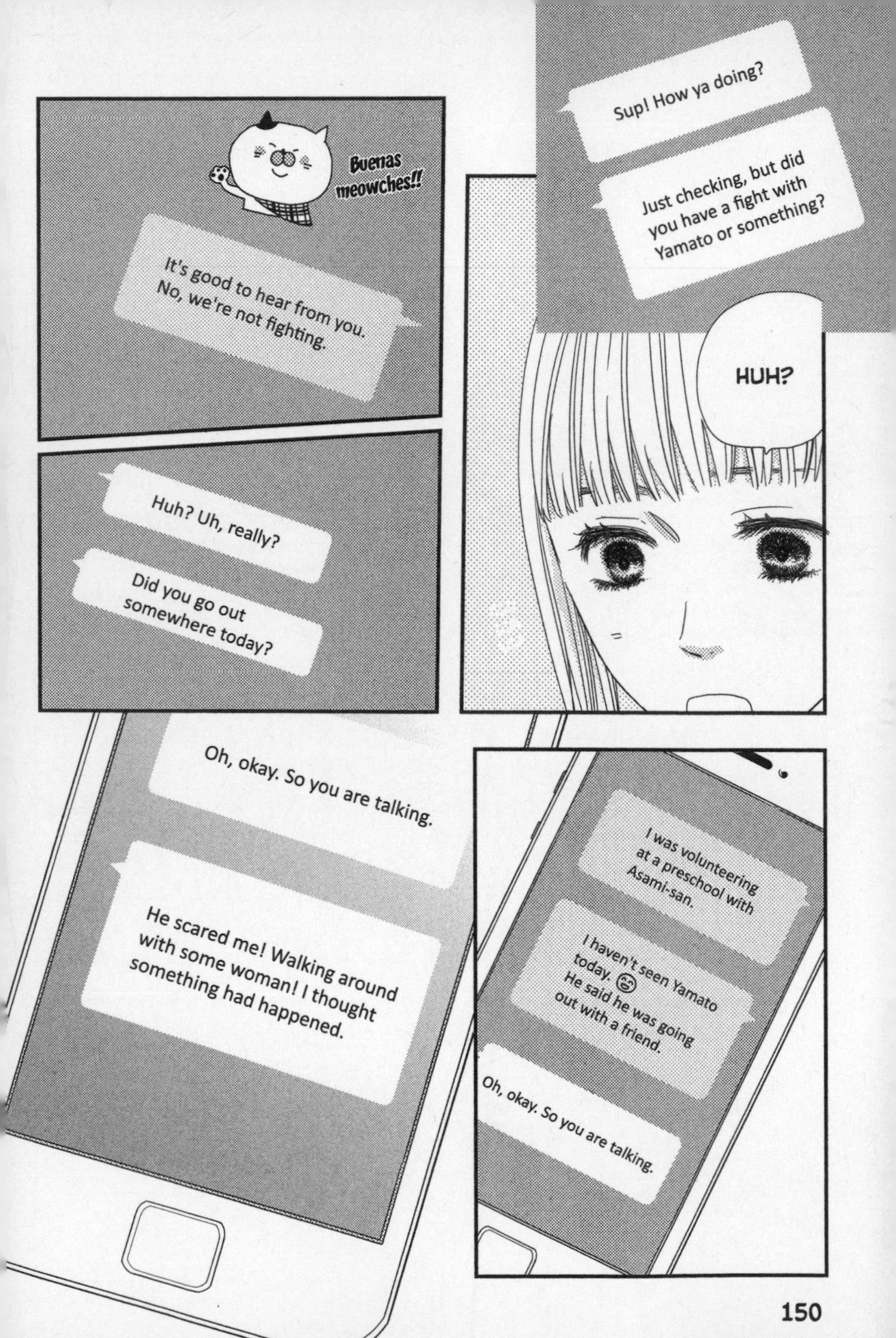

Sup! How ya doing?
Just checking, but did you have a fight with Yamato or something?
HUH?
Buenas meowches!!
It's good to hear from you. No, we're not fighting.
Huh? Uh, really?
Did you go out somewhere today?
I was volunteering at a preschool with Asami-san.
I haven't seen Yamato today. He said he was going out with a friend.
Oh, okay. So you are talking.
Oh, okay. So you are talking.
He scared me! Walking around with some woman! I thought something had happened.

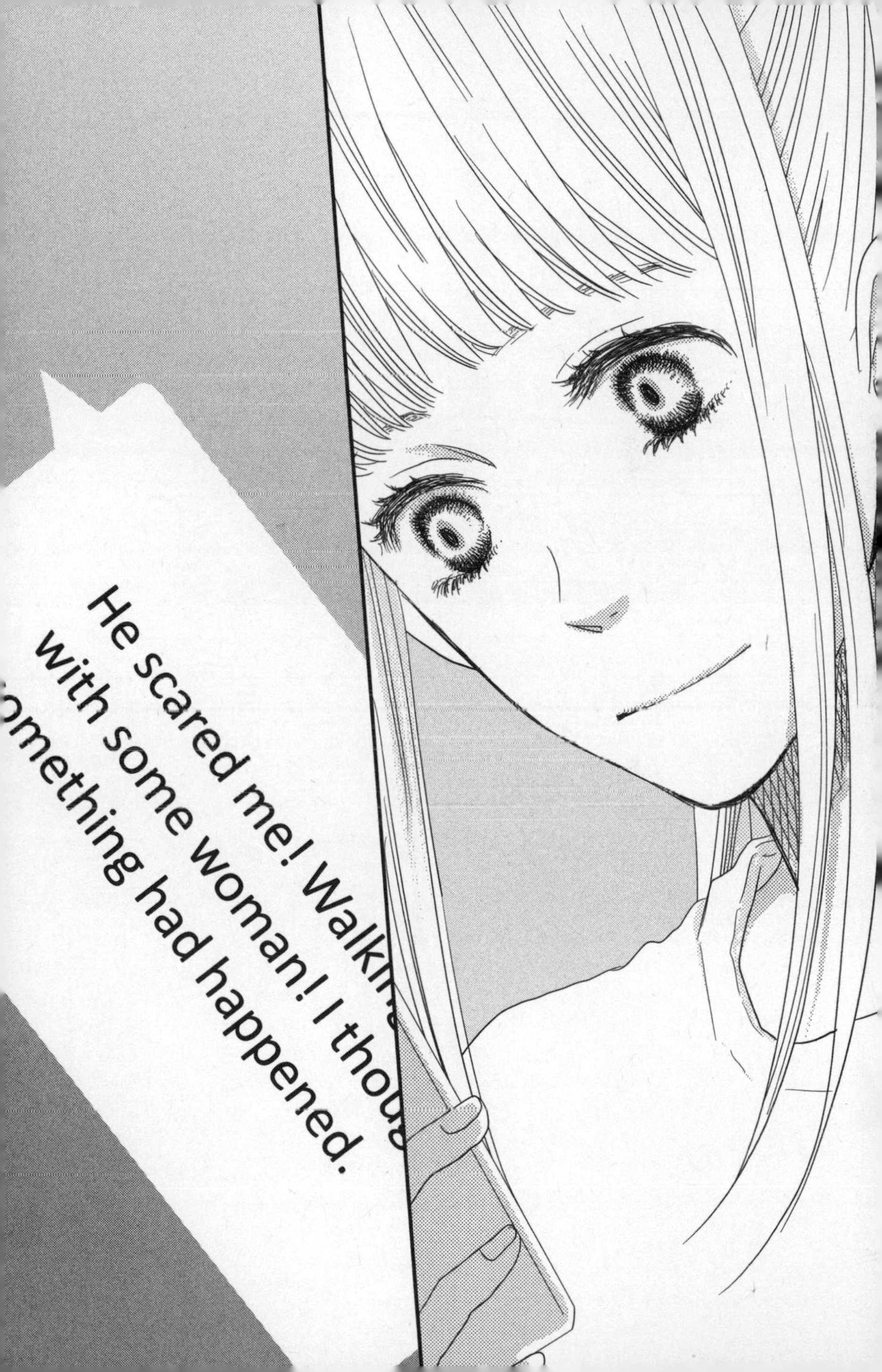
He scared me! Walki
with some woman! I thou
omething had happened.

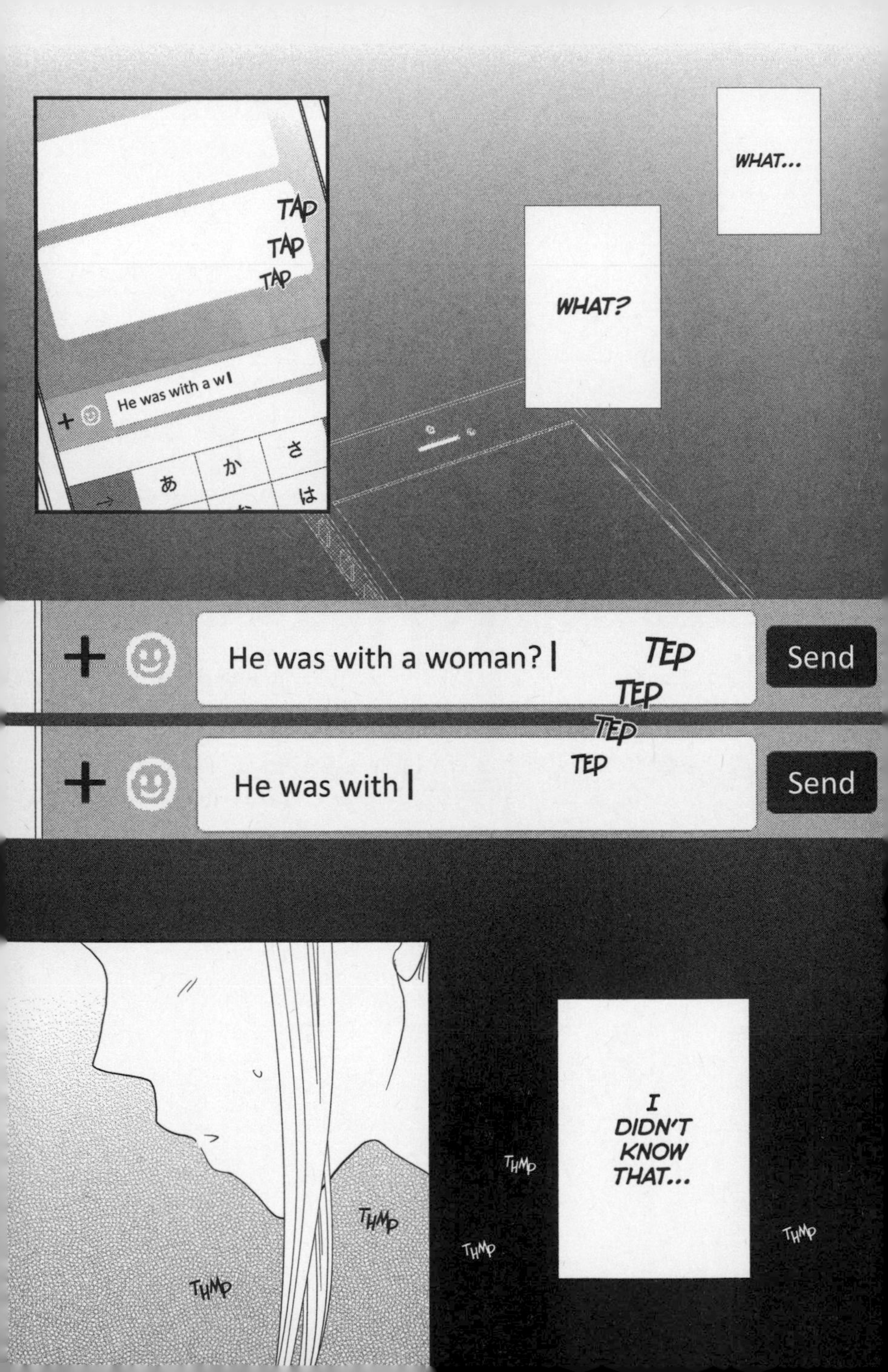
WHAT...
WHAT?
TAP
TAP
TAP
He was with a w
さ
か
あ
は
Send
TEP
He was with a woman?
TEP
TEP
TEP
Send
He was with
THMP
I DIDN'T KNOW THAT...
THMP
THMP
THMP
THMP

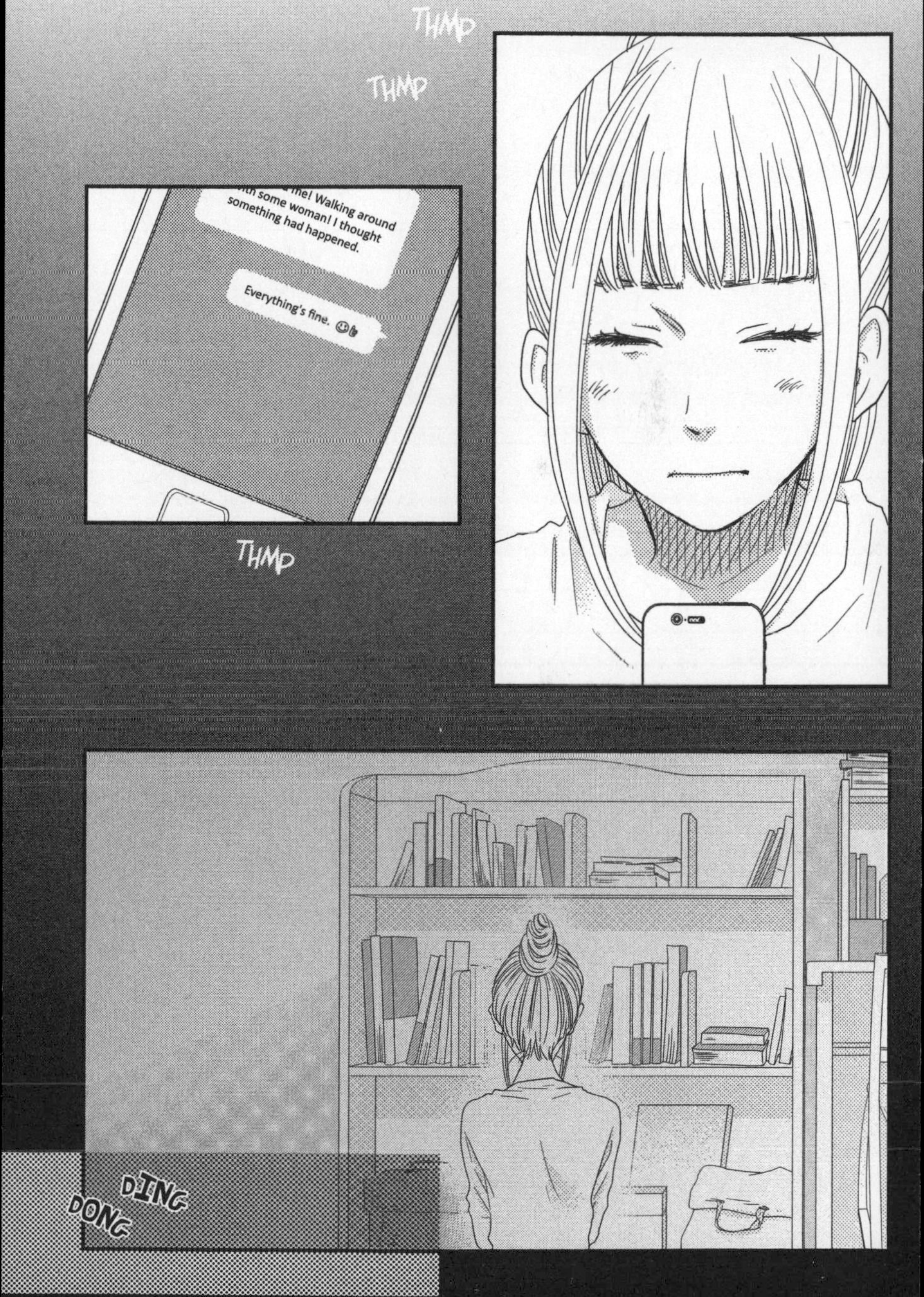
THMP
THMP
me! Walking around
ith some woman! I thought
something had happened.
Everything's fine.
THMP
DING DONG

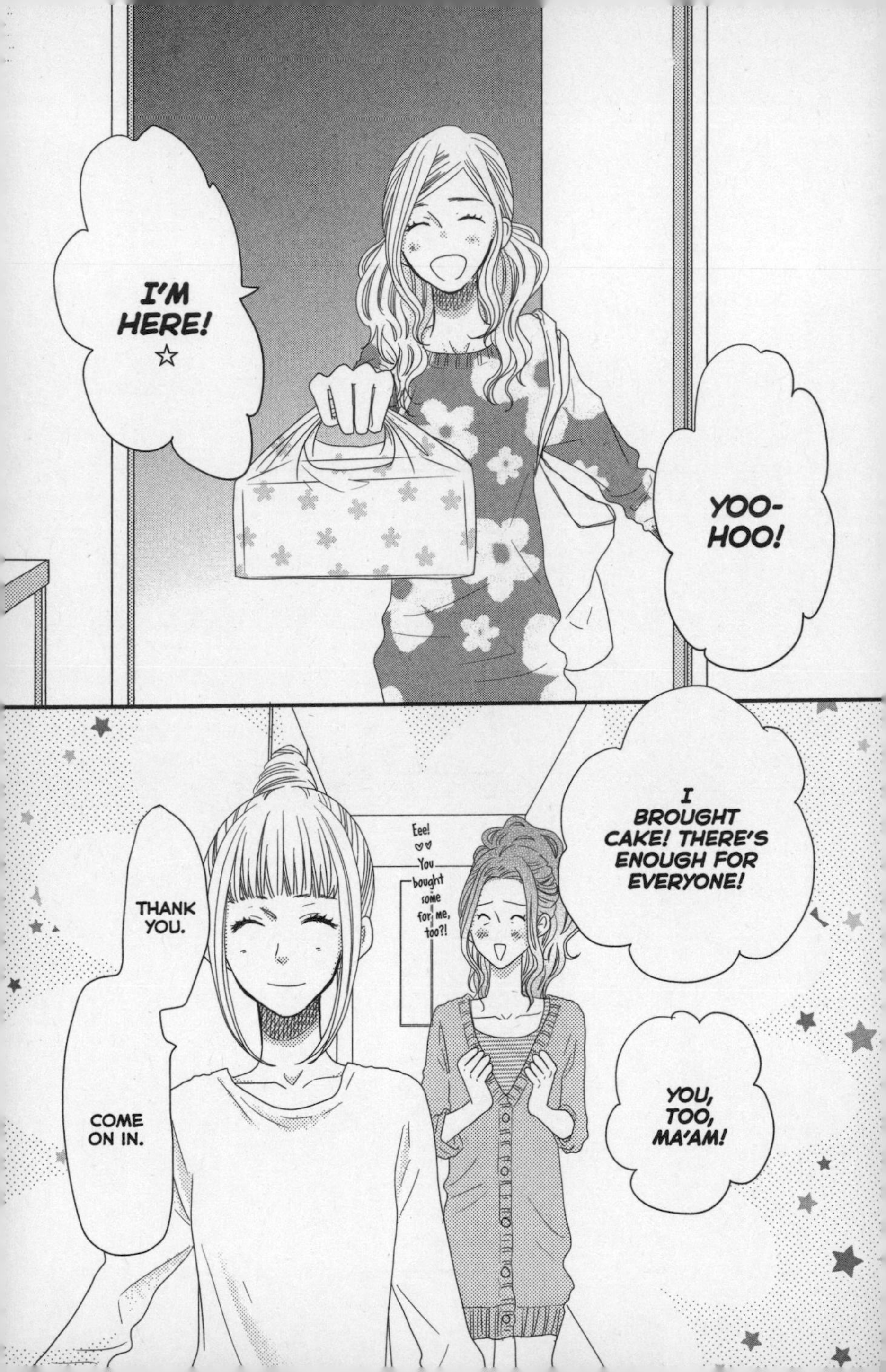
YOO-HOO!
I'M HERE! ☆
I BROUGHT CAKE! THERE'S ENOUGH FOR EVERYONE!
YOU, TOO, MA'AM!
Eee! ♡♡ You bought some for me, too?!
THANK YOU.
COME ON IN.

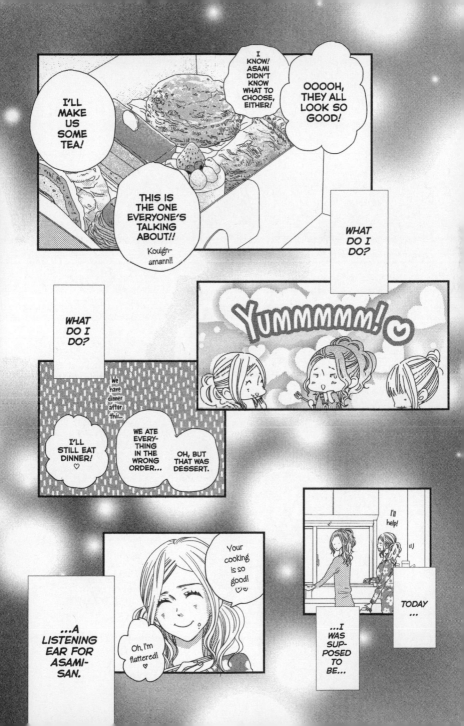

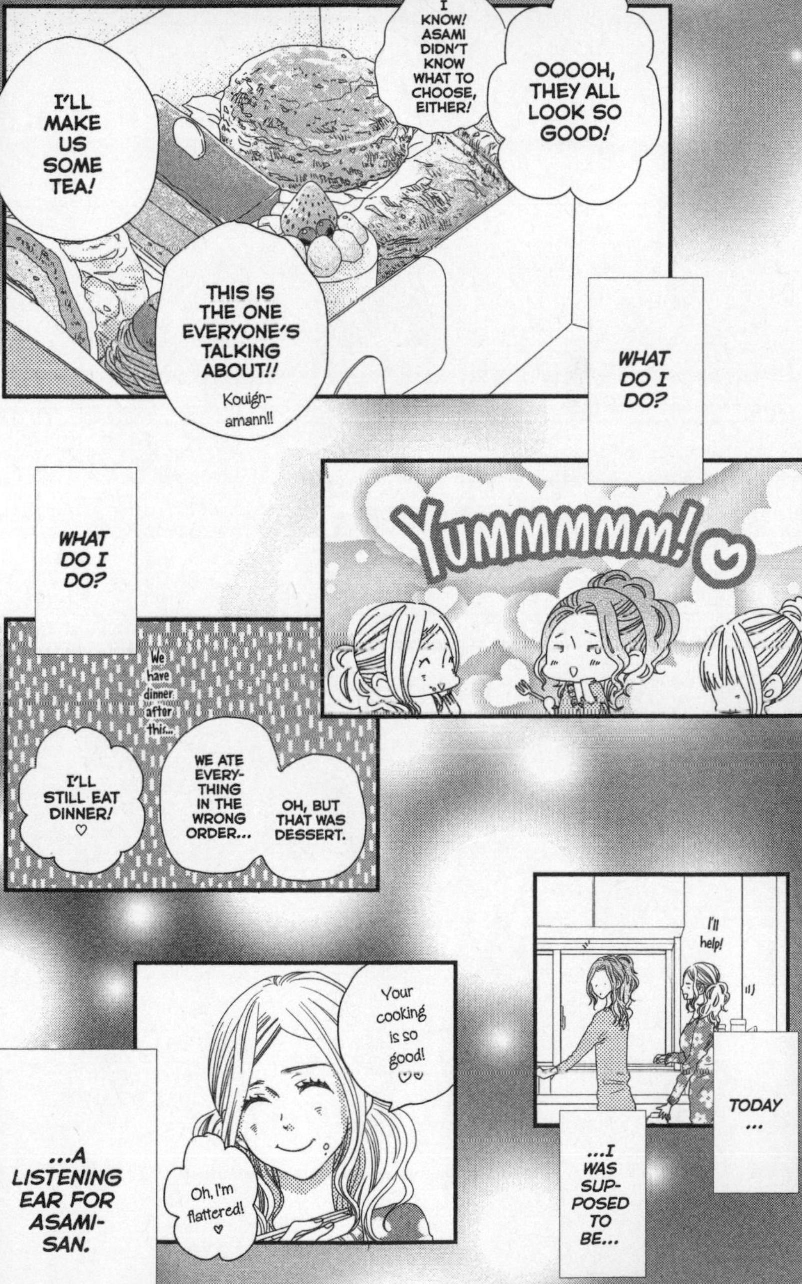
OOOOH, THEY ALL LOOK SO GOOD!
I KNOW! ASAMI DIDN'T KNOW WHAT TO CHOOSE, EITHER!
I'LL MAKE US SOME TEA!
THIS IS THE ONE EVERYONE'S TALKING ABOUT!!
Kouign-amann!!
WHAT DO I DO?
YUMMMMM! ♡
WHAT DO I DO?
We have dinner after this...
OH, BUT THAT WAS DESSERT.
WE ATE EVERYTHING IN THE WRONG ORDER...
I'LL STILL EAT DINNER! ♡
I'll help!
TODAY...
...I WAS SUPPOSED TO BE...
Your cooking is so good! ♡♡
Oh, I'm flattered! ♡
...A LISTENING EAR FOR ASAMI-SAN.

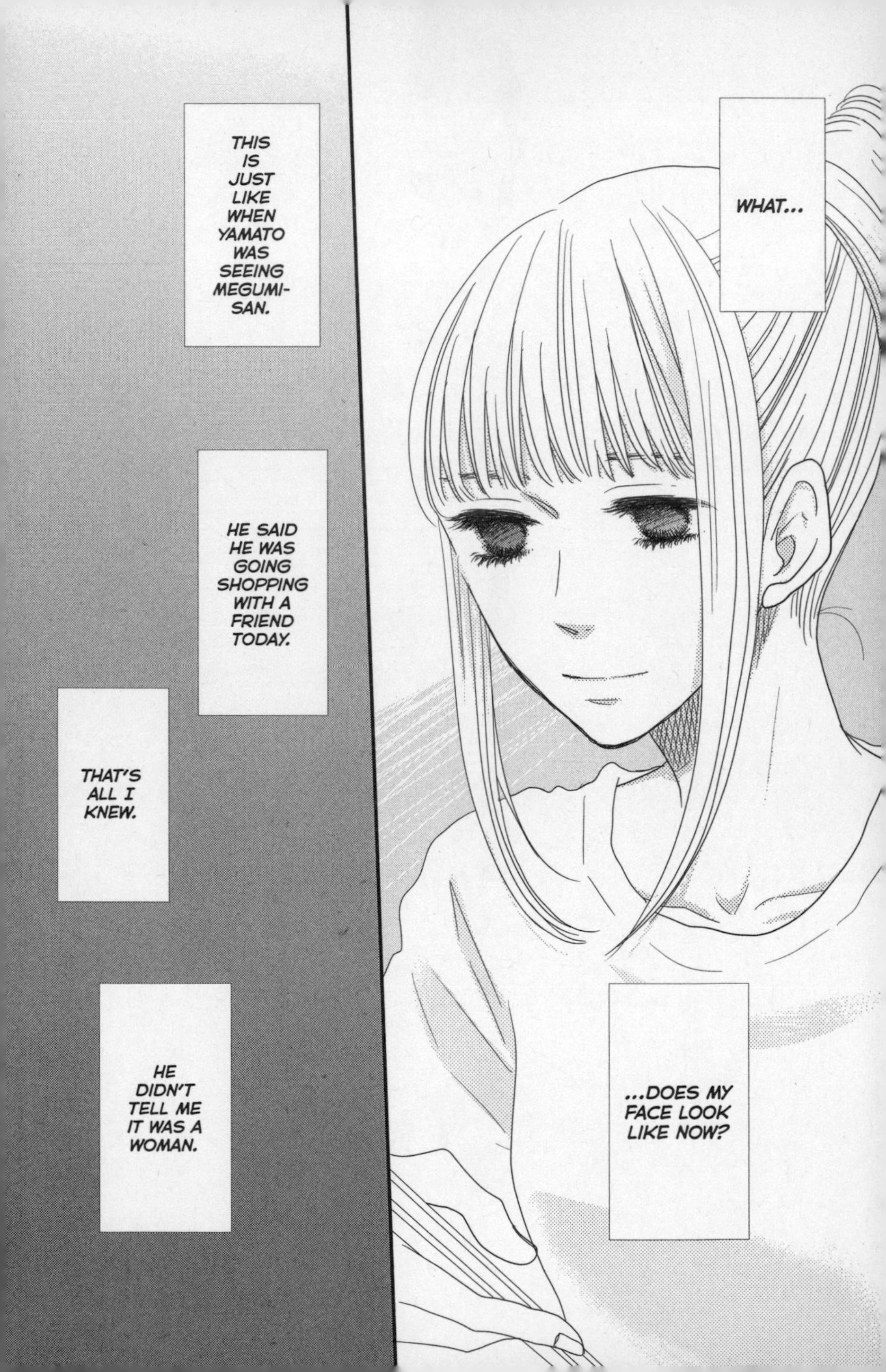
WHAT...
...DOES MY FACE LOOK LIKE NOW?
THIS IS JUST LIKE WHEN YAMATO WAS SEEING MEGUMI-SAN.
HE SAID HE WAS GOING SHOPPING WITH A FRIEND TODAY.
THAT'S ALL I KNEW.
HE DIDN'T TELL ME IT WAS A WOMAN.

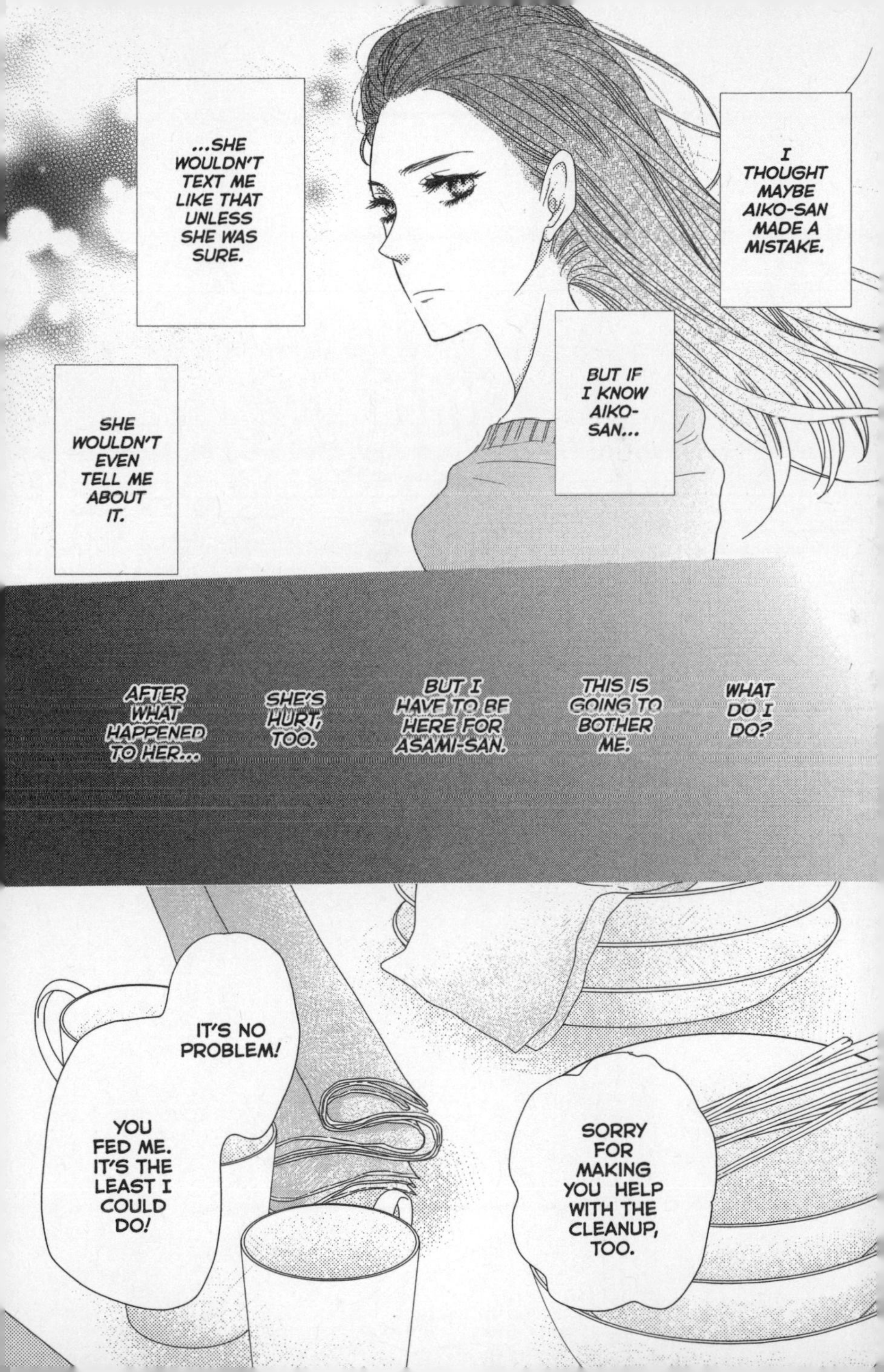
I THOUGHT MAYBE AIKO-SAN MADE A MISTAKE.
BUT IF I KNOW AIKO-SAN...
...SHE WOULDN'T TEXT ME LIKE THAT UNLESS SHE WAS SURE.
SHE WOULDN'T EVEN TELL ME ABOUT IT.
WHAT DO I DO?
THIS IS GOING TO BOTHER ME.
BUT I HAVE TO BE HERE FOR ASAMI-SAN.
SHE'S HURT, TOO.
AFTER WHAT HAPPENED TO HER...
SORRY FOR MAKING YOU HELP WITH THE CLEANUP, TOO.
IT'S NO PROBLEM!
YOU FED ME. IT'S THE LEAST I COULD DO!

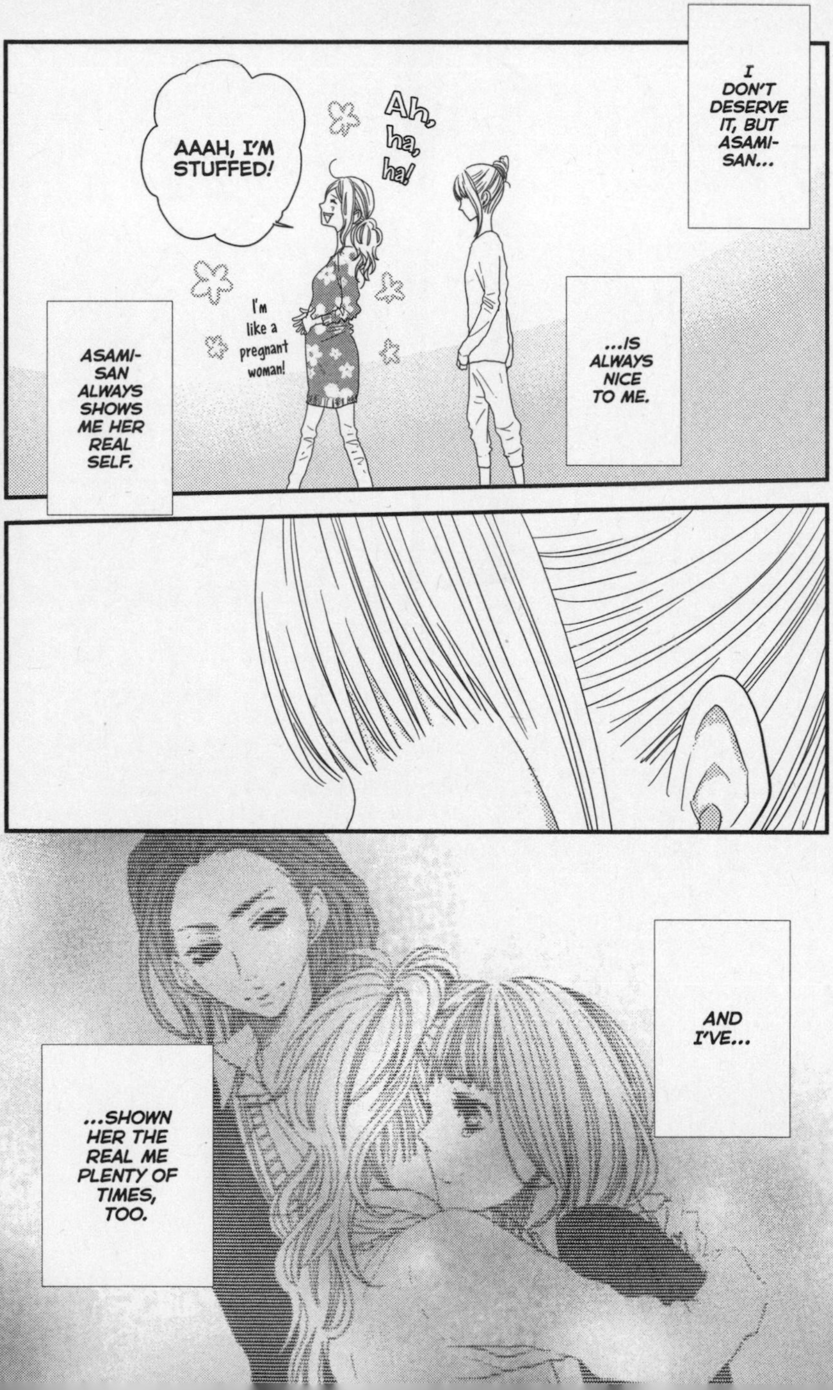
I DON'T DESERVE IT, BUT ASAMI-SAN...
...IS ALWAYS NICE TO ME.
Ah, ha, ha!
AAAH, I'M STUFFED!
I'm like a pregnant woman!
ASAMI-SAN ALWAYS SHOWS ME HER REAL SELF.
AND I'VE...
...SHOWN HER THE REAL ME PLENTY OF TIMES, TOO.

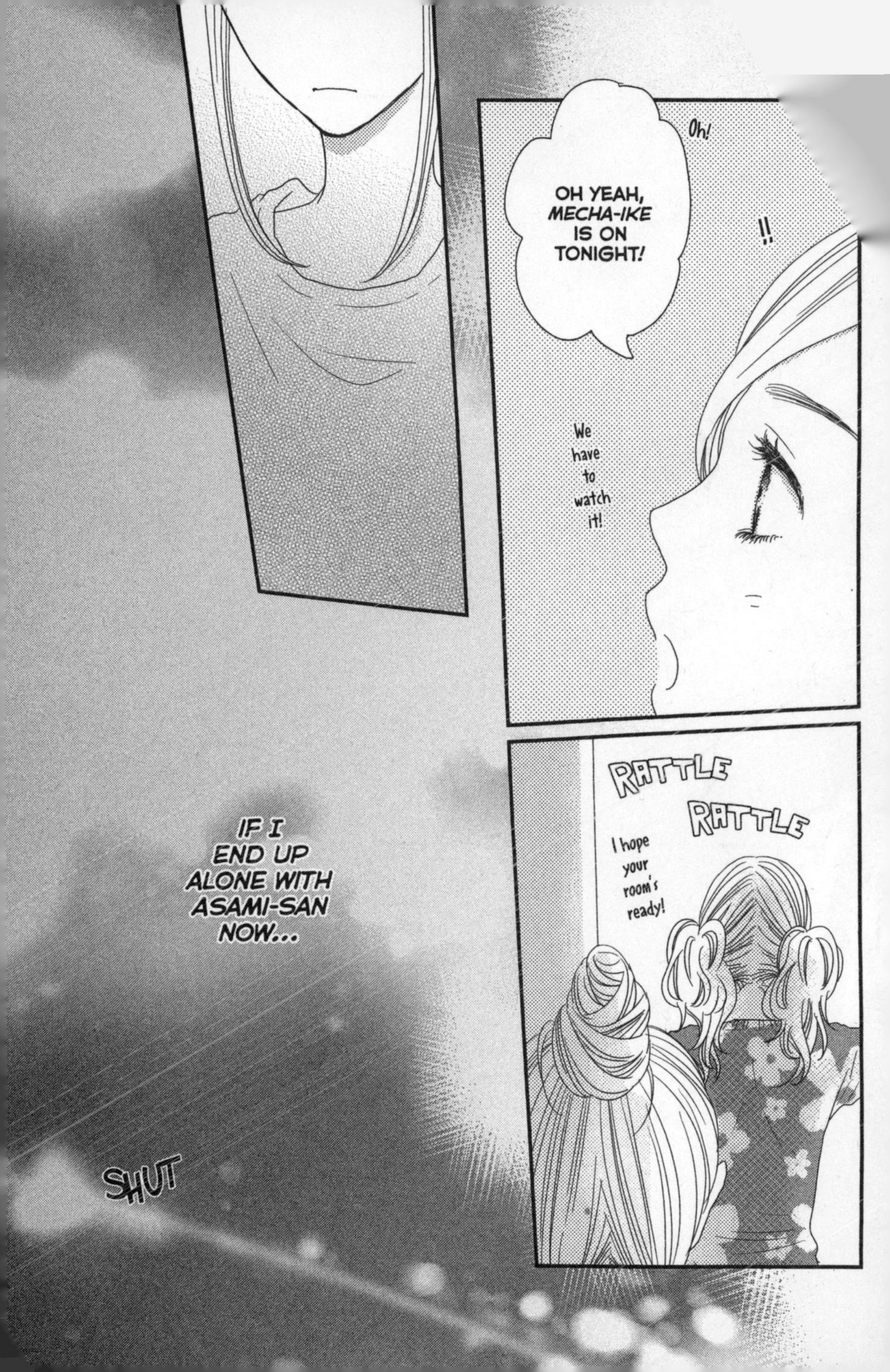
Oh!
OH YEAH, MECHA-IKE IS ON TONIGHT!
!!
We have to watch it!
RATTLE
RATTLE
I hope your room's ready!
IF I END UP ALONE WITH ASAMI-SAN NOW...
SHUT

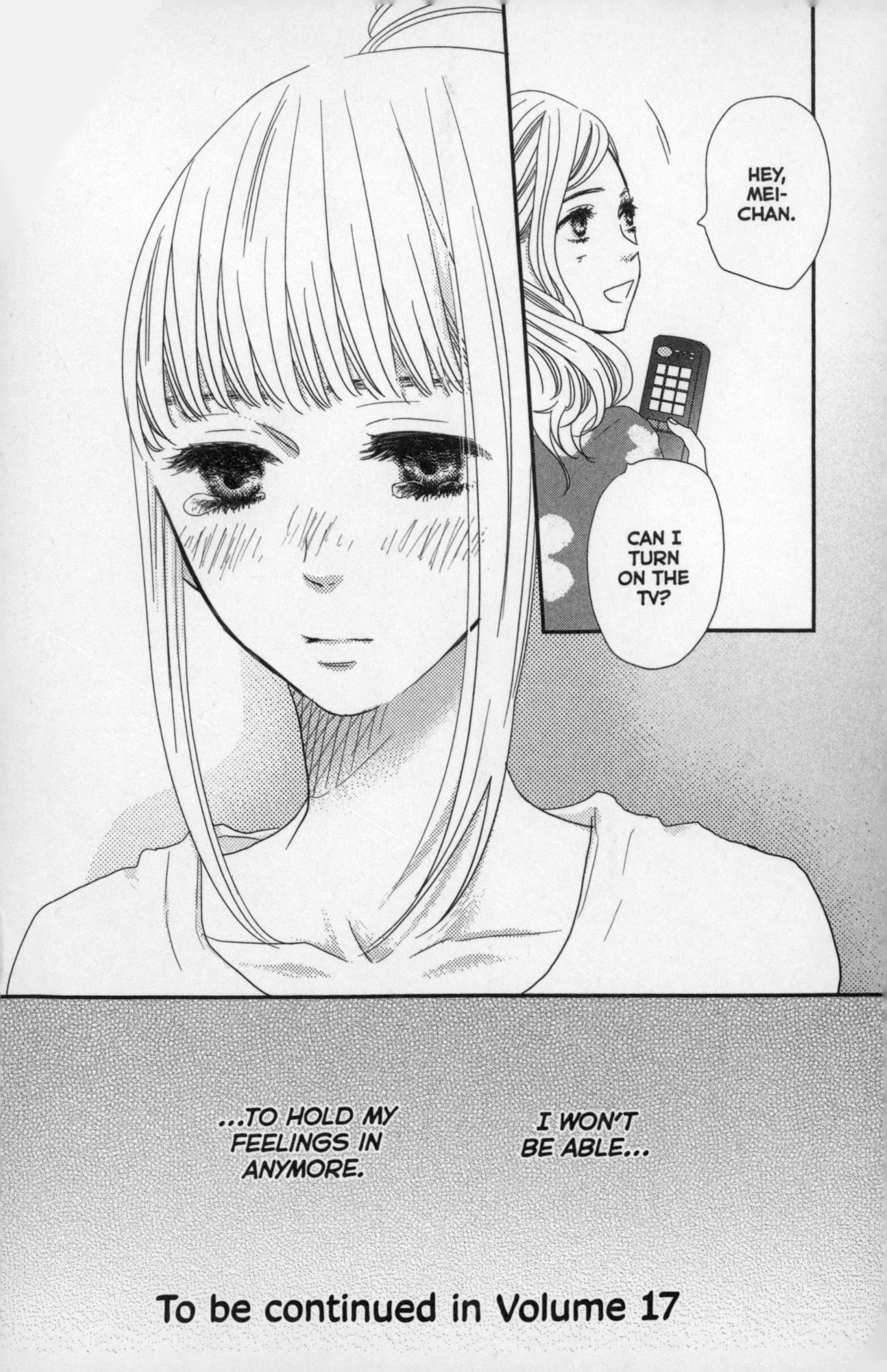
HEY, MEI-CHAN.
CAN I TURN ON THE TV?
I WON'T BE ABLE...
...TO HOLD MY FEELINGS IN ANYMORE.

To be continued in Volume 17

Say "I love you".

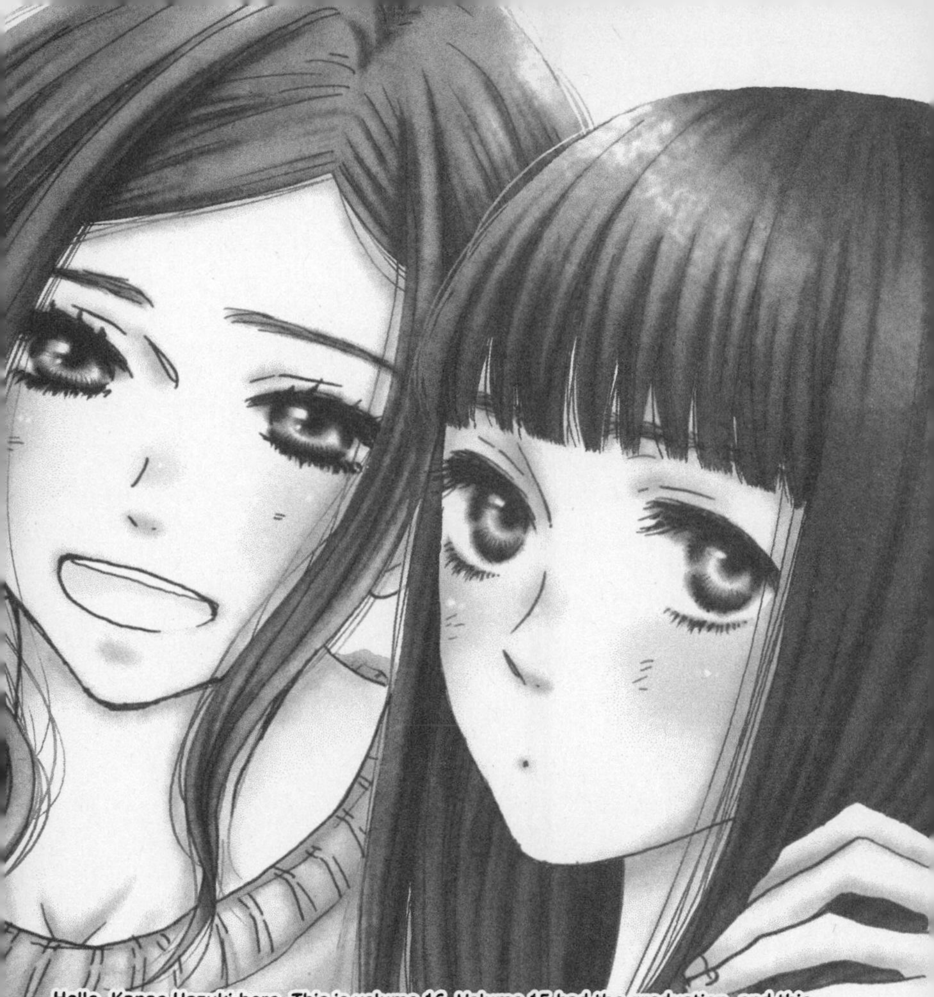

Hello, Kanae Hazuki here. This is volume 16. Volume 15 had the graduation, and this volume is the start of the college/vocational school arc. They're beginning their separate lives as they work for each other's future... Unlike high school, where they saw each other all the time, they can't see each other every day, and they can only communicate via cell phone. They start spending time with new people, and I think there's a lot of insecurity in all of that. Especially as you get older, it really gets harder and less common to become good friends with new people.

When you're little, you don't really think about it, you just say, "Hey, let's be friends," "Okay," and the friendship is formed. But it doesn't work that way for adults. We think about things, like how do we tear down and build up our old selves in order to get along with people.

I think a lot of the time, as we grow up, we start overthinking everything. We actually become more negative about things and start to feel like life is hard. How can we improve ourselves and grow as adults through that? But I think that the reality is, the more you think life is hard, the more you've grown. The more you worry about things when you're young, the more you can use that once you've become an adult and put on more years.

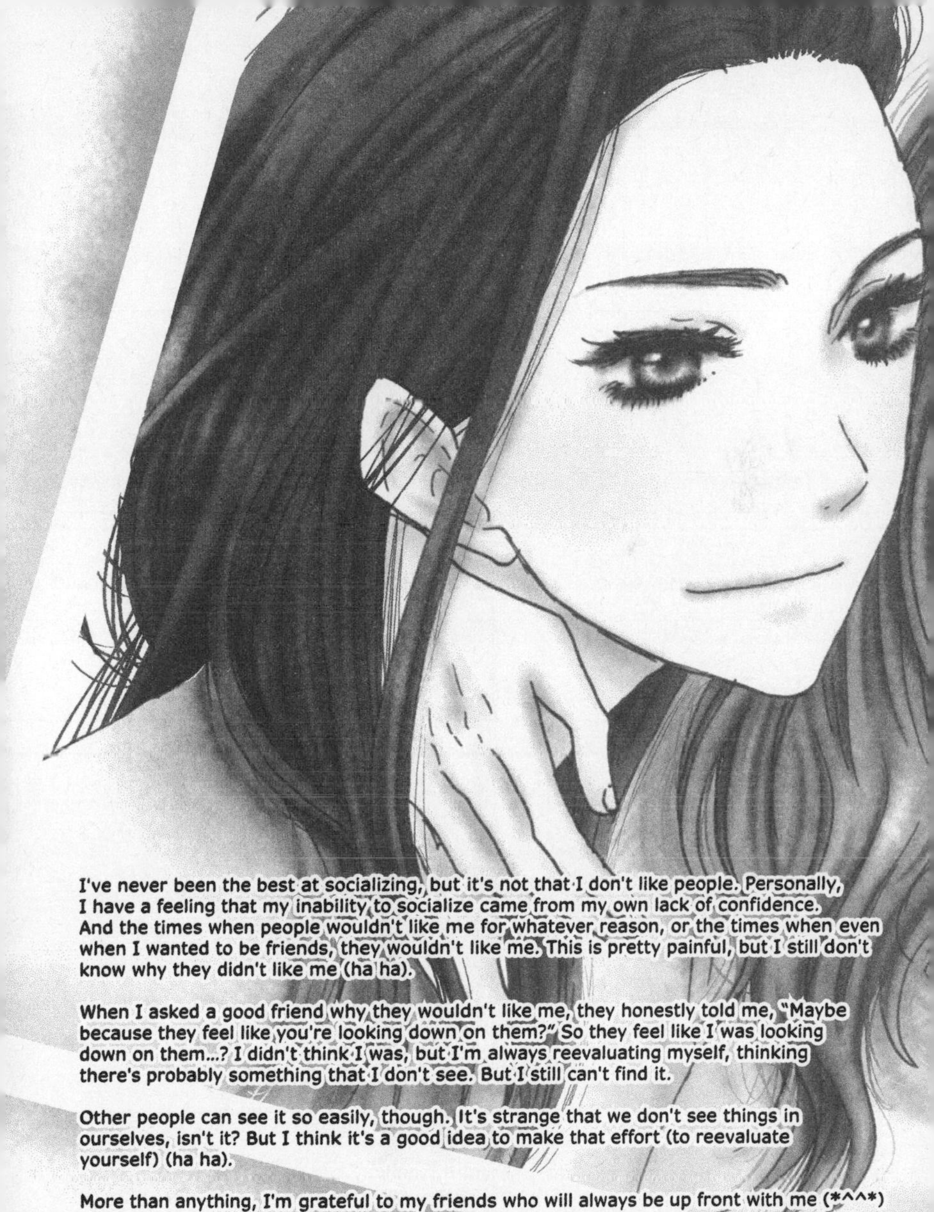

I've never been the best at socializing, but it's not that I don't like people. Personally, I have a feeling that my inability to socialize came from my own lack of confidence. And the times when people wouldn't like me for whatever reason, or the times when even when I wanted to be friends, they wouldn't like me. This is pretty painful, but I still don't know why they didn't like me (ha ha).

When I asked a good friend why they wouldn't like me, they honestly told me, "Maybe because they feel like you're looking down on them?" So they feel like I was looking down on them...? I didn't think I was, but I'm always reevaluating myself, thinking there's probably something that I don't see. But I still can't find it.

Other people can see it so easily, though. It's strange that we don't see things in ourselves, isn't it? But I think it's a good idea to make that effort (to reevaluate yourself) (ha ha).

More than anything, I'm grateful to my friends who will always be up front with me (*^^*)

Well, I went off on a tangent again. Actually, *Say I Love You.* is getting pretty close to entering its climax. I really owe my editor a lot, for answering all my questions and getting me information, especially for the college arc.

My knowledge is limited, in large part because I didn't take any schooling after high school. So it really is a big help. But I want to write and draw an ending that makes everybody glad that they read through it. I hope you'll stay with me just a little longer. Well, I'll see you in the next volume.

TRANSLATION NOTES

Smoking age, page 26
Yamato apologizes to Natsuki for accidentally catching her doing something naughty. He thought she was his age, which would make it illegal for her to smoke in Japan. The legal smoking (and drinking) age in Japan is 20.

Purikura, page 33
Also seen in volume 9, *purikura* (or a "Print Club"') is something like a photo booth, only instead of taking pictures, the people taking the pictures can choose borders and write on the pictures, then print them out onto a sticker sheet.

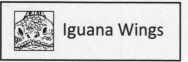

Iguana Wings, page 35
Another possible translation of Hano's username is "Iguana Feathers". Although reptiles don't have wings or feathers, the name makes sense for Hano, as the ha in her name means "wing" or "feather".

Why did you name him Pedro?

Because he's the color of sludge, but I'd feel bad naming him *Hedoro**.

Hedoro versus Pedro, page 36

To get from the word *hedoro* (sludge) to the Japanese pronunciation of the name Pedro, or *pedoro,* is not a very large jump. Using the Japanese writing system, the words are spelled with the same three characters. All it takes to get from sludge to Pedro is a little circle next to the *he,* which changes its pronunciation to *pe.*

WHAT?

HEY, HEY, DOES THAT MEAN YOU CAN PLAY, LIKE, ANIME SONGS?!

Like Yo-kai Watch?

Yo-kai Watch, page 103

A hit media franchise of role-playing games, anime, manga, and more that is very popular with children in Japan. The games involve using a special watch that can detect monsters based on traditional Japanese spirits, or *yokai,* that players can befriend and summon in battle. Although the series is targeted to kids, it has become a household name, hence a college student like Asami knowing it!

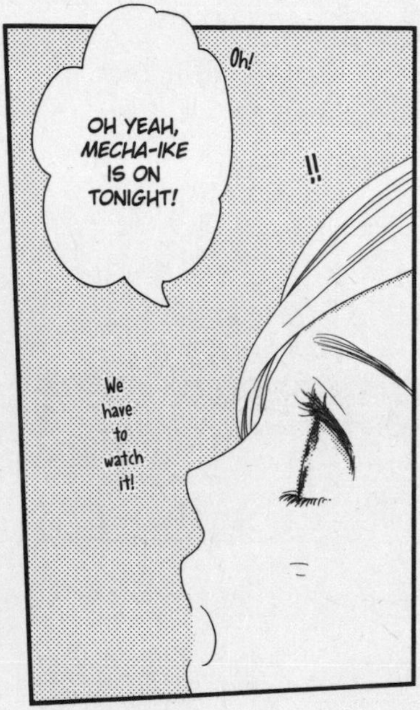
Oh!
OH YEAH, MECHA-IKE IS ON TONIGHT!
!!
We have to watch it!

***Mecha-Ike*, page 159**
Short for *Mecha Mecha Iketeru,* this is a popular Japanese show, hosted by the comedic duo Ninety-Nine. It features games and sketch comedy.

SWAPPED WITH A KISS?!

Class troublemaker Ryu Yamada is already having a bad day when he stumbles down a staircase along with star student Urara Shiraishi. When he wakes up, he realizes they have switched bodies—and that Ryu has the power to trade places with anyone just by kissing them! Ryu and Urara take full advantage of the situation to improve their lives, but with such an oddly amazing power, just how long will they be able to keep their secret under wraps?

Available now in print and digitally!

A Kodansha Comics Trade Paperback Original
Say I Love You. volume 16 copyright © 2016 Kanae Hazuki
English translation copyright © 2016 Kanae Hazuki

Published in the United States by Kodansha Comics, an imprint of
Kodansha USA Publishing, LLC, New York.

Publication rights for this English edition arranged through
Kodansha Ltd, Tokyo.

First published in Japan in 2016 by Kodansha Ltd., Tokyo
as *Sukitte iinayo.* volume 16.

ISBN 978-1-63236-302-2

Printed in the United States of America.

www.kodanshacomics.com

9 8 7 6 5 4 3 2 1
Translation: Alethea and Athena Nibley
Lettering: Jennifer Skarupa
Editing: Ajani Oloye
Kodansha Comics edition cover design: Phil Balsman